T0361224

THE DEVELOPMENT OF THE WEST OF SCOTLAND 1750–1960

THE UK

THE DEVELOPMENT OF THE WEST OF SCOTLAND 1750–1960

ANTHONY SLAVEN

Routledge
Taylor & Francis Group

LONDON AND NEW YORK

First published in 1975

Reprinted in 2006 by
Routledge
2 Park Square, Milton Park, Abingdon, Oxon, OX14 4RN

Routledge is an imprint of Taylor & Francis Group

Transferred to Digital Print 2010

© 1975 Anthony Slaven

All rights reserved. No part of this book may be reprinted or reproduced or
utilized in any form or by any electronic, mechanical, or other means, now
known or hereafter invented, including photocopying and recording, or in
any information storage or retrieval system, without permission in writing
from the publishers.

The publishers have made every effort to contact authors and copyright
holders of the works reprinted in the *Economic History* series. This has not
been possible in every case, however, and we would welcome
correspondence from those individuals or organisations we have been
unable to trace.

These reprints are taken from original copies of each book. In many cases
the condition of these originals is not perfect. The publisher has gone to
great lengths to ensure the quality of these reprints, but wishes to point out
that certain characteristics of the original copies will, of necessity, be
apparent in reprints thereof.

British Library Cataloguing in Publication Data
A CIP catalogue record for this book
is available from the British Library

The Development of the West of Scotland 1750–1960
ISBN 0-415-37868-0 (volume)
ISBN 0-415-37841-9 (subset)
ISBN 0-415-28619-0 (set)

Routledge Library Editions: Economic History

The development of the
west of Scotland: 1750 - 1960

Regional History of the British Isles

General Editor:

Professor J. R. Harris
Department of Economic and Social History,
University of Birmingham

The development of the
west of Scotland: 1750 - 1960

Anthony Slaven
Department of Economic History,
University of Glasgow

Routledge & Kegan Paul
London and Boston

First published in 1975
by Routledge & Kegan Paul Ltd
Broadway House, 68–74 Carter Lane,
London EC4V 5EL and
9 Park Street,
Boston, Mass. 02108, USA
Set in Monotype Ehrhardt

© *Anthony Slaven 1975*
No part of this book may be reproduced in
any form without permission from the
publisher, except for the quotation of brief
passages in criticism

ISBN 0 7100 8097 2

For
Isabelle, Zabele
and
Isabella

Contents

General editor's preface   xiii

Preface   xv

1   Introduction: the making of the region   1

Part One: 1750 - 1870
2   The commercial framework:
    trade, transport and banking   19
3   Change in the countryside   58
4   The industrial base: the triumph of textiles   79
5   The industrial base: the rise of the heavy industries   111
6   Population, housing, health and income   135

Part Two: 1870 - 1960
7   Industrial maturity   163
8   Dislocation   183
9   The managed economy   210
10 The region's people   230

Select bibliography   260

Index   264

Maps

1	The west of Scotland: Location	2
2	Glasgow and Central Clydeside conurbation	4
3	Railways in operation, 1830–50	43
4	West of Scotland iron industry, 1850	119

Tables

1	Percentage distribution of employment, 1951	3
2	Official values of Scottish imports, exports and re-exports, 1755–1800	24
3	West of Scotland banks, 1750–1870	49
4	Royal Bank of Scotland, Glasgow Agency, bills discounted, 1794–1836	53
5	Acreage under main crops, 1855–70	75
6	Changes in farm livestock population, 1855–70	76
7	Linen cloth stamped for sale, 1727–1822	83
8	Cotton mills and factory workforce in Scotland, 1812–71	109
9	Shipments of Scottish pig-iron, 1847–70	121
10	Output, employment and collieries in operation, 1854–70	123
11	Coalowners by rank, 1854 and 1870	124
12	Steam tonnage built in Britain and on the Clyde, 1812–70	127
13	Regional distribution of population, 1755–1871	136
14	Birth-, death- and natural increase-rates, 1855–70	140
15	Origin of immigrants to West Scotland, 1851 and 1871	143
16	Urbanisation: Scotland and West Scotland, 1801 and 1871	145
17	Average wages per week: Glasgow area, 1790–1870	156
18	Average prices, selected commodities, 1790–1870	157
19	Output, employment and collieries in operation, 1870 and 1913	167
20	Output and changing consumption of pig-iron, 1870 and 1913	171
21	Output of coal, iron, steel and ships, 1911–37	184

22 Output, employment, productivity and profitability,
    coal, 1948–60   214
23 Merchant tonnage launched and tanker tonnage launched
    on River Clyde, 1946–60   220
24 Rates of birth, death, infant mortality and natural
    increase, 1871–1960   231
25 Net gains and losses by migration, 1871–1960   233
26 Percentage urban population by county in West Scotland,
    1871–1961   235
27 Death-rate from principal epidemic diseases and certain
    others, 1871–1915   242
28 Percentage of households without exclusive use of household
    amenities in 1951   251
29 Estimates of income per head of population, 1924–60   258

General editor's preface

This volume inaugurates a new series of histories of the main regions of Britain, concentrating on their economic and social aspects in the period from the Industrial Revolution to the present day. The volumes will all be written by scholars who have made a special study of the region concerned and will incorporate the latest findings of research into its history. The aim, however, is to produce volumes for the widest possible readership consistent with this standard of scholarship, and for this reason alone there has been an avoidance of the references and footnotes which often accompany academic writing. Above all, the series seeks to keep alive the tradition of regional studies which has, for many decades, been a vital element in the study of the economic and social history of Britain.

JRH

Preface

Writing regional economic history leads an author to agree with Dr Johnson that 'a man will turn over half a library to make one book'. In the end, however, some selection must be made. The principle followed here has been to give due weight to factors at times when they played an important part in shaping the character of the region. Hence agricultural change figures prominently before 1870, but not thereafter. Further, certain themes like education and unionism, which are more part of a national history, have been referred to only in the context of specifically regional events. Consequently this history is not intended to be an exhaustive account: the aim has been to sketch the main outline of change, and to focus on the major elements involved at particular periods.

Many debts have been incurred in the course of writing, and certain acknowledgments must be made. To Professor J. R. Harris, as general editor, for his encouragement and advice. To Professors S. G. Checkland and P. L. Payne who read the text in earlier drafts and made many helpful suggestions. The librarians of the University and Mitchell Libraries in Glasgow and the staff of the Scottish Record Office in Edinburgh have been unfailingly generous with their time and assistance.

Colleagues and students, past and present, have contributed more than they know through their interest. A special debt is owed to many friends in adult education classes who raised questions, to some of which I have tried to provide an answer here.

The tedium of typing has been borne by a number of patient ladies. Jenny Hughes, Isabel Burnside, Orla Henry, Nancy Porter and Fiona

Porter have at various times coped with my manuscripts. My wife has assisted greatly in this and many other respects. The heavy burden of typing the final drafts has mainly been undertaken by Jean Verth, to whom particular thanks are due. She and Joan Porter helped correct drafts and have saved me from many failings in style.

The work of seeing the manuscript through its final stages has been much eased by the grant of a term's leave of absence by my University, for which I am specially grateful. Many others have helped in innumerable ways. I thank them all most sincerely, and hope they will find something of interest in the book they have helped to make.

UNIVERSITY OF GLASGOW   AS

1

Introduction: the making of the region

The region

In the western half of the Scottish Lowlands a great triangle can be drawn to join Arrochar at the head of Loch Long, Dolphinton on the eastern rim of Lanarkshire, and Ballantrae on the south Ayrshire coast. Within it lies the region of the west of Scotland, nestling between the rugged masses of the Highlands and the Southern Uplands. The area is commonly called 'lowland' but barely half is under 600 feet (Map 1). The landscape is cluttered with hummocks of sands, clays and gravels left behind from the Ice Age, and cut by deep valleys formed by the biting incision of small and active streams. Their vigour gave the power for the initial industrial expansion in textiles, but in cutting into the earth they uncovered a successor. Coal seams were exposed on numerous valley sides, and the Clyde and Ayrshire lowlands were found to be underlain by Scotland's richest coal and iron fields. The west of Scotland built its industrial success on these resources.

In the 1950s the west of Scotland was a mature industrial area, Scotland's manufacturing region *par excellence*. Its initial prosperity had rested on textiles followed by metals, coal, heavy engineering and ships. These specialisations had persisted. In 1951 over 60 per cent of all manufacturing jobs in Scotland were in the west; in the metal-working group the proportion was over 70 per cent (Table 1). Glasgow, at the centre of the region, appeared to have a more diversified economy than the surrounding counties, 60 per cent of its jobs being in service trades. Yet this was deceptive. These activities were closely dependent on the prosperity of

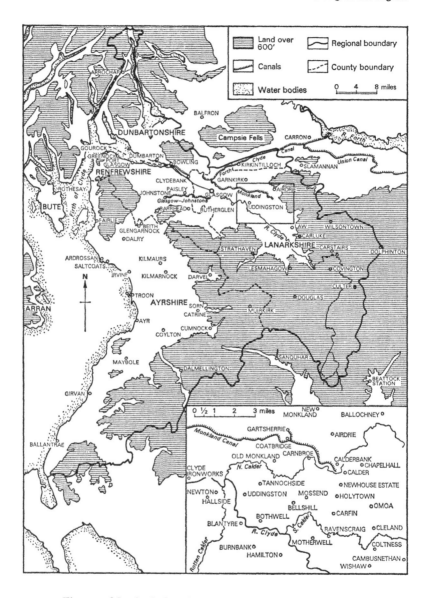

MAP 1   *The west of Scotland: Location*

TABLE I   *Percentage distribution of employment, 1951*

Major industrial groups	Lanark	Renfrew	Dun-barton	Ayr	Glasgow	W. Scot.	Scot-land
Agriculture, forestry and fishing	4·4	1·6	2·8	7·5	0·1	2·2	7·4
Mining and quarrying	10·9	0·2	3·2	9·7	0·2	3·5	4·5
Metal mfr and engineering	28·0	32·1	45·8	11·1	20·3	24·0	16·3
Miscellaneous mfr	6·9	7·1	3·6	11·2	9·0	8·3	8·2
Textiles	4·7	15·0	4·3	12·0	8·0	8·7	7·6
Total mfr	39·6	54·2	53·7	34·3	37·3	41·0	32·1
Service industries	45·1	43·9	40·2	48·6	62·3	53·3	55·8

West of Scotland share of total employment in each group (1951)

Major industrial groups	% employment in West of Scotland
Agriculture, forestry, fishing	14·5
Mining and quarrying	37·2
Metal mfr and engineering	70·7
Miscellaneous mfr	48·4
Textiles	55·0
Total mfr	61·3
Services	56·5

Source : Compiled from Census of Scotland, 1951

the staple industries in the region. When these faltered the Glasgow economy could not escape stagnation for long.

The west of Scotland is a small region, covering barely 2,500 square miles, about 8 per cent of the Scottish land area. Yet almost half Scotland's population lived there in 1951, and one Scot in five dwelt within the 60 square-mile area of Glasgow. Ninety-five per cent of the region's people were urban dwellers, most living within the complex and virtually continuous zone of built-up settlement known as the Central Clydeside conurbation (Map 2). One consequence was poor housing for many of the region's inhabitants.

This complex urban-industrial society was a far cry from the west of Scotland of James Watt, Adam Smith or Robert Burns. Two centuries ago the west was an empty region with only seven people for every 100 living there in 1951; 181,000 inhabitants instead of 2·5 million. At that

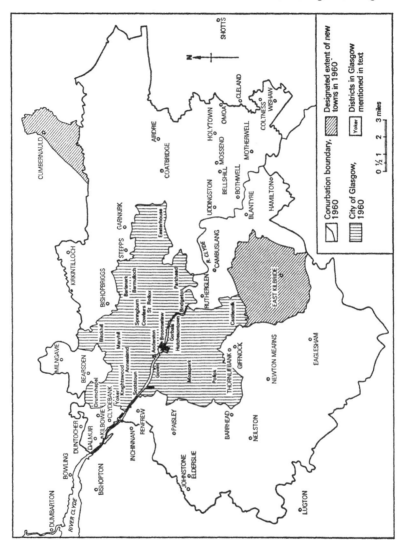

MAP 2 *Glasgow and Central Clydeside conurbation*

time over half the population lived in tiny hamlets with fewer than 300 persons; only one person in five lived in a settlement of 1,000 or more inhabitants. Glasgow had a population of only 23,544, Paisley 6,799, Greenock 3,858. Most other towns were much smaller.

This was a small-scale world where the wheeled vehicle was still uncommon. Few jobs were beyond the strength of man or animal power, and water served for the bigger tasks. Individual insecurity was common, expectation of life at birth being scarcely thirty years. The harvest was the single most important event of the year, for scarcity if not outright starvation was still common in this agrarian society. Some two-thirds of the population probably lived and worked on the land which lay derelict under the weight of ignorance and centuries of misuse.

In the middle of the eighteenth century it is impossible to identify a west of Scotland region, much less an integrated economy with dominant characteristics of the kind recognisable in the 1950s. Two hundred years ago there was a small colonial trade economy based on the infant Clyde ports. In the small towns and villages there was a linen textile economy; in the countryside itself, an agrarian economy struggling with unproductive land. No influence had yet emerged to weld these into a distinctive region. The gap between life in the region in the 1750s and the 1950s is remarkably wide, and in the 1750s there were few signs of the spectacular changes to come. Yet from these discouraging beginnings much was to be achieved in a very short space of time; the old society crumpled with remarkable speed.

The processes which transformed the pre-industrial region to its present form were linked to five broad and complementary upheavals. One major influence was the unprecedented population growth which turned the empty region into the congested area of the mid-twentieth century. A second was the series of improvements in transport which linked the region and its resources in productive ways. A third was the enormous expansion of foreign trade which drew the region into contact with world markets. The other two revolutionary changes embraced the reform of agriculture, and last, the crowning achievement of the age, the creation of machine-powered manufacturing industry. These great developments meshed with each other in a complex way and revolutionised the way of life of the region and its people.

The transformation was worked out over two centuries. In the first hundred years the west of Scotland climbed to world leadership in industrial strength while in the second century, from the decade 1870–80, the region slipped steadily out of the world limelight and became preoccupied with internal difficulties. The explanations of the upswing to prominence and the decline to relative insignificance are not simple. A brief outline of the pattern of change over the past 200 years will serve as a basis for the discussion to follow.

The first hundred years

Trade and the land

The west of Scotland moved from rural poverty to industrial prosperity in the century after 1760. The transformation of the countryside was a central part of this process, but rapid change was at first most evident in the striking growth of trade, especially the import and re-export of American tobacco.

This trade was still a small affair in the 1740s, with imports of around 10 million lbs of tobacco annually. But by 1770 imports had quadrupled and Glasgow controlled about half the entire British tobacco trade. Shorter sailing routes, superior credit facilities and commercial organisation, and regular outlets to the French tobacco monopoly carried the Scots to a position of pre-eminence. This had scarcely been attained before the trade was ruptured by the American War of Independence. Some bankruptcies ensued and trade faltered for a time, but commercial foresight permitted a steady switch of capital and enterprise into the trade with the West Indies. Sugar, molasses, rum and cotton replaced tobacco as the mainstays of foreign commerce.

The tobacco trade was short-lived, it was controlled by relatively few firms, and it was not closely linked to other activities in the region. Nevertheless, it strongly influenced two longer-term developments. Its scale threw great strains on the carrying capacity of the River Clyde and on local facilities for handling capital.

Between 1760 and 1800 the advice and work of Smeaton, Golborne and Rennie began the long conversion of the Clyde from unnavigable mud-flats to a ship canal. At the same time the Forth and Clyde Canal was opened to stimulate east-west trade and provide Glasgow merchants with a water outlet to European markets. These improvements in communications met some of the immediate needs of the growing merchant community, but the supply of credit was more pressing still.

The tobacco trade poured liquid capital into the region, and some of the new trading élite placed their money in new banks; mercantile capital supported the small Ship, Arms and Thistle banks. But others were also involved. The security of landed property attracted loans to support a new life style, and landed wealth underwrote a number of the regional banks. After 1750 the interests and actions of merchants, landowners and bankers became intimately interwoven. The *nouveaux riches* edged into ownership of failing estates, bringing with them the discipline and expectations of business. This infusion helped break the inertia of custom and encouraged the move toward agricultural improvement.

In principle, the new agriculture involved basic changes in the organisation of the farmland, the introduction of new ways of working the land, together with new crops and livestock, and the use of improved implements. Scattered strips were consolidated in compact farms; land was levelled, drained and fertilised; new crop rotations and improved livestock capitalised on these innovations. This movement gained momentum from the 1760s, but its effects were not widely felt till the end of the century. Only then did growing urban demand combine with inflationary prices during the Napoleonic wars to transform the region's agriculture. The new techniques loosened the harsh control of the physical environment and made possible an increase in output and productivity at a time when towns and industry were beginning to make unprecedented demands for more food and a new labour force. The key influence in the industrial developments was the emergence of the new cotton-textile industry.

Textiles

It was the dramatic impact of the textile industries which first gave a regional identity to the west of Scotland. From 1727 the Board of Trustees for Improving Fisheries and Manufactures employed modest funds and powerful persuasion in stimulating economic activity. In particular the linen industry responded to careful attention to the quality of flax, and improvements in spinning and finishing. In the west of Scotland emphasis was placed on quality and skill, and the domestic industry was gradually taken over by town-based yarn merchants. These men provided credit and yarn, and linked town and countryside as never before. Between 1748 and 1778 the region's output more than doubled to 3·3 million yards of cloth, the value increasing from one-third to 40 per cent of the Scottish total. A decade later this had declined to 15 per cent by value, although the region's output remained the same. After 1780 the east-coast industry strode ahead as linen merchants in the west found their attention drawn to a new product.

Cotton was the new star on the horizon, and the English had already demonstrated what could be done with the simple mechanical inventions of the spinning jenny, water-frame and mule. Its sudden and dramatic growth transformed the economic base of the west of Scotland and separated the old generation, who looked back to the land as the normal way of life, from the new one whose members became the first real urban dwellers in the modern sense of the term. Even so, the old and new ways of life were not yet completely divorced. The first spinning mills were sited in the countryside and supported many out-workers in spinning and weaving. Textile workers could still live and work in the countryside, even though the first step toward the appearance of the factory wage-earner had been taken.

The next step attracted mills to the towns and widened the gulf between the old and new societies. This came after 1800 as steam power contributed its regular untiring motion to driving textile machinery. The urban mill was dominant by 1830, though the illusion of a link to the old way of life and work in the countryside was maintained by the rural mills. This was strengthened by the lack of refinement of the early power looms which permitted growing numbers of hand-loom weavers to maintain some independence and avoid total absorption into the new factory system. Immigrant Irish and Highlanders joined their ranks, as well as entering the spinning mills. Their swelling numbers finally solved the labour-supply problem, since previously the new mills could not readily attract the literate lowland Scot. Indeed, the new factory labour force and the new urban society in the west of Scotland rested upon the illiterate, the hungry, the dispossessed and the immigrant. The western towns were the harsh frontier for the decaying peasant and expanding industrial societies.

This new urban frontier had grown substantially by 1830. Glasgow alone was a city of over 200,000, housing nearly one-third of the region's 628,000 people; almost two-thirds of these were already urban dwellers. Between 1755 and 1831 the region's population grew three-and-a-half fold. Natural increase, the decanting of surplus rural dwellers, and the influx of Irish and Highlanders combined to create the fabric of the west of Scotland's urban life in these years. With so many of the incomers lacking skill and education, they added their minimal social standards to the unpreparedness of town authorities. Together, these produced the roots of squalor and slumdom which have typified Scottish industrial communities.

These momentous changes were intermixed with an astonishing improvement in communications. The canals attracted much contemporary attention, but, placed in perspective, they played a relatively small and specialised part in the economic and social transformation of the region. The new developments were supported by a more prosaic, but more widespread, improvement in roads. In spite of the deepening of the Clyde and cutting of the canals, the urban and rural cotton mills were heavily dependent on road transport. Similarly, the early ironworks at Muirkirk, Wilsontown and Clyde all relied on roads. Moreover, the revolution in the countryside, which enabled people and food to flow to the towns, was equally dependent on the building of a dense network of roads and bridges.

By 1830 these changes, which made up the first stage of the industrial revolution, had begun to weave the parochial world of the west of Scotland into a recognisable economic unit. In the countryside the new commercial farming catered for the local urban markets: in the towns and villages a thriving textile industry rivalled the prestige if not the scale of cotton in Lancashire: on the Clyde, the coast-wise trade was being bound together by the most extensive system of steamship services anywhere in

Britain or Europe. The west of Scotland had evolved a base from which a broad thrust into industrialisation could be sustained in the decades from 1830 to 1870.

Coal and iron

In England the momentum in industrialisation had been carried forward on the two prongs of the new technology in cotton and the revolution in the production of iron following Darby's use of coke instead of charcoal in the furnace, and Henry Cort's processes of puddling and rolling to remove impurities and convert crude pig-iron to the more valuable bar- or wrought-iron. Scotland has successfully borrowed the new technology in cotton production but the iron revolution was not transferred so easily. Production was constrained because of poor-quality coking coals and phosphoric iron ores which produced a weak and brittle, yet high-cost, pig-iron from the small furnaces. Ten ironworks were established between 1759 and 1801, seven of them in the region; but total output was only 22,800 tons in 1806, and still only 29,000 tons in 1825.

The great innovation which freed Scottish ironmakers from high-cost, low-quality production was the introduction by James Neilson of his hot-blast technique between 1828 and 1832. This raised the temperature of the small and inefficient furnaces and made an acceptable pig-iron from local ironstone, the black-band, coal-measure iron ores discovered by David Mushet in 1801. When raw splint coal was substituted for coke this, together with other refinements, cut coal consumption in local furnaces by up to two-thirds, increased the yield, and gave Scottish ironmasters an immediate and major cost advantage over English and Welsh producers. These were the first uniquely Scottish contributions to the processes of the industrial revolution and the consequence was a prodigious Scottish investment in ironworks and coal mines, for the major ironmakers were also the main coal masters.

The transformation was dramatic. Iron output leapt from 29,000 tons in 1829 to 240,000 in 1840, and over 1 million tons by 1870. The region's coal production swept upward too, from perhaps 650,000–750,000 tons in 1800 to about 5 million in 1854. By 1870, 11 million of Scotland's 15 million tons were produced in the west. This prodigious expansion shifted the focus of industrial growth from the textile towns of Glasgow and Paisley to the empty areas of north Lanarkshire and north Ayrshire. The Monklands became the core area of rapid growth, and produced Scotland's first region of industrial concentration, where blast-furnaces lit up the night sky and ironwork and coalmine slag-heaps sterilised the landscape. These were the visible signs of expansion, and since people and work were brought to formerly empty areas, the despoliation no doubt seemed a small price to pay for the achievement.

While the coalmine, the blast-furnace and the railways provided the economic framework of the region, new skills of engineering in iron and steam encouraged the iron shipbuilding industry to emerge on the Clyde. Building on the foundation established by Bell with his *Comet* in 1812, and the pioneering work of the Napiers and other shipbuilders who emerged from their yards, the Clyde had by 1850 established a commanding lead in building vessels in iron and powering them by steam and the screw propeller. This dominance was sustained throughout the first three-quarters of the nineteenth century, and by 1870, the 'heavy industrial region' had been consolidated in the west of Scotland.

But although the main developments in these years were in coal, iron and ships, the textile industries still employed more labour than these three growth industries taken together in 1870. Glasgow and the towns in Renfrewshire and Dunbartonshire were still largely textile centres. Broadly speaking, the economic region now lay in two parts. North and east of Glasgow, coal and iron held north Lanarkshire and the Clyde basin under their sway, while south and west of the city, textiles were still dominant. Glasgow united the two parts as the commercial capital, and the River Clyde, emerging as a great port and shipbuilding centre, linked the thriving industries to the outside world. This commercial and industrial core was surrounded by a more rural fringe, supporting industrial salients in north Ayrshire, but characterised by highly com-mercialised mixed farming geared to the needs of the urban-industrial towns which now sheltered over 80 per cent of the region's people.

The second hundred years

Between 1870 and 1939 the region experienced unprecedented industrial prosperity, the dislocation of the First World War and the aftermath of two decades of unparalleled economic and social distress. These were the years when the first industrial revolution worked itself out, when the industries it created lost their momentum, and when the west of Scot-land's earlier industrial strengths turned into its major economic weaknesses.

Steel and ships

In the last quarter of the nineteenth century, textiles were finally over-taken by the combined strengths of steel, ships, engineering and coal. Shipbuilding emerged as the growth leader, building upon a steel industry producing plates and sections to order, and an engineering industry tailored to its needs. The new Steel Company of Scotland, established in 1871 at Hallside, pioneered the production of steel ships' plates. The suitability of steel was demonstrated to the satisfaction of Lloyds and the

Admiralty by 1877, and thereafter the substitution of steel for iron was mainly a question of comparative costs. Steel plates were cheaper than iron by the mid-1880s and this was reflected in Clyde launchings: steel tonnage represented 10 per cent of Clyde launchings in 1879, but 97 per cent by 1889. The steel industry supported this growth by importing rich non-phosphoric ores and producing high quality acid steel, while the progress of shipbuilding also rested on continuous improvements in technology. Triple-expansion engines, high-pressure boilers, and finally . steam turbines and diesel engines were all drawn into service to keep the Clyde in the forefront of world shipbuilding. In the last five years before 1914 the Clyde launched 36 per cent of British tonnage and 21 per cent of world output. This was a prodigious achievement for one small and narrow river.

This vigorous expansion drew the region's coal production upward from 11 million to 23·5 million tons between 1870 and 1913. Even so, the eastern coalfields expanded more rapidly, and the region's share in Scottish output had declined from over 78 per cent to just over half in the same period. Nevertheless, the local coal industry supported the development of the region's manufacturing, and by 1913 the west of Scotland had evolved a highly complex industrial structure and a heavily urbanised society. Over 2 million of Scotland's 4·7 million inhabitants lived there; 90 per cent were urban dwellers.

The region's economy was so successful at this time because its industries supported each other. Coal supplied the power and fed the iron and steel plants. Iron and steel supported a complex array of shipbuilding and engineering industries which in turn were linked to the needs of marine and land transport. The prosperity rested heavily on the single group of metal and engineering industries, and the whole structure was geared to supply capital goods to developing nations. The world needed ships, rails, bridges, locomotives, coal and machinery, and Glasgow and the west of Scotland were well placed to meet the demands.

Yet the position was vulnerable. If export demand slackened, the economic health of the region was likely to be at risk, particularly since newer industries, chemicals, synthetics, vehicles and electrical equipment had barely penetrated this export-oriented heavy industry community.

Staples in decline

The first shock to this pattern of dependence came when the First World War cut off overseas markets, though this loss was quickly compensated for by insatiable demands for war materials. Fears that cessation of war demand would plunge the country into depression were calmed when a frantic post-war replenishing boom set in and kept the region's industries busy: few suspected that grave difficulties were to follow. But almost overnight from mid-1920 the demand for the region's traditional products shrank to a cripplingly low level. There it remained for most of the period between the two world wars.

The tragedy of the 1920s was that few people believed world markets would not revive and provide work for the region. The wartime establishment of indigenous metal, engineering and coal industries in former markets was not taken seriously. Scottish goods, frequently produced by war-strained plant, found price competition increasingly severe: the modest overvaluation of the pound when Britain reverted to the gold standard in 1925 compounded this difficulty. Consequently, Scottish industries worked at a low ebb and employment in the region's coal, ship and metal industries declined by over 42,000 men in the decade. Worse was to follow in the economic blizzard of 1929–32. The fragmentation of the international economy, the declining confidence in paper currencies and full-blooded deflation at home forced heavy under-utilisation of resources and plunged the economy deep into depression. In 1932, over 360,000 were unemployed in Scotland, 210,000 of them being concentrated in the west. Over 20 per cent of the workforce remained out of work throughout the 1930s.

In the depths of such a calamity it was natural to blame the collapse on the failure of the traditional export industries; this analysis produced the counter-cry for 'diversification'. But the fault was not simply in a lack of diversification. The weakness lay in the tightly-integrated economic structure which produced goods no longer in growing demand. Diversification by attracting new industries could provide a few jobs, but it could not quickly create a new interacting industrial structure producing the goods the world wanted. The efforts which set up Hillington and three smaller industrial estates on the eve of the Second World War may well have used resources that could have been better employed in aiding the traditional industries to adjust their product range toward new commodities. Ships' plates were in slack demand but strip steel was already feeling the demands of the new consumer durable industries. In the event neither the staple nor the new industries did well, and in 1938 the region still had 113,000 unemployed.

The inter-war years exposed the scale of the west of Scotland's pre-1914 achievements and the appalling depths of its subsequent failure. The region was unusual in that while textiles transformed Lancashire, coal and steel reshaped South Wales, and coal, engineering and ships revolutionised the north-east of England, the west of Scotland was affected by each and every one of these. Each development overlay an earlier one and the impact was concentrated in a small geographical area. As long as work was fairly regular, the social deprivation of 2·5 million people crushed into hurriedly-erected towns and villages escaped the full glare of exposure. But when the region's economy crumbled the hopelessness of poor housing, poor environment, poor health and poor job prospects was revealed.

A century of rapid economic growth and urbanisation had social costs, and the bleak conditions between the wars brought the situation to a head. Over half the population of Glasgow lived in houses of two rooms or less. The infant mortality-rate at 87 per thousand was the highest in Great Britain; tuberculosis still bit deeply into the adult population. If we had previously identified the west as a 'textile' region and then a 'coal and iron' region, the inter-war years produced the 'depressed' region. The image of social and economic depression was branded on the minds of a generation and has coloured the attitude to every development in the area since that time.

The 'development' region

The Second World War brought a prosperity that had been unknown for a generation, but it also confirmed the region in its traditional economic structure; in the long run this was to prove unfortunate. But at the end of the war this was not apparent. The truly global scale of the devastation ensured that post-war reconstruction would be prolonged. In Britain, though the problems of reconversion to peacetime were grave, nationalisation rescued the mines and sustained the railways, while prolonged fuel shortages ensured an unsatisfied demand for coal. Moreover, with Continental and Japanese shipyards in disarray, the market prospects were bright for the region's shipyards, steel mills and engineering shops. The west of Scotland was back in business.

The return of a Labour government also emphasised economic planning. The drive to attract new industry to old regions was stepped up with the Distribution of Industry Act 1945, which designated the west of Scotland as one of a number of 'development areas'. The Board of Trade was empowered to offer financial aid to incoming industries, to build 'advance' factories, and rent premises at favourable rates. This legislation was renewed in 1950 and remained in force till replaced by the Local Employment Act of 1960. There were then nineteen industrial estates and twenty-eight individual factory sites in the region, set up under the development area policies. This was less than it might have been since the policy was severely cut back after 1949 when effort was temporarily redirected to correct the balance of payments deficit. Then, after 1950, it appeared that the region's employment problems had been solved since the staple industries had returned to full capacity working. Consequently, it seemed less urgent to attract newer industry, which came in a much reduced flow in the 1950s.

Between 1945 and 1960 the traditional industries were busy, though with the exception of iron and steel, they were not growing. The region's coal production declined by half, while tonnage launched from the Clyde began to decrease from the mid-1950s. All the basic industries, including iron and steel, continued to cut back on manpower, just as they had done between the wars. In spite of considerable prosperity, unemployment in the west of Scotland averaged 3 per cent to 3·5 per cent, twice the British level. Underlying this was the serious problem that industrial (and total) production grew more slowly in the region than in Britain; consequently the local workforce also grew less quickly. Throughout this period, industrial production in the staple trades contracted more sharply than additions could be made from other sectors of the economy.

The peculiar demand conditions of the early post-war years could not last. World shipbuilding capacity began to overtake demand between 1955 and 1958. At the same time, coal found its markets contracting as Britain began to enter upon the oil revolution. By the onset of the 1958 recession the staple industries found themselves facing familiar problems as the pattern of the 1920s and 1930s began to re-emerge. Increasing unemployment seemed once more to be linked to dependence on a narrow range of export-oriented heavy industries. All the effort to introduce new industries had done little to reshape the basic industrial structure of the region. The new jobs were beneficial, but the economic health of the district demanded that the basic industries be successful. This in turn demanded extensive investment, modernisation and some adjustment in product range toward meeting the basic material requirements of the newer industries. Not all the old trades could make such an adjustment, but without some realignment neither the old nor the new industries in the region could grow satisfactorily. The encouragement of such changes had been neglected in favour of simply providing new jobs. The 1958 recession highlighted this weakness, and in the 1960s the west of Scotland began to undertake the long and painful task of establishing a new interacting and self-reinforcing industrial structure.

The pattern of economic development in the west of Scotland has been classically simple in outline. Trade, textiles, coal and iron, steel, ships and engineering have made their contributions and have helped bridge the gap between the region of 1750 and that of today. The growth and success of the regional economy rested on the development of these industries, and now the region's problems are linked to the decline which has overtaken them. The life-cycle of the region has in some ways come full circle in the past 200 years. In the 1750s the west of Scotland was an underdeveloped area, beginning to build a self-supporting industrial economy based on imported English capital and technology linked to local skills and resources. By the 1950s this phase had long passed and the west of Scotland had reverted to being a backward region once more requiring the injection of outside capital and technology to assist it toward self-sustained growth. In the eighteenth and nineteenth centuries private initiative and investment had driven the region to commercial and industrial success, but in the mid-twentieth century such methods could not be entirely relied upon. The region was no longer an empty backwater, but a crowded industrial area, suffering from economic and social decay. Industrial rejuvenation and environmental rehabilitation were both necessary. The 'development area' policies were introduced as one means toward these ends, while after 1947 the plans for new towns at East Kilbride and Cumbernauld were attempts to combine industrial, social and environmental renewal schemes.

As the region moved into the 1960s, planners, politicians and industrialists expressed confidence that the economic ills and social malaise of the region could be cured in time. The strategy for future growth had been sketched out, based on the 'development area' policies. However, economic planning, even in the short run, is a risky business. Long-term projections are notoriously unreliable, and even an optimistic assessment of the region's prospects at that time would have been forced to concede that there was no certainty that the design would succeed. Consequently, there was no estimate of how long it would be before the west of Scotland would make the transition from the status of 'development area' to once more being a region of vigorous and prosperous growth.

Part One: 1750 - 1870

2

The commercial framework: trade, transport and banking

Advanced industrial societies are set apart from their more numerous neighbours by having passed through a series of changes loosely referred to as an 'industrial revolution'. The process of change is long and complex and it is rarely possible to identify the origins. But the rise of the west of Scotland in the eighteenth century was so dramatic that it is possible to isolate the leading sector. Foreign trade fostered a commercial revolution and set the region on the path of rapid economic growth. This is not to say that foreign trade was the only generator of the region's industrial revolution, but it was the hinge on which the west of Scotland began to swing away from an impoverished pre-industrial condition towards its modern form. It is not surprising that the momentum for change should first have become evident in the trading sphere. Scotsmen had long appreciated the benefits which flowed from active trading links. They knew that foreign trade broadened the potential market for domestic goods and could introduce a wider choice of articles to the local economy, and that the business of exchange encouraged the development of a merchant community and its specialised services, as well as directly influencing the general level of economic activity.

European markets dominated Scotland's international trade till the eighteenth century, even though the Atlantic trade to the Americas and the West Indies was growing rapidly. The west of Scotland lay on the outer rim of this European trading world and the opportunities open to local merchants had consequently been limited. But while the Clyde turned its back on Europe, its broad estuary flowed into Britain's inland sea, the Irish Sea, and linked the region to a network of small and active

Irish and English ports, which throve on the interchange of coal, salt, wool and linen, Irish leather, tallow, butter and horses. Intermittent contact was also maintained with the Low Countries and the Mediterranean ports, and before 1700 links had been forged with the British empire in the West Indies and North America, even though Scots traders were legally excluded from the colonial trade under the provisions of the English Navigation Acts. When the Union of Parliaments in 1707 opened the door to the colonial trade it did not require great astuteness on the part of Scotsmen to appreciate that the west of Scotland was advantageously located for the Atlantic trade. The route to Virginia and Maryland going north round Ireland from the Clyde was much the shortest from any river and port on the British mainland.

The opportunity to engage in the Atlantic trade was critical for the general development of the west of Scotland. Left to its own devices and its traditional trading pattern there was little hope of any significant advance in the regional economy. An insecure agriculture provided occasional saleable surpluses of oats, indifferent wool and scrawny cattle. The slender resources and dubious skills of the sprinkling of local craftsmen produced coarse linen and woollen cloth, inferior leather and ironwork, and a limited range of tools, utensils and clothing. Herring and salt and some coal were also part of the local resource base. But the district produced little that was different from any other country in pre-industrial Europe, and much that was inferior. It was mainly the cheapness of Scottish wares which found them a market, and this narrow range of goods placed severe limits on the extent to which the trade and crafts of the region could expand. Growth depended on the availability by re-export of goods more in demand in continental markets. The colonial trade allowed the west of Scotland to acquire such commodities; for the Navigation Acts required all colonial produce, wherever destined, to pass through a British port, thereby concentrating the new world trade in British hands. This legal quirk gave the Scots the chance to play a traditional and well-mastered role, that of middlemen, and presented them with access to a range of colonial produce greatly in demand in Europe, that is, sugar, rum, molasses, tobacco and cotton. Merchants in the west of Scotland therefore launched themselves into international commerce on the foundation of a legal restriction, a favoured geographical position in relation to trade routes and their tenacity and expertise as middlemen and pedlars. Within thirty years of the Union the traditional trade to Ireland and England was overshadowed by this new intercourse, which relied on relatively few exotic products. Of these, the tobacco trade has been seen as the single most important factor in the eighteenth century.

Tobacco was undoubtedly a powerful influence on the life and development of the region, but its most striking feature was its transience. In

the thirty years between the two rebellions of 1715 and 1745 the importation of tobacco to Scotland increased steadily from 2·5 million lbs to
13·6 million lbs, some 20 per cent of the British tobacco trade. Almost
all of this came to the Clyde to Glasgow's out-ports of Port Glasgow and
Greenock. It was the next thirty years which witnessed Glasgow's
meteoric rise to being Britain's premier tobacco port, and her commanding
position was the result of two great surges in imports. The early 1750s
gave some indication of things to come with imports of over 21 million
lbs and 24 million lbs in 1752 and 1753 respectively. This was enough to
capture 30 per cent of the British trade and was the prelude to an enormous
acceleration. Average annual imports increased by over 60 per cent to
almost 28 million lbs of tobacco between 1760 and 1764, compared with
the previous five years, and in 1765 Scotland controlled 40 per cent of the
total trade. This coincided with the latter years of the Seven Years' War
and trade routes to the Clyde were much safer from French privateers
than those which ended in the channel. A second great surge between
1771 and 1775 raised imports again by over 40 per cent to 44·8 million
lbs per year. Scotland's share in the trade was over 50 per cent in 1769–70,
and then fluctuated between 45 and 50 per cent up to the outbreak of the
American War of Independence. The tobacco era therefore spanned a
brief thirty years from 1745 to 1775, and tobacco was in a supreme position in the economy of the west of Scotland for only half of that time
during the fifteen years from 1760 to 1775. At the peak of the trade over
98 per cent of all Scottish tobacco imports came to the Clyde.

The Glasgow tobacco magnates controlled a far-flung mercantile
empire and this achievement, even though ephemeral, was possible
because of long hard years of work and investment aimed at capitalising
natural and human advantage. Much also depended on efficient organisation in purchasing and loading of tobacco on the American side. Since
the Scots came relatively late to a well-established trade they found that
the English had already entrenched themselves at the major tidewater
collecting points for the plantation products. But as tobacco-growing
extended further inland, up over the fall-line that separated the coastal
plain from the foothills of the Appalachians, Scots traders followed in the
wake of the planters, pursuing their customers in the time-honoured
fashion of the travelling chapman. It was an easy step from this initiative
to set up their own trading posts at critical locations in the small communities along the fall-line, where the rivers finally became unnavigable.
The Scots merchants then added a new feature to the familiar trading
post set-up. They ceased to act as consignment agents, who transported
the planters' tobacco and sold it for a percentage of the proceeds; instead
they instituted a system of stores operated by factors, whereby they
purchased the tobacco direct from the farmer and then themselves bore
the risk of selling. The factors themselves frequently held shares in the

companies and were relied upon to purchase tobacco and store it against the arrival of a ship, and to pay for the tobacco with goods instead of cash, wherever this was possible. These features enabled the Scottish merchants to organise the sailings of their vessels and, consequently, the turn-round time of Scottish ships was frequently as short as 2 or 3 weeks, while ships relying on the consignment system occasionally waited 3 or 4 months before a full cargo was obtained. Scots vessels therefore had a shorter voyage, a quicker turn-round time, usually sailed with full cargoes, and occasionally managed two round trips in the season when one trip was the rule. These dividends flowed from the investment in, and organisation of, the store system. By the 1760s tobacco purchasing had become big business. The major Glasgow companies operated chains of stores in Maryland and Virginia; the two Cunninghame companies of William Cunninghame & Co. and Cunninghame Finlay & Co. operated twenty-one stores, seven being in Maryland and fourteen in Virginia. John Glassford & Co. had nine in Virginia alone. Virginia was the most important tobacco producer and, on the eve of the American War of Independence, it was estimated that Glasgow firms had no fewer than 112 stores in operation there.

Such stores were the outlets for the sale of Scottish exports as well as the collection points for American tobacco. The planter's great need was for credit to tide him over between planting and the sale of his crop the following season. In providing this and in buying up crops against future delivery, the Glasgow merchants became middlemen in credit. This was most frequently extended in the form of goods, cloth, metalware, gunpowder, tools, all the necessities which could not be produced by the farmer himself. While this tied the small farmer to the storehouses, it also involved the Glasgow companies in a sizeable outlay on goods, and occasionally cash, an extension of credit they themselves had to find. The tobacco trade largely generated its own sources of capital to finance this credit. In the 1740s and 1750s most tobacco coming to Scotland was purchased by the Farmers General of the French customs. The main Scottish agents were initially Andrew Buchanan & Co. of Glasgow and William Alexander & Sons of Edinburgh. Latterly, the contract was held exclusively by Alexander, who was also a director of the Royal Bank of Scotland. The regular payments by the French underwrote an extensive business in bills of exchange drawn on London and handled by the Royal Bank. This was complemented by the local banks which developed in Glasgow in the 1750s, and in which prominent tobacco merchants were partners.*

The result of better organisation, quicker transport, and effective credit arrangements was lower costs, which made the Glasgow merchants the most efficient element in the tobacco trade. This competitive edge

* See p. 48.

took time to create, but it was beginning to bite in the 1740s; a decade later the tide of competition moved irresistibly in favour of Glasgow, Whitehaven fell behind and Liverpool began to divert her energies toward the slave trade, leaving Glasgow clear of the field in tobacco. There is, incidentally, no evidence of direct Glasgow participation in slaving.

The extent of tobacco's domination of Scotland's trade was quite astonishing. In the 5 years between 1771 and 1775 the tobacco pouring through the hands of the Glasgow merchants represented, at official values, 38 per cent of all Scottish imports, and almost 56 per cent of all exports. When re-exports alone are considered, tobacco took up four-fifths of the total. Between 1771 and 1775 some 193 million lbs of tobacco were exported from the Clyde to the main European markets. France took over 44 per cent, the Dutch 37·5 per cent. At this stage, only the Navigation Acts supported the Clyde's precarious position on the pinnacle of the tobacco trade, for both these customers were well able to supply their own shipping to carry tobacco to meet the craving for snuff, but were excluded by the Navigation Acts from doing so. Smuggling was already lessening the effectiveness of the legislation, and the outbreak of war with the colonies in 1776 broke Glasgow's hold on the trade with startling abruptness. The day of the middleman was over. Imports of tobacco which stood at almost 46 million lbs in 1775 dwindled to 7·4 million lbs the following year, and dropped to an insignificant 294,896 lbs in 1777. Re-exports were briefly sustained by tobacco already stored in Clyde warehouses, then that most lucrative part of the trade sank abruptly into insignificance as the supplies of tobacco bypassed Glasgow and made direct for European ports. This new pattern was maintained after the ending of the war in 1782 and the import of tobacco to the Clyde never regained more than a shadow of its former importance. This is not to say that Glasgow merchants lost all contact with the trade. Glasgow money and Glasgow ships re-entered the trade but rarely called in the Clyde, going direct to the major outlets in Europe with their cargoes.

At first sight, the sudden demise of tobacco had drastic short- and long-term effects on the scale and value of Scotland's foreign trade. Comparing 1776–80 with the immediately preceding period, the value of imports declined by 36 per cent, exports were down 41·5 per cent and re-exports were less than a third of their previous value (Table 2). In the longer term, some 15 years elapsed before imports were back to the immediate pre-war level and over 25 years passed before the total value of exports exceeded the pre-war figures. The trade of Scotland, and especially the west, would appear to have been seriously damaged.

On closer inspection, however, it is possible to argue that this was far from being the case. In spite of the American War of Independence and the later European involvement on the side of the American states –

TABLE 2 *Official values of Scottish imports, exports and re-exports, 1755–1800*
(*values in £000*)

Annual average	Imports	Home-produced exports	Re-exports	Total exports
1755–9	566·1	344·5	408·5	753·0
1771–5	1,236·4	456·2	1,048·8	1,505·0
1776–80	793·4	549·3	331·8	881·1
1781–5	1,030·7	621·5	215·3	836·8
1786–90	1,444·4	769·2	355·6	1,124·8
1791–5	1,569·3	857·2	265·5	1,122·7
1796–1800	1,934·9	1,402·4	291·7	1,694·1

Source: PRO Customs 14; H. Hamilton, *Economic History of Scotland in the Eighteenth Century*, Oxford University Press, 1963

intrusions which should have disrupted Scottish trade – the export of home-produced goods grew regularly. When tobacco is deducted from the import figures to give an idea of the value of the other imports, the remaining incoming trade diminished only slightly from an average of £771,000 per year to £731,000 in the first years of the conflict. By 1781–5 non-tobacco imports were already up by 40 per cent over the pre-war values. The simple truth appears to be that when the re-export trade in tobacco disappeared it left the vital interchange of other commodities untouched. Even the exports which formerly went to America still found their way there during the war by way of Newfoundland, Nova Scotia and Canada, and this helps explain the vigour and resilience of the normal pattern of commodity trade. But since tobacco was concentrated so heavily on the Clyde one might expect the effect of its collapse to be most serious there. This appears to have been so in the short run. The tobacco came to Port Glasgow and Greenock, and between 1772 and 1785, customs dues collected there declined by more than half. Port Glasgow was the specialist tobacco port and there the decline was 77 per cent, while at Greenock, with more general trade and more West Indian connections, the shortfall was only 15 per cent. Ten years later Greenock had grown considerably, though by then Port Glasgow had been bypassed as Glasgow's major out-port, and its trade had not recovered.

This minor effect on Greenock, and its rapid recovery, indicates that the general commodity trade of the Clyde was as little affected as in the overall Scottish case. This new growth was not simply an extension of coast-wise and European trading, but included a vigorous development of the West Indian connection, encouraged by the establishment in Glasgow in 1783 of Britain's first Chamber of Commerce. Imports of sugar swelled more than two-and-a-half times between 1775 and 1800, and imports of cotton wool, which reached 153,000 lbs before the war, rose to more than 5 million lbs by 1800. The transfer from American to West Indian products was encouraged in part by the fact that West Indian transactions still enjoyed the protection of the Navigation Acts. Trade in sugar and rum also retained part of the former habits of the middleman and re-export business, though the new trade increasingly reflected the import needs and export surpluses of the region's manufacturers.

The growth of the formerly neglected areas of trade in the West Indies was doubtless aided by the fact that Glasgow merchants survived the collapse of tobacco without extensive financial losses. Partly this was due to the fact that the war was not unexpected. There had been a number of attempts among the administrations of the thirteen American colonies to break the hold of English and Scottish merchants on colonial trade by introducing embargoes on the import of British goods. They were ineffective, but they were straws in the wind. The factors of the Scottish stores were also skilled collectors and interpreters of information, and it seems that Glasgow merchants were already beginning to call in the debts owing them from the middle of 1774. Since credit had been extended mainly in small sums of £10–£30, in goods more than in cash, and on the security of the delivery of the next year's crop of tobacco, the loans proved relatively easy to collect. Between June 1774 and May 1775 the *Caledonian Mercury* reported that there had been a steady collection of debts and fierce buying up of tobacco stocks in America, and that by May 1775 the amount owing to Scottish merchants was trifling. There were a number of failures, the most important being Buchanan Hastie & Co., and many firms still had considerable sums uncollected. The Cunninghame group alone made claims after the war for repayment of outstanding debts of over £135,000. This was an enormous sum and, as far as one can judge, exceptional.

The virtual stability of general trade following the collapse of tobacco imports, together with the fact that almost all the tobacco was re-exported without processing, has encouraged the view that the tobacco trade had few links with the local economy. It is beyond dispute that the trade never relied on Scotland as a market for the sale of tobacco and that much of the trade was financed through the profits made by re-exporting the commodity to Europe. None the less, the purchase and resale of tobacco depended ultimately on a secure foundation of trade in general commodities many of which were generated by local industry. In the peak years of the tobacco trade one-quarter of Scotland's exports were composed of home-produced goods, and half of these found outlets in America. It is clear that much of this was English and Irish cloth and leather, for the west of Scotland could not supply the great range or scale of American requirements from its own resources. But when all allowance

B*

is made for this, it cannot have been pure coincidence that in the full vigour of the tobacco trade, the west of Scotland supported the establishment of its first iron foundries and ironworks, developed its fine linen industry to its highest point, laid down many great bleachfields and spawned a large number of manufactures. Glasgow and the surrounding towns supported new distilleries, nail and earthenware works, shoe, boot and saddle making, furniture making and many other crafts. The flowering of these industries could not have been entirely unrelated to the demands of the colonial market, and it is unlikely that the small local population could have supported the growth on its own. There is very little evidence to suggest that the merchants who engaged in foreign trade actively were involved in the new industrial enterprises, nor is there adequate ground for supposing that the profits of the tobacco trade financed the new manufacturing ventures. However, the commercial expansion of the mid-eighteenth century held out the prospect of substantial profits to be earned by catering to colonial demand, and this must have been influential in encouraging the establishment of the region's first range of manufacturing firms outside the control of the old craft guilds. It is not possible to link these developments directly to the tobacco trade, which was largely encapsulated, but one can discern the suggestion of a linkage to colonial demand in general. The link to the establishment of banking is also clear, and as we shall see, there was also a great pressure brought to bear to improve the region's communications.

After the war vigorous efforts were made to re-establish the old links with America and in 1790 the American trade and West Indian trade attracted roughly the same number of vessels from the Clyde. By that time, however, the swelling importance of raw cotton imports from the West Indies had made trade with that sphere the most valuable for Glasgow merchants, and this reflected the growing interdependence of the trade and industry of the region. Cotton wool poured inward, and cotton piece-goods flowed out, marking the birth in the region of a strong export base, together with well-defined markets overseas.

The region's new trade pattern had become well established by the 1790s. Almost half the vessels entering and clearing from the Clyde were engaged in the coasting trade. The foreign trade focused on the eastern seaboard of North America, on the West Indies and on Europe. The broadly equal division between coast-wise and foreign trade remained unchanged at least till 1870, although the commodities and relative importance of the markets altered, as did the importance of the major ports on the Clyde. Till 1775 Port Glasgow was the leading port, and tobacco dominated cargoes inward from America and outward to France and Holland. After the war foreign trade switched to Greenock and its contacts with the West Indies. Sugar, rum, molasses and cotton replaced the inflow of tobacco, and this more diversified trade kept Greenock in the forefront till about 1840. It partly held its place since no ocean-going vessel came up-river to the Broomielaw until 1818, and as late as the 1840s many vessels still had to off-load part of their cargo at the Tail-of-the-Bank before proceeding up-river. The major export throughout the period was textiles; linen until about 1790, and cotton piece-goods thereafter, the West Indies, the Low Countries and France being the most important outlets.

It was only in the 1840s that the river was sufficiently deepened to enable the harbour of Glasgow to come into its own. Once berthage and a deep channel were provided trade bypassed Greenock and Port Glasgow and swept into Glasgow at the heart of the new industrial region. And with the rise of Glasgow the character of trade changed once more. Basic food in the form of wheat, maize and flour contributed 240,000 tons of foreign imports to Glasgow Harbour in 1870, more than half the entire inward tonnage. This represented a strong upsurge of imports from North America, the West Indies now being more important as an export market, since the sugar trade drew over half its supplies from Java and European sugar-beet. In 1870, nearly 206,000 tons of raw sugar were landed, virtually all of it at Greenock; Greenock was by then most noted for its imports of sugar and exports of coal, while Port Glasgow dealt in the timber trade. Foreign exports from all Clyde ports were valued at over £10 million in 1868, £9·7 million from Glasgow; this was a measure of the dominance attained in the years after 1840. The foreign exports reflected the new industrial strength of the region. Iron, iron products, machinery, and coal represented 479,000 of the 504,000 tons of foreign exports from Glasgow. North America, France and Portugal were major markets for pig-iron and iron goods, while India was a major purchaser of textiles, which still represented over 60 per cent by value of all the exports of the region.

In strong contrast to 1770, the trade of the Clyde in 1870 reflected a region with an almost self-sufficient industrial base. Grain and food products dominated the imports, and only cotton, now largely brought in coast-wise from Liverpool, represented a significant dependence on external industrial resources. The thriving iron and engineering industries were supported by their own iron ore, their own fuel, and their own smelting and refining industries. The region's problem was not now to find a means to import scarce foreign resources to develop home-based industry, but rather to extend overseas markets regularly for its coal, iron and machinery, to enable its thriving industries to continue to grow. The effectiveness with which this trade could be prosecuted depended not only on the quality, price and range of commodities, but also on the smooth delivery of the goods to the ports for distribution. One of the earliest and continuing pressures generated by foreign and coast-wise trade in the local economy was the need to improve internal communications. Understandably, the pressures first proved greatest in water transport.

Ports

Increasing trade and industry involved Port Glasgow, Greenock and Glasgow in a century of conflict and competition for ascendancy on the Clyde, where Glasgow had both the greatest advantages and disadvantages for the development of a port. The advantages were embryonic while the disadvantages were immediate. Glasgow's advantages, actual or potential, were that the city was the lowest bridging point on the river; it lay at the centre of the new commercial and industrial developments in the west of Scotland, and was already the largest town serving a potentially rich industrial hinterland. In the mid-eighteenth century it also enjoyed the services of a substantial and wealthy merchant community. But Glasgow was twenty-five miles inland at the head of an estuarine obstacle course over which the Clyde crept reluctantly to the sea. The river spilled over a marshy flood plain and tidal mud-flats. In places the channel shifted erratically and every approach up-river was impeded by sandbanks and shoals. The Clyde below Glasgow was more a ditch than a channel and only the smallest river craft could reach the city from the sea. It was a grim prospect for a place with aspirations to become a great port.

Such difficulties could not easily be overcome. The supremacy on the Clyde went first to Port Glasgow, which was also the official harbour of Glasgow established in 1668 and under the direct control of the magistrates and merchants of the city. The main rival was Greenock, but in the bonanza years of the tobacco trade Port Glasgow overtook Greenock, and Glasgow took steps to underwrite this superiority by building the first dry dock in Scotland there in 1762, to a plan by James Watt. The outport was so important to Glasgow that a separate administrative body, the Commissioners of Port Glasgow Harbour, was created in 1772, and by the following year they had deepened the harbour and built a new quay to cope with the large American trade. Although in the shadow of Port Glasgow, Greenock merchants were actively developing their own port. Extra land for port extension was acquired on three occasions between 1762 and 1772 and in 1773 Greenock also established its 'Trustees of the Harbour' to supervise and promote port development. The tide of events was flowing rapidly in their favour, for the American war and the demise of the tobacco trade greatly reduced the shipping making use of Port Glasgow and gave Greenock an opportunity to consolidate its position. The upsurge in the West Indies trade focused on Greenock and the Harbour Trustees added a dry dock to their facilities in 1786 at a cost of £4,000. Port Glasgow did not give up its leading position lightly and in 1801 the Commissioners had the harbour extended to take in a tidal area of seven acres. The effort was in vain, for Greenock had yet grander plans in mind. The Trustees took powers in 1803 to build another dry dock and engaged John Rennie to prepare plans for a new harbour. Construction commenced in 1805 and the new East India Harbour was opened in 1809. It enclosed a water area of nine acres and had cost £43,836 exclusive of ground.

Port Glasgow and Glasgow had thus for a time lost the struggle for ascendancy to Greenock. The Glasgow merchants and magistrates now turned their attention away from Port Glasgow to focus on making Glasgow into a harbour easily accessible to all kinds of shipping. The conquest of the Clyde was accomplished in three stages. The first ran roughly from 1755 to 1799 and enabled coasting vessels to come up to Glasgow Bridge; the second from 1800 to 1839 threw Glasgow open to the new steam coastal and packet trade, while the third stage from 1840 to 1870 drew the shipping of the world into the heart of the city. The first stage involved the attempt to create a recognisable and navigable channel from an ill-defined water-course by deepening the river and confining its course. The work was carried out under powers granted by two Acts of Parliament based on the advice of three civil engineers. The obstacles were clearly charted by John Smeaton in 1755 when his survey revealed twelve major shoals in the river between Glasgow and Renfrew. His recommendations involved the construction of a dam and a lock four miles down-river from Glasgow Bridge at Marlin Ford, this to give a depth of 4 ft 6 in. in the harbour at all times. The town council took powers to implement this proposal in the first Act relating to the deepening of the Clyde in 1759. However, the contemporary improvements undertaken at Port Glasgow seem to have met the immediate needs of Glasgow's merchant community, and Smeaton's proposals were not implemented. Another decade passed before interest in improving the Clyde up to Glasgow again came to the fore, and this time John Golborne of Chester was invited to make a survey. Golborne's view was that the Clyde was 'in a state of nature'. He proposed contracting the river by constructing a system of rubble jetties to force the current into a narrow path and enable the strength of the river to scour and deepen its own channel. His estimate, including some dredging, was £8,640. The next year, James Watt surveyed the whole channel to make sure the problem areas were located. The scheme was simple, cheap and effective and in 1773 Golborne was given a second contract to tackle the major obstacle of Dumbuck Ford twelve miles downstream from the harbour. The town council desired a 300-foot wide channel, giving 6 feet of water at low tide, and the contract price was £2,300. Two years later Golborne had provided a channel 10 inches deeper than requested, and a grateful town council presented him with an additional £1,500 and a silver cup. This meant that in the 1780s and 1790s vessels of about 100 tons could come up-river to Glasgow as against small craft of 20 or 30 tons before 1755. But even that improvement did not permit the larger vessels trading to England and Ireland to come direct to Glasgow with their cargoes.

The second stage in improving the channel was ushered in by John Rennie's report of 1799. He found that Golborne's jetties had created a channel with ragged edges and that shoals frequently grew between the groynes, hampering the flow of water. He advised that greater depth could be obtained by building some new jetties and joining up their ends to form a continuous smooth retaining wall on each side of the river. More than 200 new jetties were undertaken and in 1806 Thomas Telford confirmed Rennie's advice in a lengthy report to which Rennie once more added his weight in 1807. In 1809 the town council obtained a third River Improvement Act to deepen the Clyde to give 9 feet of water at neap tides, and to set up an administrative body, the Trustees of the Clyde Navigation, to carry out the improvements. The conversion of the Clyde into a ship canal was under way. A fourth Act of 1825 aimed to increase the depth of water to 13 feet all the way from Port Glasgow to Glasgow Bridge. This involved the continuous deepening and straightening of the channel, the work being much eased in 1824 with the introduction of the first steam dredger. The benefits were immediate, and in 1828 almost 700,000 tons of shipping arrived in the harbour of Glasgow, over two-thirds being coastal steam tonnage, which was less affected by tide and current. As a result of these schemes, by 1836 there was between 7 and 8 feet of water at the Broomielaw at low water, 12 feet at neap tides and 15 feet at spring tides. This was sufficient to enable ships of 300–400 tons to come up-river to the heart of the city, and represented the work of over 60 years and an expenditure of about £1·5 million. Enough had been done to tilt the scales of port ascendancy away from Greenock in favour of Glasgow itself in spite of vast outlays in improvement at Greenock Harbour.

Even with this improvement many ocean-going ships still had to unload part of their cargoes at the Tail-of-the-Bank before proceeding up to Glasgow, taking two or three tides to come to the harbour. Deeper water was still required and the foundation for the third stage in river improvement was laid with the Act of 1840 which made provision for a 17-foot deep channel. This was to be achieved by increasing the tidal volume reaching Glasgow and extending the time over which the tide flowed into the harbour. This meant undoing much of the work of the years from 1800 to 1840 which had progressively narrowed the channel. The new aim seemed to require a substantial broadening of the navigable channel and more intensive dredging. This set the pattern for the next thirty years and was the last Act dealing specifically with improvement of the channel. By 1870 neap tides gave between 24 and 26 feet of water at Glasgow and ships of 3,000 tons could come up to the harbour on a single tide.

Glasgow was at last a major port accessible to the largest vessels afloat. Progress would have been even more remarkable but for the obstacle of the Elderslie rock, brought to light in 1854 when the *Glasgow*, a steamer en route for New York, grounded on it. This proved to be a huge whinstone intrusion, 100 yards wide and over 300 yards in length. Fifteen years and £16,000 later, underwater blasting operations had carved a channel giving 14 feet of water over half its width at low tide.

With such dramatic progress in deepening the river, the next strain was on harbour accommodation in Glasgow. Another seven Acts of Parliament between 1846 and 1870 dealt with various aspects of the harbour improvements. In 1840 total quayage was only 1,800 yards and this had been extended to over 6,000 yards by 1870. Moreover, after fourteen reports from eight different engineers between 1806 and 1855, the harbour Trustees eventually constructed the first wet dock, Kingston Dock. Growing pressure on berthage space on the river had finally forced this move. When opened in 1867, the dock enclosed over 5 acres of water and provided another 830 yards of quays. This was quickly followed by the more ambitious proposals in 1870 for Stobcross Docks (later Queen's Docks), these bringing in a fourth phase of improvement which lasted till the First World War and concentrated on the construction of wet docks.

After a century of continuous work the Clyde Navigation Trust had expended some £6·5 million in improving the Clyde and Glasgow harbour and had earned a revenue of nearly £3·5 million. In the last phase of massive improvement Greenock made a heroic effort to hold on to her leading position, opening the Victoria Harbour in 1850 at a cost of £120,000. This was followed in 1862 by the Albert Harbour, costing some £250,000, the Prince's Pier being constructed at the same time for a further £100,000. Nearly £500,000 was spent within fifteen years, but even this could not halt Glasgow's climb to pre-eminence. In 1872 Glasgow Harbour cleared 2·3 million tons of shipping compared with only 769,000 tons for Greenock and a mere 82,000 for Port Glasgow. Glasgow's long catalogue of disadvantages had been overcome and her inherent advantages now attracted the shipping of the world into the heart of industrial Scotland.

Canals

While the magistrates of Glasgow bent their will and resources to make the Clyde navigable, merchants, landowners and industrialists looked for similar ways to improve their own situation. Water was the easiest way to move large tonnages of coal, grain and timber, and the striking success of the Duke of Bridgewater's canal in cutting the cost of conveying his coal to Manchester was well known. His achievement sparked off a period of frantic canal-building in England, and the mania spread to Scotland.

But only two canals of any commercial significance were ever built in Scotland, and both had their origins in the urge to imitate the English developments in the 1760s. These were the Forth and Clyde Navigation and the Monkland Canals. A third canal within the region, the Glasgow, Paisley and Johnstone Canal, had its origins in the second canal mania of the 1790s. These three canals were built with very different purposes in mind. The narrow waist of central Scotland between the Forth and Clyde had long presented itself as a natural isthmus to be spanned by a waterway, and the Forth and Clyde Canal was conceived in the 1760s as a coast-to-coast ship canal, linking the merchants of Edinburgh and the east of Scotland to the Atlantic trade, and opening up the Baltic to the penetration of Glasgow traders. The Monkland Canal, in contrast, was designed purely as an inland navigation way, specifically to open up the coal seams of north Lanarkshire. Somewhat later the Glasgow, Paisley and Ardrossan Canal was planned to make Ardrossan an international port linking Glasgow with the outside world. Not all of these hopes were to be realised.

The plan to link the firths of Clyde and Forth was the first to be mooted. A private survey, sponsored by Lord Napier in 1762, interested the Board of Trustees, who commissioned John Smeaton to investigate the possibilities. His report of 1764 charted two routes, the first to run from Abbotshaugh on the River Carron to the River Kelvin, and hence to the Clyde at Yoker. The other route began on the Forth north of Stirling, linked to the River Endrick, and hence into Loch Lomond and out to the Clyde at Dumbarton by way of the River Leven. The provisional estimate for the first route was £80,000, and the cost and alternative routes excited much discussion in Edinburgh and Glasgow. Glasgow merchants preferred a route terminating in Glasgow, and presented their own Parliamentary Bill for a 'small canal' in 1767. This was to run from Carronshore on the Forth to Glasgow, and was to be 24 feet wide and 4 feet deep. The estimated cost, including a link to Bo'ness, was around £50,000. Two Glasgow tobacco lords, John Glassford and John Ritchie, immediately took up 242 of the 400 shares offered to subscribers at £100 per share. The wrath and indignation of Edinburgh and east-coast merchants was unleashed in invective condemning the Glasgow venture, and in immediate action to promote a 'great canal' which would properly serve the national interest. A competing Bill was hurried before Parliament in May 1767, and a promise of compensation, and the inclusion of canal cuts to Glasgow and Bo'ness persuaded the promoters of the 'small canal' to withdraw their Bill. John Smeaton was again set to work to provide a route to take vessels of sixty tons, and recommended the link from the River Carron to the Clyde at Dalmuir, at a cost of £147,337. The Act for construction was finally passed in March 1768 and authorised the raising of £150,000 in £100 shares, with power to raise a further £50,000 if necessary. Of the original subscriptions offered, £128,700 was eventually paid up.

Digging began at the eastern end in June 1768. By August 1773 the canal had been brought as far west as Kirkintilloch, and the canal basin at Stockingfield, two miles north of Glasgow, had been laid out. Two years later, the canal had linked up with the Stockingfield basin and work had come to a halt, the entire subscribed funds being exhausted and a debt of £31,000 accumulated. Boats were already running on the open section of the canal and the small annual revenue of under £5,000 could not carry the work forward into Glasgow. However, in May 1776 a major proprietor, Sir Lawrence Dundas, seems to have made a loan sufficient to plan the Hamiltonhill basin one mile north of Glasgow, and by November 1777 the branch from Stockingfield to Hamiltonhill had been cut, partly, it appears, on the initiative and money of the Glasgow merchants. By mid-1778, ten years after construction had commenced, the proprietors had spent £157,372 on the main canal and £7,169 on the Glasgow branch and still needed £60,000 to finish the task. An application for government support had been made in 1776 but had been unsuccessful, being swept aside in the troubles of the war with America, but in 1784 a new request obtained a loan secured on the revenue. This was a sum of £50,000 drawn from the proceeds of the sales of annexed and forfeited estates. With funds available, the last section was resurveyed and the western terminus changed to Bowling. The canal was finally opened in July 1790, almost exactly twenty-two years after construction commenced. It was 38¾ miles in length, incorporated thirty-nine locks and was opened at an average depth of eight feet.

The Monkland Canal suffered an equally protracted construction, in spite of the urgency with which Glasgow magistrates and merchants wanted to break the monopoly of local coalmasters in the supply of coal. James Watt provided two proposals for a canal from the Monklands to Glasgow in 1769, each beginning at Woodhall and running through Coatbridge to Drumpellier. From there the canal could either be continued to the Clyde near Glasgow Green at a cost of over £20,000, or could end near Germiston and be linked to Glasgow by a short waggonway at a cost of £9,653. Economy triumphed, the second scheme was accepted and a Bill obtained from Parliament in 1770. This permitted the raising of £10,000 in shares of £100, with another £5,000 to be raised if required. The sum was quickly subscribed by the landowners through whose property the canal would pass and by those interested in the prosperity of the city. These included major merchants like James Buchanan, Alexander Spiers and John Glassford, as well as bodies like the Trades House, the university and several of the incorporated trades like the maltmen and bakers. James Watt was retained to supervise construction, which began in the Monklands at Sheepford in June 1770.

In May 1773 the canal had progressed just over seven miles. Soon after, all work ceased, the entire subscribed capital having been expended. In the aftermath of the collapse of the Ayr Bank neither credit nor increased subscriptions could be obtained, and the canal remained two miles short of Glasgow until 1782. Subscribers refused to meet a 10 per cent call on their shares in 1780, and in 1781 the shares were offered for sale in batches of five for £150. All but eleven shares were quickly acquired by Andrew Stirling of Drumpellier, the major coalowner on the canal route, and by his brothers, John and James Stirling, bleachers and dyers in the Vale of Leven. Work was recommenced, but the canal had to overcome considerable obstacles before penetrating to the city. The major difficulty was the series of locks required at Blackhill to link the eastern and western sections of the canal over a rise of 96 feet. It was not till November 1793 that through navigation was complete all the way from the Monklands to the Port Dundas basin, which had linked the Forth and Clyde Canal to the Monkland in 1791. The canal was 12¼ miles in length and had taken over 23 years to complete at a cost of some £120,000.

The final opening of these two canals coincided with the birth of the idea for the third canal from Ardrossan to Glasgow, sponsored by the twelfth Earl of Eglinton. His hope was that 'Ardrossan would be to Glasgow what Liverpool is to Manchester'. Two surveys by John Rennie in 1800 and by Rennie and Ainslie in 1804 sketched out a route which was modified by Thomas Telford in a third survey in 1805. This outlined plans for a canal thirty-two miles long at an estimated cost of £134,500. The enabling Act was passed in 1806, offering £50 shares to a total of £140,000. Only a little over £44,000 was subscribed, a further £61,000 being raised by loans among the proprietors. Digging began at Tradeston in May 1807 and the whole section of eleven miles between Glasgow and Johnstone was opened in October 1811, all the money raised having been spent. Hopes of completing the work finally died in 1816 when the government refused an application for a loan of £135,000, and though an attempt was made to link Ardrossan to Johnstone by a railway in 1827, the poor response in subscriptions only carried the line to Kilwinning. The link to Johnstone had to wait until 1840, when the Ardrossan Railway Co. linked up with the Glasgow, Paisley, Kilmarnock and Ayr Railway.

These canals had three unfortunate features in common. They took a long time to construct, the Ardrossan venture never being completed; they cost much more than anticipated; and the return on the investment had an exceptionally long gestation period. In all three cases the estimated costs were greatly exceeded. The Forth and Clyde was initially planned to cost £147,337, but almost £330,000 had been spent before it opened. The Monkland was originally intended to cost £7,653, but over £120,000 had gone into the enterprise by 1793, and the Ardrossan to Glasgow venture used up its estimated cost of £134,500 in a third of the distance between Glasgow and Johnstone. This investment of £580,000 in three canals produced little quick return. The Monkland did not pay a dividend until 1807, some 14 years after opening and 37 years after construction began. The Forth and Clyde was a little better and paid out its first dividend of 10 per cent in 1800, 30 years after commencement and 10 years after completion. The ill-fated Glasgow, Paisley and Johnstone never paid a dividend to its original subscribers. The commercial optimism which had lain behind the ventures was clearly misplaced, being based on an exaggerated notion of the ability of the canals to create trade, and fostered by the spurious precision of the estimates furnished by the civil engineers. Although every canal Bill took account of the unknown in costs by providing for a 50 per cent increase in authorised capital, if required, even this was insufficient to cover the margin of error contained in the guesswork of the surveyors. But once begun, the investment was so heavy that capital had to be poured in endlessly to bring the projects to a point where some return would be obtained. Had the surveyors been capable of accurate costing, and produced original estimates on the scale of the final costs of construction, it is doubtful if any of these canals would ever have been built.

It is arguable, too, that the Forth and Clyde Canal never fulfilled its original purpose; that the Monkland Canal was built in advance of requirements, and if any justification ever existed for the Ardrossan to Glasgow venture it had disappeared before construction was undertaken. The Forth and Clyde never became a great ship canal. Ocean-going ships outgrew the lock sizes and the Napoleonic Wars curtailed the trade eastward to the Baltic and the Low Countries. The canal became an inland waterway for coal from Port Dundas to Grangemouth, while the western end from Bowling to Maryhill became a feeder of raw materials to the factories that grew along its banks. This was profitable enough, dividends rising from the 10 per cent in 1800 to a peak of 30 per cent by 1840. At the other extreme the Ardrossan venture aimed to provide an ocean outlet for Glasgow, but this was overtaken by the rapid deepening of the channel of the Clyde, even while plans for the projected canal were under consideration. The stretch finally opened to Johnstone had a brief period of success in the 1830s, when it pioneered rapid-transit passenger barges and carried over 420,000 passengers in 1836. In contrast, the Monkland Canal eventually exceeded all expectations, but the gestation period between design and achievement was a long one. The hope was that the link to the Monkland would pour cheap coal into Glasgow, but this was only partially achieved because, first, the Glasgow market in the 1780s and 1790s failed to generate the demand the proprietors of the canal had anticipated, and secondly, the landowners along the canal kept coal production and supply in check in an attempt to force up prices. By 1806 only four collieries were in production along its banks, and although they

produced 130,000 tons of coal, only 60–80 tons of coal were delivered
each day to Glasgow by canal as late as 1813, a mere 20,000–25,000 tons
per year. The real worth of the canal was not exploited until the 1820s,
when short cuts were established to the ironworks at Calder, Gartsherrie,
Langloan and Dundyvan. Coal and iron then began to pour along the
canal and out to England, Ireland and the Continent by the Clyde, and
for the rest of its working life over four-fifths of all tonnage carried was of
coal and iron.

All three canals eventually fell under the control of the railways and
this undoubtedly shortened their working life. The Paisley and Johnstone
Canal was never of much economic significance. It was taken over by the
Glasgow and South Western Railway in 1869, and closed in 1881. The
Monkland and Forth and Clyde Canals amalgamated in 1846, and both
were taken over by the Caledonian Railway Co. in 1867, after which the
traffic began to decline. The Monkland was the more important of these
two in the economic life of the region, but even then its significant years
were only those between the 1820s and the 1860s. The canals were
highly specific, in that they served limited areas and carried the raw
materials and products of relatively few industries. The north of
Lanarkshire was linked to Glasgow by a flow of coal and iron and this
moulded the industrial geography of the region at a critical and early stage
of growth. The canals were undoubtedly an enormous advantage to the
coal- and ironmasters, moving bulky products smoothly and economically,
but they did not free the region and its resources from the general
immobility imposed by poor transport links; that was the task first of the
roads and then of the railways.

Roads

The importance of canals has tended to overshadow the significance of
roads in the development of the west of Scotland, but on balance the
roads were probably more important. The region could undoubtedly
have developed its resources in the absence of its canals, but without roads
little could have been achieved. Before the coming of the railways, and
to an extent afterward, only roads could link every hamlet to the major
towns. A growing region required improved means of communication
and a network of roads offered the only hope of exchanging general
isolation for widespread mobility. The task confronting the roadmakers
was immense. In the mid-eighteenth century the only made roads in the
region were a few miles of town streets. In the broad expanse of the
countryside the traveller had to depend on roughly-graded tracks of clay
and gravel, though important routes usually had a stone or gravel cause-
way in the centre, enabling horses to travel in wet weather. For all
practical purposes the wheel might as well not have existed; the pack-

horse and the horse-drawn sledge were the common carriers of the day. Such conditions meant that Glasgow was only saved from complete isolation from the rest of Britain because of the sea-lanes, for travel overland to Glasgow was extremely difficult. Even within the city the wheel was almost unknown. In 1744 it was reported that neither hackneys nor post-chaises could be found in Glasgow, the visitor having to entrust himself to the two or three sedan-chair carriers who plied the streets. Three years later, Provost Andrew Cochran set out for London to seek compensation for Glasgow's losses during the 1745 rebellion. To do so he had to have a carriage built for the journey and had to travel first to Edinburgh before heading south, since there was no route capable of taking a wheeled vehicle going direct from Glasgow. The journey took him and his party thirteen days. Overland communication was difficult, even hazardous, and the journey to Edinburgh took twelve hours by carriage and two days for carts.

This state of affairs existed a century after legislation had made provision for improving roads, but during which little had been done because of lack of demand, lack of money, and lack of technical know-how. But by 1750 a vigorous foreign, coastal and overland trade, the stirrings of agricultural improvement and the beginning of rapid population growth provided the need for more effective land transport, and the earlier legislation was a starting-point for new developments. The Act of 1669 had introduced statute labour, empowering sheriffs and justices of the peace to call on tenants, cottars and servants to provide up to six days' labour yearly for a man and a horse, between seed-time and harvest, for the purpose of making and repairing roads. Provision was also made to lay a tax on the 'Heritors of the Shire' (the larger landowners) at a rate not exceeding 10 shillings Scots in each £100 Scots of valued rent in one year. The legislation also allowed for the levying of moderate customs at bridges, causeways and ferries, the proceeds to go towards their upkeep. The terms of the Act therefore provided for a management body for roadmaking, a pool of labour, and a moderate source of capital by assessment and occasional toll charges. The system was ineffective, since the sheriffs and justices met irregularly, and statute labour was forced labour given unwillingly and available only at certain times of the year. Moreover, supervision was inadequate and the quality of work thus extremely poor. There was need for regular administration, regular construction and supervision and more adequate finance. After 1750 these requirements were met, partly by gradually commuting the labour services to money payments to build and maintain the group of roads which came to be known as the 'statute-labour' roads. This was a local solution applicable at the parish level and effective also for private roads on estates. The solution for main routes emerged from the idea of charging tolls for the use of roads and bridges, the revenue to be used to construct and main-

tain the highway. This was the turnpike road which, together with the
statute-labour and private roads, formed the framework for road improvement after 1750.

The more dramatic improvements came with the turnpike roads.
Ayrshire led the way in western Scotland with two general Turnpike Acts
in 1766–7 and 1774. These set up a body of turnpike trustees drawn from
the heritors of the shire, and this county trust in turn delegated authority
to numerous district committees to appoint surveyors, hire labour and
supervise the construction and administration of the improved roads.
The Acts provided for borrowing powers, the sum to be secured on the
tolls charged, though much of the capital came from funds advanced by
local landowners, and a little from direct investment by persons hoping
for a profitable dividend. Ayrshire's modern road pattern was substantially laid out by 1800 under these two enactments, the period between 1780 and 1800 being particularly busy in road construction.

The initial aims were modest. The new roads were planned to be
between 24 and 30 feet wide, but only the central half of the road was to
be metalled, the remainder to be left as 'a summer road'. The prevailing
wisdom was for solid foundations, with bottoming frequently 3 feet deep,
the road proper to consist of heavy stones, the surface to be a 3-inch
layer 'with no stone bigger than a goose egg'. This gave a road depth of
not less than 15 inches at the centre, declining to 12 inches at the outer
edge to encourage water to drain off. This was a vain hope, for the water
inevitably percolated through the layers, eroded the subsoil and undermined the foundations, with the result that the bottom boulders quickly
rose to the surface to shatter carriage wheels. It was this constructional
problem which preoccupied John Loudon McAdam, when he was
appointed a trustee in 1787. He set out to keep the subsoil dry and hence
to stabilise the foundations by making the road surface impervious to
water. He dispensed with the deep and expensive bottoming and laid a
thin veneer of road metal in three layers directly on the subsoil. Instead of
using rounded stones and gravel as before, his principle was 'to put
broken stone upon a road which shall unite by its own angles so as to
form a solid hard surface'. The angular broken stones interlocked and
eliminated the movement common with the use of rounded road metal,
and surface drainage was achieved by imparting a camber of not more
than 3 inches on a 30-foot-wide road. With an impervious surface and
dry stable foundations the road could carry considerable loads. Even so,
his method was not quickly adopted, for as late as 1793 Ayrshire roads
normally accommodated cart loads of only 10–12 cwt, while the paved
roads in Glasgow could bear three times that burden in a single cart.

Construction was not the only problem. Finding a route was also
difficult, since many landowners objected to having their plantations and
enclosures encroached upon. Also, in the interest of economy, the line of

a new road was frequently tied closely to the old route, where land previously used could be returned to the landowner in compensation for new land taken up by the highway, hence saving on the cost of acquiring land by purchase. This sometimes resulted in poor alignment and steep gradients, and McAdam felt that in the early phase of road-building much money was laid out with little effect. The roads of the 1780s were still poor, and when the commissioners of supply and justices of the peace of Lanarkshire and Ayrshire joined forces in 1787 to promote a road from Glasgow through Strathaven, Muirkirk and Sanquhar, and hence south to Dumfries and Carlisle, they found great difficulties in their way. Their surveyor, John Ainslie, reported that 'the road from Muirkirk to Strathaven in its present condition is so wretchedly bad that it is next to an impossibility to travel upon it without a guide and even then very dangerous and altogether impassable for any carriage'. An effective and short Glasgow to Carlisle route over Beattock did not come until that promoted by an Act of 1816, engineered by Thomas Telford and contracted for construction between 1817 and 1824. This was only completed with a loan of £50,000 from the government, administered through James Hope, the Edinburgh agent of the Commissioners for Highland Roads and Bridges, a body established in 1803 to promote road and bridge building in the Highlands and other remote areas. A further £35,897 was subscribed privately. The administration was in the hands of the Commissioners for the Glasgow to Carlisle road. Construction was undertaken in numerous short sections by different builders and the total cost was £89,035, about £1,200 per mile, inclusive of all bridges and eight toll houses. The road was built to Telford's specifications, which demanded a solid stone foundation overlaid by two seven-inch layers of stone packed firmly by hand. It was a more expensive and less durable technique than McAdam's, and in the 1820s many turnpikes were remaking their roads by McAdam's method. This was forced on the trustees, for road surfaces long remained the weak point in construction. As late as 1818 many Ayrshire turnpikes retained a favourable toll charge of 1½d.–2½d. for sledges or 'carts without wheels', since they did less damage to the road surface. Even the great Glasgow to Carlisle road conceded half rates to carts with broad wheels for the same reason.

The skeleton of today's road system was well established by 1800. By 1830 the major constructional problems having been overcome, the region and its towns were well served by all-weather turnpikes. Statute-labour roads were less durable in remote areas, but provided a generally serviceable and dense network of local roads. The barriers of distance and time had been reduced to the minimum possible in the age of the horse. On the best roads average speeds of 10 miles per hour could be achieved by the 1830s. Edinburgh lay within 4½ hours of Glasgow and London could be reached in 72 hours instead of 12 or 13 days. Where the region had had virtually no mileage of all-weather roads in 1750, it had over 1,100 miles of turnpike in 1830 and at least as much mileage of statute-labour roads. Thirty years later there were 1,464 miles of turnpike and 2,000 miles of statute roads. These were the inland lifelines of the region before the coming of the railway. Rural Scotland depended on its roads for the movement of its lime, its manure and its coals, and all farm products flowed along local roads on to turnpikes and into the growing markets of the industrial towns. The cotton industry in both its urban and rural locations depended almost entirely on heavy carts to bring its raw materials to the factory and distribute its cloth and yarn to the docks and inland markets. Heavy industrial transport also depended greatly on the roads. The canals were short and could serve only their immediate locality. It was roads that poured coal on to the canals, and in 1830 over 300,000 tons of coal came directly into Glasgow on local roads. Within the towns themselves there was, of course, no alternative to road transport. In the 1820s coaches flowed daily from Glasgow to London, Edinburgh and Perth, as well as to the main towns in the region. A decade later a small town like Hamilton had seven daily coaches and a mail coach connecting with Glasgow, while Lanark was connected twice daily in summer and once per day in winter, as well as having regular freight services provided by a number of carriers.

Yet in spite of these dramatic improvements, all was not well with the road system. Statute-labour roads were variable in quality and the turnpikes were heavily in debt. In 1859 the region's 1,400 miles of turnpike carried an accumulated burden of over £731,000. Nearly £207,000 of this was simply unpaid interest on monies lent to the trusts and was virtually unrecoverable. The first charge on the revenue of the Scottish trusts was the maintenance and repair of the road and this left little to pay off the subscribed capital. Much of the debt was also held by the railways, who assumed it as one way of stifling opposition to their Parliamentary Bills. The Caledonian Railway took over £15,000 of the private creditors' debt of the Glasgow to Carlisle road for this purpose, and over half the indebtedness of Renfrewshire's turnpikes was held by railway companies, who clearly expected no return on their investment. Nevertheless, the existence of a large debt, even though it took this curious form, made it difficult to end the turnpike system. Toll roads were not finally abandoned until the 1880s. Not only were the turnpikes encumbered with debt; their administration was complicated and clumsy. The coming of the railways forced, in places, a rationalisation of administration as in Ayrshire where, after 1847, both turnpike and statute-labour roads were administered by one body of trustees. But in Lanarkshire the twenty-three turnpikes each had their separate body. Uniformity in management was therefore difficult to achieve and made it hard to reduce the large number of toll points on single roads. The Cambuslang to Muirkirk road had twelve tolls within 55 miles and the Glasgow to Ayr road had ten tollhouses within 34 miles. Such circumstances were clearly a discouragement to road traffic. After 1840 the volume of traffic declined sharply as the railways destroyed the coaching service, captured mails and passengers, and took over the inland transportation of heavy and bulky commodities. Roads remained important in the remoter countryside, in towns and as feeders to the railway station, but road transport played a diminished role after 1840. It had to await the motor-car in the present century before it could once more offer speed, economy and flexibility of carriage on a scale sufficient to compete with the railway.

Railways

In the absence of reliable roads, the usual solution to the problem of moving bulky goods had been to make use of water transport, by river, sea, or by man-made canals. But by the mid-eighteenth century a practicable alternative had been discovered. For short distances, the laying of wooden or metal tracks for wheeled vehicles was found to be superior to the making of a primitive road surface that constantly required renewal. These tramways or plateways were generally used for coal or mineral traffic. With few exceptions they were designed to connect coal or iron-works to water, to a river, a canal or a port. As early as the 1750s two such tramways linked the pits of Wm Dixon at Govan and John Dixon at Knightswood to the Clyde at Windmillcroft and Yoker respectively. A similar link of coal to water transport was developed in Ayrshire in the 1770s. Two lines joined local pits to the harbour at Ayr and Newton-upon-Ayr, and a third line operated from Irvine Colliery to Irvine harbour. A canal connection was made in 1820 by the Hurlet Coal and Lime Works, with a two-mile line to the Glasgow and Johnstone Canal at Paisley. These tramways solved distribution problems for coal, but they could also be used simply for the collection and delivery of raw materials in iron production. Between 1805 and 1813 Lanarkshire's early landlocked works at Omoa, Shotts and Wilsontown also had short lines to transport coal and ore to and from their furnaces.

The idea of moving heavy loads on wheeled carriages along special tracks was clearly well understood in the west of Scotland, but the full development of the principle had to await the railway age. This revolution in transport came in three short stages between 1825 and 1850. The region's rail network was begun with the mineral lines between 1825 and 1835, was then extended by the town-to-town lines between 1838 and 1842, and finally was tied into a growing national system with the building of the Anglo-Scottish routes between 1845 and 1850. Each period of building was associated with a flurry of intensive investment in railway construction in Britain generally, the speculation being particularly severe in the two railway manias of 1835–7 and 1845–7.

The birthplace of Scotland's modern railway system was the Monklands mineral fields. The first line authorised in Scotland to use a locomotive for haulage was the Monkland and Kirkintilloch Railway, opened in 1826. This short line of ten-and-a-half miles linked the eastern end of the Monkland Canal to the Forth and Clyde Canal at Kirkintilloch. It opened up a quicker route to Edinburgh, and short-circuited the Blackhill locks on the Monkland Canal by enabling coal to come into Glasgow on the Forth and Clyde Canal. Two years later the Kipps colliery branch of the M&K was extended four miles eastward to the Arden Colliery in the Ballochney Railway. These lines were transitional from the plateway to the true railway. Both used the edge-rail instead of plates, and though authorised to use a locomotive, both still used horse haulage. This link was then extended south and eastward by the Wishaw and Coltness line, opened in stages between 1833 and 1843, while the Ballochney merged eastward into the Slamannan Railway built between 1835 and 1840 to give a link with the Union Canal at Causewayend, and through it, quick access to the Edinburgh market (Map 3).

The two original lines, the M&K and the Ballochney, and their extensions in the Wishaw and Coltness and Slamannan railways were conceived as feeders to the canals. Their promoters sought to break the monopoly of the few coalmasters along the banks of the Monkland Canal by opening up a wider hinterland of exploitable coal, and to extend the market for coal in Edinburgh and Glasgow. The promoters were coalmasters, ironmakers and landowners in the Monklands and Glasgow, but they were canal-minded. Though they built the new railway routes, they were reluctant to become involved in providing a haulage service. They preferred customers to use their own carriages and horses, and to pay a toll for the use of the track. These early lines were more like iron turnpikes than modern railways.

The initiative which turned this transitional system into the core of Scotland's modern railway network was the Garnkirk and Glasgow Railway, opened in 1831. Only 8¼ miles long, it ran a line of double tracks parallel to the Monkland Canal from Gartsherrie to St Rollox and transformed the idea of the railway from that of a feeder to a competitor of the canal. It also employed steam locomotives from the outset and inaugurated its service by undercutting the canal rates by 25 per cent. It forced the canal rapidly to reduce its own rates by a third and left the proprietors of the other local lines with no alternative but to introduce steam locomotives and make the transition from operators of railway turnpikes to railways proper by providing their own rolling stock, haulage and services. The railway age had arrived by 1831, with 24 miles of operating track in the Monklands, all only 4 ft 6 in. in width, all

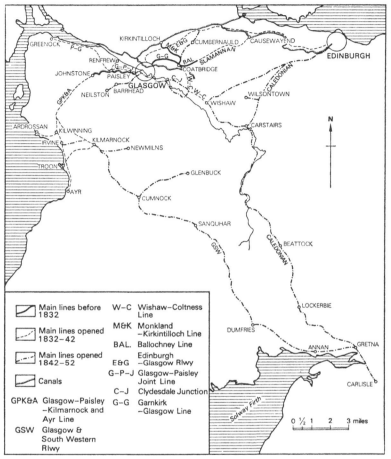

MAP 3 *Railways in operation, 1830–50*

carrying some passengers, but all being primarily designed to carry coal, ironstone, iron and other minerals. The effect on coal prices in Glasgow was dramatic. Between 1826 and 1828 the M&K was instrumental in cutting the delivered price of coal from about 12s. to 6s. per ton, and between 1832 and 1836 the Garnkirk and Glasgow brought cartage rates down from about 5d. to 2d. per ton mile. Such economy had potent effects on tonnages carried. In 1832, its first full year of operation, the Garnkirk and Glasgow carried 114,114 tons of minerals and goods, 62,605 passengers and earned a revenue of £6,476. By 1845, its last full year of independent operation, revenue had increased to £24,600, mineral and goods tonnage had grown to 354,616 tons, and passengers carried had increased to 282,000. Throughout the period the revenue earned by carrying passengers was only 30 per cent of total revenue, and this was typical of these essentially mineral-carrying lines.

The provision of passenger services was taken up more fully in the second stage of construction, when the town-to-town links were established between 1838 and 1842. Four routes were important here. The Glasgow–Paisley Joint line, and the Glasgow, Paisley, Kilmarnock and Ayr opened in 1840; the Glasgow, Paisley and Greenock which began operations in 1841, and the Edinburgh and Glasgow line in 1842. The GPK&A completed what the Earl of Eglinton had set out to do with the Glasgow–Ardrossan Canal in 1806, and which the Ardrossan to Johnstone Railway (authorised in 1827) had failed to do by reaching only to Kilwinning. It opened up the mineral fields of north Ayrshire, linked Glasgow quickly to the Irish Sea and established a system of steam packet services to Clyde holiday resorts, England and Ireland. The route also became the focus for a number of Ayrshire's ironworks, notably Glengarnock, Blair and Eglinton. The Glasgow, Paisley and Greenock linked the busy south-bank towns and drew off the passengers from the lucrative river-boat services, by making the journey to Greenock in under an hour, while the boat took 2 to 3 hours, the time depending on the state of the tide. The Glasgow and Paisley route also quickly attracted the profitable passenger and parcel trade from the Glasgow–Johnstone Canal and the same fate befell the Forth and Clyde Canal when the E&G line opened in 1842, cutting the time from 4 hours by canal and road to 2½ hours by rail. Cost, however, was even more important than speed. The E&G Railway set its goods rates at 25 per cent below the Forth and Clyde and Union canals, and its passenger fares equal to the canal rates. In spite of substantial canal rate reductions, the Union Canal was quickly in trouble. It was purchased by the E&G in 1849.

The E&G was a significant line in a number of ways. It was the first line designed as a high-speed trunk connection, to cater for passengers and goods services between Scotland's two major cities. It was also a standard gauge line of 4 ft 8½ in., as distinct from the 4 ft 6 in. of the mineral lines, and it marked a radical departure in the scale and provision of finance for railway building in Scotland. The Monkland mineral lines had been both cheap and largely locally financed. The M&K cost only £3,700 per mile; it had numbered James Merry, a local coalmaster, and Charles Tennant of St Rollox among its main shareholders. The Garnkirk and Glasgow, with its double track, cost under £12,000 per mile and three local families, the Bairds, the Tennants and the Sprotts, were major investors. Compared with this, the E&G, built as a high-speed inter-city line, cost about £26,000 per mile of double track, and

90 per cent of its capital was English in origin. This reflected both the widening appeal of railway investment as the capital market developed, and indicated the need to widen the sources of finance as construction costs rose.

With links established between the main towns in Lowland Scotland, and connections made between the new coalfields, ironworks, local markets and ports, pressure increased to take the next step and link up the local lines with England. Two possible routes presented themselves. The first was the more direct, following the Glasgow–Carlisle Turnpike up the Clyde valley, over Beattock summit and down Annandale to Lockerbie, Gretna and Carlisle. The second lay further west and was attractive to the GPK&A, which could extend from Kilmarnock through Auchinleck and down the valley of the Nith to Sanquhar and Dumfries. The merits of both routes raised considerable debate, the problem of the gradient over Beattock causing particular concern. Opinion eventually favoured this line and it became the main route of the English-controlled Caledonian Railway Company. The GPK&A was left to build its own way south in stages between 1845 and 1850, at one time pulling up the track on a premature Newmilns–Galston line for re-laying on the trunk route. The hope had been that the small Glasgow, Dumfries and Carlisle line would build energetically northward to meet the GPK&A, but the final link was not made until 1850, when the smaller line merged with the GPK&A to become the Glasgow and South Western Railway. Even after establishing links with England the GSW remained a regional line, dominated by Scottish investment, only 16 per cent of its capital coming from England in 1852, and 64 per cent being concentrated in the hands of Glasgow and west of Scotland shareholders.

The shorter trunk route constructed by the Caledonian was opened in 1848, the link as with the GPK&A depending upon a degree of amalgamation. The Caledonian branched at Carstairs to go east to Edinburgh and west down the Clyde valley towards Glasgow, where it found its way barred by the E&G and the Monkland mineral lines. The door to Glasgow was opened by ensnaring the Wishaw and Coltness and Garnkirk and Glasgow lines with offers of between $8\frac{1}{2}$ and 10 per cent dividends on their stock for leasing their lines to the Caledonian. The agreement took effect in 1846 and gave the Caledonian a dominant position in the Clyde valley, and an entrée to the rich mineral fields of north Lanarkshire. One effect was to cause the M&K and Ballochney and Slamannan lines to amalgamate in 1847, to form the Monkland Railways and to convert to standard-gauge lines. This small but important company straddled the heart of the iron and coal districts, and remained independent until 1865, when on successive days it amalgamated with the E&G, which was then taken over by the North British Railway.

The construction of the Anglo-Scottish routes by 1850 set the pattern of railway control and competition in the west of Scotland. The Caledonian split Lowland Scotland in two, controlled the Clyde valley and had important routes in the north Lanarkshire coalfield and into Glasgow on the north bank of the Clyde. The Monkland Railways and the E&G, the forerunners of the North British in the area, were dominant in the east–west traffic in the Forth-Clyde valley, and the GSW controlled the south-west, Ayrshire, and routes into Glasgow on the south bank. The lure of access to the south of Glasgow also drew the Caledonian, which entered the territory of the GPK&A in 1848 with its Glasgow, Barrhead and Neilston direct line, terminating in the south-side station at the end of Gorbals main street. Access to the Clyde was important for mineral traffic, and the General Terminus and Glasgow Harbour Railway linked with the Clydesdale Junction Railway to give common access to General Terminus quay in 1848. At that time the GPK&A and Glasgow and Paisley railways shared a terminus at Bridge Street, the E&G came into Queen Street, and the Caledonian opened Buchanan Street station in 1849.

Each of the railways had its main territory and competition tended to be on the periphery of the areas of influence, though the Caledonian competed on the Edinburgh to Glasgow route and continually sought to penetrate the territory of the GPK&A to tap the rich Ayrshire mineral traffic. Apart from this the main area of competition was in Glasgow itself, where the missing link was a line across the Clyde to connect the north- and south-side systems. Proposals for bridging the Clyde in the 1840s were swept aside by opposition from the Corporation and river trustees, who feared an obstacle to the smooth working of the harbour. The road-bridge trustees were also hostile, wishing to protect their income from the tolls on the goods traffic that crossed the city bridges. The development of the perimeter stations was a temporary solution and by the 1860s the need for a link across the Clyde had become a major issue once more. In 1864, the GSW and the E&G, the main rivals to the Caledonian, joined forces to promote the City of Glasgow Union Railway, the North British becoming the GSW's partner after the amalgamations of 1865. In its final form this scheme brought the GSW line north of the Caledonian's south-side station, swept it through the Gorbals on a raised line and across the river at Hutchesontown, then bent back westward to draw into a new station at St Enoch Square. The North British system was linked up on the north side by a new Clyde Junction and a Coatbridge branch which established a new route to Edinburgh through Coatbridge and Bathgate. The north side developments involved the purchase of the University site in the High Street, the transfer of the University to Gilmorehill in 1870, and the construction of a large passenger and goods station, College Station, on the old University site. The CGU took eleven years to build and St Enoch station was not finally opened till 1876, establishing through routes between the north and south sides of the city. Since this scheme effectively excluded the Caledonian from any meaningful participation, it pursued its own scheme to cross the river downstream from Glasgow bridge. An enabling Act was obtained in 1873 and a second modified scheme was approved in 1875, the new bridge and Central Station between Argyle and Gordon Streets eventually opening for traffic in 1879.

While the railway struggle for Glasgow was brewing in the 1850s and 1860s, the main system was gradually filled out with branch-line building and rationalised by amalgamations. The 1850s was a quiet decade after the mania of the late 1840s and the GSW extended its system, taking over the Ardrossan Railway in 1854 and the Ayr and Dalmellington in 1858. The most significant new line in the 1850s was the north-bank Glasgow, Dumbarton and Helensburgh line, opened in 1858, which effectively undermined the north-bank steamer services, just as the Glasgow, Paisley and Greenock had done on the south bank in the 1840s. In the 1860s there was a substantial extension by branch line construction, particularly in the Clyde valley, where the Caledonian drew Strathaven, Lanark, Douglas and the Lesmahagow district into its network, and further amalgamation rationalised the E&G and Monkland railways into the North British system.

The region was served by a comprehensive network of railways by 1870. The mines, ironworks and ports were joined by an intensive web of branch lines and this was reflected in the traffic of the major routes. The Monkland railways remained mineral-carrying lines throughout, earning under 10 per cent of revenue from passenger traffic in 1865 at the time of the takeover by North British. The GSW was also heavily dependent on mineral and goods traffic after the mineral traffic built up from 1848. In 1852 goods and mineral revenue was £122,665 as against £84,886 for passengers; in the year ending July 1870 the earnings were £424,514 for goods and £214,844 for passengers. The North British and Caledonian also handled large mineral tonnages, but passenger transport was important. The Caledonian brought 2,760,000 passengers into Glasgow in 1864, and nearly twice that number in the early 1870s. Even so, neither the Caledonian nor the North British earned more than 40 per cent of their revenue from the passenger trade.

The railways were clearly instrumental in opening up the land-locked coalfields and then in carrying cheap coal to a market they themselves made larger by their extent, speed and economy. The speed factor was important in eliminating the coaching traffic and river packet boats in the 1840s, but the reduction in freight costs, the increase in freight capacity and the improvement in reliability of deliveries were more significant, enabling manufacturers to carry smaller stocks and use their capacity more productively. Farmers quickly developed the liquid milk trade from the remoter parts of south Ayrshire and Lanarkshire, and rural land values rose, as did those in towns wherever the railway passed through. The urban consumer undoubtedly gained from a reduction in coal costs and increased supplies of fruit and vegetables, and the growth of the travel habit and the development of excursion and holiday trains thronged the Clyde and Ayrshire resorts with evening and summer visitors in the 1850s and 1860s. The railways also ended regional seclusion and linked the local economy into a national framework, with the effective creation of a national market in Britain. One consequence was a run-down in certain categories of coastal shipping. Trade in textiles particularly declined as the traffic deserted the sea-lanes for the railways, since virtual door-to-door delivery was important for the manufacturer and retailer.

The integration of the regional into the national economy was also marked in the investment sphere. The joint-stock company form of the railways gave reasonable security to the small investor and popularised the investment habit, and part and parcel of this investment revolution was the evolution of institutions to handle large flows and volumes of capital. This effect of the railway links directly to a key feature of the commercial revolution, the appearance of a banking and financial framework.

Banking

In the mid-eighteenth century Scotland was by European standards a poor country severely constrained in its development by a chronic shortage of coin and bullion. Liquid funds, that is, readily available and usable cash, were in particularly short supply. In this capital-scarce environment the west of Scotland emerged as a favoured enclave, for its thriving mercantile community provided from the involvement in the colonial trade Scotland's major supply of liquid capital. Consequently, it is not surprising to find that the region's first banking houses, the Ship Bank and the Arms Bank, were promoted by prominent merchants. The Ship Bank was formed in 1749 as Dunlop, Houston & Co., supported by six partners, while the Arms Bank, Cochran Murdoch & Co., 1750, had no less than twenty-six partners. Eleven years later, in 1761, a third company, Maxwell Ritchie & Co., was formed as the Thistle Bank, also with six partners (Table 3). Alexander Houston, Andrew Murdoch and Peter Murdoch were partners in the Cunninghame group of tobacco companies, while James Ritchie was the leading partner in James Ritchie & Co., also tobacco traders.

This Glasgow initiative intruded into a banking scene dominated by Edinburgh, with its two great chartered banks, the Bank of Scotland formed in 1695 and the Royal Bank of Scotland opened in 1727. These two banks had in half a century evolved the framework of a banking

TABLE 3   *West of Scotland banks, 1750–1870*

Name	Opened	Closed	Joined
1 Glasgow Ship Bank	1749		1836 (Glasgow Bank)
2 Glasgow Arms Bank	1750	1793 (failed)	
3 Thistle Bank Co., Glasgow	1761		1836 (Union Bank of Glasgow)
4 David Watson, Glasgow (becomes James & Robt Watson)	1762 1793	1832 (failed)	
5 James McAdam & Co., Ayr	1763		1771 (Ayr Bank)
6 Alex Johnson, Hugh Lawson & Co., Dumfries	1770		1771 (Ayr Bank)
7 Merchant Banking Co., Glasgow	1769	1772 (closed, re-sumed, retired 1793)	
8 Douglas, Heron & Co. (Ayr Bank)	1769	1772 (failed)	
9 Hunter & Co., Ayr	1773		1843 (Glasgow Union Bank)
10 Paisley Banking Co.	1783		1837 (British Linen Co.)
11 Andrew, George & Andrew Thomson, Glasgow	1785	1793 (failed)	
12 Greenock Banking Co.	1785		1843 (Western Bank)
13 Paisley Union Bank	1788		1838 (Glasgow Union Bank)
14 Renfrewshire Banking Co.	1802	1829 (failed)	
15 Kilmarnock Banking Co.	1802		1821 (Hunter's & Co.)
16 Dumfries Banking Co.	1804	1808 (failed)	
17 Galloway Banking Co.	1806	1821 (retired)	
18 Glasgow Bank Co.	1809		1836 (becomes Glasgow and Ship Bank) 1843 (to Glasgow Union Bank)
19 Ayrshire Banking Co.	1830		1847 (Western Bank)
20 Glasgow Union Bank	1830		1843 (becomes Union Bank of Scotland)
21 Western Bank of Scotland	1832	1857 (failed)	
22 Clydesdale Banking Co.	1838		
23 Paisley Commercial Bank	1838		1844 (Western Bank)
24 City of Glasgow Bank	1839	1878 (failed)	
25 Glasgow Joint Stock Bank	1840		1844 (Edinburgh and Glasgow Bank) 1858 (Clydesdale Bank)
26 Greenock Union Bank	1840		1843 (Clydesdale Bank)
27 Glasgow Banking Co.	1843		1844 (Western Bank)

Source: A. W. Kerr, *History of Banking in Scotland*, Glasgow, 1884, corrected from unpublished data kindly made available by Professor S. G. Checkland

C

system designed to ease Scotland's shortage of money and credit. Banks are essentially businesses which deal in cash, mobilise savings and extend credit, and the two chartered banks had developed four areas of banking to meet these needs. First, the shortage of circulating currency was attacked by both banks pushing the issue of their own notes to take the place of gold and silver in everyday transactions. Second, the public acceptance and confidence in their notes had the effect of attracting business to the banks and enabled them to extend credit. This extension of credit was supported by the cultivation of deposit banking by encouraging interest-bearing deposits, the Bank of Scotland taking this step first in 1729. Third, the lending business of the banks had been extended by the development of a system of overdrafts, or cash credits, by which means a customer could obtain credit by persuading two or more persons to be guarantors to the bank for his loan. This simple device made it possible for men of small means to obtain credit, and was introduced by the Royal Bank in 1728. Fourth, there had been some attempt to extend banking facilities by establishing branch banks, but this had not been successful. The Bank of Scotland had had short-lived branches in 1696 at Glasgow, Dundee and Aberdeen, and in 1731 at Glasgow. The branch business was first successfully pioneered by the British Linen Co., incorporated in 1746. This company began issuing its own notes in 1752, but it was not until 1849 that it was formally recognised as a banking corporation. Branch banking, however, only began to emerge properly after 1780. Before 1750 the few private banks, Coutts & Co., Alexander & Sons, and Mansfield Hunter & Co., were also Edinburgh-based, but most towns had pseudo-bankers, merchants of repute who did some banking business, borrowing and lending, and discounting bills of exchange. The chartered banks inevitably used these agencies as parts of their banking system. It was this cultivation of business through merchant bankers and private bankers which in part involved the two Edinburgh banks in the establishment of the Ship and Arms banks. The Bank of Scotland helped set up the Ship Bank and the Royal Bank the Arms Bank, each expecting these Glasgow-based banks to act as captive branches and issue the notes of the respective chartered banks. They were disappointed in this, for both the Ship and Arms banks issued their own notes and successfully withstood a period of pressure in the early 1750s when the Edinburgh banks sought to undermine their position.

The anxiety of Glasgow to establish its own banks, and the lack of favour with which Edinburgh bankers viewed this development, suggests that banking was a profitable business in the growing economy of the 1750s. An element of monopoly power and caution appears to have influenced Edinburgh opinion in the conduct of banking, for in spite of the slim provision of banking facilities there was considerable resistance to a proliferation of new banking houses. The real power lay in Edinburgh and access to banking services remained uneven. Geographically, the east of Scotland was better served than the west, and landowners obtained loans more easily than most on the security of their rent rolls. The Glasgow banks were a small counterweight favouring commercial loans, and together with the other private banks helped tie the system together through the active discounting of bills of exchange. In the absence of numerous branches it was the widespread use of paper notes and bills of exchange which articulated the banking system and gave it a national importance.

But even these national characteristics could not overcome all the deficiencies of what was still a regional and local banking system. It was this weakness, allied to the prospect of profit to be earned by meeting the growing demands for credit, which encouraged the Ayrshire squirearchy to promote in 1769 the Ayr Bank of Douglas, Heron & Co. Ayrshire lacked banking services, but was on the edge of extensive agrarian improvement and could afford to support its bank with its core of landed wealth and fringe of commercial enterprise. This was a deviant from the system. It was a joint-stock bank of 136 subscribers or shareholders, with a paid-up capital of £96,000. Its main promoters were great landowners and it extended cash accounts liberally to both landed and commercial interests. When advances outran resources, the gap was filled by a huge issue of notes which flooded the country and represented up to two-thirds of the notes in circulation. The inevitable outcome was an inability to redeem the notes in specie when they came back to the bank for conversion. This induced a short-lived attempt to keep things going by arranging a continuously renewable and growing bridging loan, by negotiating loans in London through a chain of bills of exchange based on fictitious transactions. As the Bank of England and the main Scottish banks moved to refuse acceptance of Ayr Bank notes, this circulating bill device enabled the Ayr Bank directors to obtain negotiable notes, but at the price of borrowing at 8 per cent and lending at 5 per cent. The continuation of business rested on a fragile chain of confidence, which linked the Ayr Bank to its London agents and to many Edinburgh private banks who could not resist the generous commission the Ayr Bank was prepared to pay to have its bills accepted in return for negotiable drafts, which could be drawn on London and Edinburgh. The whole process was highly speculative and inflationary and collapsed quickly following the failure of the London banking house of Neale, James, Fordyce & Brown. The Ayr Bank connection was revealed in the ensuing collapse and the run on its branches in Ayr and Edinburgh soon exhausted the small supplies of coin and forced closure on 25 June 1772, a mere two weeks after news of the London failure had reached Edinburgh. The Ayr Bank was left with liabilities of over £1·25 million, some £400,000 being in advances to its own partners. All outstanding claims were eventually met in full, but at the price of liquidating about £750,000 of property by the proprietors, who had to bear a loss of over £663,000. The excesses of the Ayr Bank had also ensnared most of the private and pseudo-banks, since they had accepted large numbers of Ayr Bank notes. All but three Edinburgh houses, and the two Glasgow Banks which had not been involved in the Ayr Bank transactions, failed in 1772. The banking system was purged in a most dramatic way, leaving a vacuum in note issue and discounting facilities which the survivors only hesitantly began to fill.

In the ensuing sixty years there were only two bursts of bank formation. In the 1780s small private banks with transferable shares, but with un-limited liability, were formed in Greenock and Paisley, these having agents operating in Glasgow. This extended the local banking network to towns of vigour and enterprise; Greenock was capturing the West Indian trade and emerging as the chief port on the Clyde, while Paisley was the busiest centre of the new cotton industry. At the same time the Royal Bank opened a solitary branch in Glasgow in 1783, the Bank of Scotland having already filled part of the vacuum left by the Ayr Bank by establish-ing branches in the west at Dumfries in 1774 and in Ayr and Kilmar-nock the following year. Twenty years later, in 1804, it opened a branch in Glasgow in the middle of a decade which produced a second group of new banks in the region. Three new banks were formed between 1800 and 1810, the Kilmarnock Banking Co., the Renfrewshire Banking Co., and the Glasgow Bank Co. (Table 3, see p. 49).

This burst of activity substantially filled the gap left in Glasgow by the closure of the Arms Bank and the Glasgow Merchants' Bank during the crisis of 1793, a panic provoked by the political instability and com-mercial uncertainty following on the outbreak of war with France. These bank formations in the first decade of the nineteenth century were part of a new movement away from the small private bank towards larger joint-stock enterprises, this being most explicitly the case with the formation in Edinburgh of the Commercial Bank of Scotland in 1810. The fact that the Commercial Bank located itself in Edinburgh underlined the continuing dominance of Edinburgh over Glasgow and highlighted the fact that the initiative of the Glasgow bankers of the 1750s and 1780s had been overtaken by their Edinburgh rivals. In the absence of local enterprise the branch of the Royal Bank came to dominate banking in Glasgow from the 1790s to the 1830s. Its connections with the Bank of England gave it resources beyond the reach of the smaller Glasgow banks, and it drew to its Glasgow branch a very large business in discounting commercial bills. An idea of the scale of the Royal Bank's business is indicated in Table 4. The Glasgow agency was supporting the business community with over £6 million in credit as early as 1807. If the ratio of Glasgow to other bills remained fairly constant, the annual extension of over £4 million in Glasgow bills in the 1820s and 1830s must have represented some £10–£12

TABLE 4 *Royal Bank of Scotland: Glasgow Agency*, bills discounted, 1794–1836*

Period	Glasgow bills discounted at any one time (£000)	Estimated annual† value of bills discounted (£000)
1794	400	1,600
1802	530	2,120
1807	636	2,544
1817–21	977	3,908
1822–6	1,042	4,168
1827–31	951	3,804
1836	1,038	4,152

Abstract of bills discounted in the Royal Bank Glasgow, 12 September 1806–11 September 1807 (£)

Glasgow bills	2,766,552
Edinburgh bills	1,231,113
London bills	2,301,042
All bills	6,298,707

† Obtained by multiplying Column 1 by 4. Assuming the bills were 3-month bills, the bank must therefore have had at least four times this sum extended in credit to cover the transactions in a full year. This is borne out by the evidence of 1807. On 27 February 1807, the Glasgow Agency had £636,000 extended in discounted bills. Multiplying by four gives an estimate of £2,544,000 for the year. The actual figure for Glasgow bills for the period 12 September 1806–11 September 1807 was £2,766,000. When the credit made available in Edinburgh and London bills is added, Glasgow bills extended at any one time represented about 10 per cent of the annual extension of credit. If this ratio holds throughout the period, some idea of the scale of business of the Glasgow Agency is obtained
* Data prepared from unpublished material kindly made available by Professor S. G. Checkland

million in credit made available to the west of Scotland by this one branch of the Royal Bank of Scotland.

This was an enormous extension of credit. Nevertheless, it is clear that the needs of the region rapidly outgrew the willingness and possibly the ability of the Royal Bank, and the other local banks, to finance the demands for credit. The Edinburgh banks followed a uniform policy of low and stable interest rates on deposits, of substantial investments in government securities, frequently up to one-third of their funds being so invested.

This induced both caution and inflexibility in the system and both the Commercial Bank (1810) and the National Bank (1825) had briefly shaken up the system with vigorous branch creation and lending policies before reaching an accommodation with the older banks. The real challenge to Edinburgh dominance came with the resurgence of Glasgow-based banks in the 1830s and the early 1840s. No fewer than nine new banks emerged, all on the joint-stock principle and all with unlimited liability.

Why banking expanded in Glasgow at this time is not clear. The Edinburgh banks had been founded on landed wealth, making secure loans on the rent rolls of the great estates in the east of Scotland. The Ayr Bank had attempted a similar involvement, drawing its funds from Ayrshire estates, but actively participating in commerce and industry. Its calamitous failure had cut off landed support for banks in the west of Scotland, and it appears that a new foundation only grew in the 1830s and 1840s with the rise of industry on the secure base of coal, iron and engineering. Once this new pool of wealth began to emerge, the prospects for local banks took on a new lease of life and seems to have encouraged the appearance of Glasgow-based banking houses. Four of these, the Glasgow Union Bank, the Western Bank, the Clydesdale Banking Co. and the City of Glasgow Bank, were specially vigorous and represented the antithesis of Edinburgh policy. They offered higher interest rates to attract deposits; they spurned the habit of holding large parts of their funds in government stocks and thus operated with low reserve ratios; they actively pursued the business of discounting commercial bills and were aggressive in extending their note issue. They also pursued a growth policy through amalgamation and branch extension.

The amalgamation movement was begun by the Glasgow Union Bank, which took over the Thistle Bank in 1836. The Paisley Union Bank joined with it in 1838 and five years later Hunter & Co. of Ayr and the Glasgow and Ship Bank were also taken over. The whole collection took the name of the Union Bank of Scotland in 1843. The Western Bank pursued a similar policy, successively taking over the Paisley Commercial Bank and the Glasgow Banking Co. in 1844 and the Ayrshire Banking Co. in 1847. In the same period the Clydesdale moved more slowly, acquiring the Greenock Union Bank in 1843, and then it was not until 1858 that it acquired the Edinburgh and Glasgow Bank, which had itself absorbed the Glasgow Joint Stock Bank in 1844. The result was that banking in Glasgow and the west of Scotland was dominated, by 1850, by four large joint-stock banks, the Union, Clydesdale, Western and City of Glasgow. Their success had forced a dramatic change in the policies of the Edinburgh banks. Their practice of paying low rates of interest on deposits was challenged; they had reduced their holdings of government stock by up to half and had used the extra funds to move more extensively into the discounting business. One consequence was that the cash credit arrangements began to diminish in importance. The Edinburgh banks found that Glasgow was the growth centre for new lending, that their profitability was declining and that their control of the system had been irretrievably broken by the new joint-stock banks.

Unhappily, both the Western Bank and the City of Glasgow Bank failed. Their collapse had serious consequences for the economic health of the region. The Western Bank pioneered the path of expansion and brinkmanship. It held tiny reserves and pushed its lending to the limit, and twice – in 1833 and 1838 – it had to appeal to the Edinburgh banks for funds to help it out of difficulty. In 1857 it had over 100 branches, paid-up capital of £1·5 million and deposits of over £5 million. However, its funds were stretched in accommodating trade bills and in 1857 a commercial crisis in America first caused the failure of the bank's New York discount agency, and then all American remittances to Britain were temporarily stopped. This placed many solvent British firms in the position of being unable to meet payments for trade bills, since their own remittances had been held up. Four prominent Glasgow firms were so affected and could not meet liabilities of £1·6 million owing to the Western Bank. An advance of £510,000 from the Edinburgh banks and £100,000 from the Clydesdale could not halt the run on the bank's reserves, as depositors sought to withdraw their funds, and in the absence of further help from Edinburgh the Western closed its doors on 9 November with total liabilities of £8,911,932. Two calls of £125 per share were made on the shareholders, and together with the Bank's capital assets this was sufficient to pay the liabilities in full.

The City of Glasgow Bank also closed its doors for one month at this time. It was to survive until 1878. When it failed, it was not so much through unrestrained lending as from extensive graft and corruption on the part of the directors. The investigating accountants revealed that fraudulent balance sheets treated £7,345,357 of bad debts as assets, and four of the bank's directors owed £5,792,394 under this arrangement. All liabilities were eventually met, but at the expense to the shareholders of calls to the total of 2,750 per cent of shares held. As in 1857, this collapse induced many business closures throughout the country.

The banking system of the region in its century of rapid economic growth withstood three great failures among Scottish banks: the Ayr Bank in 1772, the Western Bank in 1857 and the City of Glasgow Bank in 1878. Each failure reveals different dangers inherent in the development of the system. The Ayr Bank effectively was a land bank, which apart from the wildness of its note issue, fell into the trap of borrowing short and lending long, so that its liabilities were immediate but its assets were illiquid, locked up in long-term loans to landowners, yielding small returns over a long period of time. The Western and City of Glasgow, on the other hand, could broadly be described as 'commercial', even 'industrial', banks, whose lending policies were strongly influenced by the urge to accommodate the credit requirements of businessmen. In the case of the Western Bank the accommodation was pursued by lending large amounts to few concerns, without adequate reference to the security and reserve positions of the bank. Since the lending risk was not well spread, the limited reserve position inevitably made the bank vulnerable whenever a few of its clients were for some reason unable to meet their liabilities. The City of Glasgow episode highlights this danger in another way, by emphasising the impropriety of involvement by bank directors for large unsecured loans made available for their personal gain.

These three ventures are important in another way. The men behind them acted with the conviction that a bank had a part to play in economic development, that banks and bankers had a responsibility to promote the development of agriculture, trade and industry. This attempt to involve the banks in the economy in a direct way depended upon the isolated initiative of a few small groups of men, and was in opposition to British practice, where banks on the whole took the view that their responsibility was to their shareholders, not to businessmen or to the economy in general. In these circumstances, experimental banking unsupported by the system was almost bound to fail.

The failures brought great, if momentary, distress to the region, but neither this nor the slender provision of banking facilities appear seriously to have hindered the growth of the regional economy. Local businessmen found that the community as a whole tended to provide social overhead investment in roads, ports, schools and hospitals, though many, like David Dale, had to build their own factory village, just as did the coalmasters with their miners' rows. Moreover, businessmen relied on their own resources, on savings, on personal loans, and occasionally on convenient marriages to provide capital to set up the firm and build up fixed capital in plant and machinery. Partnerships and family firms were the keys to an entry into the business world. William Dixon joined briefly with David Mushet of black-band ore fame, and James Creelman, a pottery manufacturer, to purchase the Calder ironworks. Robert Owen married David Dale's daughter; the Buchanans and Finlays were intermarried, and Alexander Baird's daughter, Jane, married Thomas Jackson of the Coats ironworks. Such unions, together with the habit of ploughing back profit in a continuous addition to capital, sufficed for the provision of fixed capital and made the local businessmen largely independent of the banks.

The main link between business, industry and banks was the urgent need for working capital, credit to pay the wages, purchase stocks and service the day-to-day needs of the business. It was here that the banks and business made use of the bill of exchange, a short-term credit note drawn against the account of the purchaser and secured against the value of the goods in process of sale. The buying and selling (discounting) of these trade bills was a lucrative business and there is little evidence to suggest that businessmen regularly found the banks unwilling or unable to meet their working capital requirements. Industrialisation may have been hampered by a deficiency of banking provision before 1780, but thereafter, and especially in the first half of the nineteenth century, banking seems to have responded quickly and flexibly to the demands of industry and commerce in the region.

3

Change in the countryside

The traditional system

It is doubtful if agrarian society in the west of Scotland was ever truly self-subsistent, meeting all the needs of its inhabitants from its own resources. Even with a tiny population of 180,000 in 1750, scarcity was never far away, and the need to supplement the local produce with imports from more favoured regions was a recurring one. Any potential for regular surplus production lay behind the barriers of low productivity and primitive techniques. In summer, the greenness of the landscape did not mirror good farmland, but was a reflection of heavy rainfall, the inability to drain, and the dominance of rushes, sedges and moss over great tracts of heavy soils. In winter, the noted mildness of the climate diminished rapidly away from the coastal fringes, and upward with altitude, for the western region, though part of lowland Scotland, still lies deep within highland Britain. Above 600 feet heavy rainfall and low temperatures combined to impose severe limits on the use of the land; about half of the region lies above this altitude, drenched with more than 50 inches of rain each year, and with fewer than five months with mean temperatures in excess of 50°F. Crops can be grown in these conditions, but ripening is uncertain, and once above 750 feet the chances of successful cropping are slight, particularly when exposure and wind are added to the other disadvantages. The farmer in the west of Scotland was confronted with excessive moisture, a fugitive sun, and soils which, when not waterlogged alluvial loams, were mostly stiff, wet clays or stony sand and gravels. He had to evolve a system of agriculture which could cope with soils, exposure and local climates varying dramatically within short distances.

His response was little different from that of peasant cultivators in many other lands with similar physical conditions.

The simplest system of land use which can properly be called farming is shifting cultivation, in which the cultivator clears a small patch of land, crops and grazes it to exhaustion, then moves on and repeats the sequence, the exhausted plots being allowed to regenerate themselves over time, One stage further advanced is a 'one-field' system, in which one piece of land is farmed continuously, sections being used for crops, pasture and fallow, in a crude rotation, in an attempt to maintain at least a low level of fertility in the soil. The system which evolved in Scotland tended to combine features of both types in a single community. The land was commonly divided into two parts, known as the 'infield' and the 'outfield'. The Scottish system of farming has hence been called a two-field system, but in effect it was more a modified one-field system, since the outfield was not a field in the strict sense of the term.

The 'infield', usually, was both the best land and the land nearest to the houses; this was the arable land which was ploughed and worked in strips or rigs. The rigs varied from 12 to 18 feet in width, rose to 4 feet at the crest, and generally ran up and down hill, the ditches between acting as crude drains. The unique feature of this infield was that the tenancy of the rigs was initially re-allocated among the tenants every one to three years, to give each a fair share of good and indifferent soils. This system of rotating the tenure of the rigs has given the practice the name of 'run-rig'. Re-allocation of rigs had disappeared entirely from the region by 1750, but even when the tenant held his rigs, or portions of rigs, permanently, his acreage was still made up of patches scattered at random throughout the infield, and few tenants had made much headway in consolidating their holdings. Moreover, since Scotland was a very poor country, few individuals possessed the resources to work the land on their own, and consequently it was held and worked in common, dates of ploughing, sowing and harvest being as much influenced by custom as by climate. The land of the infield was also entirely open, with at best temporary fences to keep cattle and sheep out of the crops in summer. Thereafter, livestock roamed freely on the stubble the disadvantage of their trampling the land into muddy pools being offset by the manure which the infield received in the process. The outfield, in contrast, was not a field at all. It usually comprised a number of scattered patches of land higher up the slope. Not all of the patches would be under crop at any given time, nor was there any standard size. Its extent varied with the size of the community, the fertility of the soil and the availability of infield land. It was used very much like the patch of land in the shifting cultivation system, while the infield enjoyed a rudimentary rotation similar to that employed in primitive one-field agriculture.

This infield–outfield system, with its run-rig farming, was a very flexible, if simple, form of land use, closely in harmony with the environment. It could be employed by any size of community, and could cope with any combination of good and indifferent land, by simply expanding or contracting either the infield or outfield, and hence bringing about the balance of arable and pastoral activity best suited in the circumstances. Infield–outfield farming was therefore the standard form of land use. The houses of the farmers typically clustered around the edge of the infield to form the 'fermetouns', which were quite unlike the well-spaced nucleated villages of midland and southern England. Where the land could be drained sufficiently to take the plough and produce a crop, the rural landscape in the west of Scotland was crowded with a dense network of tiny settlements, the fermetouns, frequently of only three or four houses or hovels. These settlements took their names from one or other of the tenants, past or present, the landowner, a local feature, an occupation or activity. Hence, settlements like Gibbiestown, Kerstown or Finlayston, Hairy Boggs, Moss Neuk or Windyhills, Colehills, Coleholes and Limehills.

The fermetoun with its infield and outfield was universal: the system was designed to squeeze some arable production out of an environment that favoured pastoral activities. By employing its flexibility, the local farmers had achieved a considerable degree of adaptation to environment by the mid-eighteenth century. Although sheep and cattle could be found everywhere in the region, the moorland fringes of Lanarkshire and Ayrshire already showed some specialisation as sheepwalks, stocked mainly with the native Scottish mountain breed, a small coarse-woolled, black-faced animal. Conversely, the lower and better-drained land in the lower ward of Lanarkshire, the middle parts of Renfrewshire and northern Ayrshire, were dominantly under arable, sustaining their rotation of oats, oats and barley. The wetter haughlands and the lower slopes from 600 to 850 feet were also beginning to carry sheep and cattle for fattening, and occasionally horses for breeding. This was as far as adaptation to environment had gone. The further stage of commercial specialisation had to wait for improvements in transport.

Landholding

The practice of feuing land, granting perpetual heritable tenure in return for a down payment and a fixed annual money rent, consolidated the ownership of land in Scotland into the hands of great families. This began as early as the fifteenth century, and gained great momentum in the orgy of re-feuing which followed upon the annexation of church lands after the Reformation, when the Crown seized the chance of replenishing its coffers by taking control of all such estates and selling them off. By the eighteenth century the pattern of landholding in the west of Scotland was well entrenched; about three-quarters of all the land was held in the hands of a small number of families. At the top were the estates of the landed aristocracy. In Ayrshire these were men like the Duke of Portland, and the Earls of Eglinton and Loudon; in Lanarkshire, the Dukes of Hamilton, the Earl of Home and Lord Blantyre; in Renfrewshire, Lord Blantyre, Lord Cathcart and the Earl of Glasgow; in Dunbartonshire, the Duke of Argyll, Lord Stonefield and Lord Elphinstone. Somewhat lower in the social scale there came the next, but equally important stratum of landowners, the lairds, frequently of family as ancient and distinguished as that of the aristocracy, the Colquhouns in Dunbartonshire, the Fergussons, Blairs and Cunninghames in Ayrshire, the Houstons in Renfrewshire, the Lockharts in Lanarkshire. The landed aristocracy and the lowland lairds together formed a small band of powerful families with extensive control of the land, and the people who worked on it. At the other end of the scale there was the land belonging to most towns, which lay in plots and gardens between the outlying houses and on the perimeter of the settlement. This was used for grazing purposes, for cultivation by intensive labour, usually by spadework. Finally, there was a multitude of small landholders, the bonnet-lairds, most prevalent in north Ayrshire, Lanarkshire and Dunbartonshire, where holdings were frequently less than 50 acres, and some smaller than 20 acres.

The land in the west of Scotland was thus held by a wide range of owners, with properties extending from only a few acres to as many as 100,000. In the large holdings most owners reserved portions for their own use, whether for grazing or cultivation, while at the level of the bonnet-lairds, the land-holding was so small that many were forced to work their plots co-operatively.

But it was almost universal for most of the lands of the nobility and lairds to be rented by tenants. In the arable areas of Lanarkshire and Dunbartonshire most such farms were small, from 50 to 80 acres, while in Renfrewshire and Ayrshire a ploughgate of 104 acres was fairly common. Hill farms were larger, ranging from as few as 600 acres to over 2,000 in the remote parts of Dunbartonshire, Lanarkshire and Ayrshire. In both arable and livestock farms the tenancies were frequently shared among two, four or even eight farmers; as late as the 1750s some of these were still co-tenancies, in the sense that the tenants not only worked the land co-operatively, but lived together in the clustering hovels of the ferme-toun. More usually, the farming families had already split up, forming their own family fermetouns close to their own section of the land. Under this system only about half the arable area would be under the plough at any one time, and the shares of the tenants would not necessarily be equal, but in proportion to their ability to pay a portion of the rent. This depended on the resources which each tenant could command in stock, implements and labour.

The ability to pay rent was the key to access to the land. But even by 1750, it was rare for rentals to be paid in cash. It was still customary to pay rents in kind, and in services. Commonly, one-third of the produce of the farm went on rental, and each tenant was also encumbered by services; the requirement of working several days each week at critical times like ploughing and harvest was one of long standing, and stretched back into feudal times. The same origin was true of other services, such as cutting and carrying peats for the proprietor, and also the system of each tenant being thirled to a mill. Another burden was the tiend, the payment of a tenth part of the corn crop to the minister and the church.

All of these tenures were held on some form of lease arrangement, which obliged the tenant to observe the burdens and rents as a condition of access to the land. Leases had a long history in Scotland, but until the eighteenth century it was rare for small tenants to have a lease of any length of time. Three, five or seven years might be granted, but at the beginning of the eighteenth century many tenants in the west of Scotland held their miserable plots on a year-to-year basis, on what amounted to a kindly, or customary tenancy, with little or no legal entitlement to continued access. But in the case of larger tenancies the 19-year lease had been employed as early as 1700; this was gradually extended and was probably general in the region after 1750.

The pattern of land-holding in the region therefore broadened downward from the few great families who owned the land, to the multitude of tenants and joint tenants who toiled and lived on it. This lower stratum in turn gave shelter and employment to the least-favoured groups, the cottars and the labourers. The cottar lived in the fermetoun with the tenant, and provided him with labour in return for a few acres of the infield, and the privilege of grazing a cow and a few sheep. The cottars held their land at will from the tenant, and were exposed to any change which upset the established routine. The farm labourer was also vulnerable, but had even less to lose. He frequently lived in the tenant's house and rarely had any land of his own. He was the forerunner of the landless day-wage labourer, who was to become increasingly important as the old system was gradually reshaped from subsistence to commercial agriculture.

Farming practice

Landowner, tenant, cottar and labourer were equally impotent before the forces of nature. On the average farm the land received the roughest of preparation before the crop was planted. One ploughing was frequently the only breaking-up of the soil, for that was all that time allowed, since the primitive equipment made ploughing a slow and laborious process. The heavy rains of December and January rarely permitted the plough to begin its work before the beginning of February, and then it had to contend with cold, wet and stiff clays; its principal harvest was the endless variety of stones and boulders left behind by the glaciers. Such conditions demanded a specialised response, and the answer was the old Scotch plough. This was a large, sturdy, but enormously clumsy instrument, up to thirteen feet long. Its weight and strength allowed it to tear great gouges in intractable soils. When the plough had done its work, rudimentary wooden-toothed harrows ineffectively broke up the furrows. This was followed by simply broadcasting the seed. Oats were rarely sown before April, through fear of late frosts, and barley was sown even later. This slow start to the farming year committed the farmer to uncertainty in his harvest, for the length of time required to grow the crop carried it into late September. Once the seed was committed to the ground, little other attention was given. The livestock was kept off the ridges by temporary fences, or by a cowherd and his dog. But nothing was done to keep out weeds. They grew in profusion among the crops, and flourished in the stagnant ditches between the ridges. If the grain survived the choking of the weeds it still had to face the battering of wind and rain. In autumn, at harvest, the grain was torn rather than cut by the crude, toothed, sickle. Thereafter, it was further abused by primitive flails, often bunches of twiggy heather tied to a pole, and then winnowed by the simple process of throwing it in the air to allow the wind to separate the grain from the chaff. Even in a good year the farmer rarely expected to get more than a four-fold return for the grain planted, and that was scarcely enough to meet the demands of rent, food, fodder and a seed crop for the following year.

This cycle of impotence and hopelessness was endlessly repeated in a rotation of oats, oats, barley and grass. The crops drew the meagre nutrients from the soil, and the random dunging from wandering animals could never fully replace it. In spite of dung and the rotation of crops the fertility of the infield suffered from chronic soil exhaustion, redeemed occasionally and briefly by a year in grass.

To make matters worse the land was also over-stocked. Lean black, and brown, cattle with crooked horns were found on every farm, and often shared the pasturage with the native Scottish black-faced sheep, small and scrawny animals, carrying the coarsest of wool. Since the cultivation of hay was not a part of Scottish farm practice at that time, feeding the animals in winter was a recurring problem. Those which survived starved through the winter on mashed whin and coarse grass; the others were weeded out in the autumn slaughter and the carcases salted for preservation. The need to have sufficient livestock to make up the winter losses, and to provide power for ploughing and cartage, encouraged overstocking, and this in turn perpetuated the winter killing.

The deficiencies of the old Scottish system of agriculture appear endless. Small fragmented plots, a soil-exhausting rotation, primitive implements, poor-quality livestock and crops, combined to hold farming stagnant. The uncertain climate and the inability to cope with drainage, the lack of knowledge of fertilisers, crop and animal selection and better practice, all contributed to the erratic harvest. With weak stock and inadequate seed the farmer, in most years, struggled from brief summer hope to autumn disappointment. Scarcity was never far from the door and made both tenant and landlord vulnerable to the vicissitudes of the weather. Poverty was the common bond between cottar, tenant, and all but the largest landowner. This more than any other single factor made it very difficult to set out upon the task of improvement.

The coming of improvement

The old system of farming did not exclude change. It was flexible, constantly undergoing small modifications. But inefficient organisation and primitive techniques enforced a low ceiling on production, and any change took place within narrow limits, without altering the basic structure.

This traditional system was held in its place by two sets of factors. One was its internal organisation and characteristics, which the farmer manipulated, but because of their mutual reinforcement, could not fundamentally change. The other set of factors at work was the external order and organisation of the society within which the farming system operated. The Scottish farmer, in his ignorance and poverty, clung to the familiar, hoping to do just a little better than his father and grandfather before him. It was changes in the broader external environment, over which the farmer-tenant had no direct control, that created a new situation. When the social and economic environment altered, even the relatively stable traditional system of farming could not resist change.

The landowner was the link between the common farmer and these external changes, and his world altered swiftly in the eighteenth century. The ending of the Scottish Parliament in 1707 sent landed gentlemen to London to the new centre of government. The financial needs of the landowner increased in proportion to the speed with which he sought to acquire English standards and habits. Some outran their resources; one effect of this was to inject a cash demand into rentals. The abolition in 1748 of the privileges of heritable jurisdiction (which had given lords of regality powers equivalent to sheriffs on their own lands) meant that a broader spectrum of Scottish landowners was drawn into the service of the courts and government, and landlord aspirations were again affected. Moreover, the compensation paid for the loss of these powers enabled men like the Earls of Eglinton and Loudon to begin to introduce change into the countryside. A trickle of development capital was swollen by new families buying into landed society. Many small landowners found that their old rent rolls could not support their new interests, and sold out to new men who had achieved some status and wealth in the growing commercial and industrial economy. Thus James Ritchie, a Glasgow tobacco merchant and partner in the Thistle Bank, bought Busby estate near Kilmaurs in 1763, and Claude Alexander, a merchant who had made his fortune in the East India Company, purchased Ballochmyle estate in 1786. This injection of energy and wealth was a fundamental impulse to the improving movement.

Both the old and new landlords were also deeply affected by the spirit of intellectual inquiry into the nature of better farming. The first body to promote such investigation was the 'Society for Improving in the Knowledge of Agriculture', set up in Edinburgh in 1723. Its membership included a number of landowners from the west of Scotland, like Lord Cathcart and the Earl of Stair, their aim being to make known the best methods of husbandry, and to encourage their use by offering prizes and premia. At the local level, the Earl of Eglinton formed the 'Society for Improving of Agriculture and Manufactures in the Shire of Ayr', in 1748, and promoted indemnity schemes and a farming periodical to encourage tenants to adopt the new methods. Local farming societies spread rapidly after 1760, and by 1800 virtually every parish had its own farmers' club, or shared one with neighbouring parishes. These clubs were the means of bringing the new ideas to the attention of the small farmer, and their work was supported by a stream of practical and theoretical publications on the new farming.

Landlords in the west of Scotland could scarcely have avoided contact with the new ideas in the second half of the eighteenth century. Treatises on enclosing, fallowing, rotations, planting, animal husbandry, drainage and fertilisers abounded. Some proprietors, like the Earls of Eglinton and Loudon, the Hamiltons of Dalziel, and the Dukes of Argyll and Portland, could not resist the challenge to experiment on their own estates. Eglinton introduced a farmer from the Lothians to instruct him in new rotations and methods; the Earl of Loudon, and the Hamiltons, began to clothe the countryside with thousands of young trees. The enthusiasm of such men stretched to an attempted reorganisation of every aspect of estate life.

They were particularly concerned to improve the roads. Most land-owners were heavily involved in the turnpike trusts, and in the administration of statute labour, with the result that the region was served by adequate roads by 1800. The consequences for rural life were profound. Isolation was broken down, as the active interchange of commodities and ideas superseded the encapsulation of early eighteenth-century life. The influence of the market place steadily began to erode former habits of self-subsistence and independence.

The proprietors could move in these directions because earlier developments had given them a secure title to their land, and land-ownership opened up avenues of credit not available to other men. Enactments of 1661, 1669 and 1685 had provided for straightening estate boundaries by exchange of parcels of land, and for fencing by sharing the cost between adjacent proprietors. Further legislation in 1695 enabled owners of inter-mixed estates to exchange scattered strips and consolidate their holdings, and to establish proprietorship over uncultivated common land. This legislation provided for settlements between land-owners in areas where the legal title of those concerned was not well defined. It was a tidying-up of the pattern of landholding, and did not deal with an owner's rights on his own land: landowners could make changes on their land if they saw fit, since tenants had no rights at common law in Scotland, though customary practice could be a powerful influence in staying the proprietor's hand.

Since an owner's control over his land was substantial, and since niceties of boundaries, fences and the exchange of parcels of land could be accomplished by the simple device of making application before a sheriff, landed estates in Scotland became an acceptable security for the raising of capital. About one-third of the land in Scotland was under entail, by which the estate was in the unalienable ownership of one family, and could neither be burdened by debt, nor sold off. But landowners of other estates were not subject to these restrictions, and it became common practice to raise capital by selling land on twenty years' purchase, interest being paid on the mortgage, and the capital sum redeemed at the end of the period. This was a clumsy way of raising funds, and from the middle of the eighteenth century the public and the emerging private banks gave both long-term loans and shorter cash-credit facilities to landowners on the security of their rent rolls. This in turn encouraged proprietors to increase their rent revenue, and the success of even modest improvements in achieving this finally broke the borrowing barrier for owners of entailed estates in 1770. Thereafter they could borrow up to the extent of six years' rent for the purpose of improvement, and were permitted to pass on to their heirs up to three-quarters of the debt incurred.

The world of the landowner was powerfully influenced by new aspirations, new proprietors, new avenues of credit, and new ideas. The pressures making for change increased steadily during the eighteenth century, and were complemented by other changes outside the farming sector. The population of the west of Scotland increased from 181,000 to 331,000 between 1755 and 1801. These increasing numbers clustered more and more in villages and towns, following non-agricultural occupations. The tide of commerce and industry broadened into a new economic base for life in the region, as textile mills, coalmines, sugar refineries, glassworks, forges and foundries increased in number. New roads, new

institutions for credit, new industries, new occupations and a growing
population merged to form a young and vigorous industrial–commercial
community, which provided a regular and expanding market for agricultural produce. New and old landowners were drawn irresistibly into the
new economy. When they ceased to be prepared to tolerate the old ways,
the tenant was obliged to change his ways. He persisted in his old life as
long as he could, but the environment which had supported the traditional
system melted away, and this cleared the way for the new agriculture.

The new agriculture: 1750–1820

The new agriculture was designed to break the old system at its most
inhibitive points: low productivity of crops and animals, primitive
methods and unwieldy organisation. Against these it offered a new
husbandry, advances in technology, and improvements in farming
organisation. These were the three supports of the new agriculture. The
old system had been confirmed in its place through a poverty of ideas and
capital. New ideas and new capital became available in the eighteenth
century. Combined with new crops and animals, new tools and new
organisation, they raised agricultural productivity.

The new husbandry first attacked the shortage of fodder and attempted
to rescue the soil from exhaustion. The critical innovation here was the
introduction of root and grass crops in new rotations. In the late seventeenth century clovers, sainfoin, rye grasses and the turnip appeared in
England; they first came to Scotland in the fertile Lothians early in the
eighteenth century. The new grasses and the turnip were nitrogenous
plants. They fixed nitrogen from the atmosphere and fed it into the soil.
The dense growth of the grasses smothered the weeds and provided rich
crops of hay. When ploughed in, the sward was the foundation for humus
to enrich the soil further. The sowing-down of land to the new grasses
and turnips broke the cycle of soil depletion and fodder shortage in one
simple operation. This was the basis for increasing numbers of livestock,
which in turn generated more manure to sustain the new-found productivity of the soil.

While the new husbandry techniques were the fundamental source of
increased productivity, contemporaries were much concerned also with
the organisation of farming. They deplored short leases, small and fragmented farms, scattered and unenclosed strips of land, and fields without
adequate boundaries. Many contemporaries stressed the need to re-
organise these farming arrangements as a prerequisite for all other
improvements. Hence in England the emphasis on enclosure, and in
Scotland, in faithful imitation, the efforts of the early agricultural writers
to encourage improving landlords to enclose their lands, lower and
straighten the rigs, consolidate and enlarge the farms and lengthen the

leases. This aspect of the new agriculture provides today the most striking features of the landscape. The neat rectangular fields, trim hedgerows, dykes and fences, and well-spaced, moderately-sized farms, all bear witness to the enterprise of the improvers. Indeed, it is perhaps easy to exaggerate the significance of this visible transformation. On the whole, the effects of new methods, new crops and animals were more immediate in improving productivity than those of new organisation, especially since the reorganisation of the landscape proceeded slowly over a long period.

In the first phase of improvement between 1750 and 1820 enclosure created compact farms out of the clusters of fermetouns. It effectively divided livestock from crops, a first step towards better farming practice. There had been some enclosure before the mid-eighteenth century, around country seats for parkland, near towns for garden ground, and larger areas set aside for bleachers and dyers in the linen industry. But larger-scale agricultural enclosure began in a few pioneer areas in the middle of the century. In Ayrshire, tentative enclosure and the new farming had begun as early as the 1730s near the River Irvine on the lands of Loudon and Eglinton; within twenty years it spread to neighbouring estates, and in the 1770s and 1780s it extended southward from the Cunninghame district on to the estates of the Blairs, Brisbanes and Dunlops. This outward spread from a few pioneer areas was repeated in the other counties. In Renfrewshire the lands of Fullwood and Craigends were among the first to be enclosed; this was followed by Alexander Spiers on his Houston and Elderslie estates in the 1770s. In Lanarkshire, the lands closest to Glasgow were the earliest to be set out to the new farms. Thereafter, enclosure moved south-eastward up the Clyde valley in the wake of the new roads.

In Scotland, enclosure meant simply fencing and dividing off the fields. The most common method was to construct a ditch and hedge. Deep ditches surrounded the fields, the excavated earth forming an inner mound on top of which a hedge was planted. One disadvantage indicated by Colonel Fullarton in his survey of farming in Ayrshire in 1793 was that 'the pernicious custom of deep ditches fronting the road . . . endanger the neck of the traveller'. The ditches were also intended to help drain the land, and some attempt was made to straighten the ridges within the enclosing ditch to encourage water to run off in the furrows. Some feeder ditches were opened, and a few farmers constructed rubble-filled and stone-covered drains. These were expensive and easily blocked, causing this first attempt at underground, as distinct from surface drainage, to be unpopular.

The investment in this first stage of enclosure and drainage must have been substantial. Simple ditch and hedging cost 2s. to 2s. 6d. per fall (a measure of about 6 yards); covered stone drains could cost £3–£5 per acre. The results were disappointing. The ditches silted up, the hedges died on their mounds, and attempts to level the ridges exposed poor subsoil through pulling the topsoil into the furrows. More careful levelling was expensive and rigs remained high and wide in many districts. Effective drainage over large areas proved impossible, and a heavy reliance was placed on the extensive use of lime in an attempt to offset high acidity in the persistently wet soils. Enclosure had at best given the landscape an incomplete facelift by 1815. The basic problems of drainage, fencing and smoothing the ridges remained to be fully solved.

Initial experiments with the new husbandry were equally unsuccessful. The innovation of winter ploughing foundered on the wet, sticky clays of Lanarkshire and Ayrshire. Early sowing, in imitation of best English practice, failed in the face of long, cold springs and late frosts. Summer fallowing to kill off weeds exposed sticky clays to the wind and sun, and produced an impenetrable hard pan; it only succeeded on lighter, better-drained soils. The prevalence of heavy clays and poor drainage proved to be insuperable barriers to the direct transplantation of English methods. Even more disappointing, the heavy clays resisted the innovation of the turnip, and banished it to the few areas of light, warm, well-drained soil.

But the mixed success in imitating developments brought to fruition in other parts of Britain, was followed by years of intensive trial-and-error improvement. The last quarter of the eighteenth century witnessed an abandonment of standardisation and imitation. Solutions and adaptations were sought which took account of local and regional conditions. By 1794, John Naismith, writing the county survey of agriculture in Clydesdale, could say of Lanarkshire, 'rotations are as various as the climate and soil', and this was symptomatic of the response in the region. As in England and the Lothians, the farmers broke the routine of successive grain crops by interspersing them with green crops. Since turnips only answered well in limited areas, and peas and beans remained largely garden crops, the main innovation in the west of Scotland was to use grass crops. Throughout the region, between 1770 and 1800, the new farms slowly introduced rotations including red, white, and yellow clovers, together with rye grass. Temporary lay-farming became common, with land in grass for up to 5 years in an 8-year rotation, and in the west of Scotland hay and grass replaced the turnip as fodder for animals, and green crop between grains. Since new crops and new sequences of sowing could be employed without radically altering the existing arrangements of farms and tenancies, the new crop rotations spread fairly rapidly, though in Dunbartonshire about a quarter of the arable land still suffered the traditional three-year cycle of oats, oats and barley.

The variety of rotations was accompanied by an uneven innovation of new tools to help the farmer in his work. There was a universal intermixture of the old Scotch plough with various new types. The heavy

plough was difficult to beat on stiff clay lands, but was rapidly disappear-
ing on lighter soils, in the face of the competition from James Small's
plough, introduced about 1763. The improved Rotherham plough was
also in use, and these two new light ploughs, with metal-covered mould-
boards, reduced the time and labour required for the re-ploughing of
fallow land, and gradually were ousting the Scotch plough from much
first ploughing as well. Many districts had their own variants, as local
smiths adapted the basic innovation by adding refinements of their own.
Thus, in parts of Lanarkshire, the Rutherglen plough found great favour,
giving a deep strong furrow. However, even in the midst of experimentation with the plough, many upland areas in Dunbartonshire still
used the Highland spade; in Luss and Arrochar, teams of eight to ten
men and women worked together, cutting a deep slit and throwing over
the whole sod like a furrow. But this was exceptional. Elsewhere the new
ploughs broke up the land ready for the new metal-toothed harrows,
which prepared the soil for the seed.

But there the chain of improvement faltered. The hand method of
broadcasting seed was still preferred to the new seed drill. Further on,
at harvest, there was another gap in the sequence of improvement.
Crops were universally taken by the old toothed sickle, the scythe having
made little headway.

At the next stage of separating the grain from the straw, the mechanical
thresher re-established the new technology, and the last stage, sifting the
grain from the chaff, was also accomplished by a mechanical winnowing
machine. The winnower, or fanner, had been introduced from Holland
in 1710 by James Meikle; and his son, Andrew, produced the first
practical thresher about 1775. In the 1790s, fanners were being added to
the threshers, and these combined machines were appearing in Lanarkshire and Ayrshire.

The diffusion of the new machines and tools was imperfect, and in
spite of the more general acceptance of new crops and rotations, the
improvement of the arable sector was by no means complete by 1800.
Success depended greatly on the drive of the landowner. If he took the
view that his tenants were responsible for improvements, this slowed
down the spread of the new system. In Ayrshire, Colonel Fullarton
maintained that 'improvements have in general been established not by
the farmers, who can ill afford such speculations; but as they ought to be,
at the expense of the landholder'. However, the expense and uncertainty
involved was a challenge to even the richest landowner. Alexander
Fairlie of Fairlie overcame this problem by enclosing farm by farm as
old leases fell due. This was a phased method, which spread the cost of
improvement, and it became the preferred procedure. This type of outlay
was not beyond the capacity of the smaller proprietor. In Lanarkshire,
Naismith maintained that, 'The proprietors of small estates frequently

cultivate the whole or a considerable part of their own land, and much improvement of the county is owing to their efforts and example.'

Some landowners were active, but there is little evidence that the tenants were much involved in improvement, if not being directed to be so by the terms of their leases. This practice was common by the last quarter of the eighteenth century. The most potent brake on tenant initiative, however, seems to have been the practice of auctioning off the leases of the new farms to the highest bidder. This destroyed confidence in continuity of tenancy, and by appropriating the tenant's liquid capital in lease rents, left him with little to invest in improving his farm. Moreover, tenants regarded even the nineteen-year lease as far too short to give back any benefit from the work and capital required as investments in the new agriculture. Consequently, the benefits of the first phase of improvement were by 1800 marred by half-completed tasks and slovenly farming practice. Even in the main improvement of enriching the grasslands, tenants compromised by sowing mixtures of seeds, heavily adulterated by poor-quality annual rye grasses. In this they were partly at the mercy of unscrupulous seed merchants, who sold them inferior qualities of seed, and this was reflected in the patchy improvement of grassland.

Nevertheless, in a region naturally suited to pastoral activities, the improvement in the grassland was sufficient to support the less publicised, but vital, revolution in livestock production. The region's farmers traditionally fattened Irish and Highland cattle for sale locally and in England. In Ayrshire the Galloway breed was equally important for beef and milk: Galloways sold in great numbers in England, fetching £5–£10 per head during the Napoleonic wars. The beef-cattle sector was well developed, but dairying received less attention, the local breeds being poor milkers, and perishable dairy products difficult to market.

The problem of indifferent milk yield was attacked by developing a new breed of dairy cow in north Ayrshire. In the early eighteenth century, both the Earl of Marchmont and John Dunlop of Dunlop appear to have introduced Teeswater, or Lincoln cattle, for cross-breeding with local stock. By the 1780s the hybrid had developed into a brown-and-white mottled breed, first called Dunlop cattle, and later the Ayrshire. These cattle could give 3–4 gallons of milk per day in the summer, and had become the main dairy cows in north Ayrshire by the 1790s, and had also penetrated the other counties close to the Glasgow market.

But dairy practice lagged. The necessary spur to improvement was the prospect of profit. In his 1794 report Naismith maintained:

> it was not till after the first Peace of Paris when the rapid progress
> of commerce and manufactures brought a new influx of wealth
> among the inhabitants, and greatly increased the price of butter
> and cheese, that attention to the dairy became general.

The price rise of the Napoleonic Wars built on this. Even then the effects varied with distance from the market. In south Ayrshire, the upper ward of Lanarkshire, and Dunbartonshire, most dairy produce was consumed locally. Cheese and butter mainly went to Glasgow from the north of Ayrshire, and central Lanarkshire, but liquid milk was not yet important, since the needs of most towns were still met by their own dairy herds.

The new commercialism also influenced sheep rearing and horse breeding. By 1800 the native whitefaced sheep had been replaced by the hardier blackface, and large areas of land around Glasgow were rented by jobbers each year to fatten both sheep and cattle for market. The farmers of the region also evolved the Clydesdale or Lanarkshire workhorse to take over the work of the farm as oxen disappeared as draft animals. A good breeding mare could cost £30–£40, more than many small farmers earned in a year. Their needs were satisfied by developing the import of large numbers of lighter horses from Ireland, which sold at £10–£15.

Growing demand and rising incomes clearly helped develop the agriculture of the west. The region's farmers also discovered that their improved livestock found willing buyers outside the district. Ayrshire cattle spread far afield; Clydesdale horses were much sought after in England, and the wool of the new blackfaced sheep was prized by Yorkshire merchants. This was a bonus on top of the local demand, which drew great quantities of butter, cheese and oats into the towns to support the budding industrial growth.

The second stage: 1820–1870

The first main stage of improvement from 1750 to 1820 brought order out of chaos on the land. Enclosures, rotations, improved livestock and mixed farming brought increased yields, rents and profits. But after 1819 the momentum was lost. Further expansion was inhibited by persistently wet land, diminishing returns from heavy applications of lime to sweeten and fertilise the soil, the mediocre milk yields of good Ayrshire cows growing lean on meagre diets in winter time, and the inability of hand labour to till the land and gather the harvest in years when bad weather cut the season perilously close to the minimum growing period for grain.

The key to further improvement was furrow draining and subsoil ploughing. Ditches dug across the field simply fed water into the deep perimeter ditches, and these proved ineffective in draining away water from heavy land. Some farmers in Ayrshire, particularly in Sorn parish, attempted to remedy this by laying parallel stone drains. This was fairly effective, but expensive, and a simpler solution had to be found. The answer came from farmers in Essex, Suffolk and Staffordshire, where by the end of the Napoleonic wars water was being drained effectively by laying tile tubes. The practice spread north to Cumberland, where Sir James Graham developed 'tiles of varying diameters', and in turn this was taken up in Ayrshire by the Duke of Portland. He built a tileworks in 1825, and demonstrated the benefits of the new principle by laying out a fifteen-acre field to tile drains in 1826. True underground drainage had arrived.

The Duke drained about 12,000 acres on his Ayrshire estates in the next twenty years: at a cost of £5–£7 per acre the outlay could scarcely have been less than £60,000. Much of the expense was for labour in trenching, though this was partly overcome by 1831 with the introduction of James Smith's 'subsoil plough'. This reached depths of up to two feet below an ordinary furrow, loosened the soil, and made trenching easy. The benefits were obvious, and by the 1830s most districts were experimenting with tile drains, local agricultural societies offered them as prizes at ploughing matches, and tileworks were established in many areas. This was essential, since the early tiles were brittle and had to be made close to the point of use. Furrow draining demanded that the tiles be laid in parallel ditches 15–18 feet apart; and this innovation also made it possible to lower and straighten the old ridges in a systematic way, and though ridges remained, they had a gentle low profile, the track of the new drains being marked by the regular shallow furrows.

In spite of this advance it was not till after 1845 that the draining revolution drew the water out of the wet clays of the west of Scotland. The timing was influenced by two developments. The early tiles had flat bottoms, normally of wood, and required great care in laying. However, about 1841–2, a Kentish farm worker invented the cylindrical tile, overcoming this problem. Several tileworks were producing the new tile in 1843 and this coincided with government subsidies in aid of drainage. An Act of 1845 set aside £2 million to be used in loans, claimed by application to the Enclosure Commissioners. This stimulated an intensive phase of draining in Scotland, loans being made for 22 years at $6\frac{1}{2}$ per cent interest, payment of which extinguished the loan at the end of the period. Tenants could apply for loans, but most were taken up by the landowner, the tenants simply paying him the interest on the outlay. Following on this the best heavy land was dried out and many mosses were reclaimed. The major obstacle to good farming was therefore brought under control between 1845 and 1870. This advance opened the way to the better use of new manures and machines.

The fertiliser problem was in two parts. No farm generated sufficient manure for its own needs, and supplies from town stables were expensive. The chemistry of manures was imperfectly understood. Lord Dundonald had published his treatise on *Agriculture and Chemistry* in 1795, but his initial preference for heavy liming had produced disappointing results after an early improvement. Alternatives like woollen rags, coke from gasworks, and seaweed helped, but did not provide a universal solution. The answer clearly lay in artificial fertilisers. Scottish farmers conducted a series of experiments in the 1820s, applying salt, soot, nitre and bones to a range of common crops. Bones in any form supplied phosphates and nitrogen, and were in wide use from the later 1820s. But the big step forward came with the first importations of Peruvian guano in 1842. Its appearance and normal manure-like smell encouraged experimentation under the auspices of the Highland and Agricultural Society, between 1843 and 1845. The Society subsequently appointed Dr Thomas Anderson as research chemist, and his results quickly demonstrated the beneficial effects of nitrogenous and phosphatic manures.

Under Anderson's guidance the consumption of artificial manures in Scotland increased from about 3,000 tons in 1842 to 85,000 tons in 1872. At the outset, bones provided two-thirds of the manure and guano the remainder. Guano consumption then increased steadily to 50,000 tons in 1862, supplying two-thirds of all artificial manures on Scottish farms, though after that its importance decreased with a fall-off in quality. Nitrate of soda also began to be used in the 1850s, and together with sulphate of ammonia, supplied 18 per cent of requirements in 1872: bones still provided one-third of artificial manure at that time. The benefits were more in obtaining a regularly good yield than in dramatically increasing the product of particular crops.

Thorough draining and extensive fertilising were important advances, for they partly neutralised the effects of cold, wet soils and uncertain weather and gave the farmer the expectation of regular returns on his investment and work. This was a new prospect, and was underwritten by the introduction of more efficient implements. Refinements in the plough were continuous, improving its weight and manoeuvrability: Wilkie's iron plough was very popular around Hamilton in the 1830s, and Gray's plough, made at Uddingston, was coming into more general use at the same time. Steam ploughing was given a trial in the 1860s, but did not do well on undulating surfaces in small fields. The iron harrow, grubber, horsedrawn hoe and seed drill met with more success, and were widely used by the 1860s, and larger farms even used machines for broadcasting grain.

Machinery also brought greater security to the harvest. Early mechanical reapers were introduced by James Smith of Deanston between 1811 and 1835, and the Reverend Patrick Bell in 1825, but serious trials did not begin till the Americans, McCormick and Hussey, displayed their machines at the Great Exhibition of 1851. The results were impressive; most farms over 100 acres were employing mechanical reapers by 1860. The design of threshing machines also advanced, and fixed machines worked by two horses were common, though larger, steam-driven mobile threshers also toured the region in the 1860s, and could be hired to do the work with great speed and efficiency.

The third critical element in this second phase of agricultural improvement was the increasing use of animal feeding-stuffs which had been bought in instead of being produced on the farm. Linseed cake was in use in the 1830s, and was quickly followed by rape cake and cotton-seed cake. This last type became the most important. The farmer's expenditure on feeding-stuffs was thought, in many cases, to equal the rent of his farm. This innovation prefaced a dramatic change in the nature of the region's farming. The first phase of improvement had replaced subsistence cultivation by mixed farming: mixed farming now began to give way to a more commercialised form of factory-like farming. Seeds, stock and food were purchased off the farm and livestock was quickly fattened for sale in nearby urban markets. The self-contained nature of mixed farming disappeared. As a result there was a sharp contraction of the area sown to crops, and an extension of the acreage under grass (Table 5). Livestock increased its dominance in the farm economy (Table 6) and dairy products assumed an even greater importance. Liquid milk played a greater part, though even in Ayrshire it represented only £40,000 of the £418,000 valuation of the county's dairy produce in 1867. Farmers increasingly adjusted their production to local demands. The Ayrshire

TABLE 5 *Acreage under main crops, 1855–70 (West Scotland)*

Crops	1855	(%)	1870	(%)
White Crops				
Wheat	27,023		16,982	
Oats	142,682		118,332	
Barley	4,104		3,099	
Total	173,809	31·0	138,413	23·4
Green Crops				
Turnips	33,722		23,311	
Potatoes	24,280		22,147	
Total	58,002	10·3	45,458	7·7
Rotation and improved grass	329,800	58·6	406,600	68·8
Total under crops and grass	561,611		590,471	

Sources: 1855, Trans. Highland and Agricultural Society; 1870, Dept of Agriculture, Agricultural Returns

coast between Ayr and Girvan developed the early seed-potato trade, while the middle Clyde valley smallholders extended the fruit-growing districts, adding strawberries and gooseberries for the jam factories to the traditional orchard crops. Closer to Glasgow, market gardening was well established, specialising in cabbages, carrots and other vegetables.

TABLE 6 *Changes in farm livestock population, 1855–70 (West Scotland)*

Livestock	1855	1870
Horses for		
agricultural purposes	20,593	13,939
Milk cows	86,203	92,318
Other cows		
(including calves)	104,163	81,823
Sheep	321,016	384,672
Lambs .	187,868	230,074
Swine	22,999	27,505
Total	742,842	830,331

Sources: 1855, Trans. Highland and Agricultural Society; 1870, Dept of Agriculture, Agricultural Returns

By 1870, a highly commercial pattern of land use was well established. The central areas were still dominated by a modified mixed farming and dairying economy, and this merged into specialised liquid milk dairying and market gardening close to the towns. Around this core there was a broad zone of general mixed farming in which stock fattening played a prominent part, and as the zone merged with the moorland edge, extensive sheep raising took over. The adaptations to environment, already evident in the region's farming in 1750, had been extended and given a secure commercial foundation by 1870.

Landlord, tenant and labourer

The century of agricultural improvement greatly changed the positions of landlord, tenant and labourer, both absolutely and in relation to one another. Change was least marked in ownership: in 1873 there were more than 23,000 proprietors in the region, but most of the land was still held in a few hands. Three landlords owned 40 per cent of the acreage in Renfrewshire; seven held over one-third of the land in Ayrshire; one, Sir James Colquhoun, owned over half the acreage in Dunbartonshire, and four families controlled almost one-third of Lanarkshire. At the other extreme, fewer than 15 per cent of the farmers who worked the land actually owned it. The gulf between proprietor and tenant was already wide in 1750, but it became even more marked as ties of mutual support were replaced by obligations of money rent. Increasing rentals represented the real change for the landowner. In 1790 the real rent of the land in the west of Scotland was £251,000, probably double the level of 1760. In 1811–12, at the height of wartime inflation, rental had increased to £818,530, and reached £3,685,389 in 1870. This was an increase of at least fifteen times in less than 100 years.

This was in part a reflection of the great changes at the level of tenant and labourer. The small fermetoun and scattered parcels of unenclosed land had given way to the compact tenant farm, and this had enforced a change of status for many people. Joint tenancies disappeared and landless labourers undoubtedly increased in number. But it is impossible to be precise about the scale of change: we cannot even be certain of changes in the total farm labour force. The census of 1801 recorded 57,416 persons in the region as mainly dependent upon agriculture, but it is not clear how this should be interpreted. In 1851, 53,208 persons were engaged in agriculture, forestry and fishing, and this had declined to 31,634 in 1871. The agrarian revolution does not appear to have produced a severe contraction in the farming population before 1840 or 1850, though it must have altered their position on the land. It is difficult to say more than that the majority of the agricultural population probably rented a little land of their own at the beginning of the period, but only a minority survived as tenants in 1870. The purely farming population was just over 26,000 persons in 1870; only 6,000 were farmers and their families, but 40 per cent were outdoor labourers, and over a third were hired indoor servants.

These people worked on 8,343 farms in 1870. Nearly half of these were smaller than 50 acres while only 30 per cent were larger than 100 acres. The farmers were assisted not only by their families and permanent hired help, but by a well-developed supply of gang labour, composed of the wives and daughters of Irishmen and miners. The gangs represented a mobile supply of seasonal labour, working on piece rates during a 9–10 hour day, and involved no charge upon the farmer for maintenance or food. The end-product of the changes in status flowing from agricultural improvement was that the region's farms were held by a small number of tenants who paid rentals to generally absentee landlords. The work was carried out by family labour, hired help and seasonal workers. This concentrated the profits of the farming year into a relatively few hands and enabled the tenant to meet the demands of proprietor and labourer alike.

The demands of proprietors seem to have been more pressing than those of labour. Aggregate rental increased more than fifteen-fold, though that represented the yield on formerly unproductive land as well as long-standing farmland. On the scant evidence available, wage labour did less well. A ploughman earned £10–£12 per year in the early 1790s, and this tripled to £30–£35 in the peak years of the Napoleonic wars, only to fall back to £18–£22 in 1870, though a top ploughman could still earn £25–£30. However, such wages were commonly increased by bed and board for an unmarried labourer, and a house and garden for a married man. There was also a supplementary allowance of oatmeal, potatoes and the right to keep a cow, though all these were being replaced by direct cash payments towards the end of the period.

The changes of these 100 years made obsolete an unproductive communal system of farming and brought an efficient commercial one in its place. Wage labour came to play a prominent part in the system. The traditional underemployment of labour was replaced by an intensive use of men and machinery. The result was a dramatic increase in rentals. This rested upon an increase in the value of output which appears to have been four-fold between 1790 and 1840, and to have doubled again by 1870. In the latter stages this was achieved by a diminishing labour force, an increased capital investment, and an upsurge in productivity which, contrary to common belief, could scarcely have been equalled in the industrial field.

4

The industrial base:
the triumph of textiles

Scotland, like England, took the first step into the factory age in the textile sector. Cotton, however, was a late-comer in Scottish textiles. It was built upon the foundations slowly and painstakingly erected in the linen industry. The rise of cotton was a considerable achievement, for following upon the Union of 1707 Scotland had found herself at a competitive disadvantage with England in most manufacturing activities. The Scottish economy was still strongly agricultural and the people still lived mostly in small towns and scattered hamlets. Where manufacturing did exist it was based either on the traditional crafts of spinning and weaving in the home, or in the specialisations of the craft guilds in the small towns. Production was everywhere small-scale, inefficiently organised and burdened by the long acceptance of modest skills and poor-quality products. But by a strange quirk it was these very characteristics of cheapness and coarseness which underlay the early success of the linen industry as its cheap fabrics found an expanding market in the English plantations.

The rise of linen

In response to English demand, linen cloth had become Scotland's most important manufactured export at the beginning of the eighteenth century. But though the volume of output was increasing, the structure of the industry remained a ramshackle affair. Cloth production was loosely organised, depending on the work of independent spinners and weavers who frequently alternated their work at the spinning wheel and loom with labour on the land, and who brought their products to market in an irregular way. The disposal of the yarn or cloth could be as infrequent as annual fairs, though there were sometimes more regular outlets through the visits of linen merchants' agents from the towns of Paisley and Glasgow. Consequently, neither output nor marketing could respond quickly to new demands. The growth of the industry was hampered further by the large volume of capital tied up in the bleaching process, which could extend over six to eight months. The first concerted move to overcome these difficulties was taken in 1726, when the Convention of Royal Burghs suggested to the government a scheme for promoting manufactures, and in 1727 the 'Board of Trustees for Improving Fisheries and Manufactures in Scotland' was established. Modest funds of up to £6,000 per year were available to the Board for this purpose under the financial provisions of the Union of 1707 and of the malt tax legislation of 1729, and though only a small part of this was ever diverted into linen, the Board of Trustees became an important influence on the development of the linen industry.

From the outset, the Board identified the central weakness of the industry as one of quality of work and product. It attacked these deficiencies in a number of ways. Much of the early effort of the trustees concentrated upon improving the quantity and quality of home-grown flax by paying a subsidy of first 15s., and ultimately 20s., per acre laid down to flax. These efforts met with only modest success and in the 1750s Scotland seldom provided more than half her own requirements. The difficulty was that the unimproved agriculture of Scotland could provide neither the space nor the skills required to produce this demanding crop in adequate quantities. The problem of supply and quality was ultimately met by importation, some three-quarters of the raw material coming from overseas in the 1780s. This favoured the west of Scotland whose traditional markets in Ireland and the Low Countries supplied her with better-quality flax than that obtained by the east-coast producers who relied mainly on the Baltic lands for their supplies.

While the Board's attempts to increase the supplies of home-grown flax were not particularly successful, the effort to improve the preparation of flax and the quality of the cloth was better rewarded. The traditional method of preparation involved steeping the flax in water for up to ten days to loosen the fibre from the woody stock, then hanging the soggy mass on a board and beating it with a wooden blade to complete the separation, a process called 'scutching'. This was followed by 'heckling', in which the fibre was teased with a steel-toothed comb to sub-divide the strands in preparation for the spinning-wheel. These hand processes were inefficient and the Board was quick to seek improvements. As on many previous occasions the Continent provided the example. In 1728 James Spalding of Bonnington Mills was dispatched to observe Continental methods. On his return he built an improved scutch mill, on a Dutch model, which employed sharp-edged blades set on a flywheel driven at great speed by water power. The machine cost about £25 and quickly proved itself; within 50 years there were seventy-two scutch or lint mills in operation in the west of Scotland and 252 in the whole country. The Board next imported improved Dutch heckles, and it became common for the new lint mills and heckleries to be erected side by side. These improvements in preparing the flax made it all the more essential to tackle the deficiencies in spinning and weaving, since even good flax could be ruined by careless workers and crude equipment. Again following a common practice of earlier centuries, the Board persuaded foreign weavers to come to Scotland to teach their skills. This met two needs, for while the men taught weaving methods, their wives were frequently employed to demonstrate the best ways of spinning the finer yarns. Spinning was also promoted through the spinning schools established from 1729, and although many were frequented out of interest by 'ladies of quality', others more practically motivated also attended, and twenty-four such schools were in operation within 20 years.

The Board attacked the problem of quality on a broad front, bringing its influence to bear on the growing of the flax, on the basic preparation and on spinning and weaving. There remained the problems of finishing the cloth and then marketing the product. The Board once more took the lead in seeking out improvements. The most time-consuming and expensive part of the finishing processes was bleaching. This was a capital-intensive activity, and between 1727 and 1772 the Board subsidised the laying down of bleachfields at up to £50 per acre. Among the early fields developed with this assistance was the extension of the Dalquhurn field on the River Leven, the laying out of the Cameron field at Loch Lomond, and Grays Green at Glasgow. There were seventeen large bleachfields in operation in the region by 1772, and a further seventy-five elsewhere in Scotland.

In the effort to improve bleaching the Board again resorted to imported skills, this time both of Dutch and Irish bleachers. The Dutch supplied the methods and skills for finishing the finest linen, while the Irish techniques were best suited for use with the medium and coarser grades of cloth. Bleaching involved first the application of a mild alkali, normally a lye of wood ashes or kelp (seaweed ash), followed by steeping in a dilute acid, which until about 1750, was usually sour milk. The alkali removed impurities and dirt, and the acid disposed of earthy substances which prevented even dyeing of the cloth. The cloth was then washed and exposed to sunlight, the process being repeated until the required whiteness was obtained. The Board encouraged the use of kelp and the importation of fine wood-ash to improve the alkalis available, but the significant revolution came with the use of sulphuric acid in place of sour milk.

D

Sulphuric acid had begun to be imported from Holland in the 1740s where its bleaching properties were undoubtedly known, and by 1750, working at the request of the Board of Trustees, Professor Black of Glasgow, and Francis Home and William Cullen of Edinburgh, had demonstrated a satisfactory procedure for employing this acid. This reduced the time taken in the souring part of bleaching from four or five months to the same number of days, and freed the industry from seasonality and reliance on sunshine. This coincided with the commercial production of the acid by Dr Roebuck at Prestonpans from 1749. These advances helped release the industry from a large part of the crippling burden of capital locked up in unfinished cloth. The final breakthrough in bleaching was only to come through the discovery of the properties of chlorine by Berthollet in 1784, and the perfection of dry bleaching powder by Charles Mackintosh and Charles Tennant in 1799. These measures finally rescued bleaching from its rural setting and made it possible to perform the whole process indoors, thus releasing great bleachfields for agricultural use.

These improvements in finishing the cloth left the control of quality and marketing to be organised. The Board supervised the quality of the cloth by employing an elaborate structure of travelling inspectors who affixed the Stampmasters' mark to cloth of approved quality; only cloth bearing the stamp could be offered for sale. The disposal of the cloth itself was assisted by legislation; the Bounty Act of 1742 offered premiums on certain types of linen exported, and in 1748 the embargo on the importation and wear of French cambrics increased the demand for fine home-produced linens.

Active as the Board was, it remained essentially an administrative organisation. It encouraged the search for improvement, and demonstrated and supported innovations by small cash grants, but it could not finance the application of these new methods on a wide scale. The provision of finance and credit required a deeper involvement than the Board was designed to give, and from the initiative of one of its members, Lord Milton, there emerged in 1746 the British Linen Company. This organisation was established in Edinburgh and quickly had a warehouse in Glasgow. It set out to promote the manufacture of linen by purchasing raw flax, preparing it and giving it out on credit to spinners, re-purchasing the yarn and repeating the process with weavers. Its business increased rapidly and agencies were established over a wide area in which yarn was distributed and cloth collected. In 1747 the Company began to issue its own chits or notes to weavers against the value of the cloth produced, and these notes passed rapidly into circulation. This proved to be very profitable and the Company gradually began to withdraw from active involvement in spinning, weaving and marketing, and concentrated on extending credit to weavers and larger manufacturers to tide them over the long wait which the bleaching process imposed between the manufacture and the sale of cloth. Because the Company was a body incorporated by charter its shareholders enjoyed limited liability; moreover, it could enter into any activity not prohibited by its charter: it thus had authority both to bank and to trade: the Bank of Scotland and the Royal Bank of Scotland could do only the former. The Company soon extended its banking functions and eventually was to become the British Linen Bank.

Thus by 1760, some of the problems of promoting the linen industry had been lifted from the shoulders of individual entrepreneurs through the work of the Board of Trustees and the contribution of the British Linen Company. The response of the industry was quite dramatic. Total production increased five-fold between 1728 and 1758 and the west of Scotland had emerged as a region of high-quality manufacture, producing only 30 per cent of the yardage but 40 per cent of the total value of cloth stamped for sale in 1758 (Table 7). This was an immense achievement

TABLE 7   *Linen cloth stamped for sale, 1727–1822*

Area	1727–8 (Yds)	(£)	1757–8 (Yds)	(£)	1767–8 (Yds)	(£)
Ayr	26,699	2,087	139,161	7,481	123,543	6,591
Dunbarton	66,027	2,356	310,827	23,940	52,650	2,557
Lanark	272,658	9,968	1,951,693	86,531	1,994,906	172,764
Renfrew	85,527	6,853	788,491	51,660	674,178	66,387
W. Scotland	450,911	21,264	3,190,172	169,612	2,845,277	248,299
Scotland	2,183,978	103,312	10,624,436	424,141	11,795,437	599,689
% W. Scotland	20·6	20·6	30·04	39·9	24·1	41·4

Area	1777–8 (Yds)	(£)	1787–8 (Yds)	(£)	1821–2 (Yds)	(£)
Ayr	50,826	3,000	54,110	6,591	20,826	3,197
Dunbarton	31,541	1,290	74,295	3,097	11,331	647
Lanark	1,748,674	142,446	1,362,150	109,440	22,869	1,951
Renfrew	1,467,935	96,201	1,671,346	115,817	25,685	3,107
W. Scotland	3,298,976	242,937	3,161,901	234,945	80,711	8,902
Scotland	13,264,411	592,023	20,506,310	854,901	36,268,530	1,396,296
% W. Scotland	24·7	41·0	15·4	27·4	0·22	0·64

Sources: Reports of the Board of Trustees for Improving Fisheries and Manufactures in Scotland; H. Hamilton, *Economic History of Scotland in the Eighteenth Century*, Oxford University Press, 1963

for a small country with a scattered rural population and no great store of capital, and reflected the success of the developmental programme of the Board of Trustees. The cumulative changes thus brought about had, by the middle of the century, begun to produce a new type of organisation and a new scale of production in the industry. For when changes were introduced in the preparation of the flax and yarn, these altered the established relationships among the different stages of production and precipitated new developments at other points in the production line.

The initial point of disruption was in scutching and heckling. The improvements which resulted in the construction of the new water-powered lint mills called for investment on a new and larger scale. Each new mill represented an outlay of £80 or £100. Being water driven, this also initiated a search for suitable water sites around which the previously scattered domestic industry began to coalesce. This new level of investment was far beyond the means of most individual spinners or weavers. It encouraged the dominance of merchant capitalists, men who were already important in the working of an industry whose scattered production demanded a knowledgeable middleman to organise supplies of flax and to keep in touch with the changing demands of distant and, frequently, specialised markets. Such men often owned the materials through all the stages of production, and carried the financial risk involved by having their capital tied up in raw materials, goods in production and stocks in process of sale. Merchant-middlemen, together with the British Linen Co., provided the vital short-term credit in the domestically organised industry. When scutching mills were introduced, capital requirements were extended, and the burden of fixed capital in buildings and machinery had to be added to the costs of working capital locked up in materials and goods, thus pushing the control of the growing industry further into the hands of men of capital.

These departures from previous practice resulted in a rapid expansion in the quantity of flax prepared for spinning. The increased flow of raw material brought new pressures to bear both on spinners and weavers, pushing them in the direction of full-time work at the spinning wheel and loom. The innovations in technology had already encouraged a capitalistic structure in the preparatory processes, but now centralised production in spinning and weaving resulted in an organisational revolution. The big change was the extension of central control by the merchant manufacturers in the towns, and the big gain was an increasing regularity of production and the establishment of communities of skilled spinners and weavers. The weavers were the first to concentrate in loom shops in and around the towns where the merchants had their yarn warehouses, and many quickly became full-time employees who no longer even owned their own looms. These merchant manufacturers flourished as the old problem of poor quality production was overcome. Better preparation of flax and a rationalisation of processes permitted a new capitalistic structure in the industry by 1760. The same merchant manufacturers enhanced the new quality by importing fine-grade flax and yarn from Ireland and the Low Countries. The chemical revolution had also encouraged a concentration of capital in the finishing processes. Here, however, it was not usually the merchant manufacturers who controlled the industry, but another group of capitalists, the bleachers and dyers often operating bleachfields and printfields side by side.

The Board of Trustees had begun assisting the laying out of bleach-fields from 1727, and similar help was extended to the laying out of print-fields. Both Dutch and English printers were encouraged to come to Scotland to teach their skills. In 1742 calico printing was introduced into the west of Scotland. Archibald Ingram, in partnership with some merchants in the West Indian trade, opened a print work at Pollokshaws to the south of Glasgow. The next works was set up in 1750 on the Kelvin at Dalsholm by William Stirling who moved in 1770 to Cordale on the River Leven, a site adjoining his uncle's bleachfield and dyeworks at Dalquhurn. This branch of the trade grew rapidly from 1770, especially under the influence of the Crum family who had begun business with a small printfield in the Gallowgate. In 1771 they opened the Levern printfield and followed this with the Fereneze and Thornliebank fields in 1773 and 1779 respectively. By the 1780s most of the bleachers were dyers and printers as well, the combination of all three processes being encouraged by the common need for plentiful supplies of clean soft water, and initially for space to lay out the cloth. After 1785, block printing began to be superseded by William Bell's invention of cylinder printing, and this furthered the alliance between the manufacturers involved in these capital-intensive processes. These pressures con-centrated the industry around Glasgow in small, specialised, settlements like Maryhill, Pollokshaws, Thornliebank and Dalsholm. Further from the city other centres emerged at Lennoxtown in Stirlingshire, on the rivers Cart and Levern in Renfrewshire, and in Bonhill, Renton and Alexandria in Dunbartonshire.

In the half century from 1730 to 1780 a highly-organised and very skilled linen industry had been created in the west of Scotland. It was not one uniform type of manufacture, but rather a number of highly specialised branches of the linen trade, each tending to concentrate in its own particular district. Glasgow was already Britain's leading linen town in 1771, with over 2 million yards of cloth stamped for sale valued at £156,000. Three-quarters of this was represented by handkerchiefs, and two fine-quality cloths known as 'bengals' and 'carolines'. Specialisa-tion had been carried much further in Paisley where, in addition to the usual cambrics and lawns, there was a thriving silk-gauze manufacture and a flourishing linen-thread industry. Silk gauze employed about

10,000 persons in and around Paisley, and the output of thread was put at £64,000 per year in the early 1780s. Similar specialisations were common throughout the region. In Lanarkshire small towns like Hamilton and Strathaven had a reputation for fine yarns, silk gauzes and Hollands; this was true also of the villages in the Monklands parishes. Most of this Lanarkshire production was controlled by the Glasgow and Paisley merchants. In the Irvine valley in Ayrshire silk and linen gauzes were a feature, while Beith was an important centre of the fine-yarn and silk-gauze trade. The plain finished articles made in all of these districts were enhanced by the labour of thousands of girls and women employed in tambour and embroidery work; this again was organised through Glasgow and Paisley manufacturing houses.

The emphasis in the region tended to be on skill and on quality, though the coarser cloths retained an important share in output. Even in Glasgow and Paisley coarse osnaburgs were manufactured, and outside the specialist centres, coarse brown linen and checked and striped linens were commonly produced. This was particularly the case in rural Ayrshire where coarse cloth was manufactured from locally-grown flax. For this grade of cloth all processes from cultivation to bleaching were carried out in the local community, the cloth either being consumed domestically or disposed of at fairs to the agents of the Glasgow and Paisley manufacturers. The output of linen stamped for sale increased sharply between 1730 and 1760, before stabilising at around 3 million yards per year. But even if the volume of output ceased to grow, the emphasis on skill and quality enabled the region to produce over 40 per cent by value of Scotland's linen cloth for some twenty years between 1758 and 1778. In the succeeding decade, however, both the volume and value of cloth produced in Scotland almost doubled, while production in the west of Scotland declined (Table 7, see p. 83).

Cotton had begun to attract attention in the west of Scotland, and in the space of the single decade from 1780 to 1790, the productive structure which had been slowly and carefully erected to foster the linen trade was switched to the exotic and lucrative cotton wool. When the last records of the Stampmaster of linen cloth were compiled in 1822 the west of Scotland then produced only 80,000 yards valued at less than £9,000. This was less than half of 1 per cent of Scottish output, and is to be compared with the region's contribution of more than 40 per cent by value in the 1770s.

Linen to cotton

The Scottish cotton industry rose to prominence in the 1780s by borrowing its technology, and by imitating the organisation and product of the local linen trade. The critical inventions which freed hand-loom weavers from part-time work and a dependence on the slow yarn output of single-spindle spinning wheels were taken *en bloc* from Lancashire. In 1764 James Hargreaves invented his first spinning jenny with eight spindles, and these had been increased to sixteen when he took out his patent in 1770. In this form, the jenny revolutionised the productivity of the spinners, and was small and cheap enough to be installed in the cottages, so that the old spinning wheels were quickly discarded. The appearance of the jenny preceded an even more significant technical advance in spinning, the water-frame, although Richard Arkwright's patent in 1769 was taken out a year before that of Hargreaves. The water-frame was able to spin a cotton yarn which was strong enough for warp thread, and created for the first time the possibility of making cotton cloth wholly from British-produced yarn. This could be woven from weft-yarn produced by the jenny and warp-yarn spun by the water-frame. The advantages of these two machines were combined when Samuel Crompton patented his mule in 1779, a machine which was capable of producing a smoother and finer yarn suitable for both weft and warp threads.

The advantages of these innovations in spinning were so obvious that every kind of textile manufacturer wanted to use them. But it was soon obvious that these early and primitive machines were better for cotton wool than for the less tractable wool and flax fibres; the implications were clear to any manufacturer who wished to employ the new methods. The west of Scotland, like Lancashire, was heavily involved in the American trade. By the 1790s there was easy access to apparently un-limited supplies of raw cotton, which was very advantageous compared with reliance on limited supplies of local wool, or on European flax the delivery of which was continually liable to disruption through warfare. Most of the capital in the early textile trade was in the form of raw materials and stocks, so that the switch to the new material did not involve writing off substantial capital investments, and the transition to the new textile fibre was rapidly and easily made. In Scotland the transition was even simpler than in England, for Lanarkshire followed Lancashire into the cotton industry with a lag of some twenty years, just sufficient time for the Lancashire producers to have proved the feasibility of the new techniques, to have discovered the insatiable market for their products and to have demonstrated that substantial profits came the way of the innovator in the new cotton industry.

The borrowing of the new machines, jennys for the home and water-frames and mules for the factories, was an obvious move for the Scottish producers, and gave them the immediate advantages of late starters, since the costs of pioneering had been borne by their Lancashire rivals. It was also logical to borrow and imitate the organisational structure which had been evolved by the local linen industry, and to carry this forward to factory production as had Arkwright and others in England.

The English experience was again imitated in the search for water-power sites and in the building of large spinning mills and factory villages. The Scottish cotton masters did not have to bear the costs of the pioneer in any of these areas; this helps to explain the speed with which cotton grew to prominence. Moreover, the Scots did not even have to experiment widely to find a range of cloths in which to specialise. Lancashire, with its earlier start, had pre-empted the market in cheaper cottons, and since the west of Scotland had specialised in working in finer linens, any attempt to imitate Lancashire products would have represented a squandering of Scottish skills in spinning and weaving. Consequently, the cotton merchants in the west of Scotland concentrated on producing a fine cotton yarn to replace fine linen yarns, and they carried on the tradition of skilled weaving by producing fine cloths; they substituted all-cotton cambrics for linen cambrics, and fine muslins for lawns. These were the essential steps which had to be taken to make the change from a linen to a cotton industry in the west of Scotland. It has long been clear that the transition rested on the basis of borrowed technology allied to local skills in spinning and weaving, but the origin of the men who enabled these steps to be taken and who guided the early growth of the cotton industry is much more debatable.

Entrepreneurs and capital

The fact that Scotland was a poor and backward country in the eighteenth century has presented problems for historians when they have sought to explain the rapid development of the cotton industry after 1780, particularly when it seemed obvious that large outlays of capital were called for. In an effort to fill this capital vacuum and present a convincing explanation, earlier historians were attracted to the rough coincidence in time of the collapse of the lucrative tobacco trade in the later 1770s, and the rise of the cotton industry from 1780. Accordingly, there grew up an assumption that there had been a transfer of funds from the profits of tobacco into the new machinery and mills of cotton spinning. But on closer investigation this explanation is not convincing. Of all the great tobacco families who made fortunes in the middle of the century, there are perhaps only two or three possible links with the new cotton industry. The most firmly established connection is that of Robert Dunmore, a Virginian merchant who financed the Ballindalloch cotton mill at Balfron, and is thought also to have contributed to Monteith's mill at Pollokshaws in 1793. Dunmore is also known to have contributed £100 with Robert Bogle, another tobacco merchant, to the short-lived Spinningdale mill in Sutherland. But this is scanty evidence on which to build the assumption that the profits of the tobacco trade financed the cotton industry.

However, dismissing this possible source of capital in a country which was notoriously poor, leaves us with the problem in an even more acute form. Later historians have attempted to bridge the gap by arguing that there was indirect investment in cotton, the funds passing from trade into the landed estate in which so many successful merchants sought to acquire respectability, position and influence, and thence into cotton. There is, in fact, a great deal of evidence to suggest that landed capital found an attractive investment in cotton. Claude Alexander of Ballochmyle invested with David Dale in the great mills at Catrine in Ayrshire, and Dale also had lairds like Sir William Douglas as partners at the Newton Stewart mill, and George Dempster at the Spinningdale enterprise. Dempster was himself also the founder of the great mills at Stanley in Perthshire. Indeed Robert Dunmore, the tobacco merchant who financed the mill at Balfron, only did so after he had purchased the estates of Ballindalloch and Ballinkinrain, and when the fortunes of Alexander and Dempster are investigated it is clear that Alexander acquired his capital as an official of the East India Company, while the Dempster fortune was begun by the grandfather as a merchant in Dundee. Dempster then bought the estate of Dunnichen, and the family fortune was extended by the grandson, George, who was also a director of the East India Company. The evidence is strong that it was not so much capital earned and based on rent-rolls from the land which flowed into cotton, but money which had first been earned in trade, then securely invested in land, but which subsequently sought other outlets where the return was more rapid than from improving agriculture. If capital did flow from the Virginia and the East and West Indies traders to cotton it was by this indirect route through land, and it was poured in by the sons and grandsons of the original Virginian and West Indian merchants, the survivors among whom would have been too old to have taken an active part in the new industry.

Even this more convincing explanation of sources of capital and enterprise overlooks the most obvious source of funds and expertise for the new industry. Since cotton was based on imported technology and local skills employed within the established framework of the linen trade, the men to effect the change were those already deeply involved in the textile industries. The connections of many of the major cotton producers with the earlier textile trades are strikingly clear. David Dale, perhaps the most famous of the first generation of Scottish spinners, began as a hand-loom weaver in fine linen, became a weaving master and importer of fine French and Flemish yarns, and by 1783 was rich enough to spend £6,000, the price of a fair-sized cotton mill, on erecting an elegant town house in Charlotte Street in Glasgow. Dale was deeply involved in cotton, founding New Lanark, and at various times being in partnership at Catrine, Blantyre, Spinningdale, Newton Stewart, Stanley and Rothesay. The Finlay family, ultimately to be the largest in cotton in

D*

Scotland, established themselves first as linen-weaving masters in Glasgow and Paisley, moved into yarn importing and exporting, and entered the cotton industry in 1798 when Kirkman Finlay purchased the Ballindalloch mill. The Finlays were also related to the Buchanans who were Arkwright's agents in Scotland. The Buchanans founded Deanston, managed Catrine and owned Stanley in Perthshire, and they too began as 'English merchants', marketing Scottish linens through a network of pedlars or packmen. Yet another famous cotton family, the Monteiths, were involved in linen, James Monteith being the most important yarn importer in Glasgow in the 1770s. His sons, James, Henry and John, were all to become prominent members of the cotton community as spinners and calico printers, and it was James who purchased the Blantyre mill from David Dale. Lesser-known linen merchants were also involved. John Freeland was a linen manufacturer who founded a spinning mill at Houston in Renfrewshire, and William Gillespie, a bleacher and weaving master in linen, built the first spinning mill in the Barony of Glasgow at Woodside in 1784. David Todd of Todd & Stevenson was a similar case in Glasgow, while the founders of Paisley's cotton mills, the Carlisles, Orrs, Browns, and the later thread dynasties of Coats and Clark, all entered the cotton industry from the existing linen and silk-gauze trades.

The importance of these men is emphasised when we take another look at the source of investment from trade and the land, for few lairds ventured into the exotic world of cotton on their own. They preferred the company of men with more experience. Thus, as we have seen, David Dale partnered Alexander at Catrine, Dempster at Spinningdale and Stanley, and Sir William Douglas at Newton Stewart, while Dunmore joined with the Buchanans at Ballindalloch and with the Monteiths at Pollokshaws. The evidence is overwhelming that it was a small band of influential former linen merchants and manufacturers who, alone or in partnership, provided the main stream of enterprise and finance in the new cotton industry. The willingness of the landed interests to link up with these men suggests that it was individuals like Dale, Finlay, Monteith and the other linen merchants who alone in Scotland had sufficient knowledge of the organisation of production and markets in textiles to have a reasonable chance of success in the new industry. Indeed, their organising skill, their established contacts in the trade, and their knowledge of markets were possibly as important as their ability to supply capital for the new mills.

One contribution which should not be overlooked is the link between Scotland and England and the influx of English skill and capital. The first mill in the west of Scotland, that at Rothesay in 1779, was built with English capital by a group of Sheffield businessmen, though later purchased by Dale in 1785. Benjamin Flounders, a Quaker, came to the rescue of Deanston, purchasing it from the bankrupt Buchanan of Carston in 1793, and Robert Owen came north from the Manchester area to manage New Lanark in 1799. In the same year, Henry Houldsworth came from Manchester to take over Gillespie's Woodside mill, and then built another at Anderston in 1801. The infusion is not large, but the individuals involved are significant, and symptomatic of the very close ties that operated between the two main cotton-manufacturing areas.

Finally, there were the banks, but the evidence of substantial bank investment in the new industry is slight. It is well known that Dale was the Glasgow agent of the Royal Bank of Scotland, and that by the 1780s the west of Scotland was becoming better served by local banks. The service, however, seems to have been confined to the discounting of bills of exchange, probably also the extension of short-term loans on the cash-credit system, rather than being in the nature of an advance to assist in the foundation or expansion of a cotton mill. There were, however, exceptions. The Renfrewshire Bank and the Glasgow Ship Bank were heavily involved at Rothesay mill; Bertram Gardner & Co., Edinburgh bankers, were involved at the Pennicuik mill; Sir William Douglas, who partnered Dale at Newton Stewart, was a founder of the Galloway Bank and it is likely that he was able to draw on bank finance. In the eighteenth century men of capital were involved in many enterprises, and any attempt to unravel the sources of their capital can be difficult. However, it is even more difficult to establish the scale of investment.

Little is known with any certainty concerning the average capital investment. The Newton Stewart mill built in 1787 is known to have cost £20,000, and the larger establishments which were built at Catrine and New Lanark could not have cost less. In 1790, John Dunlop and Hugh Hamilton of Pinmore planned to set up a cotton mill in some old sugar houses and estimated they would need £4,000, besides the price of the houses, to set up a mill containing 9,360 jennys, and other machinery sufficient to employ 170 hands. By 1796 there were thirty-nine twist mills in Scotland which Brown, in his *History of Glasgow* (1797), valued at £490,200, an average of more than £12,500 per mill; some mills like New Lanark*, Blantyre, Linwood, and Catrine were substantially bigger than this. In 1812, the total capital invested in cotton was estimated by Sinclair to amount to £1,400,000, and since there were then 120 cotton mills in operation the average capitalisation was only just over £11,600. The average was undoubtedly pulled down by many small mills, for in 1833 Houldsworth assured the Select Committee on Commerce and Shipping that an investment of £10,000 to £12,000 for machinery and buildings would only suffice to set up a small spinning mill, and such an establishment would have little hope of survival. The major league of

---

* Owen and his partners bought New Lanark from David Dale in 1799 for £60,000. At the next change of partnership in 1814 the establishment went to Owen and his partners at auction for £120,000.

producers clearly required very substantial investments in fixed capital, often sums in excess of £20,000, and it should be remembered that the outlay of fixed capital was usually the smallest part of the investment, since most capital was usually tied up in the stocks of raw materials and goods in process of sale. It is not surprising, then, that the linen merchants welcomed partnerships with men in trade and men of property. The varied origins of the capital is a reflection of the rapidity with which the industry grew and the 'lumpiness' of the investment required to get into cotton spinning in a big way.

The establishment of cotton

Even as linen production climbed to its peak in the west of Scotland, the imports of raw cotton suggest that cotton yarn was being increasingly used in mixtures with linen and wool. Between 1756 and 1760 the annual importation averaged 94,000 lbs and this had more than doubled to over 208,000 lbs by 1780. This was before the establishment of the great cotton spinning mills; the yarn was absorbed in the elaborate structure of production and marketing controlled by the linen merchants. Cotton was clearly being consumed in substantial quantities before 1780, but as yet, Scotland did not have a true cotton industry. Lancashire was already well established in the new textile, and in view of the profitability of the cotton industry at this time, it is pertinent to ask why Scotland only began to enter the trade from 1780. It can be argued that the buoyancy of the linen trade delayed the rise of cotton, and that it was only after the entry of France and Holland into the American War of Independence in 1778 that real difficulty was experienced in maintaining the supplies of flax from the Continent. Moreover, the vagaries of fashion had produced severe distress in the specialist Paisley silk-gauze trade, and it could be suggested that textile manufacturers were more favourably disposed to considering new types of enterprise than was the case before. But the problems of raw material supply and changes of taste in fashion had always been a feature of the linen trade; they did not suddenly appear around 1780 to push the manufacturers out of linen and into cotton. The critical factors in explaining the late entry into cotton are that up to 1780 conditions in the home linen trade were generally favourable and did not push enterprise into the new fibre, and that earlier conditions in the cotton trade were such as to actively discourage entry by the Scots.

The success of linen in the west of Scotland rested on the skill of the spinners and weavers, and this kept the Scottish textile manufacturers out of cotton until the new machinery had improved sufficiently to spin a yarn fine enough to require the skills of Scottish weavers. Until about 1780, the skill of the local hand-spinners was better employed in producing fine linen yarns than in working up the finer cotton yarns on spinning jennies, since this yarn was weak and suited only for the weft in cloths of mixed fibres. But when Richard Arkwright patented his water-frame in 1769 the obstacles to producing strong cotton yarns began to diminish, and the other difficulty of spinning a smooth yarn was overcome in 1779 when Samuel Crompton introduced his mule. It was then technically possible to produce cotton cloth either by combining the strong power-spun warp yarn from Arkwright's frame with the smooth weft yarn of the hand-operated jenny and mule, or entirely from the fine, strong, mule yarn. This was at last the type of yarn suited to the skills of Scottish weavers. It could hardly have been a coincidence that Scotland's first cotton mill was opened at Pennicuik in 1778 to be followed quickly by others at Rothesay in 1779, Neilston in 1780, Johnstone in 1782 and respectively at East Kilbride, Woodside and New Lanark in each of the next three years. This first phase of rapid growth continued till in 1793 there were some thirty-nine water-spinning mills in operation or under construction. The imports of raw cotton had increased ten-fold from 260,000 lbs to 2·6 million lbs between 1779 and 1793. These were the obvious features of the revolution in cotton spinning. They were paralleled by a switch from linen to cotton weaving in the towns and villages of the west of Scotland. In the single decade from 1784 to 1793 fine muslin had completely replaced silk gauze in Paisley, and the 3,000 looms at work in the Barony of Glasgow had changed from the production of lawns and cambrics to the weaving of muslins.

The initial expansion in the fifteen years from 1778 to 1793 left the industry with a number of distinguishing features. Above all, it was the era of water power, when production was dominated by the large spinning mill with a capacity in excess of 10,000 spindles; indeed, in 1793 the two mills at New Lanark and Catrine together consumed more than 20 per cent of the raw cotton imported into Scotland. These were planned establishments, and as with similar mills at Blantyre, Linwood and Loch-winnoch, they had their own factory villages to house the labour force, since the search for adequate water power had taken many of the larger mills to isolated locations. The distribution of these mills was at once both scattered and concentrated. The scatter took mills to the River Tay (Stanley), to the Teith (Deanston), to the Ayr (Catrine), and to the Clyde at New Lanark and Blantyre. But in Renfrewshire the rivers Levern and Black Cart attracted many mills. Such was the importance of contacts with the Glasgow and Paisley yarn merchants and warehousemen that of the thirty-nine mills in operation by the early 1790s, all but a few were to be found within twenty-five miles of Glasgow. Even so, the spinning and weaving sections were frequently some distance apart, and it was the attraction of the yarn market and the warehouse and credit facilities in Glasgow and Paisley which drew the elements of the industry together.

Another distinguishing feature of the industry was the way in which different types of organisation worked side by side. It is true that the great water-powered mills with their large and disciplined labour forces were the dominant feature, but in the excitement of the expansion other forms of organisation could flourish. Even at the great mills not all the work was rationalised and carried on within the new establishment. Much of the initial cleaning of the raw cotton was carried out by women in their own homes. Moreover, it was not uncommon for a great water mill to have hand-powered jennies and mules at work in some of its shops. It was also part of the price paid for rapid growth that old grain mills or other buildings were pressed into use and converted to take the new spinning machinery. This improvisation was more common among the smaller mills which flourished in the early 1790s, when in almost every parish 'public-spirited gentlemen' sought to bring the benefits of employment to their own areas. Thus in Lanarkshire small mills sprang up at Douglas, Carmacoup, Cambuslang and Strathaven. In Ayrshire there were similar establishments at Dalry, Monkton, Irvine and Kilwinning, while in Renfrewshire, they appeared in smaller villages like Kilbarchan, as well as side by side with the larger mills. Most of these were jenny-houses with fifteen to thirty jennies or mules driven by hand or animal power, employing thirty to seventy persons, and some, like those at Kilwinning or Dalry, would also have a small carding mill driven by horses or water. Not only was it possible for small-scale local enterprise to prosper side by side with the capital-intensive water-spinning mills, but both the large and small components of the new industrial organisation linked forward into an equally mixed situation in weaving.

The control of weaving by yarn merchants had been well established in the linen trade and this was carried over into cotton. Large mills like Catrine, New Lanark and Blantyre initially sent the bulk of their yarn by carrier to Glasgow, where yarn merchants organised the weaving side of the trade. The new spinning mills, however, quickly attracted their own communities of weavers, and as weavers began to be employed directly by the mills the processes of spinning and weaving were in some cases brought under the control of single firms. But although the work of producing cloth was being integrated in this way, the weavers did not organise themselves in any systematic fashion. Most of the urban weavers were not corporately organised, and in rural areas the traditional guild structure of master, journeyman and apprentice still persisted. In this case the master weaver was the intermediary who took on the work contracted out by the mill or the yarn merchant. This form of production lasted into the third quarter of the nineteenth century in rural Ayrshire.

The structure of the cotton trade which evolved from the linen industry between 1780 and the early 1790s was fluid and subject to rapid change. It was a very mixed affair with large and small mills in which traditional and newer features worked together. It was the era of water power. The fabric of the new industry was extensively based on borrowing and imitating the first generation inventions in textile machinery made by the English. But from the 1790s the Scots began to invent and innovate for themselves, and this coincided with the beginnings of the second stage of growth in the cotton industry associated with the adoption of steam power.

The introduction of steam: 1792–1830

In 1793 there was only one spinning mill driven by steam power in the whole of Scotland. This was the Springfield mill in the east end of Glasgow, erected by Scott, Stevenson & Co. in 1792, a small establishment employing 100 workers. This departure from previous practice, though modest, was significant. For all the most convenient and economic water-power sites had been exploited, and only steam power, employing Watt's new rotative engine, could break the limitation on growth imposed by a shortage of power. Even so, the use of steam power spread slowly and in 1800 only eight steam engines with a total capacity of 128 horse-power were at work in Scottish cotton mills. But then the culmination of several developments cleared the way for a more rapid expansion.

During the years when water power was being applied to cotton spinning, both the new factory organisation and the domestic system throve side by side, since both the spinning jenny and the mule could be worked by hand and were effective competitors with the water-frame. Moreover, the mule initially was dependent on the jenny to produce its rovings prior to spinning into yarn, and so the jenny had not immediately been displaced. But in 1782 John Swindells of Stockport introduced his 'slubbing billy', a machine which could produce rovings of any fineness from the carded cotton; these rovings were suitable for spinning by the jenny, the mule, and the water-frame. As the slubbing billy came into use the jenny was no longer required to produce rovings, and the mule, as a superior spinning machine, began to gain precedence over it. It is at this stage in the developments that Scottish innovation began the final elimination of the domestic system in spinning.

In 1790, William Kelly, the manager at New Lanark, applied power to the mule making it possible for one man to operate two standard 144-spindle machines. He followed this up in 1792 by applying power to move the carriage on the mule, after which a child was able to operate two machines, as was already the case with the water-frame. Though this application of power was only partially successful (a true self-acting mule was not perfected till 1825 by Richard Roberts) Kelly's work enabled the mule to be increased in size, and since it too could now be worked by children it began rapidly to replace the water-frame as the main spinning equipment. The superior quality of the mule yarn was an important factor in this switch, and with increasing numbers of spindles per machine, and faster speeds in working, the output of yarn per spinner began to climb steeply. In turn, these developments enlarged the demands for cleaned and processed raw cotton. The preparatory cleaning processes had normally been done by hand, partly in the mill, and partly by children and old women in their own homes, but when this began to prove ineffective in keeping up with the demands of the spinners, it was a Glasgow man, Neil Snodgrass, who introduced an improved scutching machine in 1797 to clean and prepare the raw material.

This widening of the capacity to produce by accelerating and cheapening the cleaning, roving, and spinning processes, made possible a dramatic expansion of output, building up in the decade from 1790 to 1800. In 1793, thirty-nine cotton mills were in operation employing 124,800 water-frame spindles, 100,800 jenny spindles and 86,400 mule spindles, some 312,000 spindles in all. In the five years up to 1796 the average annual import of raw cotton was 2·1 million lbs and the value of cotton consumed in 1796 was placed at £462,904; the capital sunk in plant and machinery was estimated to be £490,200 and the value of the yarn produced placed at £1,256,412. In the decade after 1800, the scale of the industry was dramatically increased from 39 mills in 1796 to 120 in 1812, although eight of these were not working in the latter year. The expansion was facilitated by the expiry of James Watt's patent in 1800, a freeing of experimentation on the steam engine, and a loosening of the bottleneck in the production and supply of steam engines, for engineers and engine builders were as yet a scarce breed of men. Although there are no figures for the number of steam engines in the 112 working mills in 1812, the previous exhaustion of water-power sites must have meant that virtually all the new additions would be powered by steam. Moreover, many of the existing water mills installed steam engines to increase their power. By 1812, the number of spindles in Scottish mills had trebled to around 900,000, and the effects of applying power to the mule were such that 800,000 of these were mule spindles, and only 100,000 were of the water-frame variety. The fixed capital in the industry was now estimated at £1,400,000, and the volume of cotton imported was 8·7 million lbs.

In this phase of expansion the location of new mills was powerfully affected by the attraction of the import and export facilities and yarn markets and credit arrangements of Glasgow and Paisley. The steam engine gave a new mobility to the industry, allowing these factors to operate. Virtually all the new building was concentrated in the Glasgow–Paisley area. Of the 134 mills in existence in 1833, no fewer than 74 were located in Lanarkshire, but only the large mills at New Lanark and Blantyre were outside the city and its near neighbourhood. In Renfrewshire there were 41 mills; nearly all were congregated in the Johnstone, Barrhead, Neilston, Paisley and Elderslie districts. The Lanarkshire and

Renfrewshire mills together accounted for 1,353,860 of Scotland's 1,728,628 spindles and consumed 78 per cent of the Scottish supplies of raw cotton. Therefore, while the enormous expansion from 1796 to 1812 was characterised by a great growth in the number of mills, the substantial development from 1812 to the early 1830s was marked by an increase in the scale of many of the mills already in existence. The average spindles per mill in 1793 was 8,000; by 1812 this had fallen to 7,000 in view of the vast increase in the numbers of small and medium-sized mills, but by 1833, the average number of spindles per mill was just over 12,000. The largest mills were to be found in Lanarkshire and Renfrewshire, and the average capacity of forty-four Lanarkshire mills examined by James Cleland in 1831 was over 14,500 spindles, while in 1833 an average of some 13,000 spindles were installed in each of the six Neilston mills. By this time it was no longer possible for men of small capital to make a successful entry into the spinning sector of the cotton trade.

Hand loom to power loom

When the first cotton mills were being built in Scotland it is thought that there were up to 20,000 skilled weavers at work in the region, most of whom were to make the transition from linen to cotton quickly and easily, simply accepting the new fibre and continuing to rely on the established network of domestic production and town warehousing. Although the weavers clung to work in their own homes and resisted factory-like organisation, many were already concentrated in loom-shops in and around Glasgow and Paisley, Glasgow having about 4,000 looms, and Paisley some 5,000 employed in various branches of the linen and silk trades. Outside the two large towns most small towns and villages were also dominated by weavers; Airdrie was said to be a town of weavers, as was Strathaven with more than 300 looms. In every parish in the western counties looms were at this time turning to the weaving of muslin, and by 1791 the Glasgow manufacturers alone are said to have employed some 15,000 hand looms in the area from Girvan in the south to Stirling in the north.

Domestic out-work was still important in the 1790s, the whole family frequently assisting the father at the loom, but the spread of power spinning was soon to disrupt this old family unit of production. The women in the household had previously spun their own fine yarn and kept the man of the house in intermittent work at weaving, but with large quantities of fine machine-spun yarn becoming available the men found it profitable to leave farming and become full-time weavers, while the women and girls took up the new jobs of dotting, tambouring and flowering of muslin. This trade was also engrossed by the Glasgow and Paisley cotton merchants, and Ayrshire women soon achieved distinction, their embroidered muslin selling as 'Ayrshire Needlework'. The labour force was becoming sectionalised. Local women and girls frequently took up needlework; local men specialised in weaving, and the incoming Irish, Highlanders, and their children went into the spinning mills.

As improved mechanisation brought more and more of the operations in spinning within the capabilities of young women and children, even the male Irish and Highlanders began to filter into the weaving sector, normally taking up work in the coarser branches of the trade. This was the beginning of a vast expansion in the ranks of the hand-loom weavers, for there was no restriction on entry. The basic technique could quickly be acquired, and in conditions of high profitability the city merchants were willing to rent out hand looms to all comers. By 1831, John Ure estimated that there were 45,000 hand-loom operatives in the west of Scotland, most of them on the books of the Glasgow and Paisley manufacturers. On Ure's reckoning there were 7,000 hand-loom weavers in Ayrshire, 2,000 in Dunbartonshire, 7,000 in Lanarkshire excluding Glasgow, and a further 20,000 in Glasgow itself. Renfrewshire had some 6,000 looms in Paisley, and another 3,000 were scattered throughout the county.

The advantages of such a system were very great for the manufacturer and very slight for the hand-loom weaver. As the minister of Ardrossan parish, contributing to the first Statistical Account of Scotland, pointed out in 1793, weavers outside the main towns 'bore all the inconvenience of distance from the chief seats of manufacture; they are always the first who feel the disadvantages arising from the stagnation of trade and the last who benefited from its revival'. In other words, the manufacturer used the domestic system to cushion himself from the down-turns in trade. He employed large numbers of weavers to build up stocks in good times, and paid them off in slack times, making them bear the brunt of declining markets and falling prices. As long as the growing army of hand-workers so conveniently met manufacturers' requirements, it is not surprising that they were reluctant to burden themselves with the fixed capital investment required to set up weaving factories and install power looms. But as the early power looms were improved it became apparent that even the poorest-paid hand-loom weaver could not produce some grades of cloth as cheaply as the new looms, and manufacturers in Scotland began to experiment in that direction.

The major defect in the early power loom as designed by Edmund Cartwright in 1784 was the need for frequent stopping to dress the warp with paste as it unrolled from the beam, thus enabling the yarn to take the continual strain of being lifted and lowered by the heddles. This obstacle was overcome by dressing the warp before it was placed on the beam, a dressing machine to do this being patented by Messrs Radcliffe and Ross of Stockport. Subsequent refinements to the loom by Horrocks of

Preston, and Radcliffe of Mellor, had made it a commercial prospect by 1806, but even before this Scottish manufacturers had made a beginning in power weaving.

The first attempt had a comic aspect, for the power was supplied by a large Newfoundland dog walking the treadmill in a drum or cylinder. This was an experiment made in an Argyle Street basement in 1793 by James Lewis Robertson of Dunblane, who had purchased a couple of looms from the prison hulks in London. The following year a more serious attempt was made by Andrew Kinloch of Glasgow, who installed forty looms developed from Robertson's in a mill at Milton in Dunbarton; these proved uneconomic, though capable of producing calicoes for printing. Thereafter, power weaving in Scotland languished until 1801, when John Monteith installed 200 power looms in part of his spinning mill at Pollokshaws. These were built by Robert Miller of Glasgow. Pollokshaws can claim to have been the first commercially successful power-weaving establishment in Britain. Monteith then seems to have persuaded Archibald Buchanan of the Catrine mill to use his mechanical skill to improve the looms, and by 1807, probably by adapting the improvements pioneered by Horrocks, Buchanan had built a strong and compact loom, improved the dressing machine, and integrated the processes of warping, dressing and power weaving in a single factory. As these improvements accumulated power weaving began to be added to other spinning mills in the region. Foster and Corbet introduced power weaving in Glasgow, while Messrs Crum added looms to their works at Thornliebank. These early looms were all employed on plain and simple fabrics like calicoes, tweeds, checks and shirtings. In 1812 Sir John Sinclair enumerated 1,560 power looms in Scotland, each loom being valued at about £10, and all were concentrated into fifteen weaving factories, most of which were simple appendages to existing spinning mills. Nearly all of these looms were in the west of Scotland. Six years later Glasgow had eighteen steam-weaving factories employing 2,800 looms.

Power weaving spread very slowly indeed in the first quarter of the nineteenth century, there being no shortage of hand-loom weavers in the manufacturing districts. In fact there seems always to have been an over-supply of hand-workers, and the power looms were initially confined to weaving fabrics which had not previously been produced in the Glasgow area. However, introduction accelerated in the 1820s, and by 1831 some 15,000 looms were at work in over sixty power-weaving establishments. There were on average about 200 looms per factory, though some cotton manufacturers like Monteith at Blantyre, Todd at Hutchesontown and Finlay at Catrine, employed 500 looms or more. The capacity of the weaving sector widened enormously between 1800 and 1830 as both power-weaving and hand-weaving grew side by side. By 1831, with some 15,000 power looms in operation, the Glasgow manufacturers also controlled some 30,000 hand-loom weavers, and the Paisley merchants had a further 15,000 on their books.

In the brief span of fifty years from 1780 to 1830, the cotton industry grew from a position of insignificance to industrial leadership in the west of Scotland. The revolution was primarily in power spinning, and the new industrial organisation rested mainly on water power, half the total power used in cotton mills still coming from that source in 1830. Steam power complemented water power and sustained the rapid expansion of the industry after 1800, and factory organisation now gradually began to penetrate the weaving sector. This enormous growth and the equally dramatic changes in the work of spinning and weaving were not accomplished easily. In its first half-century the progress of the industry was characterised by substantial fluctuations in activity and basic changes in the types of cloth produced.

It has already been suggested that Scotland's late entry into the cotton industry was related to the introduction of fine spinning with the innovation of the mule, this providing a thread fine enough to make good use of Scottish weaving skills. Indeed, building on the basis of native skill, there seems little doubt that Scotland first entered the cotton industry by concentrating on the production of fine muslins. In the 1780s, Scottish and Lancashire manufacturers were struggling for supremacy in fine cotton cloths, and by 1790 Scotland had established herself in this field. A process of regional specialisation was taking place in which the various manufacturing districts adopted cotton fabrics nearest to the grade of goods they had been accustomed to produce in linen. Thus Bolton produced coarse and fine jaconets and the heavier grades of checked and striped muslins, while in Glasgow, book, mull and leno muslins, and jaconets of lighter descriptions were manufactured. Sewed and tamboured muslins concentrated in Paisley, as did the fancy trade, though the Anderston district of Glasgow also had a strong trade in fancy goods. Because of this tradition of skill and quality, it is not surprising to find that muslins accounted for almost 64 per cent by value of the pure cotton goods exported from Scotland in 1793. Moreover this basis of skill was extended into even more specialised fields such as the Paisley shawl from 1805. The shawl was a very specialised article in which the weaver attempted to produce on the loom the effect created by the needle in the Indian cashmere shawl. This speciality began to develop extensively in the first decade of the nineteenth century and by 1834 the production of shawls was valued at £1 million per year. The most expensive shawls were mixtures of silk and cashmere wool for the warp, and cotton for the weft, while the cheapest were entirely made from cotton.

This concentration on fine and fancy work in Scotland, together with the fact that the Paisley merchants were heavily involved in the highly-skilled tambouring and flowering of muslins in the finishing trade, has led some historians to the view that the product of the Scottish cotton industry was too highly specialised. Since articles like the Paisley shawl were at the mercy of quick changes in fashion, it has also been argued that this specialisation made the industry vulnerable and that its success rested on insecure foundations. But while no one would dispute that the industry was established on a basis of specialisation, it is hard to see how it can be maintained that the industry remained over-specialised in the period of rapid growth. The initial production of fine muslins and fancy fabrics was clearly for a limited quality market, and even rapidly falling prices could not bring these products into mass consumption.

While these products remained a feature of the Scottish industry, the vast expansion after 1800, exemplified in the increasing number of mills, weavers and imports of raw cotton, could only be sustained by producing heavier and coarser qualities of cotton cloth. Thus in 1812 Sir John Sinclair found that the average number or count of yarn spun in Scotland was only 48 and in 1816, giving evidence to the commissioners investigating the conditions of children employed in manufactories, Henry Houldsworth stated that he was the only spinner in Scotland who regularly spun counts in excess of 100, and that in the whole of Britain only five or six mills were engaged in such fine spinning. Robert Owen declared that New Lanark spun coarse yarns; Adam Bogle said Blantyre mill was currently spinning 70–74s, and Houldsworth said the average coarser yarn spun in Britain would be about the 40s or 50s. Since most mills clearly spun medium and low counts, the thousands of hand-loom weavers in Scotland must also have been engaged in producing heavier cloths. This is borne out by the export figures of 1818, when with fewer than 2,000 power looms in operation, 80 per cent of Scotland's cotton exports by value were of plain calicoes, fustians and other heavier fabrics, and the fine muslins which in 1793 had accounted for two-thirds of the cotton cloth exported now represented only 19·4 per cent.

It is difficult to sustain an argument of over-specialisation on these figures. This move into producing goods of wide appeal and lower price was also conditioned by the growing competition in formerly secure European markets, where after 1815 France and Switzerland established their cotton industries producing fine hand-loom goods of the type supplied by Scotland. It seems quite clear that in this phase of rapid expansion from 1800 to 1815 the Scottish cotton industry moved into lines of production which were distinguished from the products of their English rivals more in design and style than in the grade of yarn or quality of workmanship.

The fortunes of the Scottish cotton industry from 1780 to 1830 are clearly reflected in the annual figures of cotton imports. The upward progress of the industry only suffered marked checks in 1794, 1808, 1812–16 and 1824. The sharp down-turn in 1794, the effects of which lingered to 1797, can be related directly to the commencement of the Napoleonic wars and the disruption of the important European markets for Scottish cloth and Scottish yarn. The sharp decrease in activity during 1808 is closely linked to the introduction of the restrictions and embargoes which eventually culminated in the Continental System of 1810, and the disruption of the American market. On the other hand, the long depression from 1812 to 1816 was begun by a collapse of overseas markets, which in turn included a run on banking houses in Glasgow and a restriction on credit; recovery was prevented by the outbreak of war with America, and there was severe distress in the trade till the end of 1816. The next phase of slackness came in 1824 and again in 1826. The first down-turn was occasioned by a protracted strike of the operative spinners from September 1824 into January 1825; the slackness of 1826 again involved local factors when the employers and employees were in dispute. The mills were sometimes wholly idle, sometimes working half or two-thirds time, and this was capped by an extensive drought which put many water mills out of operation. The disruption was unfortunate for the mill owners, for there was a great boom in overseas trade, generally, in 1826, of which they could not take advantage.

It is quite clear that there was also much speculative investment in the industry throughout these years. Cotton was certainly profitable, but vulnerable, and this is reflected in the pattern of ownership. Sole control, or even a single family in control of a mill was rare, and the normal structure of ownership was the partnership. This often appeared to involve only a few persons, but it frequently was a large partnership made up of a number of investors, many of whom played no active part in the conduct of the business. Thus, when Robert Owen joined David Dale at New Lanark he headed a large number of English backers, including Jeremy Bentham. Not only was the risk spread over many partners, but the vulnerability is also shown in the rapid turnover in the ownership of many mills. The Rothesay mill is a famous case; built by James Kenyon and an English partnership in 1779, it was sold to Dale in 1785, who then sold it to Lord Bute, and it eventually passed to William Kelly and Robert Thom in 1813. The great Blantyre mills passed from Dale to Monteith in 1793, and Gillespie's Woodside mill was bought up by Houldsworth in 1799. There are many more examples of changing ownership. The Finlays were perhaps the most persistent purchasers, buying their way into the cotton trade at Deanston in 1793, Catrine in 1822 and Ballindalloch in 1825. However, in spite of its speculative nature, the industry grew prodigiously in the first third of the nineteenth century. But from 1830 it was to encounter less favourable trends.

An end to growth: 1830–70

The forty years of hectic expansion from 1790 to 1830 were followed by another forty years of less consistent progress. The industry ceased to grow rapidly and at least to 1850 was deeply affected by the problems arising from the long-drawn-out decline of the hand-loom weavers. The blame for the impoverished circumstances into which this class of operatives was plunged in the 1830s and 1840s is often laid on the shoulders of the mill owners who introduced power looms and deprived their workers of a livelihood. Any objective reading of the facts must suggest that this was a contributory factor, but not the root cause of the hand-loom weavers' distress.

In the 1780s it was estimated that there were about 20,000 hand-loom weavers in the west of Scotland. In Glasgow in 1791 these men earned from 12s. 0d. to 20s. 0d. per week, depending on the class of goods they worked, and in Paisley, the centre of the highest quality work, an industrious and highly-skilled weaver could have earned from 25s. 0d. to 30s. 0d., though the average was probably nearer £1. The weavers initially enjoyed a scarcity value which held their earnings high, but by 1810 there were some 35,000 hand-loom workers in the west of Scotland, and average wages in Glasgow varied from 6s. 0d. to 15s. 0d. per week, this again depending on the class of cloth woven. At that time there were fewer than 1,500 power looms in the entire country, and the low wages of the weavers were obviously due to a glut of labour trying to get into the trade, and to the poor market conditions operating during the Napoleonic wars. In the bad year of 1819, Cleland recorded the average wages of Glasgow weavers as between 4s. 0d. and 7s. 3d. per week, and this, too, was long before the power loom had made any significant impact. Wage levels rose to 13s. 0d. or 14s. 0d. per week in the early 1820s, but from 1825 began to decline, falling to 6s. 6d. in 1831, recovering to 8s. 9d. in 1836 and declining again to 6s. 9d. by 1840. At the latter date, hand-loom weavers of the finest plain goods could command 9s. 0d. to 10s. 0d. per week: but among the 45,000 weavers in the west of Scotland only about one-third worked in finer fabrics and could earn the higher wages. Those who worked in plainer cloths eked out an existence on the pittance they earned for long hours of hard labour.

As the average weekly wages of hand-loom workers declined the number of power looms increased; there was a dramatic increase between 1820 and 1835 from 2,800 to 17,531. One explanation could be that the six-fold increase in power looms pushed down hand-loom earnings by one-third. Hand-loom weavers' earnings had, however, been even lower than this during periods of dull trade in 1810 and 1819, long before there was any competition from the power loom. Consequently, since conditions of trade could have a serious effect, it would be unreasonable to explain the entire decline in wages as due to increased competition from the power loom. On the contrary, the evidence suggests that with the exception of brief periods of modest prosperity the earnings of the hand-loom weavers had consistently been low from the early 1800s, and were kept low mainly by a chronic over-supply of weavers in the trade. This was due to the influx of Irish and Highlanders who found the weavers' trade easy to enter and learn, and their numbers were swelled by countless women and children who joined the ranks of the weavers working up the coarser grades of cloth. It was the massive increase in numbers of hand-loom workers from 20,000 in 1790 to 35,000 or 40,000 in 1810 which helped the cotton industry to grow so rapidly, but high earnings were quickly banished for all save those of the highest skill working on the most intricate fabrics. Indeed, far from causing the plight of the hand-loom worker, the power loom was adopted much more slowly than it might have been because there was no shortage of weavers who were willing to produce even the coarser cloths more cheaply than could the early power looms. The cotton industry consistently commanded more labour than it required, wages consequently remained low, and power looms only came in slowly to produce fabrics which either were not produced by hand, or which, owing to continually falling prices, could no longer be woven quickly enough by hand to guarantee even a few shillings per week.

In the 1820s and 1830s the increasing technical efficiency of the cotton industry cut prices and profit per unit of production so rapidly that more and more types of cloth had to be woven by power, or not at all, for no hand-loom weaver could produce them cheaply enough, or would accept work in these lines. Hence the major switch to power looms took place in the 1820s without reducing the numbers of hand-loom opera-tives. They continued to increase in number in spite of consistently low earnings, until in 1840 there were between 45,000 and 50,000 in the west of Scotland. By 1840 it was the complexity of pattern rather than fineness of yarn which held back the power loom, and since fashion increasingly demanded crowded patterns, this left a largely unchallenged specialised sector of some 15,000 hand-loom weavers employed in the fancy goods trade, most working in the thriving Paisley shawl business. The growing cheapness of coarser cloths made it impossible for the remaining 35,000 or 40,000 weavers to earn high wages, but, perversely, they stayed in the trade. The real culprit in this situation was neither the power loom, nor the capitalist manufacturer; it was the pressure of labour from areas of low income and employment, men who crowded into weaving because, in spite of its limitations, it provided a way of life preferable to what they had left. The immature nature of the regional economy also contributed to the problem. There were as yet few new industrial jobs for males in the towns. The mines, shipyards and ironworks were still small and could offer few men employment. Consequently, when the immigrant male came to the towns, hand-loom weaving was the obvious choice, and this increased the hardship in this occupation. As long as there were few other jobs, even the severest crisis and the lowest rates would not diminish the numbers clinging to the trade.

Consequently, it was not simply the severity of the two depressions of the hungry 1840s which broke up the hand-loom weaving population in Scotland, for wage rates were no lower then than they had been in other slumps. Rather this coincided with increasing job opportunities in mines, shipyards and ironworks; there was at long last somewhere else for the weavers to go. There followed a rapid contraction of weavers from 45,000 in 1840 to 10,000 in 1860. Significantly when the second large increase in power weaving came in the 1850s, virtually all the hand-weavers of plain and coarse goods had disappeared. The power looms were brought in to fill the vacuum as these men found work in other trades. The 10,000 remaining weavers were the hard core of the 15,000 fine and fancy hand-workers who were in employment in the 1830s. In 1870 a similar number were still working on the shawl and fancy fabrics in Paisley and district, and in the Irvine valley on fine muslins and special curtain materials.

Cotton under stress

The demise of the hand-loom weavers and the popular unrest associated with this class in its distress has overshadowed other developments in the industry between 1830 and 1870 which were of greater long-term significance. From the 1830s, cotton was in a continuing period of difficulty and this encouraged far-reaching changes in the structure of the industry. The major problems were associated with technology, labour relations, and competition in the industry's major products and markets.

The spinning technology of the Scottish cotton industry had been designed to foster expansion in the medium and coarse ranges of cotton cloth between 1800 and 1820, but in the 1820s there was a rapid increase in competition in the markets for coarse goods. Most European countries had now established their own cotton industries, and the American cotton manufacturers were rapidly cutting into the lucrative markets of the New World. Piece goods prices fell steadily and profit margins dwindled. The only way manufacturers thought they could increase their profits in a situation of falling prices was to spin and weave more efficiently, that is, to increase their production at lower unit cost. In the early 1830s there was a wave of new investment bringing much new spinning machinery and a move into power-loom weaving, all designed to halt the slide in profits. But the vastly-increased capacity of the industry produced a decade of overproduction in which prices continued to fall and profit margins further contracted. In turn, this slackened the flow of funds available for reinvestment, which cut into the technical efficiency of the Scottish cotton industry, and narrowed the basis of the Scottish textile-machine industry. The local market proved too small to support continuous experimentation with machines, and by 1833 the dominance of Manchester machine makers was no longer challenged. One prop of the Scottish industries' earlier success had therefore been removed and the local stake in technical advancement was lost. Consequently, much of the machinery installed in the 1830s came from England and America. Many of the new throstles, a development of the water-frame, were of American design, for instance the Danforth cap-spinning throstle. Others were self-acting mules of the English Sharp & Roberts pattern, or of the Scottish Smith & Orr design. Most of these machines were for spinning the familiar coarse- and medium-grade yarns, and committed the industry to production in the area of fiercest competition. There was in fact no alternative, the quality market being too limited in extent, but the resulting overcapacity did not permit the expected profits to accrue to Scottish producers. As overcapacity and declining prices defeated the hopes that the new investment would be repaid out of increased profits, Scotland fell further behind Lancashire in technical efficiency.

As the Scottish manufacturers found the cost advantages associated with technical efficiency slipping from their grasp they sought another means of reducing their costs of production. They inevitably turned their eyes to labour costs. Wage cutting was a well-known device in times of dull trade or fierce competition. But wages were already low in Scotland, for the Irish had spilled over not only into the spinning mills, but into hand-weaving and power-weaving establishments. The oversupply of labour kept wages low in all branches of the trade and made the operatives even more sensitive to any new downward pressure on their rates of pay. Even so, wages were commonly adjusted downward. In the case of male spinners low rates were accompanied by the threat of self-acting mules which could be worked by females, and would have deprived the adult male spinner of work altogether. The major confrontation came in the slump of 1837 when the mill owners sought to impose a reduction of 56 per cent in the rates of spinners. The spinners inevitably struck with the full support and involvement of the Cotton Operatives' Union, then the strongest in Scotland. During the protracted stoppage the use of blacklegs provoked assault, arson, vitriol-throwing and a murder. The masters stood united and the authorities invoked the full vigour of the law against 'conspiracy in restraint of trade'. The union leaders were arrested, charged with murder, arson and conspiracy, and sentenced in the High Court in Edinburgh to seven years' transportation on the conspiracy charge alone. The union, with its funds exhausted and its leaders in Botany Bay, was broken; a low-wage policy became characteristic of the Scottish industry and was to sustain it through the difficult years to the 1870s. The adoption of self-acting mules was also accelerated, and the traditional reliance on young and female labour further increased.

While the pressure of costs produced strains in the Scottish cotton industry leading to the adoption of a young, female, low-wage labour force, increasing competitive pressures between 1840 and 1870 induced other changes. Kirkman Finlay complained in 1833 to the Select Committee on Manufactures, Commerce and Shipping that 'now there is not a single country in which there is not a great manufacturing of cotton carried on', and foreign competition was growing rapidly in formerly preserved British markets. In reaction, the Lancashire producers began spinning more medium counts of yarn and weaving grades of cloth similar to the Scottish articles. The Scottish producers who were facing competition abroad now also found themselves squeezed by new competition in the home market. This push of the Lancashire men into the fringes of the Scottish products took Lancashire power weaving into competition with Scottish calicoes, produced mainly by the hand-loom weavers. This brought down the price of their product and made it uneconomic for hand-workers to continue in some lines. As a consequence, between 1840 and 1860, the Scottish producers added to their power-weaving capacity to take up these lines of work, and increased their stake in novelty, colour and design, in an attempt to differentiate their articles from the English product. This was not a retreat back to the specialisation in fine and fancy fabrics which had been the foundation of the early success in the industry, and which always remained at the core of the Paisley trade. In this new brand of specialisation most manufacturers tended to produce jaconets, mulls, pullicates, ginghams, and books, the quality of which, though still appropriate to the mass market, placed them at the upper rather than lower end of it. This area of the popular market was more limited than that of the bread-and-butter ranges of the heavier fabrics, but it was one in which Scotland had considerable experience. The potential for growth in it clearly depended more on rising incomes among the mass of workers at home and abroad, than on increasing numbers, but it was not so fiercely competitive and offered at least temporary stability in the difficult middle decades of the nineteenth century.

These problems of production and marketing were aggravated by the speculative financing and credit arrangements which increased the instability of many firms in the business. The buying and selling of raw cotton and yarn had always been subject to erratic price movements. Unfortunately, the speculative tendencies also began to penetrate the finance of manufacturing firms, particularly through the use of accommodation bills. It was quite normal for much of the working capital of a firm to be provided by the discounting of bills of exchange secured on the goods in process of sale.

In times of active business there were always firms seeking capital in order to expand their production, and accommodation bills came into use to 'accommodate' these needs. These bills of exchange were drawn without relation to real transactions by people who did not have the immediate means to pay them. The whole affair was based on confidence by the lender that the borrower eventually would make good use of his credit and be able to repay the loan. But in the tight conditions of the financial crises of 1857 the Western Bank sought to reduce its outstanding loans. It had unwisely concentrated its credit with three or four major cotton borrowers. When it presented bills amounting to £1·6 million for payment the firms owing the money could not meet the demand. This produced a run on the bank as depositors sought to withdraw their cash, and the Western Bank was forced to close its doors. The succeeding bankruptcies and commercial distress came as a great blow to the prosperity of the cotton industry. It has frequently been considered that it was this catastrophe which stopped the upward course of the industry, threw it into short-term collapse and, when combined with the difficulties of the cotton famine during the American Civil War, forced the industry into long-term stagnation and eventual decline. Indeed, it has been argued that the cotton industry is the first example of a major industry going into stagnation and decline in modern Scotland, and that this was evident from the crisis of 1857. The lack of production statistics makes it difficult to determine the course of events precisely, but other information on the number of mills, spindles, looms and employees helps to clarify the situation.

Table 8 indicates the progress of the industry from 1812 to 1871, and it is clear that the number of spindles and looms employed is a better guide to the state of the industry than is the number of mills, which contracted from 168 to 152 between 1850 and 1856, while spindle capacity increased to over 2 million at the height of the speculation. Indeed, mills, looms and labour force were all contracting in these years while spindle capacity increased by over 20 per cent. The short-run impact of the crisis of 1857 seems to have been limited to a 5 per cent reduction in spindles between 1856 and 1861 while the numbers of mills, looms and workers employed all increased, presumably to catch up on some of the surplus spinning capacity installed in the early 1850s. The evidence here does not support the view that the 1857 crisis threw the industry into short-term collapse.

In contrast, the effect of the American Civil War is much more pronounced. Cloth and yarn exports declined between 1861 and 1864. Cloth exported contracted from 150·7 to 94·7 million yards. However, the combined value of cloth and yarn exports increased from £3·1 to £3·5

TABLE 8 *Cotton mills and factory workforce in Scotland, 1812–71*

Year	Mills	Spindles	Looms	Labour	Spindles/Mill
1812	120	c. 900,000	1,560	c. 20,000	7,500
1833	134	1,728,628	14,970	c. 30,000	12,900
1850	168	1,683,043	23,574	36,325	10,000
1856	152	2,041,129	21,624	36,698	13,400
1861	163	1,951,398	30,110	41,237	12,000
1868	131	1,583,674	31,864	39,809	12,000
1871	98	1,487,871	25,903	30,960	15,000

Sources: Factory Inspectors' reports, 1850–71; D. Bremner, *Industries of Scotland* 1812; Sir J. Sinclair, General Report 1833; E. Baines, *History of the Cotton Manufacture of Great Britain*

million. This pattern was continued through to 1867. This anomalous situation was achieved through a sustained speculation in yarn purchases which drove prices up while the cotton famine deepened, and many mills went on a third- or half-time working. It is here that the delayed effects of the 1857 crisis became apparent. The financial position of the industry had undoubtedly been weakened and the sustained pressure of the early 1860s could not be withstood. The whole decade of the 1860s became one prolonged contraction; between 1861 and 1871 the number of mills contracted by 40 per cent and spindles and workforce by a quarter. The same pattern is evident in estimates of the consumption of raw cotton in the industry. Between 1840 and 1860, about 40 to 45 million lbs of cotton were consumed each year. In 1866, the industry consumed 2,500 bales per week. Contemporaries allowed a fifty-one week working year and an average of 375 lbs per bale, making about 47·8 million lbs consumed. In 1867, as the post-war boom collapsed, bales consumed fell to 1,700 per week or about 32 million lbs per year. During the rest of the decade, weekly consumption averaged 1,500 to 2,000 bales, or somewhere between 28 and 38 million lbs of raw cotton per year, a reduction of about a quarter to a third from the levels of the twenty years from 1840 to 1860. Even if we allow some margin for increased efficiency and reductions in losses through waste, it is clear that the industry was operating on a new and much reduced scale from the 1860s.

However, it is also clear that it was the spinning sector of the industry which bore the brunt of the contraction; this is not surprising since there was a long history of speculative investment in this sector. Years of surplus capacity were stripped away in a single decade, and while the number of spinning mills contracted, the numbers of spindles per mill increased from 12,000 in 1861 to 15,000 in 1871. It was the smaller and the more speculative establishments which suffered most, and the capacity of the industry was being reduced to a core of more efficient and larger units. This was more a period of rationalisation than of stagnation, for the industry stabilised at its new level and the real demise did not occur till the twenty years preceding the First World War.

5

The industrial base:
the rise of the heavy industries

Foundations

Coal and iron were the sinews of Scotland's economic revolution in the
nineteenth century, but before that time they grew haltingly and were
not greatly dependent on each other. Technical problems limited the
expansion of both industries. It was coalmining which made the greater
progress in the eighteenth and early nineteenth centuries. Scotland had
a long history in the working of coal; small pits were common throughout
the Central Lowlands by 1750. The industry was dominated by the
collieries along the Firth of Forth since landowners there enjoyed easy
access to coal seams, reliable communications by road and coaster, and
well-established contacts with markets on the Continent. The mines in
the West of Scotland were too isolated to share in this traditional trade and
remained largely undeveloped till the local market began to expand in the
eighteenth century. As we have seen, the political and economic union of
1707 diminished the importance of the European orientation and carried
the west of Scotland out of its rural remoteness. Overseas trading was
pushed dramatically westward, and successful manipulation of the new
opportunities resulted in unprecedented commercial expansion. A
rapidly-growing population and the development of small industries
supplying the colonial trade stimulated domestic and industrial demand
for coal. This placed the capacity of the scattered diggings under great
strain.

The problem was that the coal industry, generally, was limited in
its response to its market opportunities through primitive technology
and an inadequate labour force composed partly of independent workers

and partly of serf labour. As mines grew deeper in the eighteenth century the technical problems of drainage, haulage and ventilation limited expansion of output as never before. Drainage was the crucial constraint, since it confined mining to shallow inclined seams from which water could be drawn off by gravity. This limitation was partly overcome by adits or tunnels driven upward into the seam from further down the hillside, but this solution was expensive and time consuming. Buckets and chains were also employed but the 'fire engine' or early steam engine of Thomas Newcomen was the first significant artificial aid applied in Scotland. This was an atmospheric pump the working stroke of which relied on air pressure to depress a piston after steam in a cylinder had been cooled to create a partial vacuum. It worked in a jerky fashion but could raise water about 150 feet. Fourteen or fifteen such engines were at work in Scottish mines by the 1760s. By this time, James Watt at Glasgow University was already working on an improved steam pump with a separate condenser which employed steam on both sides of the piston; it was to be smoother in action, more reliable and much more economic in fuel. However, fuel economy was not important at a coalmine, and Watt's more sophisticated pump was not quickly adopted. In fact, for a time the problem of drainage seems to have been circumvented by opening more shallow pits rather than by employing steam pumps. But by 1800 steam technology was sufficiently advanced to permit the raising of coal and water speedily and efficiently from as deep as 900 feet, a level not attained by any mine in Scotland at that time. Over thirty engines were at work in mines in the west by then.

As long as most mines remained small and shallow the haulage of coal continued to depend upon human and animal muscle. Small boys dragged the corves or wicker baskets of coal from the face to the bottom of the shaft. In the larger pits the horse and pony were introduced underground soon after 1700, and in some cases wooden rails were laid in main roadways and wheeled bogies or 'whirlies' replaced the corves. This, the most advanced solution to the haulage problem, was unfortunately not typical of the industry, even in the east, where deeper and larger mines were more common. There, women and girls were taken into the workforce where they not only dragged the coal from the face to the pit bottom, but in the notorious 'stair-pits' they carried it in baskets on their backs up flights of ladders to the coalhill on the surface. Women and girls also worked underground in the west of Scotland but the practice was not so common as in the east. However, such exploitation permitted output to meet the increasing demands of the emerging industrial society.

While the limitations on drainage and haulage were being overcome there remained the threat of suffocation, fire and explosion from choke-damp and firedamp. The remedy was obvious enough to contemporary coalowners; it was a question of adequate ventilation. The passage of air through the mine was commonly encouraged by suspending a fire-basket down the single shaft or by constructing a furnace at the foot of it. The furnace long remained the major device for stimulating a current of air, but with deeper mines neither the fire-basket nor the furnace were wholly satisfactory on their own. In the last quarter of the eighteenth century some collieries improved the flow of air by dividing the shaft in two with a wooden partition thus creating an up-cast and down-cast circulation for the air. This was a compromise, and cheaper than constructing two separate shafts to achieve an improved circulation; it was taken up by a few collieries. The latter also employed the complex system of trap-doors opened and closed by young boy 'trappers' to conduct the stream of air through every portion of the pit. These were the first solutions to the problem of ventilation and enabled pits to enjoy a longer life and produce more coal from a single shaft.

The major obstacles to expanding the output of the coal industry were overcome in a piecemeal way. But as the technical difficulties receded, the problem of attracting labour into the mines came to the fore. The imposition of serfdom on Scottish colliers in the middle of the seventeenth century had turned collier villages into relatively closed self-perpetuating communities. The stigma of serfdom and an ingrained repugnance to working underground effectively limited recruitment. Even in the west of Scotland where the local coalmasters could not afford the costs of a tied labour force, and independent colliers were more common, the problem of increasing the labour force was causing concern. There was a growing opinion in favour of improving the status of the collier. The first modest step was taken in the Act of 1775 by which colliers could work off their serfdom over periods of time which varied with the age of the individual. This provision proved to be defective. The whole shameful structure of serfdom was finally swept away with the Act of 1799. The solvents of serfdom were the need to recruit more labour, the possibilities of keeping wage claims in check when a plentiful labour force had been secured, and the benefit of being able to expand output to meet the new demands. Labour supply was the last of the great bottlenecks restricting expansion. The abolition of serfdom coincided with the beginnings of Highland and Irish immigration to the Central Lowlands.

The changes in mining during the eighteenth century were reflected in the rising output of coal. Production was around 500,000 tons at the time of the Union in 1707, and the number of colliers as distinct from boys, women and girls in their families who also worked in the pits, could scarcely have been in excess of 2,500. In 1800 output stood between 1·6 and 1·9 million tons, and the number of colliers must have been in the order of 7,000–8,000. At the same time coal production in the west of Scotland grew from perhaps 100,000 tons to 600,000 or 700,000

E

tons. The collier community there could have been as small as 500 at the Union and had increased to perhaps 2,000 or 2,500 men at the beginning of the nineteenth century.

Indeed, after a century of change and growth, coalmining was still on a very small scale in the west of Scotland. Most of the pits were small, serving their local areas, their market radiating outward to a distance of 8–12 miles. The cost of carriage made coal too expensive beyond this range except where no alternative supply existed, as in the upper ward of Lanarkshire where coal had to be supplied from Douglas, or where the coal had special properties, such as Lesmahagow cannel coal which gave sufficient light for illumination, and later was used in making gas. This coal could bear the cost of being carried distances of 40 or 50 miles in the 1790s and had a good market in Glasgow.

A steady general demand for coal consolidated the pattern of mining activity and by 1830 there were two main zones of exploitation in Lanarkshire. The more important swept in a great crescent along the northern rim of the central coalfield where the seams were either exposed or close to the surface; this took in the districts of the Monklands, Bothwell, Shotts, Cambusnethan and Carnwath. South of the River Clyde there was a parallel line along the southern rim of the coalfield stretching from the Paisley district through Gorbals, Govan, Cambuslang and Quarter to Larkhall. Further upstream flanking the Douglas Water was the small Carmichael-Douglas field which was locally important. A similar pattern of scattered mining emerged in Ayrshire where coal seams were exposed by the deeply-entrenched rivers Garnock, Irvine, Ayr, and Girvan Water. Mines thrived along all of these. The rivers, as well as serving their own districts, carried coal downstream and out of the small Ayrshire ports to Ireland.

The scale of total exports is difficult to estimate at this period but between 1830 and 1834 the ports of Ayr and Irvine shipped out 187,760 tons of coal compared with 192,327 tons from Glasgow and Greenock, the main outlets for the central coalfield. But while exports were important it was undoubtedly the expanding Glasgow market which most encouraged the growth of coalmining in the west. This had led to the improving of the Glasgow to Edinburgh turnpike in the 1780s to bring coal more easily from the Monklands, and the same need for reliable supplies lay behind the construction of the Monkland Canal, opened in 1793. The Monkland district was being prepared for the role of Scotland's major mining area; the road and canal together with the deepening of the Clyde opened to Monkland coal both the growing Glasgow market and export opportunities. Access to seams, adequate communications and the availability of markets, the factors which had long sustained the east-coast coal industry, now began to take effect in the west of Scotland. But though the pattern seemed set for a steady growth in the first quarter of the nineteenth century, there was little in the mining scene to suggest the rapid expansion which was to follow.

This deceptive calm was a mirror of the situation in the iron industry. Ironmaking had become a steady source of demand for coal, but the link did not seem critically important. Forges and foundries had grown in number around Glasgow till by the 1770s iron was being processed at Dalnottar, Duntocher, Partick, Rutherglen and Broomielaw. This was only an extension of the traditional use of coal by the blacksmith. The demand for coal to feed blast furnaces did not appear in Scotland till 1759 with the founding of the Carron Company near Falkirk. This was the beginning of the modern coke-smelting pig-iron industry in Scotland. Carron remained the only large ironworks in Scotland for twenty years after its inception. It evolved as an integrated concern using local coal and iron in the furnaces, consuming the make of pig-iron in its own foundries, and refining it to malleable iron in its forges, slitting and rolling mills.

The modern iron industry came to the west of Scotland in 1779 with the establishment of the Wilsontown works on the Mouse Water in north Lanarkshire. The founders were three brothers, John, Robert and William Wilson, who were attracted to this isolated spot by the water supplies and rich local coal and iron ores. Yet another decade passed before there were real signs of expansion, for the industry suffered from a shortage of technical expertise. When Clyde Ironworks was founded in 1786 and Muirkirk opened in 1789 they borrowed some experience from Carron. Clyde Ironworks was established by Thomas Eddington and William Caddell; Eddington had been a traveller for the Carron Company while Caddell was an original shareholder. Eddington was also involved at Muirkirk, this time in partnership with local ironworkers, John Gillies of the Dalnottar works and William Robertson of the Smithfield or Broomielaw forge. Both these works produced pig-iron and bar-iron, and Carron was an important market for their product. These establishments were joined by Omoa (Cleland) also in 1789, Glenbuck and Devon in 1792 and Calder, Shotts and Markinch between 1795 and 1801. There were therefore ten ironworks at the beginning of the nineteenth century and, with the exception of Carron, Markinch and Devon, they were located in the west of Scotland. This Scottish investment in ironmaking was rewarded by a substantial expansion of output from 7,000 tons of pig-iron in 1788 to 22,800 tons in 1800, 9 per cent of the British total. The number of furnaces increased from the 4 at Carron in the 1760s to 27, of which 18 were in blast with an average make of 1,200 tons each per year.

Unfortunately the initial impetus was soon lost for the industry ran into difficulties. Although all the new works employed the technique of coke smelting developed by the Darbys at Coalbrookdale in 1709, they had made no significant advances in the design and size of the furnace or in smelting technology. The basic problem was that in the small low-temperature furnaces the poor-quality coking coals and local iron ores combined to produce an inferior and costly pig-iron. The disadvantages of Scottish iron were so pronounced that even during the long Napoleonic wars with their sustained military demands for iron, only the Carron works prospered, and the others limped along supplying local needs in a market protected by distance and poor communications from English and Welsh competitors. The iron industry stagnated; between 1801 and 1825 no major new works was erected and although the annual output grew to 29,000 tons, Scotland's share in British production slipped back to 5 per cent. In 1825, only 17 of 25 furnaces were in blast, and the average output had increased to about 1,700 tons per year. As late as 1825 the link between coal and iron remained weak and the regional iron industry seemed destined to remain small and backward.

The age of iron

But two events, separated by more than two decades, transformed the situation. The first occurred in 1801 when David Mushet, then manager of Dixon's Calder ironworks, discovered that the black stone called 'wild coal' by local miners was, in fact, an iron ore. It existed in nodules set in a band of black clay between the seams of coal, hence the name of black-band ironstone. Even in a raw condition the iron content varied from 35 to 50 per cent, but when calcined it could be as much as 70 per cent. This coal-measure iron ore was a very rich one indeed. But when mixed with local coking coals it produced an inferior iron, weak and brittle. For almost the next thirty years it was used only at the Calder and Clyde works, and then in mixtures with other ores. Though the economic advantages of possessing rich iron ores and coal in the same locality were appreciated, cost and quality difficulties placed serious limitations on any general exploitation of black-band.

Then, in 1828, James Beaumont Neilson took the second and crucial step. Neilson was first foreman and then manager of Glasgow Gasworks and worked there from 1817 to 1847. His improvements at the gasworks established his reputation locally as a sound chemist and engineer. Between 1824 and 1826 he had been asked to assist with the problem of the blast supplied to furnaces. In attempting to increase the volume of air supplied to a furnace at Muirkirk, he heated the air and stumbled upon the beneficial results of applying a heated blast. He then had to overcome the local ironmasters' ingrained resistance to experimentation, for no one understood the chemistry of smelting, and any furnace was only disturbed in dire necessity once a reasonable iron was obtained from it. However, with the aid of Charles MacIntosh the chemist, Neilson was allowed by Colin Dunlop and John Wilson to blow hot air into one of their furnaces at the Clyde ironworks in 1828. The first primitive device only raised the temperature of the air to 80°F but even this improved the quality of the iron. Neilson's patents for, 'The improved application of air to produce heat in fires, forges and furnaces, where bellows or other blowing apparatus are required', were taken out in England on 11 September and in Scotland on 1 October 1828. By early 1829 his device raised temperatures to 280°F and the following year temperatures of 300°F were normal.

The introduction of this technique had a revolutionary effect upon the Scottish industry. At Clyde ironworks, where the main experiments took place, the furnaces had required a little over 8 tons of coal to produce 1 ton of cold-blast iron. By early 1830 this charge had been reduced to about 5 tons 3 cwt, and by 1833 to just under 3 tons, by which time the temperature of the blast had been doubled to 600°F. The use of the hot blast not only resulted in a dramatic saving in fuel, material and costs, but in an increased production per furnace. Similar savings were achieved at Dixon's Calder works. There the furnaces had produced 5 tons 12 cwt of cold-blast iron per day in 1828; when the blast temperature was increased to 300°F in 1831 production increased by 1 ton per furnace, and in 1833, using a blast of 612°F, the output of the furnaces jumped to 9 tons of iron per day. Thus, in these works coal consumption was about one-third that of the cold-blast technique and production per furnace was raised by about one-third.

Neilson's basic invention was modified and improved by a number of men between 1828 and 1834. James Baird devised a more efficient blowing engine and arrangement of pipes. William Dixon raised the temperature of the blast to over 600°F. John Condie overcame the problem of the blowing machine nozzles melting in the heat by devising a workable water-cooled tuyère in 1834. Perhaps the greatest success of the system was the substitution by Dixon of local splint coal for the poor Scottish coke in the furnace. By 1834 the innovations combined to free Scottish ironmasters from high-cost and low-quality production. In 1829 cold-blast pig-iron was produced for £3 18s. 0d. per ton at Calder and £4 2s. 0d. at Clyde, and could not be sold at a profit for less than £6 per ton, while the average price of English pig-iron was only £5 per ton. By 1833, Clyde and Calder were producing hot-blast iron at £2 9s. 6d. and £2 7s. 6d. per ton respectively, and the product was quoted at £4 15s. 0d. on the Liverpool Exchange, compared with £6 for best Staffordshire pig.

As far as Scots ironmasters were concerned this was the fundamental innovation on which the fortunes of the pig-iron industry were based. It gave the Scottish producers immediate cost advantages over their English and Welsh competitors. The differential was increased by Scottish access to supplies of cheap Irish and Highland labour flooding into the west of Scotland. These cost advantages were reinforced by low mineral royalties of 1s. 0d. to 2s. 0d. per calcined ton of iron, and low annual rents for mineral fields, since landowners did not at first appreciate the economic significance of the minerals on their lands. The Scots had at their disposal a new technique which permitted them to exploit abundant supplies of cheap raw materials in a time of already quickening progress when iron was becoming the basic constructional element of the age. The result was prodigious investment and expansion of pig-iron production.

Between 1801 and 1825 only the short-lived Balgonnie ironworks had been opened in Scotland; the existing Wilsontown and Glenbuck ventures had become bankrupt in 1812 and 1813 respectively, though Wilsontown was brought back into production by Dixon in 1821. Only six ironworks were operational in the region in 1825. But the very high prices of that year encouraged new investment, and Chapelhall was established in 1825, Monkland the year after, and in 1828 the Bairds began to lay down their great empire at Gartsherrie. They designed the works to take advantage of the new hot-blast technique and built the first great circular furnace in Scotland, bringing it into blast in 1832. In 1825 total output of pig-iron in Scotland stood at 25,000 tons; by 1830, when the hot-blast had scarcely made its impact, this had increased to 39,500 tons. A decade later output reached the prodigious figure of 240,000 tons. In the period between 1825 and 1841, eleven new ironworks were opened in the west of Scotland; the hectic expansion continued unabated. In 1848 there were 15 ironworks in Lanarkshire with 92 furnaces, 57 in blast and most of the remainder building. In Ayrshire there were 5 works with 6 furnaces operational and a further 17 under construction or out of blast. There were only 2 works in the east of Scotland with a total of 15 furnaces. The Scottish iron industry had increased its output to 564,000 tons, more than double the figure for 1840, and more than twenty times the output of 1825. By the 1840s all the furnaces then in blast in Scotland used the hot blast, save one at Carron. The large furnaces produced 150–200 tons per week or 7,500–10,000 tons per year. Costs of producing a ton of pig-iron were about 40 per cent below the 1829 figures.

The greater part of this mushroom growth was concentrated in the Monklands, and this was not surprising. In the 1840s the Monklands had easy access to the cheap bulk transport provided by the Canal; it was also in this district that rich and extensive resources of black-band and clay-band iron ores were first proved and exploited. Here, too, the first railways were constructed. As the demand for coal and iron grew the Monkland Canal emerged as the major axis of growth, and its termini in Glasgow and the Monklands became nodes of industrial concentration. In 1848, 6 of Lanarkshire's 15 ironworks and 39 of her 57 active furnaces were concentrated around the eastern end of the Canal in the Coatbridge area (Map 4).

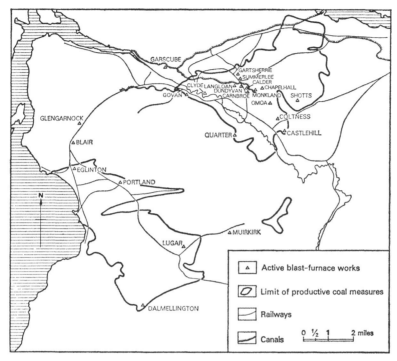

MAP 4   *West of Scotland iron industry, 1850*

This industrial concentration had been created with great speed in formerly empty areas. In 1841, Thomas Tancred, the commissioner appointed to report on the conditions in the mining districts, described the Monklands in graphic terms in evidence to the Royal Commission on the Employment of Children in Mines. He reported:

At night ascending to the hill on which the established church stands, the groups of blast furnaces on all sides might be imagined to be blazing volcanoes, at most of which smelting is continued Sunday and weekdays, by day and night without intermission. By day a perpetual steam arises from the whole length of the canal where it receives waste water from the blast engines on both sides of it, and railroads traversed by long trains of waggons drawn by locomotive engines intersect the country in all directions.

Tancred and the commissioners to the mining districts were well aware of the newness of it all, and its dependence on a tiny innovating élite.

The 1844 annual report on the mining districts described the Monklands district as 'the creation of a few men in a few years and [as] the result of the devotion of a high degree of intelligence and perseverance to one object'. In Tancred's view each of the coal and ironmasters was 'the architect of his own fortunes'. He was right in stressing the energy and determination of a small group of men. For as with the cotton industry, the men who pioneered the expansion were few in number. Most began in the smaller coalworks or ironworks, though some like the first Dixon and the first Baird were prosperous farmers before moving into minerals.

The first Dixon came from Northumberland where he had been interested both in farming and mining. Soon after coming to Scotland he became manager of the Govan colliery and later opened Calder iron-works in 1801 in association with Mushet. Subsequently, he acquired the Govan colliery and the Wilsontown ironworks, though his son closed Wilsontown in 1842 and concentrated ironmaking at Calder and Govan. In the 1820s Dixon was probably the largest coal and ironmaster in the west of Scotland. The Dunlops and Wilsons who controlled the Clyde ironworks were also involved in the great Dundyvan enterprise com-menced in 1835. The Houldsworths moved from their Anderston foundry to open an ironworks at Coltness and another at Dalmellington. However, the greatest of the iron and coal dynasties was undoubtedly that of the Bairds. They moved into ironmaking at Gartsherrie in 1828, and suc-cessively extended their empire to Eglinton in 1844, Blair in 1852 and later acquired the works at Muirkirk, Lugar and Portland, all in Ayrshire.

The industry was controlled by a small number of family and partner-ship firms and financed by the simple means of ploughing back capital. This was possible because of large turnovers and substantial profits, and the case of the Bairds is often quoted to illustrate the point. Because of their efforts to break Neilson's patent the Bairds' business figures had to be revealed, and between 31 May 1833, and 31 May 1840, a period of seven years, total profits at Gartsherrie amounted to £269,655 9s. 5d. By then the annual royalties on Neilson's patent stood at £20,000, and the Bairds, William Dixon, Alison, Merry & Cunninghame, and MacDonald of Blair ironworks combined to try to break the patent. Neilson was victorious in the ensuing struggle, and the resulting dis-agreements among the major ironmasters as they sought to apportion damages, poisoned the working relationship among the Scottish iron companies for decades. The Bairds alone settled out of court, paying £106,000 in lieu of unpaid royalties and damages to cover previous court expenses.

With the great iron districts established, the output of Scottish pig-iron moved continuously upward. The 564,000 tons of 1848 grew to 775,000 in 1852, and passed 1 million tons in 1862 with an output of 1,080,000 tons. Production then more or less stabilised, climbing only slowly to its nineteenth-century zenith of 1,206,000 tons in 1870. At this date there were 158 blast-furnaces in Scotland of which 92 were in Lanarkshire, 41 in Ayrshire, 13 in Fife, and 12 elsewhere in Scotland. Of these, 32 were inactive, 12 in Lanarkshire, 13 in Ayrshire and 7 in Fife. More than any other single factor, it was the influence of low costs of production achieved through the combined use of the hot blast, splint coal, and black-band ore which had encouraged the expansion of output and the establishment of large numbers of ironworks. The Scottish ironmasters relied mostly on a small return per ton produced, the ability to do so resting on maintaining a high volume of output.

One consequence of such rapid expansion and large-scale production was that the total product could not be absorbed by the Scottish economy. Hence, Scottish pig-iron figured prominently in export sales. As early as 1847, at the end of the first phase of most rapid growth, two-thirds of Scotland's pig-iron was exported, and by 1868–70 over half the total output was still being dispatched to markets outside Scotland (Table 9). The Scottish achievement in the export of iron was quite remarkable. During this whole period Scottish output of pig-iron averaged 25 per cent of British production, and yet Scotland was responsible for supplying between 50 and 90 per cent of British pig-iron exports. This is a startling discrepancy and highlights the fact that neither the foundry nor the forge ever consumed the bulk of Scottish output.

TABLE 9   *Shipments of Scottish pig-iron, 1847–70 (000 tons)*

Year	Output	Tons coast-wise	% Output	Tons foreign	% Output
1847	539·9	227·0	41·1	143·5	26·6
1860	937·0	321·4	34·3	255·6	27·3
1870	1,206·0	266·1*	22·1	388·8	32·2

* Includes 35,200 tons sent by rail to England
Source: R. Meade, *The Coal and Iron Industries of the United Kingdom*, London, 1882

As a result the development of the malleable-iron or forge branch of the Scottish industry was particularly slow. This has been partly attributed to the chemical constitution of Scottish pig-iron which was reputed to make it more suitable for recasting in the foundry than for working into malleable iron for use in the forge. There is little to indicate that the puddling of pig-iron to produce malleable iron was much practised in Scotland before 1836. Up to the early 1840s puddling was only regularly employed at Calderbank, Govan and Dundyvan. The Mossend Iron and

E *

Steel Company, founded by Neilson in 1845, also made bar-iron, but the total consumption of pig-iron by these malleable iron producers was only of the order of 50,000 tons per year. The upsurge in railway construction in 1846 and 1847 encouraged further developments, and the consumption of pig-iron leaped to 80,000 tons in 1846 when the existing ironmasters combined to form three regional malleable iron companies, the Ayrshire Iron Company, the West of Scotland, and the East of Scotland Malleable Iron companies. These were set up separately from the blast-furnace works and were designed to make use of some of the surplus pig-iron production in each area. But internal tensions helped to cause all three companies to fail by 1849. At that date, with nineteen pig-iron works in the west of Scotland, there were only five malleable-iron works or forges, consuming no more than 90,000 tons of pig-iron.

However, the slow start was eventually overcome, and by 1870 there were 14 malleable-iron works in Scotland with 338 puddling furnaces and 44 rolling mills. All were located in the west of Scotland, mainly around Coatbridge. They consumed 198,000 tons of pig-iron per year, while foundries, the traditional consumers of local pig-iron, disposed of 249,000 tons. The lag in malleable-iron production had virtually disappeared, but only Wilson, Dixon and Baird of the major pig-iron producers were engaged in malleable-iron production, possessing just over a quarter of the puddling furnaces in operation. The remainder was in separate hands, and the pig-iron and forge sections of the industry were poorly integrated in both ownership and location. The cleavage between these major activities was unfortunate, but up to 1870 at least, it did not seem to have a critical effect on the prosperity of the iron trade, for output had grown steadily and pig-iron dominated the economic life of the area. However, though the pig-iron makers neglected forward integration into malleable-iron production, they developed backward integration more intensively, making the major ironmasters also the major coalmasters of the region.

The link between coal and iron was very close in the west of Scotland, where every increase in the output of iron drew forth a further expansion in the production of coal during the four or five decades after 1830. In that year the Scottish iron industry consumed perhaps 170,000 tons of coal; in 1870, despite the fuel economy given by the hot blast, 3 million tons of coal, one-quarter of the region's output, was consumed in the manufacture of pig-iron. While the region had produced around $\frac{1}{2}$ million tons of coal in 1800, it raised almost 12 million tons in 1870 (Table 10), and Lanarkshire alone mined 8·1 million tons, 54 per cent of Scotland's total production. At the beginning of the century there were probably 7,000 or 8,000 miners in the country; this labour force had expanded to nearly 47,000 men working in over 400 collieries in 1870. By this time mining in the west of Scotland had overwhelmed the

TABLE 10   *Output, employment and collieries in operation, 1854–70*

	West of Scotland			Scotland		
	1854	*1865*	*1870*	*1854*	*1865*	*1870*
Coal (M tons)	*c.* 5·6	*c.* 9·9	11·9	7·4	12·8	14·9
Employment	23,245	28,113	34,732	32,969	39,223	46,984
No. of collieries	249	330	229	368	497	413
OPM*	244	353	345	224	324	317
Output per colliery	22,000	29,500	40,000	20,000	25,700	35,000

* OPM = Output per man per year in tons
Source: Returns of the Inspectors of Mines, 1854, 1865, 1870

historical superiority of the east-coast industry. Not only were almost three-quarters of the men and mines located in the region, but the productivity of both men and pits was superior to those elsewhere in Scotland.

Although much of this growth was tied closely to the development of the iron industry, the traditional sale of coal overseas continued to absorb growing tonnages. Between 1835 and 1839 over 700,000 tons of coal were exported annually. This increased to over 2 million tons per year between 1865 and 1869, about 60 per cent going to foreign markets mainly in Scandinavia, France, Italy and Russia, the remainder being shipped coast-wise to British ports. Thus the export and iron industry markets together consumed about 40 per cent of the total output of the Scottish coal industry in 1870. Another 20 per cent was consumed by industry in general, half being taken by the textile trades alone. Gasworks, railways and collieries themselves consumed a further 10 per cent, leaving about 4 million tons for general domestic consumption.

While the demands made on coal were growing rapidly, the link with iron showed few signs of weakening, and the ironmasters retained a commanding position in the control of both industries. The pattern of ownership in coal was very volatile and there was a rapid turnover of companies. Between 1854 and 1870, 91 out of 145 companies went out of operation, a turnover rate of 60 per cent: there were at the same time 122 new entrants and a net gain of 31 companies, taking the total to 176 firms in 1870. Only 4 of these companies operated 10 or more collieries, another 5 had between 5 and 9 collieries, and 24 companies owned between 2 and 4 pits. The remainder were single-colliery concerns. It was also unusual for companies to operate outside their own local district. In 1854, four companies and in 1870, nine companies, operated in more than one county. Only Merry & Cunninghame straddled the four counties in the region, and Bairds had collieries in all the counties save Renfrewshire. The mining industry was therefore characterised by single-colliery companies with a high rate of turnover, but it is significant that the few large coalowners were closely linked with ironworks. In 1854, only Finnie & Co. of the top eight coal concerns did not operate an ironworks, and this was still the case in 1870 (Table 11).

TABLE 11   *Coalowners by rank, 1854 (west of Scotland)*

Name of company	No. of collieries
1 Trustees of John Wilson	13
2 Wilsons & Co.	10
3 Merry & Cunninghame	10
4 Wm Baird & Co.	9
5 Wm Dixon	8
6 Arch. Finnie & Co.	6
7 Shotts Iron Co.	5
8 Colin Dunlop & Co.	5

Coalowners by rank, 1870 (west of Scotland)

1 Wm Baird & Co.	26*
2 Merry & Cunninghame	22
3 Wilsons & Co.	11
4 Wm and W. S. Dixon	10
5 Glasgow Iron Works	9
6 Arch. Finnie & Sons	7
7 Monkland Iron & Steel Co. (& Trustees)	7
8 Shotts Iron Co.	6
9 James Dunlop & Co.	5

* Includes 11 collieries operated under the names of the Portland and Eglinton Iron companies
Sources: 1854, R. Hunt, *Geological Survey: Mineral Statistics*; 1870, *Royal Commission on the Coal Trade, 1871*

As iron and coal flourished in Lanarkshire and Ayrshire, industry crowded into the coalfields and was serviced by an extensive network of railway lines. Coal, iron and the railways underlay the domestic industrial success of the region, and at the same time coal and iron flowed outward from the region to meet increasing demands for basic industrial materials around the world. Although the region could not process all the raw coal and iron that poured from its mines and ironworks, other developments in steam, metallurgy, and engineering combined to use some of these resources in a new and exciting way. The banks of the River Clyde began to change their appearance to accommodate slipways. Shipbuilding had come to the Clyde and was now to add its own remarkable contribution to the growth of the region.

The rise of shipbuilding

The west of Scotland and the Clyde appear to have had very little claim to the building of ships before the establishment of Scotts in Greenock in 1711. Indeed, all the early shipbuilding on the Clyde took place on the open deep-water estuary, the upper reaches being too tortuous, narrow and shallow to offer good yard sites. This was the situation for most of the eighteenth century till the American War of Independence cut off supplies of American timber and ships, and gave a boost to British construction. In the 1780s the Clyde was building over 6,000 tons of shipping per year, only 113 tons coming from Glasgow itself. This was an exceptional level of activity and in the 1790s about 1,500 tons was the average in any one year. The influence of the Napoleonic wars increased this, and by 1813–14 Clyde tonnage had grown to 4,000 tons, of which 163 tons came from Glasgow. This represented about 4·5 per cent of tonnage built in Great Britain; twenty years later launchings were at much the same level, still under 5 per cent of British tonnage. In terms of traditional building in wood, the Clyde was a very minor shipbuilding river well into the fourth decade of the nineteenth century. There is little evidence to support the proposition that the later dominance of the Clyde in shipbuilding rested on traditional skills and long-standing importance in ship construction.

The origins of the Clyde's shipbuilding greatness did not derive from traditional skills but from the cultivation of new techniques of propulsion and construction. The early foundations were laid in pioneering the development of steam, and here the Clyde district was at no disadvantage. The developing coalfields of Lanarkshire and Ayrshire had attracted their share of the early Newcomen atmospheric engines to pump water and raise coals, and from the 1780s, with Watt's development first of the separate cylinder and condenser, and then of rotary motion, steam engines became increasingly common in the cotton mills of the region. With the growth in the use of steam engines there appeared small engine shops where mechanics tinkered, repaired, coddled and refined the temperamental machines. Steam obsessed the inquiring minds of the age, and the eighteenth century is punctuated with attempts of varying degrees of success to apply the new power to transport. The early low-pressure boilers and the unreliability of the first machines gave them poor power-to-weight ratios and made the preparing of a level way, on which a carriage would move by steam, difficult to achieve. Rivers and lochs offered a level plane and less resistance to the movement of the heavy engines so that men's energies first grappled most successfully with steam-powered transport on water.

In 1788, Patrick Miller, the Edinburgh private banker, James Taylor and William Symington successfully sailed a double-hulled paddle-driven steam-boat on Dalswinton Loch in Dumfriesshire. Symington later built the *Charlotte Dundas*, a steam barge which sailed on the Forth and Clyde Canal in 1802. The first steam-boats to achieve commercial success were by Fulton in America, in 1807, and Henry Bell in Scotland, when in 1812 he launched and successfully sailed his *Comet* across the Clyde.

This is the event to which it is possible to trace the emergence of the Clyde as a famous shipbuilding and engineering river. And Bell's example was soon to be followed by others. He convincingly demonstrated that steam worked. The way in which he achieved his success encouraged competitors. Bell did not build the *Comet* himself. He designed it, but the hull was built for him by an established boatbuilder, John Wood of Port Glasgow. The boiler was made at David Napier's Camlachie foundry, and the engine itself in the Dempster Street engineering works of John Robertson. Bell in effect assembled the components to produce his *Comet*. For early steam-ship building was not the work of a single skilled man or company, but was an assembly of parts, piecing together specialist components made by sub-contractors. Once Bell demonstrated that it could be done, there was little to stop many small builders calling on the services of foundries and engineering shops who were not primarily producing marine engines, but could do so if directed to produce a particular type of engine. These were then fitted into modified wooden hulls of small tonnage.

Between 1812 and 1820 forty-two steam vessels were constructed on the Clyde, totalling 3,200 tons. John Wood, the initial builder, was quickly followed by Archibald McLauchlan of Dumbarton, James Munn of Greenock, J. W. Fife of Fairlie, John Hunter of Port Glasgow, Denny of Dumbarton, and a few others. All were actively building in the few years immediately after the launch of the *Comet*. As more builders copied Wood, so more foundries followed Napier and Robertson in making boilers and engines not only for mills and mines but also for the new steam-shipbuilders. Prominent in the first decade of steam-shipbuilding were John Thomson of Tradeston, George Dobie of Tradeston, James Cook of Tradeston, D. MacArthur of Camlachie, and the Greenhead Foundry Company, Tradeston. Without exception the foundries and engineering shops were clustered in the cotton districts of the city, where most of their previous business had been concentrated.

The Clyde therefore made a good start in steam navigation. But it was to be caught up quickly by other shipbuilding districts, for the simple assembly of engines and boilers, produced by existing engineers and placed in hulls built very like those of traditional sailing vessels, was as easily done on other rivers. While the Clyde produced some 60 per cent of all steam tonnage between 1812 and 1820 this lead was annihilated in the following decade (Table 12). This is not surprising, for increased output did not depend on increased efficiency, but on a simple multiplication of the number of small-scale units engaged in producing the vessels. The construction capacity of the Clyde was already fully stretched in the 1820s and the upsurge in steam tonnage came from large numbers of small producers entering into the field on other shipbuilding rivers.

TABLE 12   *Steam tonnage built in Britain and on the Clyde,*
1812–70 (all tonnage in 000 tons)

Period	Britain	River Clyde	% Clyde
1812–20	5·3	3·2	60
1821–30	30·5	4·2	14
1831–40	71·8	17·6	24
1841–50	122·6	81·4	66
1860–70	1,084·3	798·4	66

Sources: J. Strang, *Social and Economic Statistics of Glasgow,* 1851–61; *Glasgow Herald,* Shipbuilding and Engineering Supplement; G. R. Porter, *Progress of the Nation,* London, 1851, p. 316

By the 1830s, however, the simple assembly methods were being left behind. Rapid advances in techniques and efficiency in skilled engineering pushed the lion's share back into the hands of the Clyde marine engineers, who thenceforward played a leading part in developing the marine steam engine.

Many of the most important of the early advances came from the works of the Napier family. David Napier was the first of the ship assemblers to combine both the engineering and the shipbuilding in one firm. He had been established as an ironfounder and engineer at his Camlachie foundry before making his first marine engine in 1816. Subsequently he had several ships built for him to take his engines, the *Active,* and *Despatch* in 1817, the *Rob Roy* in 1818, the *Robert Bruce,* the *Talbot,* and the *Fingal* in 1819. In 1821 he moved his business to Lancefield, and set up a shipbuilding yard in addition to his engineering shop. By being the first steam-shipbuilder to have both construction and engine-making in his own hands, Napier was pushed into solving difficulties in both directions. By 1820 he had already designed a wedge-shaped bow to replace the bluff bow of traditional British design, and it was with this form that his *Rob Roy*, built by Denny in 1818, ventured out of the estuary and became the first sea-going steamer, plying the Glasgow to Belfast route.

It was the sea routes which presented the greatest challenge, for the early steamers required vast quantities of coal. The engines squandered steam and the boilers were weak, capable only of very low pressures, sometimes only 1½ to 2 lbs per square inch. The capturing of longer routes depended on economising on fuel. Napier attempted to solve the problem of low-pressure boilers by patenting an improved version of Watt's surface condenser in 1820–1. Watt had invented and patented both the jet and surface condenser, but the latter was expensive, complex and rarely used. The jet condenser was simple, mixing cooling water and steam in the cylinder to produce a vacuum, water returning to the boiler to be reconverted to steam. This was fine for land engines where fresh-water supplies were available for topping up, but at sea the cooling was done with salt water, and the water in the boiler became a concentration of brine. This corroded the boilers and had to be blown off to avoid explosion, and was accordingly very wasteful. The surface condenser, by keeping the steam and water separate, solved the problem of brine concentration and permitted higher pressures to be obtained without fear of explosion. But the early versions were expensive and this innovation only came fully into use after 1865. Nevertheless, Napier pioneered the process and kept searching for ways to economise on fuel. In 1830, his cousin James Napier contributed the haystack tubular boiler, which passed the hot gases up vertically through a series of tubes and out through a funnel thus cutting coal consumption by between 25 and 30 per cent. This type of boiler long remained most popular for river steamers.

Having improved the efficiency of the boiler to meet immediate needs Napier turned his attention to the marine engine. All the early engines were of a side-levered type in which the engine shaft was connected to the paddles by means of spur wheels or cogs. In 1835 Napier introduced his steeple engine which improved upon the old side-lever type, dispensing with the spurred cogs. In 1841 he further improved efficiency and economy by patenting an improved version of the feathering paddle to cut down resistance on entry and exit from the water. In the twenty years from 1816 to 1836, before he moved to London, David Napier had pioneered the integration of marine engineering and shipbuilding, the search for fuel economy and high boiler pressures, and improved engines and more efficient paddles; in addition he had paved the way to better ship design and open-sea steam navigation. He also dabbled in the novel constructional material of iron, building the *Aglaia* in 1827, the first iron steamer in the west of Scotland.

When David Napier removed himself and his business to London his

Lancefield yard was taken over by his cousin Robert Napier, who had previously occupied the Camlachie foundry after David Napier vacated it in 1821. Robert had subsequently opened the Vulcan foundry in Washington Street, close to the Lancefield works, and Robert's brother James was also in business in the same area. As we have seen, much of the early innovation sprang from this inventive family. The Napier yards and engine shops were also remarkable as being the training ground for many famous shipbuilders of later years. David Napier's Lancefield works were managed by David Tod and John MacGregor from 1821. They set up first as engineers in Carrick Street in 1834, then as shipbuilders in 1836 opposite Lancefield, before moving to Meadowside in 1845. Robert Napier's Camlachie works were managed by James Thomson from 1828, and he was joined by his brother George in 1838 at Lancefield. In 1847 they set up as independent builders at Mavisbank before moving in 1870 to Clydebank, on the site later to become John Brown's. Robert Napier also employed one of the Dennys in his drawing office, and when Napier acquired Parkhead forge in the 1840s, one of the managers persuaded to come from London was William Beardmore. The Elders also began in Napier's yards as did Charles Randolph. Randolph and Elder were co-founders of Fairfields shipyard at Govan. Later in the century William Pearce and A. C. Kirk also worked for Napier, before attaining their positions as partners and managers of Fairfields and Napiers respectively. Much of the enterprise in the early years clearly came from a small group of men. Robert Napier added shipowning to his shipbuilding interests, being a leading light in founding the forerunner of the Cunard Line in 1839; in addition to raising much of the £270,000 capital he designed and engined the first four Cunard steamers. The energy and initiative of these men in technology and in commerce stimulated the infant industry of steam-shipbuilding on the Clyde, and by 1831–40 (Table 12, see p. 127), nearly a quarter of Britain's steam tonnage flowed from Clyde slipways. This was but the beginning of the upsurge, for by 1850 two-thirds of British steam tonnage launched came from the Clyde. This was still the position in a rapidly expanding industry in 1870.

However, the initiative of the Napiers and their trained offshoots does not in itself explain the upsurge. Other significant changes contributed to the movement and gave it momentum. Up to 1870 the conquest of steam navigation revolved around three events. First, Bell's successful demonstration of steam as a motive power in 1812 inaugurated steam propulsion and raised the curtain on the next twenty-five years of invention and innovation on the Clyde, with the Napiers in a leading role and imitated on other British shipbuilding rivers. The second dramatic improvement was the development of the screw propeller in place of the paddle. Screws were well known as alternatives to paddles and had been tried experimentally by Stevens in New York as early as

1802, but in Britain, Smith, Woodcroft and Ericson all grappled with the problem to which both Smith and Ericson provided similar solutions independently of each other in 1836.

The screw had the advantage over the paddle in efficiency, but it had to revolve at very high speeds, which were difficult to sustain with early engines. Gearing had therefore to be adopted till improved boilers and engines could provide sufficient power to enable the screw to attain the required revolutions independently of gears. Speed partly depended on steam pressure and high-pressure engines were already common for locomotives. In marine engines, pressures of 5–10 lbs per square inch were attainable in the 1830s and this was raised to 40 lbs per square inch in the 1840s. At this point the use of the screw became feasible: Captain Kincaid of Greenock experimented with a screw-steamer on the Forth and Clyde Canal in 1840 and the device was rapidly adopted by Clydeside shipbuilders.

The third great innovation in the marine engine, giving much better economy and power, and making the use of the screw essential, was the introduction of the compound marine steam engine. In this device the steam was expanded successively in two cylinders, thus making double use of the energy. Compound engines had been used on land since Arthur Woolf had demonstrated the principle successfully in 1804. Moreover, forms of marine compound engines appear to have been on trial in America as early as 1834 and on the Rhine in 1847. However, it was Charles Randolph and John Elder who produced the first successful marine version in January 1853, at the same time re-introducing steam jacketing for the cylinders to cut down heat loss. Coal consumption was dramatically cut from 4–$4\frac{1}{2}$ lbs per indicated horse-power per hour to $2\frac{1}{2}$–3 lbs. This striking economy, together with the increase in power, made possible the conquest of the long ocean routes formerly the preserve of the sailing ship and ushered in the real era of steam on the world's oceans.

Invention and innovation in marine engineering dominated the progress of the industry on the Clyde in the first seventy years of the nineteenth century. The developments were all variations on Watt's simple steam engine. The Clyde area had a long tradition in tinkering with and re-pairing this device, and the expertise thus acquired was concentrated into the marine version of the engine. The energy and inventiveness of the marine engineers forced other changes of great significance on the Clyde. The early steam-ships, built of wood, were expensive in comparison with a sailing vessel. In 1825 a steam packet of 150 tons cost about £60 per ton, compared with about £10–£15 for a sailing ship. One way to make the steam-ship a more economic proposition was to make the engine more compact and efficient, in order to reduce the space given over to carrying coal and so increase the payload. Clyde engineers were already at work on this. Another possibility was to make the steam-ship large enough so that with its superior speed it could carry larger cargoes with a greater frequency of voyages. Size, however, presented problems for wooden ships. Once the keel exceeded 300 feet there was a loss of rigidity, and this placed a limit on the size of the earlier steamers. One solution was to build in a more rigid material, and the obvious choice was iron. The increasing speed of steamships also pushed builders in this direction, for the screw, operating at high revolutions, seriously weakened wooden vessels.

The move from wood to iron has another long history of experimentation. As early as 1827 David Napier built an iron vessel, the *Aglaia*, to sail on Loch Eck. In 1835 Tod and MacGregor inaugurated iron steamers on the Clyde with the *Vale of Leven*, and by 1839–40 iron steamers from the Clyde were making open sea passages. Similar trials were conducted on the Mersey and elsewhere, but even so, iron was not rapidly adopted. Many believed that an iron hull would corrode quickly in salt water and fracture easily on impact. The Navy was put off because it could not quickly patch a hole in an iron vessel, and it feared the effect of iron splinters in gun battles. The massive iron hulls deflected compasses and Lloyds, the marine underwriters, kept rates on iron vessels very high.

But the virtues of iron became increasingly appreciated as from the mid-1830s the growing number of iron sail and iron steam-ships proved their superiority. Shipowners gradually began to accept the advantages of iron; not only were iron hulls immensely stronger than those of wood, but the problem of rigidity over 300 feet was answered, as was that of the stresses caused by the pounding and vibration of engines and screws. Moreover, an iron vessel proved to be lighter than a wooden one of similar size, and owing to thinner walls the iron vessel had a much larger carrying capacity. Added to this was a vastly longer life. Though wooden hulls could, with frequent repair, last over 100 years, oak hulls could deteriorate sharply after only twenty years, and softwood vessels in less than half that. In contrast, iron could last for decades. These advantages in strength, size, speed and durability quickly increased the popularity of iron hulls. With rising production the differential in the initial cost of building iron and wooden hulls was reduced. In 1852, David Strang estimated that of vessels built on the Clyde, iron hulls cost on average £12 per ton, but wooden ones were dearer at £14.

This was no doubt partly a reflection of the Clyde's specialisation in iron, for few wooden vessels were constructed there after 1845, the year in which *Fire Queen* of 135 tons and 80 horse-power, the first iron screw-steamer to be built on the river, was launched. The advances in steam propulsion made on the Clyde committed local builders to the new material of iron. The adoption of iron in turn encouraged a rapid increase in the size and power of ships built, thus helping to increase the Clyde's share of British construction. Of ships recorded in Lloyds' Register in 1850-1 only 6,270 tons were steamers, although much larger tonnages were built but not recorded. The Clyde shipbuilders built 5,300 tons or 84 per cent of this total. At the same time the Register showed 8,020 tons of iron-hulled ships, even though separate rules for iron ships were not introduced till 1855. Of these the Clyde shipbuilders built 6,070 tons or 76 per cent. Moreover, 4,870 tons or 89 per cent were engined on the Clyde. So although the Clyde only built about 20,000 tons out of nearly 150,000 tons in Britain in 1850-1, about 14 per cent of the total, Clyde yards had established a striking lead in three critical areas, construction in iron, power by steam, and propulsion by screw propeller. In fact, between 1846 and 1852, the Clyde shipbuilders built 247 ships totalling 147,000 tons; only fourteen were of wood, accounting for 18,000 tons. Moreover, while 141 of the vessels were driven by paddles, 100 were already powered by screws. In the 1840s virtually all iron tonnage in Britain emanated from the Clyde, and even between 1851-60, when the compound engine had appeared, when surface condensers and high-pressure boilers were gaining popularity, and when Lloyds had prepared separate rules for iron ships, the Clyde produced 87 per cent of all iron tonnage in Britain and 68 per cent in the following decade. For twenty years from 1851 to 1870 the Clyde shipbuilders poured out the prodigious figure of over 70 per cent of all the iron tonnage launched in Britain.

It is tempting to link the rise of the coal and iron industries in the west of Scotland from the 1840s to the rise of iron steamship construction in a causal connection. There is no doubt that the great iron foundries and the forges and coalmines supplied the raw materials of construction, fuel and power; but the Tyne, Wear, Tees and Mersey also had access to local coal and iron industries but did not rival the early development of Clyde iron shipbuilding. The coal and iron industries must be seen as secondary features in the rise of shipbuilding, where invention and innovation in marine engineering forced the pace. It was here, as we have seen, that the Clyde shipbuilders pioneered new developments which were brought to fruition by combining them with iron as a new constructional material. There seems little doubt that Clyde shipbuilders were able to exploit these advances partly because they were local developments, and quickly became familiar among the compact group of builders on the riverside, and partly because taking risks in building in a new way gave the Clyde builders competitive advantages they could not otherwise obtain. They had no particular reputation in wood and sail construction, but the very lack of traditional skills meant they did not have to overcome the opposition of entrenched craftsmen hostile to the introduction of new methods.

The great breakthrough for the Clyde came in the 1850s when iron and steam eclipsed wood and sail. In 1850 steam represented only 6·8 per cent of British tonnage, but accounted for 30 per cent by 1860, and 70 per cent in 1870. The result was a massive increase in Clyde launchings from 200,800 tons in 1860 to 342,000 in 1870, an increase from 33 per cent to 55 per cent of the British total. By 1870, 24,000 out of 47,500 men employed in British shipbuilding were at work in Scotland. All but a few hundred of the 24,000 were on the Clyde, pouring out half the total British tonnage, a position that was to be maintained up to the First World War. In half a century the Clyde had emerged from obscurity to become Britain's main shipbuilding river, pioneering the most modern developments in the industry. This was before what are commonly regarded as the Clyde's greatest years, but already the work of the early iron and steam builders had stamped the reputation of the Clyde across the world's trade routes. Coal and iron joined with the skills of engineering to build a complex structure of steam and iron technology on the Clyde in the heart of a new heavy industrial region.

But though the economy of the west of Scotland was moulded around heavy engineering in these years, the heavy chemical industry also made a significant contribution. This activity had grown out of the bleaching and dyeing industries, and linked the old textile base to the newer heavy-industry economy. The search for improved bleaching methods had stimulated the growth of sulphuric acid manufacture and chlorine bleaching. This latter innovation had been successfully promoted by Charles Tennant with his innovation of dry bleaching powder. Further, the need to find cheaper alternatives to vegetable alkalis, manufactured from barilla and kelp, promoted experimentation in the production of soda from common salt. The critical process was evolved by Leblanc, and his method was pioneered in Scotland by Tennant at the St Rollox works.

This was a significant step, for it linked all Tennant's chemical activities into one sequence. Sulphuric acid production was necessary in the Leblanc process, and the hydrochloric acid, produced as a by-product in the soda process, became the new raw material from which the chlorine for bleaching powder was obtained. This neat interlinkage became the foundation of Tennant's success, and the business was promoted with great vigour. In addition, the Leblanc process used sulphur, which led the Tennants first to develop sulphur mines in Sicily, and later, in 1866, to join in a consortium to develop the Tharsis pyrites mines in Spain. Sulphur could be recovered from the pyrites, and residues of copper and iron were also left in commercial quantities. This sequence of events carried the St Rollox works to a peak of prominence. In the 1830s and 1840s it was already considered the largest heavy-chemical plant in Europe. By 1870 the Glasgow area was, with Tyneside and South Lancashire, one of the three main heavy-chemical districts in Britain, its products supplying bleachers and dyers, metal refiners, and agriculture both at home and overseas.

Industrial and commercial success touched virtually every branch of industry in the region in the mid-nineteenth century. Coal, iron, engineering, ships, chemicals and, to an extent, textiles, all prospered. The west of Scotland's economy was on the upswing, its success based on its local resources of raw materials, skills and enterprise. The achievement was particularly marked in metallurgy and engineering, and within this group, marine engineering was emerging to a position of prominence. These foundations were to support substantial growth in the period after 1870, and, among all the industries, it was shipbuilding which was to carry the region forward to new heights before the First World War.

6

Population, housing, health and income

Outlines

In the 500 years between 1250 and 1750 Scotland's population perhaps doubled to a total of 1·2 million. Three generations later in 1841 it had doubled again to 2·6 million and grew by more than a quarter in the next generation to reach 3·3 million in 1871. The expansion was most dramatic in the west of Scotland, where the population grew three times faster than the national average. When Dr Alexander Webster conducted his enumeration of the population between 1752 and 1755 he estimated that 181,000 persons lived in the western region. With the exception of the bleak Southern Uplands and Borders, it was then the least populous of Scotland's major regions. Only one person in seven lived in the Clyde–Ayrshire district, while over half the total population lived in the Highland counties north of a line joining the great estuaries of the Clyde and Tay. But thereafter the vigorous growth of population in the west of Scotland began to redress the balance. In each decade from 1801 to 1871 the population in the west outpaced the growth in other Scottish regions, and in the forty years of most explosive growth from 1801 to 1841, the increase was over 20 per cent per decade. The demographic expansion of the west of Scotland was inexorable, yet it was not till the decade 1861–71 that its population finally equalled and then surpassed that of the Highland counties. In 1871 nearly 1·25 million people were crowded into the region and only 86,000 fewer lived north of the Highland Line. The Highlands and west of Scotland each then contained just over one third of the total population, and both these regions supported about as many people as had been counted by Webster in the whole country in the 1750s.

Between 1750 and 1870, while the Scottish population increased more than two-and-a-half times from 1·2 to 3·3 million, the region's population grew almost seven times from 181,000 to 1·2 million. At the same time the population of all the other regions increased (Table 13). It is an oversimplification to say that the population of the west of Scotland grew by emptying the population of the Highlands and Islands into the factories and mines of the Lowlands. Some inter-regional movement was certainly part of these momentous changes, and its contribution cannot be ignored, but it is only one factor to be included in any explanation of how this dramatic increase in population was achieved.

TABLE 13   *Regional distribution of population, 1755–1871 (population in 000)*

Region	1755 (000)	(%)	1801 (000)	(%)	1841 (000)	(%)	1871 (000)	(%)
N.W. Highlands and Islands	262·6	20·7	314·6	19·6	411·8	15·7	388·3	11·6
N.E. and central Highlands	407·9	32·2	452·1	28·1	636·0	24·3	767·6	22·8
East-central	264·5	20·9	325·8	20·3	529·6	20·2	689·8	20·5
West-central	181·2	14·2	331·1	20·6	790·7	30·2	1241·9	33·9
South-east	71·6	5·7	78·0	4·8	98·9	3·8	116·8	3·5
South-west	77·5	6·1	106·7	6·6	153·1	5·8	155·5	4·6
Scotland	1265·4	100·0	1608·4	100·0	2620·2	100·0	3360·0	100·0

Sources: D. Webster, *Enumeration of the Inhabitants of Scotland in 1755; Censuses of Great Britain and Scotland,* 1801–71

Births and deaths

Changes in the size, distribution and character of any population are first linked to the changing relationship between the number of births and deaths; the other factor which is of fundamental importance is migration. When birth-rate exceeds death-rate, as it normally does, the difference, or excess of births over deaths per thousand of the population, gives the natural increase for that population. The total change over any period of time may be influenced upward or downward by the net flow of migration.

The traditional explanation of the upsurge of population in Britain in the eighteenth century has been that the main factor was a rapidly declining death-rate, combined with a high but fairly steady birth-rate. Recent re-interpretations based on research on parish registers in England have thrown some doubt upon this explanation for that country. The traditional assumptions are more difficult to confirm or disprove in

Scotland. The major difficulty is that data on births and deaths were not systematically collected in Scotland before 1855, and earlier records like the mortality bills for Glasgow and the parish registers are imperfect. When asked to give information on births, marriages and deaths for Sir John Sinclair's Statistical Account in the 1790s the parish ministers could only reply with confused and conflicting estimates of doubtful reliability. However, according to this unsatisfactory information, the death-rate for the portion of the region's people covered by the church records, excluding Glasgow, seems to have been roughly between 20 and 25 per thousand of the population, though there are many instances of rates both above and below these levels. Sixty years later, in the first years of official registration, the death rate for Scotland was 20·8 per thousand, and 23·7 per thousand for the west of Scotland, levels very close to the guesses derived from Sinclair's compilations in the earlier period. There is no significant evidence here to suggest that there was, overall, a rapid or sustained decrease in death-rate, though some localities may well have experienced improvements.

On the other hand, if the evidence on death-rate is indecisive, there is ample circumstantial evidence which suggests that any swift and persistent decrease was unlikely to have occurred. The main weight of the argument that population growth was a response to declining death-rates has always rested on the supposed impact of medical improvements, together with improvements in the environment. But in the middle of the eighteenth century the standard of medical practice was low, and most rural parishes still relied on traditional remedies, amateur doctors, and the services of 'bleeders'. Moreover, there were few hospitals and dispensaries (Glasgow Royal Infirmary was opened as late as 1794). Though medical practice had improved substantially by the end of the century the improvements were available only to a small part of the population. Even in the case of smallpox, where inoculation was recognised as a great safeguard, and where Jenner's discovery of vaccination was attracting medical interest by 1800, there was still a great resistance to the acceptance of such measures in the countryside. Writing for the Statistical Account in 1793, the minister of Kilwinning parish declared that 'every argument in support of inoculation makes no impression upon their minds', and added that because of prejudice and ignorance, the parents, far from inoculating their children, 'crowd into these houses in which the disease is of the most malignant nature'.

The evidence suggests that improved medical practice, the building of hospitals, and the control of disease did not precede the upsurge of population, but came long after the process was well under way; consequently there are few grounds for the belief that such measures appreciably affected survival or that the death-rate declined rapidly at this time. This pessimism must also be extended to the area of infant mortality in the eighteenth century. Unfortunately, much of the data on child deaths are distorted because they come primarily from the mortality bills of Glasgow, where one would expect unusually high death-rates.

Everything points to the truth of the saying that towns ate people. The mortality bills indicate that there was an appalling wastage of children, and even as late as the 1850s over half of all deaths in Glasgow each year were of children under five years of age. If we seek to explain part of the population increase by a marked decline in child mortality, we must make unsupported assumptions that the evidence of such a fall is hidden in the anonymity of the presumably healthier countryside. Environmental improvements, following on the draining of land and the building of better houses, together with regular harvests and better food, might have had such an effect. The other factors normally marshalled in support of the idea of a declining death-rate, such as better and cheaper clothes, better habits of cleanliness, improved sanitation, piped water and so on, all again only begin to make an impact well after the sustained rise in numbers was achieved, and could not materially have affected the death-rate in the early years of population growth. On these grounds it seems unlikely that a falling death-rate was the dynamic factor in Scotland's population expansion.

The other assumption is that birth-rate increased in the eighteenth century, but there is no certain evidence here either. Sporadic references to dubious baptismal figures over the years spanning Webster's and Sinclair's estimates of the population in the 1750s and 1790s do on occasion suggest substantial increases in some parishes such as Kilmarnock, where the birth-rate would seem to have increased from about 26 to 35 per thousand, and again in Beith from roughly 28 to 36 per thousand. But there is as much evidence of movement the other way, or of no change at all.

What can be said with more confidence is that some parishes and localities certainly had higher rates of birth and greater rates of natural increase than others. The fragmentary data in the Statistical Accounts of the 1790s point to the fact that the areas in which industry was growing, and where jobs were available, had substantially higher birth-rates than the more remote upland parishes which were purely agricultural, and often losing young people by emigration. In both Ayrshire and Lanarkshire there appears to have been a rough division among the parishes into those with a birth-rate in excess of 25 per thousand and those with less. In Ayrshire the parishes with low birth-rates include the more remote, like Coylton, Ballantrae, Straiton and Stewarton; in Lanarkshire the same pattern emerges for parishes such as Covington, Culter and Liberton. In both counties, the parishes in this category had birth-rates generally between 19 and 23 per thousand and death-rates between 17 and 19 per thousand.

In the more rapidly-growing parishes like Kilmarnock, Mauchline and Stevenson in Ayrshire, birth-rates were in the order of 32 to 35 per thousand, and frequently higher, while death-rates were not much different from those in the remoter parishes. The general level of death-rate was 17 to 20 per thousand, though a few parishes seemed to record very low rates of 12 or 14 per thousand. This could well be due to deficient recording, which was usual, or perhaps because inward migration had produced an unusually young age structure in the parish, and consequently deaths were temporarily less frequent. In Lanarkshire, birth-rates do not seem to have been so high in the 1780s and 1790s, and the scanty data suggest a figure of 28 to 31 per thousand for the more rapidly-expanding parishes. In Renfrewshire and Dunbartonshire, where there were concentrations of the textile industries at this time, almost every parish showed a birth-rate in excess of 30 per thousand, and death-rate, as in the other counties, in the order of 17 to 20 per thousand. In most cases the areas of increasing employment were breeding their own population by sustaining a higher birth-rate and a corresponding doubling of the rate of natural increase over that of the more rural and agricultural parishes.

Such evidence as there is therefore tends to point in the direction of higher birth-rates as the main dynamic factor in the great upsurge of population in Scotland in the second half of the eighteenth century. But why were birth-rates increasing, and the population growing after 1750, when as far as we know the population was almost stagnant between the Union of 1707 and Webster's enumeration? Contemporaries thought they knew exactly why. Writing in his *Northern Tour* in 1770, Arthur Young expounded 'It is employment that creates population. . . . Provide new employment and new hands will inevitably follow.' And about the same time, Adam Smith was writing in the *Wealth of Nations* that 'the high wages of labour encourages population'. It is an attractively simple idea that expanding industry stimulated the growth of population. But there is more to the explanation than that, for although availability of employment tends to attract migrants, enables early marriages to take place, and encourages population growth, the increase in population itself has reciprocal effects on the course of economic growth. People shifted towards the new centres of employment, and by providing a ready labour supply, allowed the transformation of the country from a rural-agrarian to an urban-industrial economy. It was only by allowing this restructuring to happen that more jobs were created and the continuous upsurge of population was sustained. The root causes of population growth therefore seem to lie in expanding employment opportunities, though the interlinkage between the demographic and economic factors is not clear, and is much more complex than contemporaries imagined. At present we can go no further than this in trying to explain the population explosion and its links to the economic growth of the country.

The argument in explaining the rise in population from 1750 to 1850 therefore rests on the assumption that birth-rates were at least differentially higher in areas of employment opportunity, even if they did not increase for all areas of Scotland. We cannot be precise in describing the trends of birth-rate and death-rate in this unrecorded century, but when registration was begun in the 1850s the new evidence lends weight to earlier assumptions. Birth-rates were considerably higher in the western counties than for Scotland as a whole, and though death-rates were also above the average, the regions of growing employment opportunities sustained a higher rate of natural increase (Table 14). The evidence at present would seem to point to the view that the genesis of the rapid growth of population in Scotland is to be found in high and possibly rising birth-rates in the eighteenth century, this being sustained into the nineteenth century, particularly in areas of increasing employment. However, the changing balance between births and deaths does not give a complete explanation of Scotland's changing population. Migration must also be considered, since the large-scale movement of people over long periods sapped the growth-rate of population in some areas, and increased it dramatically in others.

TABLE 14   *Birth-, death- and natural increase-rates, 1855–70 (rates per 000 of the population)*

Period	Scotland			W.C. Scotland (incl. Glasgow)		
	BR	DR	NI	BR	DR	NI
1855–60	34·1	20·8	13·3	38·2	23·7	14·5
1861–70	35·0	22·1	12·9	38·7	26·1	12·6

Source: Annual Reports of the Registrar General for Scotland

Migration

While it is true that the reasons for the increased rate of growth in the Scottish population lie in the balance between birth-rates and death-rates, the great expansion of the population in the west of Scotland is intimately bound up with immigration from other regions within Scotland, and also from Ireland. The absence of data before 1855 makes any assessment in the first half of the nineteenth century an uncertain business, but it is nevertheless possible to make a guess at the dimensions of the major movements, based on crude estimates of the rates of natural increase in comparison with the total population actually recorded at each census. The role of migration emerges quite strikingly.

Taking Scotland as a whole, it is clear that there was a net loss of population in each decade in the first half of the century, but that before 1841 the loss appears to have been very small. It seems that between 1801 and 1841 the natural increase of the population was in the order of 1·1 million, and that there was a total loss by emigration of only 117,000, or about 10 per cent of the total natural increase. Scotland appears to have achieved such high rates of population growth between 1801 and 1841 because the loss of population was probably under 3 per cent of the total in each of these decades.

But if the whole of Scotland lost very little of its population by migration before 1841, the losses and gains were much more marked among the regions. At the losing end of the scale the north-west Highlands and Islands were the most severely affected. Between 40 and 50 per cent of the total natural increase appears to have been lost by emigration in these years. In contrast, the remainder of the Highland area seems to have lost up to a quarter of its natural increase in this way, while the south-east and south-west counties lost about one-half and one-third respectively of their natural increase. At the same time the Central Lowland counties in the east of Scotland seem to have retained most of their increase, the outflow probably being less than 5 per cent.

At the other end of the scale the net gainer in these large movements was the west of Scotland, including Glasgow, where about 40 per cent of the total population increase between 1801 and 1841 seems to have been contributed by immigration. However, even though the whole region gained in this way, there were striking differences as between one county and another. Between 1801 and 1861 up to half the increase in population in Glasgow and Lanarkshire seems to have been due to additions by immigration. In contrast, Ayrshire may have lost between 10 and 15 per cent of its natural increase, most of the loss occurring after 1820. The ebb and flow of migration is even more complex for the counties of Dunbartonshire and Renfrewshire. Dunbartonshire grew neither faster nor slower in total population than its natural increase would have warranted, but migration was nevertheless important. There appears to have been a very high turnover of people, the incomers just exceeding the departures. Thus, while only 19 per cent of Ayrshire's population were incomers in 1841, the proportion was 50 per cent for Dunbartonshire: this compared with 29 per cent for Renfrewshire and 40 per cent for Lanarkshire including Glasgow. The great mobility of the people was certainly linked to expanding employment opportunities, and this may have been heightened in Dunbartonshire, since it was a transit zone between the Highlands and Islands on the one side, and the expanding industries of Clydeside on the other. The situation is even more complex in Renfrewshire, where up to 30 per cent of the population increase seems to have been due to additions by immigration before 1841, but between 1841 and 1861 these gains appear to have been wiped out by emigration. This would have been encouraged by the great distress among hand-loom weavers in the 1840s and 1850s, and must have been strongly influenced by the severe depression in the early 1840s when one-third of Paisley's population is reported to have been dependent on charity. This pattern of gains and losses by migration within the region was continued after 1841, for it seems that all the counties save Lanarkshire lost some of their natural increase by migration between 1841 and 1871, even though their populations were still expanding. Again, the real gainer was Lanarkshire, which added another third to its population by immigration in these years. This massive inflow of people, which was sustained throughout the period, added between a third and a half to the total population, and contributed to the very high rates of growth.

Such dramatic population movements require some explanation. Undoubtedly they owe most to the influence exerted by expanding and contracting employment opportunities within the region. In the case of the Irish and Highlanders, this attraction was complemented by an element of compulsion pushing them out of their home areas. This was particularly true in the years of most rapid population growth, up to and including the 1840s. However, after the mid-century it is apparent that the scale of population movements, into and out of the region, was also related to the wider flow of emigration from Scotland itself. When emigration from Scotland as a whole was at a high level, the inflow of people to the region, and noticeably to Glasgow, tended to be depressed. Thus, in the decade of the 1850s, following upon the gold discoveries in California, there seems to have been no net addition by migration to the region's population, the outflows from Renfrewshire, Ayrshire and Dunbartonshire just being balanced by the modest gains achieved by Lanarkshire and Glasgow. Conversely, when the flow of migration from Scotland was stemmed between 1871 and 1881, Glasgow, and all the counties except Ayrshire, made substantial gains by immigration. In a sense, the west of Scotland gained population at the expense of overseas countries, when for any reason the flow of emigration from Scotland was temporarily curbed.

The immigrants

The movement of people into the region involved both local and longer-distance migration. The environment of expanding industry and towns was steadily eroding the traditional immobility of rural life. People everywhere moved more readily from their place of birth. It is not surprising, therefore, to find that there was a substantial movement of people within the counties of the region. This type of migrant was an incomer to his county of destination, though since he had been born in the region, he would not be counted as an immigrant to the region itself. Thus, while in 1851 over 40 per cent of the population of all the counties, save Ayrshire, had not been born in these counties, about a quarter of the newcomers in each county were simply short-distance local migrants, who had been born in other counties within the region. Twenty years later, in 1871, the situation had altered very little. Local migration from adjacent counties once more contributed about a quarter of the incomers, though Dunbartonshire had a higher proportion of 43 per cent.

This interchange of population among the counties of the region was of continuing importance, but it was the longer-distance migrant who was the more powerful influence on the growth of the population in the region after 1800. We have estimated that before 1841 perhaps up to 40 per cent of the total increase in the region's population was due to immigration. In 1851 with a population of 924,000, the census showed 279,000 as migrants. In other words, 30 per cent of all the people in the region had been born outside it in 1851. By 1871 the situation was strikingly similar, the tide of immigrants still contributing almost 30 per cent of the total population (Table 15). Between 1851 and 1871 almost half of all the immigrants into the region were from other Lowland Scottish counties in the south and east, but the most homogeneous section of Scottish migrants was the Highlanders. In 1851 there were 54,000 Highlanders in the region, two-thirds being located in Lanarkshire and Glasgow. By 1871 the number was almost 79,000, and over 70 per cent were crowded into the Glasgow district. Considering the long history of Highland emigration, the total attracted to the west of Scotland is surprisingly small. It is clear that when the Highlander was shaken loose from his peasant holding, he was more inclined to go to Canada or America than gravitate to the factories, mines and labouring jobs in the western region.

TABLE 15   *Origin of immigrants to West Scotland, 1851 and 1871*

| Year | Population W. Scotland (000) | Total no. immigrants | Immigrants % total pop. | % Immigrants From | | | | |
				S. and E. Cent. Scotland	High-lands	Ire-land	Eng-land	Others
1851	962·2	279·1	30·1	27·9	19·5	45·7	5·3	1·5
1871	1,241·9	358·8	28·9	24·6	21·9	43·2	8·0	2·1

Source: Censuses, 1851 and 1871

However, even the substantial Highland influx is overshadowed by the inflow of Irish in the nineteenth century. Irish immigration to Scotland was of long standing, and like the flow of Highlanders to the region, had begun as a seasonal movement in search of harvest work. The first move was to the south-western counties, and by 1790 about two-thirds of Wigtownshire's population is thought to have been of Irish extraction. Large-scale Irish emigration only gathered momentum from the 179s, with political troubles at home. This coincided with active recruitment of labour by the factory masters for the expanding Scottish cotton industry. In the nineteenth century a further stimulus followed upon the improvement of communications and consequent fare reductions for the short crossing over the Irish Sea.

Since the Irish were part of a long-established inflow of population it is difficult to estimate the proportion of the Scottish population which is of Irish extraction. The census only records persons by their place of birth, and the second generation born of Irish parents was automatically classed as Scots. The 1841 census revealed 126,300 Irish-born in Scotland, but their historian, J. E. Handley, considers that twice this number would be nearer the figure for the population of Irish extraction. Even the census figures of 'Irish-born' represented 5 per cent of the total population, and 93,000, or nearly 74 per cent of these, lived in the west of Scotland. This was already over 13 per cent of the region's population. If Handley's suggestion is accepted this would mean that at least a quarter of the people in the region were of Irish extraction in 1841. The Irish contribution was even more concentrated than these figures suggest, for Glasgow was the great magnet for the Irish immigrant. With a population of 274,000 in 1841, Glasgow contained 44,000 Irish-born, 16 per cent of the total, and again, if Handley is right, this would mean that one person in three in the city was probably of Irish descent. By 1871 there had been seven or eight decades of sustained Irish immigration, and the Irish-born in Scotland stood at 207,700, of which 154,900, some 76 per cent, were located in the west of Scotland. This was about 13 per cent of the population. Somewhere between one-quarter and one-third of the inhabitants of the region must have been of Irish extraction. Lanarkshire and Glasgow were still the main areas of concentration, with half of all the Irish in the region.

Until 1840 the Irish coming into the west of Scotland have been described as 'self-improvers', emigrating to better their condition. But thereafter the flow was dominated by the hungry and destitute, who brought the standards of peasant Ireland to urban Scotland. They occupied the poorest housing and formed the backbone of the workforce in the least skilled occupations. The women dominated employment in the cotton mills. The men monopolised the work of the general labourer, and increasingly entered the mines. Handley estimates that at least half the Irish influx were Protestants, and it is only that factor which stopped a predominantly Presbyterian west of Scotland being turned into a Catholic enclave. The very size of the Irish community largely prevented the incomers from feeling the stresses and strains associated with minority groups. This undoubtedly eased the adaptation of the region to the acceptance of new population, and their way of life.

Urban growth

Scotland was well on the way to becoming an urban society in 1800. Although there were only two towns with populations of more than 60,000 persons, compared with five in England, Scotland did have seven towns with populations in excess of 10,000. A third of the entire population lived in settlements of 1,000 or more persons, and could reasonably be described as urban dwellers. Nearly half of these lived in the seven larger towns. Over 60 per cent of the urban population was concentrated in Edinburgh and Glasgow, with populations of 82,560 and 77,385 respectively. In the region urbanisation had gone even further. Over half the population was already urban. Two-thirds of these people lived in Glasgow, Paisley and Greenock. By 1841 70 per cent of the region's population was urban, almost three-quarters living in the six large towns of Glasgow, Paisley, Greenock, Kilmarnock, Ayr and Airdrie. Thirty years later, 60 per cent of Scotland's population and four-fifths of that of the region was urban. There were then twenty-six towns in Scotland with populations in excess of 10,000: ten of these were in the region, housing three-quarters of the urban population and 60 per cent of all the people in the west of Scotland (Table 16).

TABLE 16   *Urbanisation: Scotland and West Scotland, 1801 and 1871*

	1801		*1871*	
	Scotland	*W. Scotland*	*Scotland*	*W. Scotland*
Urban population (000)	538·9	111·9	2020	1023
% Urban	33·5	50·7	60·1	82·4
% Urban population in towns over 10,000	46·9	66·7	68·0	74·3
% Total population in towns over 10 000	15·7	33·8	41·4	61·2

Source: Censuses, 1801 and 1871

Urbanisation of the region's people proceeded with astonishing swiftness, crowding most persons into relatively few large towns. The framework for this growth was already evident in 1800. Glasgow lay at

F

the apex of a great urban triangle. One arm stretched south-east up the Clyde valley to Lanark; a second drove south-west through Paisley and the Lochwinnoch Gap to the Ayrshire coast as far south as Ayr, paralleled by a secondary route through the Lugton Gap to Kilmarnock. These two arms were linked by a long base line, running from Larkhall on the Clyde through the Irvine valley to Kilmarnock and Irvine, this route also paralleled by a more southerly line from Lanark through Douglas to Muirkirk, Cumnock and Ayr. The urban population clustered along these axes in two distinct phases before 1870.

The first phase of urbanisation lasted roughly from 1780 to 1840, begun by the influence of trade, but dominated by the expansion of cotton textiles. Though Glasgow, Greenock and Port Glasgow thrived first on the colonial trade, it was textiles which spread the influence of urbanisation throughout the region.

The search for water power established small quasi-urban communities in remote locations like New Lanark and Catrine, and also encouraged urban concentrations, as around Barrhead, Neilston, Johnstone and Paisley. Paisley almost trebled its population from 17,026 to 48,426 between 1801 and 1841, to dominate the second largest concentration of urban population in the region next to Glasgow, which grew nearly four-fold to 274,324 in the same period. Indeed, most of the thriving textile towns grew rapidly in these years: Kilmarnock expanded by 50 per cent to over 12,000 inhabitants, and Airdrie grew from insignificance to 12,418 in the same time.

The impulse from textiles weakened in the 1830s to be replaced in the second stage of growth by the development of the coal and iron industries. While urbanisation had proceeded most rapidly in Glasgow and the Renfrewshire textile towns before 1840, it now shifted to the mineral fields of north Lanarkshire. Glasgow still dominated urban growth, increasing to 477,156 in 1871, but Coatbridge grew ten-fold from 1,599 inhabitants in 1841 to 15,802 in 1871, while Wishaw increased its population five times to 10,600, and Airdrie added 25 per cent to take its total to 15,671. The new growth was also evident in the host of smaller mining communities like Calder with 1,787 persons, Mossend with 1,500 inhabitants and Cambusnethan with 1,795: all had grown from very tiny settlements in the 1830s. The influence of metals and engineering also spread the growth to the Clydeside shipbuilding towns. Dumbarton almost trebled its population, reaching 11,423 in 1871, while Govan grew from under 2,500 to 19,200 in the same period. Greenock also expanded quickly from 36,135 to 57,821, but conversely Paisley stagnated as the textile industries faltered. Its population was 48,299 in 1841, and almost the same at 48,257 in 1871.

Demographic expansion had wrought great changes in the west of Scotland between 1755 and 1871. The region increased its share of the total population from 14 to 37 per cent: this was partly due to slightly higher rates of natural increase, the region averaging 13–16 per thousand of the population as against 12–13 per thousand for Scotland as a whole between 1855 and 1871. But inward migration was more important. In 1871 nearly 40 per cent of the region's population were immigrants, and the Irish alone accounted for over 31 per cent of these. High rates of natural increase and large surges of immigrants drove the population upward and concentrated it in the few large towns and numerous mining villages in a very short period of time. It was the speed of this transformation which, more than any other factor, bred the twin problems of housing and health. These were to prove intractable, and dominated the social life of the region for the century to come.

Housing and health

Population growth and economic development were intimately linked in the nineteenth century, but so too was a related and less fortunate pairing, poor housing and poor health. Scotland had long been notorious for its primitive housing, rural squalor and overcrowding in turf-roofed hovels, typical features of the countryside. But as industry and population grew in the region, the problems of housing and health became particularly severe in the expanding industrial towns and mining villages. The situation rested on three factors: the scale and rapidity of the population increase; the inadequacy of housing; the scanty provision of public services such as water and sanitation, refuse removal and medical care. Not surprisingly, the distress was most severe in Glasgow and its suburbs.

Glasgow's problems were generated in the overwhelming tide of humanity which flooded into the city between 1770 and 1870. The population more than doubled between 1780 and 1811 from 42,800 to 100,700, then grew almost three-fold to 274,300 in 1841, and almost doubled again to reach 477,700 in 1871. The provision of physical shelter for such numbers presented almost insuperable difficulties. The solution adopted was the tenement of four storeys, to replace the old two-storey cottage-style housing of the earlier period. This was the first of Glasgow's attempts to solve its housing problems by building high-rise housing with high-density occupation. Building upward was already under way by 1760, for when Richard Pococke wrote his journal of his *Tours in Scotland* in 1760 he reported that the houses in Glasgow were 'four storeys high and some five' and mostly built of hewn stone. However, the first real phase of tenement building fell between 1780 and 1830. These early tenements gave access from the street by a close leading to a rear stair, each floor being served by a common internal passageway from which four, six or eight one- and two-roomed houses led off. These houses filled up the interstices of the old town on its axes of High Street and Trongate and were quite incapable of absorbing the growing population. The problem was intensified since all building was carried out by private property speculators and small master builders. At the time the tide of immigrants pressed hardest on the city's housing resources, the more prosperous middle classes required more salubrious housing and so attracted resources in the building industry away from the working-class areas.

Between 1780 and 1830 three middle-class 'new-town' areas were laid out in spacious grid-iron patterns. Dugald Bannatyne, Robert Smith and John Thomson headed a partnership called the Glasgow Building Company and spent over £120,000 between 1786 and 1796 in building a new town area centred on what is now George Square, in the lands of Meadowflats and Ramshorn. Though initially a middle-class housing area its convenience to the old town quickly caused it to become the new commercial core of the city. Further west the Campbells of Blythswood gradually feued out their estate, the principal developer being William Harley. By 1837, the elegant terraces and squares of 'Blythswood' had been built and the Campbells' rent revenue had increased from £223 to £12,500 per year. The third of the new developments lay south of the river, immediately west of the village of Gorbals on land feued by the Trades House and Hutchesons Hospital. The developer was David Laurie, who purchased 47 acres in 1801–2, and proposed to develop 'Laurieston' in 374 separate plots, ranging from the elegance of Carlton Place on the river to less favourable positions nearer Eglinton Toll. This project was hampered by lack of cash, and building did not accelerate till after 1815. The streets were broad and airy, the terraces prestigious, but the environment of the southern new town was distorted by the neighbouring brick and tile works, and Dixon's iron and coal works. Indeed, the whole integrity of the scheme was ruptured as early as 1809 when William Dixon unscrupulously drove a colliery waggon way through the heart of the project to carry his coal to the quay at Windmillcroft. By 1825, in spite of its impressive appearance, the commercial classes were deserting Laurieston and working-class families were taking it over.

These three middle-class schemes added only between 70 and 160 houses to Glasgow's resources each year in the second decade of the nineteenth century. They employed about 44 builders, who engaged some 1,700 masons and their labourers. Moreover, these schemes controlled up to three-quarters of all the new building land added to Glasgow between 1780 and 1830. In these circumstances, and in view of the fact that the population of the city was growing by more than 20 per cent per decade for much of this time, it was inevitable that the working classes should be disadvantaged. Since land and capital was tied up in middle-class housing schemes, the burden of providing working-class housing produced a number of unsatisfactory responses. The close-in

villages of Calton, Bridgeton, Anderston and others took much of the
strain, but in Glasgow itself, in the old city, the open spaces at the rear
of the street tenements were built over in a jumbled and uncontrolled way.
The 'backlands' tenements were inferior to earlier versions. They totally
lacked light, ventilation and sanitation. But even the old city, in its
wynds and closes, could be saturated. The safety-valve proved to be
David Laurie's failed project for middle-class housing south of the river.
Since industry had already penetrated this scheme, the middle classes
avoided it, and the speculators moved in to 'make down' the large rooms
to small single and double apartments. Intense subdivision of formerly
substantial houses answered a desperate need for shelter in the 1820s and
1830s. It is arguable that this down-grading of Laurie's estate prevented a
calamitous shortage of working-class housing at a critical period in the
growth of the city.

Such subdivision of larger terraced houses continued unabated after
1840. In addition, the pressure of population at last stimulated active
building of tenements for the working classes. Private contractors built on
a great scale in the 1850s and 1860s, adding over 28,000 houses to the
stock of accommodation between 1851 and 1871. Many of these contained
apartments of two and three rooms rented at £8–£12 per year. But such
was the demand for living space that they in their turn were sublet to
lodgers. Notwithstanding the rapid growth of housing, the working
population crowded into the older parts of the town where rents were
cheapest. By the 1860s densities of over 1,000 persons per acre were
common between the old College on High Street and the river. No
definition of overcrowding had yet been set out, but Glasgow was
certainly a grotesquely overcrowded city. In 1871 over 41 per cent of all
families in Glasgow lived in one-roomed houses, that is, in a single end.
A further 37 per cent lived in two-roomed houses. Consequently, 78·5
per cent of all families in the city lived in single-ends and room-and-
kitchens.

Glasgow was little worse off than the west of Scotland as a whole,
where 77·2 per cent of all families lived in houses of one and two rooms.
This overcrowding was generally present throughout Scotland, whether
in the towns or in the villages; the national proportion was 69·2 per cent.
So many families living in one and two rooms also meant a high density
per room. In Glasgow there were 2·1 persons for every room, while the
average for Scotland was 1·7. This problem of overcrowding was intensified by the common practice of taking in lodgers. In 1871, 23 per cent of
all families in Glasgow took in lodgers: 20 per cent of such families already
lived in single rooms, and a further 48 per cent in two rooms. Even this
elasticity of house space, and the willingness, or necessity, of taking in a
paying guest, could not absorb all the ranks of the poor and single. There
therefore grew up a system of lodging houses, offering barrack-room

accommodation at very low nightly rates of between 2*d*. and 4*d*. In 1846 it was estimated that there were up to 10,000 persons using common lodging houses in Glasgow. At that time there were 489 registered houses, though it is thought 600–700 were actually in operation.

The consequence of such overcrowding was appalling and general squalor. The dunghill with its stink and germs was the constant companion of every close, wynd and tenement. Yet it was valuable, its rotting garbage and human waste jealously guarded as a source of revenue from sale to farmers. Conditions were worst in the heart of the old city. J. C. Symonds, as Assistant Commissioner to the Royal Commission on Hand Loom Weavers, described the district in 1839: 'The wynds consist of long lanes, so narrow that a cart could with difficulty pass along them; out of these open the "closes" which are courts fifteen or twenty feet square . . . the centre of the court is the dunghill.' Captain Miller, the Superintendent of Police, thought 'the houses . . . are unfit even for sties', a view shared by Professor Cowan who, in 1840, described the wynds as 'filthy beyond measure . . . the houses . . . ruinous, ill constructed'. The lodging houses were even worse. Symonds reported them ' . . . as regards dirt, damp, and decay, such as no person of common humanity to animals would stable his horse in'.

Glasgow was not alone in discovering it had a problem of housing, overcrowding and squalor. The report on the sanitary condition of British towns in 1842 found that in Lanark most of the working classes were crushed into one apartment for the entire family, that little attention was paid to cleanliness or comfort, and that the floors were normally bare earth. In the oldest part of Ayr, the houses were generally dirty and constantly wet. The commissioners sometimes found 'a heap of horse dung under the bed, which is collected by the children from the streets, and sold when a sufficient quantity had been accumulated'. At the same time, Greenock laboured under the local nickname of 'Old-Dirty', being 'notoriously the dirtiest town in the west of Scotland', and in the east or old part of the town, overcrowding was rife, 'not the meanest outhouse [remaining] without its tenants'.

These were the costs of rapid urbanisation and industrialisation. Abysmal housing meant general ill health. The years from 1818 to 1870 became known as the fever years as typhus and cholera repeatedly ravaged the urban population. The situation was again extreme in Glasgow. Major typhus epidemics attacked the city on eight occasions between 1818 and 1871, and the disease was generally endemic in other years. Asiatic cholera swept through Glasgow in three major waves in 1832, 1848–9 and 1853–4, taking over 3,000 lives on each occasion, and recurred briefly in 1866. These epidemics raised a generally high death-rate of between 30 and 40 per thousand up to appalling peaks: in 1832, a bad cholera year, the death-rate reached 46 per thousand, and in 1846, during a massive outbreak of typhus, 56 per thousand was reached. The damage to health and life was so great that between 1821 and 1841 the expectation of life at ten years of age had been reduced by five years, and the 1821 life expectation was not reached again until the 1880s.

Since regular recording of births and deaths did not begin till 1855, one cannot give a comprehensive view of mortality in Glasgow in these years, though certain glimpses are possible. Between 1836 and 1840 over 13 per cent of all deaths were due to fever, and a similar proportion to a combination of measles, smallpox and scarlet fever. In the 1850s and 1860s roughly a quarter of all deaths were due to contagious diseases, and over 30 per cent due to lung disease, among which consumption was the major cause. Fever and tuberculosis were the great killers, especially among adults, but it was the young children who suffered most. There is some evidence to suggest that mortality among them was declining before 1820, but between 1840 and 1870 roughly half of all the deaths in Glasgow were of children under five years of age. The proportion was as low as 35 per cent in 1848, when adult deaths were dramatically increased by cholera, but child deaths under five years were again 51 per cent of the total in 1871. The main child-killers were smallpox, measles, whooping cough, scarlatina and croup.

Confronted with stinking, overcrowded houses and high death-rates, the medical profession worked unstintingly, but to little effect. Preventive medicine was unknown. This was especially serious in the case of the epidemic diseases, which in the 1820s were still frequently regarded as visitations of God. When the wrath of the Almighty began to spill over from the houses of the poor to the secluded estates of the rich in the 1830s and 1840s, such complacency was replaced by an anxious search for causes and cures. The obvious source appeared to be the rotting dunghills and filthy, damp houses and lodgings in working-class districts. The lodging houses in particular were regarded as 'the great foci of poverty, vice and crime as well as of disease'. Professor Cowan maintained they were 'the media through which the newly arrived immigrants found their way to the Fever Hospital'. But this view that poor environment was the main cause of disease gained ground only slowly, in the face of varying beliefs that disease and destitution arose from reckless addiction to 'ardent spirits', or from the 'want of good religious training'. But even when the link had been established to the satisfaction of most medical men there was no certainty on how to proceed, since the basic cause of fever was not understood. A few linked it directly to destitution, leading on to poor diets and lowered resistance to dirt and disease. Most held that the poison arose from miasmas or vapours given off by the multitude of dunghills.

The remedies proposed involved action in three directions. First the removal of the dunghills or nuisances to clear up the streets; second to open up the congested districts by pulling down the worst houses and driving new and broader streets through; and third, to exercise some control over the number of persons who could be accommodated in the smaller houses. Related to these was a fourth measure, the provision of an improved water supply, though this was not generally advocated as a major way of improving health. These measures all required powers to be obtained from parliament. Progress was at first hindered by the administrative division and jealousies between Glasgow on the one hand and the three local burghs of Calton, Gorbals and Anderston on the other, though these were incorporated in the city following the boundary extension in 1846.

The removal of dunghills was first tackled under the Police Act of 1843, with the appointment of an Inspector of Cleansing. In turn this led to a Committee on Nuisances in 1857, the establishment of a Sanitation Department and the appointment of the first Medical Officer of Health in 1862. The attack on overcrowding also stemmed from the Glasgow Police Act of 1843 which gave the Dean of Guild powers to order the demolition of old and unsafe buildings. This type of control was extended by the Common Lodging Houses Act of 1851 which entitled local authorities to inspect and regulate these establishments. In 1862 and 1866 further powers were obtained prohibiting the occupation of houses of less than 700 cubic feet of air space, and strictly limiting the occupancy of others between 700 and 2,000 cubic feet to not less than 300 cubic feet of air per adult. This was the start of 'ticketed houses', by which inspectors set plates at the entrances specifying the maximum number of occupants permitted to sleep therein. The most ambitious step toward opening up the wynds and closes came in 1866 with the City of Glasgow Improvements Act, which set up as trustees the Lord Provost, magistrates and Council, with powers to purchase a designated area of 88 acres in the centre of Glasgow to clear old houses, make thirty-nine new streets and alter twelve existing ones. By 1870 this trust was just beginning to demolish slums, but had already purchased land and laid out Alexandra Park, and spent £565,016 on acquiring slum property for clearance. The trust did not envisage building houses at this time.

In spite of this activity, none of these measures had made a significant impact on the housing problem or the death-rate by 1870. It was the piping of water from Loch Katrine, to supplement the wells and the private water companies, which had the most immediate effect. The water was led into the city in March 1860, with one dramatic result. When cholera revisited Glasgow in 1866 only 66 deaths were recorded, where over 3,000 had succumbed in previous visitations. This was more accident than deliberate plan, for doctors still associated all fever with miasmas from rotting vegetation and the dunghills. They could not distinguish between cholera and enteric fever, both transmitted by bacteria in polluted water and tainted food, and typhus fever, transmitted by the bite of the body louse, or endemic typhus, linked to the bite of the rat flea. By the provision of clean drinking water, cholera was beaten and enteric fever began to be contained. But typhus was associated with domestic and personal cleanliness. Its defeat awaited improvement in housing and scavenging and the decline of the practice of buying and wearing second-hand clothes. These were still major problems, for the whole characteristic of the period to 1870 was slum creation rather than slum clearance. Failing an effective policy, the *ad hoc* hospital provision proved helpless in the face of typhus, enteric fever and diarrhoea. Until the opening of the municipally-controlled Parliamentary Road Hospital in 1865 the Royal Infirmary bore the brunt of hospital services, though complemented by temporary fever isolation huts built in times of epidemic together with the growing care of the pauper population in Poor Law hospitals. Even so, enough had been done to reveal that the recurrence of fever had diverted attention away from more intractable killers. Measles, whooping cough, scarlet fever and smallpox decimated the city's children, and consumption debilitated and destroyed the adults with remorseless persistence.

The same problems of poor housing and poor health followed on the hasty erection of the smaller industrial and mining communities. Outside Glasgow the Monklands district was sore afflicted. In the 1840s, Baird of Gartsherrie held the accepted view that 'there is not a worse place out of hell' than the Airdrie district, and Thomas Tancred, the commissioner to the mining districts, thought that in the Monklands 'everything . . . tells of slavish labour united to brutal intemperance'. The churchmen were convinced that the problem arose from the 'stationary condition of our religious establishments amongst a rapidly increasing population'. However, most close observers shared Tancred's opinion that the problem arose from the sudden throwing together of thousands of people before the fabric of an urban society could be established to receive them. The miners had been 'thrown upon one spot as outcasts, a herd rather than a society'.

A major contribution to the dislocation and distress was the quality of collier housing. Typically, the mine-owners provided the houses in long rows or parallelograms, containing from 20 to 100 or more dwellings. The typical house in the miners' 'row' was single-storeyed with a single room on each side of a central doorway. In the early rows, the floors were of beaten earth, and the houses lacked water, light and sanitation. The accommodation was incapable of absorbing the continuing influx of men and boys in search of work, and the taking in of lodgers was as common as in the towns. In one case Tancred found a family which had taken in fourteen single men, the family and lodgers sleeping in rotation, depending on the shift to be worked below ground. Some mine-owners did attempt primitive measures of street cleansing. Wilson of Dundyvan provided

F*

dustbins and enforced their use, and Baird periodically had his village roads and open drains cleared. At this time, the best collier housing in Scotland was said to be provided by the Duke of Portland. His houses were rooms 18 feet square, the back area divided to give two bedrooms, each 6 feet by 9 feet, the front being a kitchen, 12 feet by 18 feet, containing one bed, one fireplace, a cupboard and a door.

Under the continual prodding of the commissioners and the mines inspectors the coalowners began to impose more order and cleanliness in their villages in the 1850s, but this was largely vitiated by the policy of tying the tenancy of the cottage to the period of employment. This meant that most miners could be evicted at anything from one day to one month's notice. Extreme insecurity could not promote improvement in housing. When the *Glasgow Herald* conducted a survey of miners' housing in the 1870s, its reporters found things little changed from the lurid conditions in the 1840s. In their 'Notes on miners' houses', published irregularly throughout 1875, the *Herald*'s reporters found that it was still common to have open drains and middens close by the front door; many houses had low ceilings, were very damp and had peeling walls and cracked earthen floors. Sanitation scarcely existed, water closets being practically unknown. Even piped water for the village tap was provided without due care and attention. Fever was still common in the villages. This is scarcely surprising, since in one notorious place, Carfin, 'the cooking water comes from one of Dixon's pits and is imperfectly filtered; in summer it harbours "worms and wee creepers".' The miners and their families lived in conditions every bit as cramped and unhealthy as the workers in the towns. But unlike Glasgow dwellers, they did not even have the small benefit of emerging public-health measures at this time.

The labouring population clearly bore the weight of the growing industrial society, and paid for it heavily in high mortality, poor health and squalid housing. No doubt many thought the improved earnings and more regular work an adequate compensation, for poor health and dreadful housing was nothing new. What was new was the enormous size of the problem, which now demanded action by the community at large, and on which society was as yet ill-prepared to act.

The rewards of labour

The conditions of life in the towns were one aspect of the social cost of industrialisation. Society could hardly claim to have rewarded the mass of its citizens well in this respect, and contemporary observers were also divided in their opinion of the economic compensations. Friedrich Engels, writing in the *Condition of the Working Class in England* in 1844, held that the ordinary workman had been . . .

cast into the whirlpool, [where] he must struggle through as best he can. If he is so happy as to find work . . . wages await him which scarcely suffice to keep body and soul together. . . . He knows that though he may have the means of living today, it is very uncertain whether he shall tomorrow.

In contrast, Dr John Strang, town clerk of Glasgow, in preparing his annual reports on the *Vital Social and Economic Statistics of Glasgow* in the 1850s, thought that the working man had prospered. He argued that, 'If the labour, given in money . . . be measured in bread, meal, tea, beef or sugar, the advantage in favour of the workman in 1851 over . . . 1819 is prodigious . . . [and] the industrious man never knew a period in which . . . he might more easily save money.'

These judgments were drawn from the observation of similar conditions in Manchester, Glasgow, and other large towns at roughly the same period, but the interpretations are poles apart. To an extent this is because Engels described conditions as they appeared at a moment in time without reference to what had gone before, while Strang drew a picture of comparative advance over a short period of time. Neither view is entirely objective, nor should one be regarded as a more accurate portrayal than the other. For they represent different facets of the answer to the very difficult question: What did the labouring population get out of industrialisation?

There are enormous difficulties in the way of giving a precise and objective answer to this question in the century to 1870. There are no estimates of the region's or Scotland's income by which to judge the growth of society's wealth. We cannot say whether the share of capital going to labour increased, decreased or remained constant. Nor can we say if the workers as a whole, or even groups of workers, improved their economic position. This last assessment would require series of money wages, runs of the prices of commodities, and from these the calculation of the trends of real income. None of these exist for the west of Scotland, or Scotland as a whole. What remains is the coloured opinions of contemporary observers and heterogeneous quotations of wage rates and prices, which are discontinuous in time and coverage of groups of men and goods.

In spite of this, we must still attempt to form a view of the rewards of labour, and in the absence of wage and price series we can at the moment offer a number of snapshots of wage and price quotations at intervals between 1790 and 1870 (Tables 17, 18). The gains in money terms were not large when spread over a period of almost sixty years, from 1812 to 1870, though they appear more substantial when measured from 1819. Masons' wages rose by 73 per cent, carpenters' earnings more than doubled, and colliers advanced their pay by two-thirds. Conversely, hand-loom weavers' earnings remained at a pitiful level, and female spinners, the bulwark of the cotton-mill labour force, did relatively badly, increasing their wages by a mere 20 per cent. The workforce divided clearly into better-off and disadvantaged groups. The more highly skilled craftsmen existed on a level of income which was between a third and a half greater than the unskilled labourer, the vanishing hand-loom weaver, and the poorly paid female mill-worker. The division was not entirely skilled *v.* unskilled, for one unskilled group, the colliers, maintained a level of income akin to that of the better class of tradesmen. When the 1870 earnings are compared with the high levels obtained in 1812, at the height of the Napoleonic wars, all the groups do less well. Colliers' earnings advanced by only 15 per cent, the general labourers' by 27 per cent and masons' by 44 per cent. Interestingly, agricultural workers appear to have come from behind and increased their wages more rapidly in this period than their urban counterparts, though even they advanced by less than half between 1812 and 1870.

TABLE 17   *Average wages per week: Glasgow area, 1790–1870*

Occupation	1790	1812	1819	1831	1851	1870
Blacksmiths		15s.	17s.	17s.	22s.	26s.
Carpenters	12s.	18s.	12s.	14s.	20s.	27s.
Colliers	18s.	24s. 6d.	17s.	13s.	15s.	28s.
Labourers	8s.	11s.	7s. 6d.	9s.	12s.	14s.
Machine makers		19s.	19s.	19s.	22s. 6d.	
Masons	12s.	18s.	15s.	14s.	18s.	26s.
Female spinners		15s.	15s.	15s.		19s.
Male spinners		24s.	24s.	24s.	25s.	26s.
Weavers (hand)	21s.	12s.	5s.	6s. 6d.	6s.	
Agric. workers (annual)	£15	£27	£22	£19	£29	£41
Married ploughmen (West Scotland)	£16		£24		£27 10s.	£36

Sources: Sir J. Sinclair, *Statistical Account of Scotland*; J. Cleland, *Enumeration of the Inhabitants of Glasgow*, etc.; J. Strang, 'The Wages of Labour', *Glasgow Statistics*, 1851 and 1856; A. L. Bowley, 'Statistics of wages in the United Kingdom during the last hundred years. Agricultural wages', *Journal of the Royal Statistical Society*, 62, 1899

Any gain made by these groups, as representative of the mass of the workforce, depended not solely on the increase in their money wages, but in improvements in their real income, that is, in the purchasing power of the money in the paypacket. This was determined by the movement of prices, and the scanty evidence does not suggest any universal shift in favour of the working man. Oatmeal, cheese and bread prices declined by between a fifth and a third, but beef prices rose by four-fifths, potatoes by three-quarters, and butter doubled in price. Also, rent increased steeply by over 40 per cent, the biggest jump coming after 1850.

TABLE 18   *Average prices, selected commodities, 1790–1870 (in pence per unit shown)*

	1790	1812	1815	1819	1831	1841	1851	1861	1870
Oatmeal/peck (8 lbs)	12½	21	27	15	14	10½	11¼	11½	10
Cheese/lb	4½	12	5¾	6	6	4¾	5½	5	
Beef/lb	3½	6	4	5½	5	7	4½	8½	10
Wheaten loaf (4½ lbs)	9	18½	10½	11½	8	9½	8		7
Eggs/dozen					10	12	10	10	13
Potatoes/stone			4¼	3½	4	4½	5½	7	6
Butter/lb			8	9¼	13	12	9½	14	16
Rent: 2 apts Glasgow/year (shillings)		100	100	90	85	130	–	–	129

Sources: Sir J. Sinclair, *Statistical Account of Scotland*; J. Cleland, *Enumeration of the Inhabitants of Glasgow*, etc.; J. Strang, 'The Wages of Labour', *Glasgow Statistics*, 1851 and 1856; T. R. Gourvish, 'The cost of living in Glasgow in the early nineteenth century', *Econ. Hist. Rev.* 2nd series, 25, 1972

Potatoes, beef and rent were major items in the ordinary family budget, and could only be adjusted to a limited extent by seeking poorer accommodation and cheaper cuts of meat. Price rises in these items consequently pressed hard on the workers' income at the points where weekly outlays were most firmly committed. The modest reductions in the prices of cheese and bread were undoubtedly a benefit, but it is difficult to say whether the price falls outweighed the price advances. A very rough guide can be obtained by comparing the outlay required to purchase the items for which prices are available in both 1819 and 1870. Including rent, a man had to spend 7s. 7d. in 1870 for what he could have obtained for 5s. 5d. in 1819; an increase of some 21 per cent. On the other hand, the wage bill, for the groups represented in 1819 and 1870, increased by just over half. Both averages include wide ranges of price and wage changes, but it appears that money wages just about outgrew price rises, though any improvement in the standard of living must have been slender, and confined to the highest paid, and numerically the smallest, groups of the labouring classes.

The balancing of wages and prices, in this fashion, is a very dubious procedure, and no great weight can be placed on the conclusion. The nature of the data demands extreme caution in interpretation. The average wages are based on quotations of daily wage rates multiplied by six to give a weekly wage. Such a step takes no account of short-time or overtime, of time lost by illness or slack trade: nor does it give any weight to the wide range of earnings normally found within any group of workmen. Further, it says nothing of family income, for in this period wives and children commonly worked, and any assessment of changes in the workers' standard of living on the basis of individual earnings can be very misleading.

Similar qualifications apply to the price data. The quotations take no account of changes in quality, nor the changes in price which could take place from week to week: moreover, they do not include any adjustment for differences in price which could exist for the same commodity in different districts of the same town, or in different towns in the region. Further, these prices cannot realistically be employed to deflate the money wage rate to give an idea of real wages. This technique properly requires the construction of a price index for a selected group of commodities, adjusted to take account of the relative importance, or weight, of each item in the weekly budget. A more objective assessment can only be arrived at when these conditions are met, and when the price index includes other important items like clothing, lighting and fuel. Even then, the conclusion may be indecisive. Dr Gourvish took account of such complications for the period 1810–31, and was forced to conclude tentatively that, 'The experience of Glasgow's working classes would seem to involve a very modest improvement for the more highly paid, and little or no improvement for the unskilled labourer and hand-loom weaver.'

The piecemeal evidence on the trend of real wages suggests that between 1800 and 1830 the more highly skilled workman, in the Glasgow district, probably experienced a modest advance in the order of 25–30 per cent, while the bulk of the workforce barely held its position. Neither group seems to have made much advance in the 1830s, while the 1840s was a time of great distress. Major commercial depression in 1841–2, followed by the potato crop failures between 1844 and 1847, earned the decade the title of the 'hungry forties'. Only the beginning of extensive railway construction from 1847 began to pull income and employment upward again. Dr Strang's data suggest a considerable advance in real wages in the late 1840s and early 1850s, but this was mostly cut away in the commercial crises of 1856–7. The skilled groups always rode these fluctuations more securely than the mass of unskilled labour. For the latter it appears that any general advance in real income only began to materialise in the 1860s: even then there is no certainty about the matter.

Looked at in terms of an increase in real income, the rewards of labour appear slender in the period up to 1870. It may be, however, that our standards of measurement are misplaced, being appropriate to modern ideas more than to contemporary circumstances. The price trends of food, rent and clothing may not be the only, or best, indicators of the disposable income of the labouring classes at that time. The working man may have used his income in other ways, either by habit or by choice. Certainly Dr Strang was forced to qualify his view that a Glasgow working man could save in 1851, by adding, 'if he could only be temperate and frugal'. The capacity of the working classes for drink and debauchery mesmerised middle-class observers in the nineteenth century, who saw it as a major cause of the lowly condition of the working classes. Was it also an indicator of improved earnings? The occasional blow-out could be at the expense of food, clothing and accommodation, but sustained dissipation may have been supported by some increase in disposable income.

There are some indirect measures of improvement: in the slowly improving sanitation of the towns, in the work of mines and factory inspectors as they attacked the worst aspects of working conditions. Further, at the most basic level of all, the expectancy of life at birth had increased by 10 years to just over 40 by 1870. But set against the magnificent achievements in canals and railways, in mines, factories and the overall wealth of the nation, these improvements were small reward for the labouring classes. We must still conclude that substantial gains in real income eluded the mass of workers of the region in this period.

Part Two: 1870 - 1960

7

Industrial maturity

The heavy industries grew to maturity between 1870 and 1914. As coal, marine engineering and steel ships climbed to commanding positions in the national and international economy Clydeside took its place among the world's leading centres of industry. Cotton textiles in the region did not share this success, and alone of its staple industries, slid slowly towards contraction and decline. This prospect was apparent, but by no means inevitable, in the 1870s. The stripping away of decades of surplus spinning capacity had eliminated some weaknesses, but dangers remained in the shape of obsolescent technology and limited product ranges, together with the absence of any major renovation.

Between 1830 and 1870 Scottish cotton manufacturers had stabilised their position by adopting a low wage-rate, female labour force, allied to a concentration on better-quality cloths, where skill in production, style and finish protected a specialised market. But between 1870 and 1900 increasing competition at home and abroad cut into the Scottish leadership in novelty, design and finish, and threw Scottish cloths into direct cost competition. At this stage flagging productivity weakened the industry's ability to compete. In the 1880s and 1890s, contemporaries were aware that machinery in Scottish mills had become 'archaic alongside that of similar establishments in England'. In mule spinning, the females worked the machines less rapidly than the male spinners of Lancashire; in weaving, Scottish mill girls traditionally attended two looms, while in Lancashire, women worked three looms, and men attended four. The differentials in productivity were too great to be offset by the lower wage rates of Scottish workers. Moreover, in comparison with the USA, the average Scottish productivity per employee was miserably low; by 1885 one American weaver could operate up to fifteen of the new fully-automatic looms.

In the 1880s and 1890s Scottish manufacturers were generally unable to produce cloth as cheaply as their main competitors, and this began to narrow the markets available to them. The response was not a further move into ever fancier and more complex-designed high-quality products, but a concentration on a middle range of better-quality cloths. In 1870 a considerable part of Scottish output was cloth in the grey for bleaching and dyeing. By 1900 this had been greatly reduced, succumbing to Lancashire production, and even the great bleaching and dyeing industry in the Vale of Leven had by then to rely on grey cloth brought from Lancashire for the bulk of its work. On the other hand, plain muslins of good quality survived almost intact in the east end of Glasgow, and the shirtings trade also withstood Lancashire competition well.

The main failure, in the 1870s, was the total collapse of the Paisley shawl industry. Printed imitations of the delicately woven Paisley shawl cheapened the product, and a fashion change from the crinoline to the bustle deprived the garment of any real utility. This calamity threw between 7,000 and 10,000 persons out of work. But the female contingent was quickly taken up in the expanding thread industry. Paisley had advantages here; a traditional skill in thread making, plentiful and cheap female labour, and an increasing world demand for thread as the sewing machine became popular. The local stimulus was the production of sewing machines by Singer at Clydebank, from 1884, where they had transferred from an earlier factory in Bridgeton, together with the industrial and domestic machines made by Kimball and Morton in Glasgow since 1867. Cotton thread, at least, was an expanding sector, and it was strongly located in Paisley where J. & P. Coats and J. & J. Clark were the main manufacturers.

New employment in thread-making thus prevented a serious contraction in the 1870s. Sustained in this way the industry moved into the severe depression of 1894. It emerged much reduced, a number of the smaller weaving establishments going out of business. The section worst hit was again the very fanciest fashion fabrics, which were meeting great competition overseas. French cloth invaded the North African markets with the help of tariff discrimination. In India, local producers in Bombay seriously challenged Glasgow fancy goods in the bazaars, and the picture was similar in European markets. One powerful obstacle to Scottish success in these markets was that the duties charged on imported cloths were normally specific, not *ad valorem*. Consequently, even enormous efforts to reduce costs were largely nullified by the addition of fixed duties. Moreover, the position was complicated in Glasgow's main Indian and Chinese markets, since these countries based their currencies on silver, whereas Britain was on a gold standard. In the last three decades of the nineteenth century the exchange value of silver generally fell in relation to gold, and imports into the markets of silver-based economies tended to be rising in price, thus partly offsetting the attempts of Scottish manufacturers to reduce their costs of production. In sum, it is misleading to depict the history of the Scottish cotton trade in the late nineteenth century as an attempt to survive by moving deeper into fancy high-quality fabric production at the expense of plainer cloths. Indeed, it was the highest-quality sectors, the Paisley shawl and the Glasgow fancy trade, which fared worst in this period. The area of production which survived best was that of the good-quality plain muslins and shirtings, the fabrics which had been the foundation of the cotton industry in the west of Scotland since the 1830s.

The industry certainly became increasingly specialised in this good-quality sector, and in thread making. This new pattern of specialist production was elaborated by James Hood and Andrew Morton who established the machine lace industry in the Irvine valley in the late 1880s. A decade later the Irvine valley producers had captured British leadership in lace curtain manufactures. This was achieved by building large spacious factories and equipping them with the widest and most modern lace machines. These, allied to traditionally low wages, made for handsome returns and highly competitive products. In 1911, this new industry employed about 8,000 persons. When this is added to the employment in the Paisley thread industry, and combined with the employment in the traditional cotton-spinning and weaving sector, the factory labour force in cotton manufacture was close to 30,000, only a little different from the 36,000 employed in the 1870s. New products in thread and lace saved the cotton industry from extinction, but the decline had been serious in the traditional spinning and weaving sector, where fewer than 13,000 found employment in 1911. This reduced scale was the consequence of inefficient machinery and poor labour productivity, in turn a reflection of lethargic management.

In and around Glasgow only the Glasgow Cotton Spinning Company invested in new equipment and competed successfully with Lancashire producers. For the rest, the real failure appears to have been in a lack of new investment. Plentiful cheap labour forestalled this until dwindling profit margins made it difficult for manufacturers to contemplate any heavy expenditure. It seems likely that the financial hardships of the 1850s and 1860s had left little spare capital available to manufacturers, and by the 1880s two decades of indifferent trading conditions had no doubt made the investment prospects seem bleak. The industry lacked vigour both because existing manufacturers withheld new investment, and also because no outside investment was attracted, since the region provided many more enticing opportunities. On the whole, few manufacturers deliberately left the industry. A few did, but this was generally before 1870, the Houldsworths in 1833, and the Scotts in 1869. Thereafter, the decline was by slow attrition. Losing buildings by fire appears to have been a regular means of exit from the trade; in the 1880s and 1890s, ten or twelve mills were destroyed in Glasgow and never replaced. Moreover, the early location of the industry now told seriously against it. In Anderston and Bridgeton, once open village suburbs of Glasgow, the cotton factories were enclosed by tenement buildings. Glasgow had spread and sprawled east and west from its central axis, and left no room for physical expansion of plant in the old weaving and spinning districts. Only new men and new capital in growing industries could contemplate breaking the bonds of industrial inertia and seek new open sites on the perimeter of the city. Singer did this, moving from Bridgeton to Kilbowie on the outskirts of the new shipbuilding town of Clydebank; J. & G. Thomson also moved to Clydebank from Govan, and the North British Locomotive Company located itself at Springburn. Such initiatives were beyond the will of the cotton men, and they and their industry languished in old centres of production, destined to eventual extinction. The industry which had once driven the region to industrial success, and had employed upwards of half its total population, now employed a small part of the labour force. It had been overtaken by the thriving nexus of coal and metallurgy.

Coalmining

The expansion of coal production had been crucial for the growth of the regional economy in the middle decades of the nineteenth century. The industry retained this central position before the First World War. Between 1870 and 1913 both output and employment doubled in the west of Scotland (Table 19) and this achievement has to be seen against a background of unsettled markets and increasing competition. In 1870 coal and iron had been linked closely together, both in ownership of mines and ironworks, and in the demands made by the pig-iron industry for coal as fuel in the furnaces. Over 20 per cent of total output was consumed in ironworks and this had exercised a profound influence over the progress and prosperity of the coal industry. However, this close association seems to have weakened as pig-iron production contracted in the years of the great depression, from the mid-1870s to the mid-1890s. Consequently, in 1913, the pig-iron industry consumed only 6 per cent of coal output, while the combined market of exports, bunkers and coastwise shipments took over 16 million tons, or some 38 per cent of total Scottish production. The fortunes of the industry had apparently been tied as effectively to export markets in 1913 as they had been to the iron industry in 1870.

TABLE 19   *Output, employment and collieries in operation, 1870 and 1913*

| | | *1870* | | | *1913* | |
	West Scotland	*Rest Scotland*	*Scotland*	*West Scotland*	*Rest Scotland*	*Scotland*
Output (million tons)	11·9	3·0	14·9	22·4	20·0	42·4
Employment (000s)	34·7	12·2	46·9	79·1	68·4	147·5
Collieries	292	121	413	341	201	542

Sources: Annual returns of Inspectors of Mines; Mineral Statistics of the United Kingdom and Ireland, 1870 and 1913

It was the east-coast producers who redeveloped the traditional Baltic and north European export markets, and linked their fortunes to the demands of the foreign consumer. The changing market pattern is less marked in the west of Scotland. The iron industry took less coal than before, but the new steel industry and its coke requirements more than filled the gap. In 1913, the metallurgical industries must still have consumed about 20 per cent of the west of Scotland's coal. Nevertheless, exports were important. Over 2 million tons of coal left Clyde and Ayrshire ports for overseas markets in 1913, and coastal shipments also made heavy demands, nearly 1·5 million tons being moved. More west-coast coal went east by canal and railway to swell the shipments from eastern ports. Some 12–15 per cent of the total coal production of the region must have been shipped to markets overseas.

Within the region, there remained the richest industrial and consumer markets in Scotland. While the east-coast producers made themselves vulnerable by concentrating on exports, the western coalowners appear to have found their outlets broadening. The demands were not so spectacular, but they were less liable to disruption. Even the ironmasters began to sell their coal on the regional open market. This had begun as a short-term expedient in the 1860s, but developed into a regular part of the coal trade by the 1880s.

While the output of the region doubled in response to these demands, the shifts in market emphasis were accompanied by shifts in the location of the main producing areas. Till 1870 the iron districts of the Monklands and north Lanarkshire were the core areas of coal production in the west of Scotland, but in the next twenty years several factors combined to shift the focus of production into the middle Clyde basin. Partly the move was in response to declining resources in the part of the coalfield which had been exploited earliest. The movement to the Clyde was made easier since the railway network had been extended to the middle and upper

Clyde in the 1860s. When accessibility to the district was combined with the rise in prices of the early 1870s, there appeared to be a promise of rich returns on any investment. The possibility of opening up the central Clyde district was enhanced by improvements in sinking equipment and winding gear, which brought within reach the deep seams. Extensive new developments took place in the new field from the early 1870s. As a consequence the middle Clyde valley between Cambuslang and Larkhall had, by 1900, become the major coal-producing area in the central coalfield.

The new investments in mines also introduced mechanical coal cutters and conveyor belts into the Scottish coalfields. As early as 1906, 1·3 million tons of coal were machine-cut in the west of Scotland. By 1913 Scotland raised 22 per cent of her output with the aid of machinery, using nearly 900 coal cutters and 125 conveyors. This was a much larger mechanisation than any other British mining district. Five hundred of these cutters were at work in the west of Scotland, and raised about 5 million of the 9 million tons of Scottish coal cut by machines; this represented some 20–25 per cent of the region's output.

Superficially, the coal industry in the west of Scotland was in a prosperous and progressive condition. It underwrote the industrial strength of the region; it had developed and extended its markets, doubled its output and employment and invested heavily in new power machinery. However, there were disquieting trends. In spite of the impressive growth in absolute output, the inevitable slackening of rates of growth which are built into extractive industries had overtaken the region's coal industry in this period. The major adjustment was the slowing down in growth of output of the great Lanarkshire coalfield. After the late 1880s the sustained rate of expansion of the new areas of production in Fife, Edinburgh and Linlithgow rapidly ate into the dominant position of the west of Scotland coalfields. The west produced 80 per cent of Scotland's coal in 1870; in 1913 this had been cut back to just over half the total by the astonishing growth of the eastern coalfield. This in itself was no great cause for concern, for the western region had doubled its own output and increased its working collieries (Table 19, see p. 167). The disturbing element was that by 1913 the average output per colliery in the west was much smaller than in the new eastern districts. Even in the new area in the middle Clyde basin the average output per colliery in 1900 was only 84,000 tons per year, as against 93,000 tons in Fife. In the west output per man slumped badly from 345 to 283 tons per year, while the rest of Scotland registered a marked increase. The burden of declining productivity had clearly not been offset even by the heavy investment in mechanical cutters.

The industry in the west of Scotland could not escape its geology or its history. It had expanded vigorously in the mid-nineteenth century, and the best and thickest seams had been extensively worked. By 1913 the exploitation of both deeper and thinner seams was becoming more common, and this was linked to a very large number of small one-colliery coal companies. There were too many companies, too many small concerns. The largest producers frequently were partly protected from competition, since they were raising coal for consumption in their own ironworks. One consequence was that the west of Scotland, and especially the major Lanarkshire field, was becoming a high-cost area of production. The average cost of a ton of coal at the pit head was 9s. 8d. in Scotland in 1913. Ayrshire and Dunbartonshire averaged only 9s. 1d., but Lanarkshire, the heart of the west's industry, could only raise its coal at an average cost of 11s. 5d. per ton. This compared badly with the average, and even less well with the 8s. 10d. of Linlithgow, and 9s. 0d. of Edinburgh.

Lanarkshire and the west of Scotland still dominated Scottish mining in 1913, but ominous signs for the future were already present. The most modern mines, the largest producing units and the most economic pits were all to be found in eastern Scotland. A start had been made in mechanising the western industry to overcome its geological disadvantages, but the future remained doubtful. The coal–iron link had been weakened if not entirely dissolved, and it is to iron, the other foundation of the regional economy, that we now turn.

The metal industries

Iron

The headlong expansion of the pig-iron industry which had dominated the region's life between 1830 and 1870, faltered in the early 1870s. The peak production of 1·2 million tons in 1870 was not equalled for over thirty years, till 1902. The iron industry was experiencing a period of prolonged difficulty, the roots of which could be traced to the very factors which had underlain its spectacular success in the middle nineteenth century. The earlier prosperity had rested largely on cost advantages achieved through the application of a new technique, the hot blast, to plentiful supplies of local raw materials, both iron and coal. The first serious strains to affect the industry struck at this resource base. In face of prolonged exploitation the supplies of the coal-measure iron ores inevitably began to diminish. From an average annual output of 2·2 million tons in the 1870s local iron-ore production slipped back to 1·7 million tons in the 1880s, the beginnings of sharp contraction that came after 1883. After 1900, local supplies amounted only to 600,000–700,000 tons per year, and in 1913 a mere 591,000 tons.

The iron industry lost its former position of self-sufficiency, and had to turn progressively to imported ores. Between 1875 and 1885, even before the local ore supplies began to diminish seriously, iron-ore imports into the Clyde grew from just over 15,000 tons to almost 290,000 tons. By 1900, the importation to Glasgow harbour was almost 700,000 tons, and in 1913 had grown to 1·9 million tons. While such imports could secure the basis of the industry, they could not help but add to its costs, and when hard-splint coal, for use in the furnace, also began to run into diminishing supplies, the old foundations of the industry had gone.

The Scottish pig-iron industry had risen to prominence more on its low prices than superior quality of product. When the supply of cheap raw materials failed, the product of the industry found itself very vulnerable to competition from other districts. Railways had reduced the cost of distance as a barrier to competitors; and Cleveland and Welsh producers began to penetrate the Glasgow market. The competition was fiercest from the Cleveland district, where producers enjoyed the combination of rich local resources, modern plant and lower costs, just as the Scots had done in the 1840s and 1850s. Such competition could be contained while generally rising prices affected the industry up to 1873, when Scottish pig-iron averaged £5 to £7 per ton. But when prices collapsed to £2 7s. 0d. per ton in 1879, and remained at a low level throughout the 1880s, the more efficient English producers were able to undercut Glasgow suppliers by margins of up to 20 per cent. Scottish pig-iron manufacturers came under pressure not only from rising costs in the supply of raw materials, but from increasing competition in all their major outlets, the forge, the foundry, and exports. The consequence was that the profits of the industry were squeezed mercilessly between both rising costs and falling prices. The depression of prices and the increase of competition revealed the weaknesses of the west of Scotland pig-iron industry. It was a technological anachronism. Its furnaces were small and out-dated. Its once famous hot blast now worked at lower temperatures than more modern plant, and the open-topped furnaces fed the gases to the empty air, wasting valuable by-products and defiling the environment.

The immediate response to these difficulties was to contract output by about 10 per cent throughout the 1870s and 1880s. In the circumstances, there were few alternatives, for a more positive response was hindered by a number of factors. The declining resource-base severely limited freedom of action, and the fact that most of the major pig-iron producers were also major coalmasters tended to confirm them in the established pattern. Coal at least was expanding its output, and its markets were growing, so some support must have come to the iron producers from this connection. Moreover, reduced production and low prices gave no incentive to invest heavily to renew the plant. The basic deficiency was the small scale of the furnace, but this was related to the use of raw-splint coal. Being softer than coke, it could only support a more limited charge of ore and limestone in the furnace without caving in and letting the furnace go out. The choice was effectively between increasing the size of furnaces, together with the expense of making an increasing use of coke; or sticking with the smaller furnace and continuing to use splint coal in the hope that the cheapness of this fuel would offset the lower productivity of the furnaces and the general tendency to higher costs of production. The ironmasters chose, on the whole, to stick by local splint coal. The market prospects were also inimical to creative action among the ironmasters. Since they themselves had rarely been involved in the processing of their pig-iron in forges and foundries they must have had uneasy feelings concerning investment in the new steel industry. Also, since they had rarely marketed their own product, they must have had a bleak view of the chances of any initiative taken to recapture markets which were being invaded by English, and later German producers.

TABLE 20   *Output and changing consumption of pig-iron,
1870 and 1913 (000 tons) (Scotland)*

	1870	1913
Total output, pig-iron	1,206	1,369
Of which haematite pig-iron	–	740
Used for foundry	249	424
Used for forge	198	127
Exports	650	268

Source: Mineral Statistics of the United Kingdom and
Ireland, 1870 and 1913

Having had contraction forced upon them, the Scottish iron producers reacted positively, if cautiously. The changing markets for pig-iron give a clue to the directions in which they turned (Table 20). The traditional outlets of foundry, forge and exports were still important in 1913, and the foundry side of the industry had much expanded. In contrast, pig-iron in the forge used to make malleable iron had declined from a peak of 237,000 tons in 1880 as mild steel replaced malleable iron for most purposes. An even more dramatic reversal was the decline of pig-iron exports to less than 20 per cent of the total output in 1913. This certainly reflected increasing competition in overseas markets, but more important, it represented a redirection of Scottish ironmakers' efforts. In contrast to the position before 1870, the Scottish iron industry could expect the bulk of its output to be consumed locally, and hence the ironmakers began to concentrate their efforts on supplying the home market. Even so, 613,000 tons of pig-iron came in from England in 1913, to help make up the deficiency in local supplies. However, the most dramatic change was in the production of haematite or acid pig-iron, this representing over half the total output in 1913. This innovation was a response to changes in the raw material and market situations. Diminishing local ores demanded imported ores in replacement, and the rise of the steel industry, linked to shipyard demands for acid steel, turned the ironmasters' eyes toward replacement ores of the rich haematite variety.

These ores came mainly from the north of Spain. The production of this new high-grade haematite pig-iron enforced some improvement in the plant used. This occurred first in the average size of the furnace. The average output per week in 1870 was only 200 tons per furnace, but by 1913 this had increased to 300 tons, or some 15,000–16,000 tons per year. This had been achieved by building some new plant, but mainly by mixing coke with the splint coal, to enable the furnace to take increased charges. Consequently, Scottish furnaces still produced only half as much iron per unit as the British average. Some advances were also made in increasing the temperature of the blast by making use of waste gases to heat the blast and boilers. This coincided with the introduction of distillation plants to recover tar and ammonia from the gas, a move begun by the Bairds in 1880. By 1900 every works in the west of Scotland had this type of by-product recovery plant, but only the Bairds took the further step of recovering by-products from coke-oven gas.

The improvements were small, but sufficient to move the iron industry back into increasing outputs after 1899. Production stood at 694,000 tons in the strike-hit year of 1894, but grew to over 1 million tons the following year, and the new high levels were sustained until the outbreak of war. But although the ironmasters responded positively in developing new types of pig-iron to meet new markets within Scotland, the achievement must be qualified by a sense of missed opportunity. The philosophy was 'mend and renovate', rather than 'scrap and renew'. This is borne out by the considered comment of Professor Sexton, when he reviewed the progress of the industry for the British Association meeting in Glasgow in 1900. He wrote that much reconstruction had been undertaken in the preceding decade '. . . so as to bring [the works] well up to date'. But he added that:

> whilst much of the plant is such that it would not be put into a newly designed works today, there is no reason why it should be discarded if it is doing its work well. Scotch iron masters have as a rule been wise in the slowness with which they have revolutionized the works. 'Hasten slowly' is always a good motto in such cases.

Such a cautious philosophy shaped the iron industry in the thirty years before the war, and gave little strength to the trade to withstand the troubles that lay ahead.

Steel

In the middle decades of the nineteenth century an observer might understandably have thought that the west of Scotland and its range of industries provided a sound foundation for the development of a steel industry. The making of steel is, in effect, a finishing process in the iron trade, just as was malleable-iron production. Scotland already possessed an extensive pig-iron industry, and a smaller but well-established malleable-iron sector. The problem with steelmaking, however, was the inability to produce this superior metal in large volume. Both the crucible and blister processes were well known, but produced very small quantities of high-grade steel at great expense. Such steel production was essentially a craft industry, supplying the needs of the cutlery trade, swordmakers and watch- and springmakers. As long as the production of steel depended on these techniques the metal could only be produced in small and expensive quantities. Scotland did have some steelmaking capacity in the first half of the nineteenth century, principally through the efforts of the Monkland Iron and Steel Co., but even this firm abandoned small-scale cast steel production in favour of malleable iron in the 1840s.

The solution to the problem of producing good-quality cast steel in bulk, and cheaply, came with the introduction of the Bessemer process between 1856 and 1858. Bessemer did not initially set out to mass-produce steel. His aim was to convert pig-iron into wrought, or workable malleable iron, without going through the laborious puddling and rolling stages. His method was to pour molten pig-iron into his bottle-shaped converter, whereupon great quantities of cold air, under pressure, were blown through the hot metal. In bubbling through the molten metal the air oxidised or burnt out the impurities, leaving behind pure liquid iron. However, in the course of his experiments, Bessemer had noted that, at a stage immediately following the boil, the liquid metal attained the condition of ordinary-quality cast steel. If the process was continued, and all the carbon burnt out of the metal, pure malleable iron remained. Bessemer also picked out a stage mid-way between the cast-steel and malleable-iron stage, where, if the process was stopped, the ensuing metal had marvellous properties: it had greater tensile strength than malleable iron, but was more elastic and more resistant to wear than brittle cast steel. He called this semi-steel, the quality of metal now commonly called mild steel.

His revelations on the method of producing either pure malleable iron, by completely burning out all the impurities, or various grades of steel by stopping the process at particular points, aroused great interest.* In Scotland, Jackson, the manager at Coats Iron Works, attempted the process with hastily-erected equipment in 1856, and met with complete failure. The following year William Dixon built a complete converter under Bessemer's supervision, and paid £10,000 for the Scottish rights to the process. But after numerous trials, only pure brittle crystalline iron was produced; this was worthless, shattering at the smallest blow. Bessemer was obliged to repurchase the patent from Dixon, and in Scotland, Wales and England, eager ironmasters retreated from the new miracle process in dismay and disgruntlement. It took Bessemer two years of effort and experiment, and also the help of a Swedish patentee who found the process worked perfectly with Swedish iron ores, to solve the problem. By 1858 Bessemer could demonstrate that he had perfected the process using non-phosphoric haematite pig-iron from Blaenavon. The other attempts had failed because they had used the more common phosphoric pig-irons.

The failure of the Bessemer process in Scotland, and then the solution provided, revealed two great difficulties in the way of producing large quantities of cheap steel; one was technical. The Bessemer conversion took place so rapidly, and the chemistry of ironmaking was so ill-understood, that even adding identical quantities of carbon to succeeding conversions produced different qualities of steel. Technically, the Bessemer process raised a problem of reliable quality. The other difficulty revealed in the initial failure of the Bessemer method was one of resources. Success with the Bessemer converter demanded non-phosphoric iron ores. In this context Scotland had no natural endowment, as she had had in the establishment of the pig-iron industry. She lacked high-quality haematite ores, and in addition, her coking coals were poor. The technical difficulties of quality production and the lack of appropriate ores were two powerful barriers to Scotland's entry into the steel industry.

The quality problem was the first to be solved. In the 1850s both C. W. Siemens in England and Pierre Martin in France were experimenting with the technique of making steel by the immersion of malleable iron bars in a bath of molten metal in an open hearth. In 1856 Siemens' brother Friedrich conceived the notion of applying a regenerative furnace to malleable-iron production, to save gas and increase heat. In the early 1860s William Siemens began to bring both the open hearth and regenerative furnaces together. However, it was Martin in France who first obtained consistent results with this process, and although Siemens took out a patent early in 1866, by November of that year an agreement was reached to satisfy the claims of both Siemens and Martin,

---

* In practice it was customary to finish the conversion, and then add quantities of carbon to produce the quality of steel desired.

and the Siemens-Martin open-hearth regenerative furnace was brought into use.

It had considerable advantages over the Bessemer technique. Bessemer's conversion took place in half an hour, and quality control was imperfect. The Siemens-Martin process took fourteen hours to complete, allowed extensive chemical analysis, and therefore permitted precise control of quality. Moreover, since it worked on the principle of mixing solid malleable iron into a molten bath of pig-iron to produce cast steel, it also permitted the addition of scrap, and hence the re-utilisation of old malleable iron rails and plates for conversion to steel.

There remained the problem of resources. The Siemens-Martin process, like the Bessemer, had been evolved to deal with non-phosphoric iron. The phosphoric-iron districts like the west of Scotland were still faced with the need to import acid iron ores, or pig-iron, if the new steel industry was to be set up. However, a solution seemed to present itself to one group of men in Scotland at this time, particularly since Siemens was also experimenting with a modified furnace to produce steel direct from the ore, without the necessity of having it first smelted in a blast furnace. This group of men owned neither blast furnaces nor a malleable-iron works. But some among them did control an immense quantity of non-phosphoric iron residue, a waste deposit which had been accumulating in Glasgow where the Tharsis Sulphur and Copper Company refined iron pyrites from its Spanish mines. Charles Tennant of St Rollox, various members of the Tharsis Co., Henry Dubs of Glasgow Locomotive Works, the Arrols of engineering fame, and a number of others, joined with C. W. Siemens to set up a company to exploit these non-phosphoric iron residues, using the direct conversion process of Siemens' rotary furnaces. Intensive trials were carried out in the Atlas foundry, and a private company was set up in 1871, but quickly changed to a public company in 1872, with a capital of £105,000 in £10 shares, taken up by twenty-eight persons.

This was Scotland's first steel company, appropriately called the Steel Company of Scotland. Its owners were not the great pig-iron producers, but came from the chemical industry, as the controller of the raw materials, the engineering industry, as the intending purchasers of the new steel, and from science, in the person of Siemens. The company purchased a site at Hallside, near Cambuslang, in 1871, convenient to the Tharsis Co., and well served by the Caledonian Railway. Production commenced in the autumn of 1873 from four Siemens-Martin open-hearth furnaces of traditional design. The experiment with the rotary furnaces did not get under way till 1874; good-quality malleable iron was made from a mix of iron residue and other ores, but at very high cost. The experimental plant was dismantled the following year. Thereafter, the Steel Company of Scotland concentrated on the standard open-hearth furnaces. This was a disappointment, but not a total loss, for the company could compromise on resources by using local scrap mixed with some local, and much Cleveland, iron.

The Steel Company of Scotland intended to specialise in the new and growing market for steel rails, a direction influenced by the engineering interests of some of the partners. However, the new company was caught between the rapid growth of English steel rail-making capacity, and declining prices. After 1875 it diversified into plates, bars and forgings. In particular, it developed boiler plates, and began experiments with ships' plates. This was to prove the key to rapid growth.

The Scottish steel industry therefore began a decade later than that in England, in the hope that the resource problem could be overcome, only to find it necessary to depend on imports of non-phosphoric iron.

In early 1879 there was one steel firm; by the end of 1880 there were five, and by 1885 there were ten. The new wave of firms began in May 1879, when Beardmore added steel furnaces at his Parkhead forge, and later, in the same year, the Glasgow Iron and Steel Co. added steel capacity to their Wishaw works. The following year, the Summerlee and Mossend Iron Co. and David Colville at Motherwell took up steelmaking, and the Steel Company of Scotland bought the Blochairn Ironworks at St Rollox and began converting them. All the new Scottish plants, save the Glasgow Iron and Steel Co., set up with Siemens-Martin open-hearth furnaces, using acid or haematite pig-iron; the Glasgow Iron and Steel Co. set up Bessemer converters using the acid process. In the next few years during which another five companies set up, only Merry & Cunninghame at their Glengarnock works installed Bessemer converters to use the Gilchrist-Thomas basic steel process,* and the Glasgow Iron and Steel Co. also converted their Bessemer furnaces to produce basic steel.

With these exceptions, the Scottish steel firms chose to expand in the acid-steelmaking sector. Their choice was strongly influenced by a number of factors. There was, of course, the demonstration effect of the success of the Steel Company of Scotland making acid steel. In addition, there was the declining production of local supplies of iron ore, and the successful establishment of shipments of high-grade haematite from Spain to the Clyde. Moreover, by the late 1870s, the local shipbuilders were expressing a decided preference for ships' plates made of acid steel by the open-hearth process. This was a decisive influence, and the judgment of the local shipbuilders was borne out when Lloyds placed a ban on the use of basic Bessemer steel in ship construction. This forced Merry &

---

* In 1880 Gilchrist and Thomas demonstrated that satisfactory steel could be made from phosphoric pig-iron by lining the furnace with basic firebricks; adding quicklime as a basic flux to induce a highly basic slag to form on the surface of the metal; and after-blowing of air over the slag to burn off residual phosphorus.

Cunninghame to add open-hearth furnaces to their existing Bessemer converters, and the Glasgow Iron and Steel Co. discontinued production of basic steel. The link between steelmaking and the demand of Clyde shipyards was very close. In 1873, total steel production in Scotland was only 1,199 tons. In 1879, open-hearth production was 50,593 tons, and by 1890, 485,000 tons. Between 1879 and 1890, steel tonnage launched on the Clyde grew from 18,000 tons to 326,000 tons. The Scottish steel industry therefore developed on a foundation of borrowed technology, imported ores, and exported steel ships.

Once established, the industry grew very rapidly. It also took on certain characteristics which were to have considerable influence on subsequent developments. The single most significant feature was the pattern of ownership. With few exceptions the main steelmakers emerged from the ranks of the malleable-iron producers. Major pig-iron makers like the Dunlops and Merry & Cunninghame were represented, as were engineering interests like A. J. Stewart and Menzies, but no other sector was so well represented as the malleable-iron makers. This in turn imparted other features to the industry. One important consequence was the separate location of steelworks and pig-iron-producing blast furnaces. In 1900 only three of the fifteen steelworks had been set up side by side with blast furnaces. These were at Coltness, Wishaw and Ardeer. Another three companies also worked blast furnaces, but on separate sites.

On the whole, then, pig-iron making and steel production were poorly integrated in the spatial sense. The most significant repercussion was that the Scottish steelmasters failed to develop the hot-metal process, whereby great economies were gained by transferring molten pig-iron direct from the blast furnace to the steel converter. Although the Glasgow Iron and Steel Co. at Wishaw experimented with hot-metal production in 1900, the industry generally made its steel from cold pig-iron which required to be remelted before the conversion could begin.

The seriousness of these features was quickly evident. In comparison with the Cleveland district the west of Scotland steel mills were generally smaller in scale, suffered from the dis-economies of the cold-metal process, and bore the extra burdens of additional freight charges incurred in moving the iron ore to inland sites, together with the increasing burden of the highest coal royalties of any mining district in Britain. This was reflected in the most damaging way possible, namely in the ability of Cleveland steelmakers to sell ships' plates cheaper on Clydeside than the local producers. In the 1880s, the disadvantage ran at 5–7 per cent in favour of the Cleveland steelmakers, though this was generally offset by a 5 per cent discount on Scottish plates, provided orders were regularly placed with the local suppliers. After 1900 the position deteriorated, and in 1913 even German steel plates could be landed on Clydeside at up to

G

20 per cent below the price of the local article. The industry was only saved from this damaging competition because the German plates were of basic steel and were subject to very severe inspection by Lloyds.

The Scottish steelmakers responded both positively and negatively to this situation. The most dramatic development was forward integration into shipbuilding. This step was taken by Beardmore's in 1900 when the company took over Robert Napier's yard at Govan, and then laid out a new yard at Dalmuir in 1906. More generally, the steelmakers responded by developing the use of scrap metal in the open-hearth furnaces, a technique which helped to contain costs and minimise waste. Moreover, there was a general move to seek protection by more negative means. This principally took the form of an attempt at price-fixing through the Scottish Steel Makers' Association. This body was established to control the price of boiler plates in 1897, and extended its influence to ships' plates from 1904. The Association also developed the principle of giving a rebate of 5s. 0d. per ton in addition to a 5 per cent discount to purchasers buying exclusively from its members. These steps did contain foreign and English competition, and maintained Scottish prices above Cleveland and German prices until the agreement was abolished in March 1914.

In spite of its difficulties the Scottish industry expanded quickly. In 1880, Scotland produced 101,000 tons of open-hearth steel, 40 per cent of the British output of such steel, but only 8 per cent of all steel produced. In 1900, after twenty years of rapid growth, Scotland then made 30 per cent of British open-hearth steel, with 963,000 tons, and this was about 20 per cent of total British steel output. However, after 1900, Scotland's disadvantages began to take their toll. Although total Scottish output had climbed to 1·4 million tons in 1913, this represented only 21 per cent of open-hearth production, and 18 per cent of the British steel output. Scotland had never had the commanding position in steel production which had been achieved in pig-iron making. Even her early prominence and specialisation in open-hearth acid steel was beginning to be eroded in the decade before the First World War.

Shipbuilding

The record of the Clyde in shipbuilding between 1870 and 1913 is quite astonishing. Between these dates her slipways consistently poured out a third of the total British tonnage. Launchings averaged 250,000 tons each year between 1871 and 1874, and this was more than doubled to 565,000 tons between 1909 and 1913. In the peak year of 1913 the Clyde built and launched almost three-quarters of a million tons of shipping, some 756,973 tons, a feat never to be equalled. This represented not only one-third of British tonnage, but almost 18 per cent of world output, and was more than the production of the entire shipbuilding industry of either Germany or America. The Clyde was supreme in 1870, and was still on the pinnacle in 1913. It maintained this dominant position by developing further the basis of success established in the years before 1870. The technical environment again lay at the heart of the matter and advances in construction and in marine engineering once more led the way.

The technical environment

The most rapid and dramatic innovation was in the replacement of iron by steel in ship construction. Iron had scarcely established its supremacy over wood when mild steel appeared to challenge it. Some steel ships were built on the Thames during the American Civil War, and the French Navy introduced steel in construction in 1874. The advantages of steel over wrought iron were clear. Steel was more flexible, more tensile and more elastic than iron. Builders were aware that since steel was stronger than iron, a ship of similar proportions could be built with less metal, saving up to 16 per cent in weight. The barrier to quick adoption lay in the quality and price of steel plates in comparison with iron. Bessemer steel was regarded with open suspicion by shipbuilders, and it was only the techniques of Siemens-Martin and Gilchrist-Thomas which overcame this quality difficulty. The answer to high cost was to increase the volume of production.

Scottish shipbuilders barely waited for the problem of quality to be solved, and they plunged into steel construction while costs were still high. John Elder launched two steel paddle-steamers in 1877. The following year J. & G. Thomson launched another, and in 1879 Wm Denny built the *Rotomahana*, the first ocean-going vessel constructed of mild steel. By 1881, J. & G. Thomson had built and launched the *Servia*, of 7,392 tons; this was the first Cunarder built of steel and with the exception of the *Great Eastern*, was the largest vessel then afloat. In this way the Clyde led the world into the era of steel ships. In 1879, Clyde yards launched 18,000 tons of steel shipping, some 10·3 per cent of total launchings for that year. By 1884, 133,670 tons, some 45 per cent of launchings on the Clyde, were of steel-built ships. At this stage only 15 per cent of all ships on Lloyds Register were of steel construction. Five years later, in 1889, 97·2 per cent of Clyde tonnage, some 326,136 tons, were steel-built. Iron had been quite dramatically replaced. When the Clyde initiative in steel construction began steel plates were still over 50 per cent more expensive than iron, averaging £9 12s. 6d. as against £6 per ton of iron in 1881. In 1886 the steel plates cost £6 2s. 6d. and iron had not changed. Thereafter steel was cheaper than iron, and the initiative of Clyde builders, allied to the heavy investment of local steelmakers, had established a new leadership in ship construction for the west of Scotland.

As ocean trade routes fell to the steamships, shipbuilders had to seek answers to the conflicting demands of greater size, higher speed, and greater economy. The use of steel in hulls was one solution to the size problem, and with weight reduction, contributed to economy. But the answers to speed and further economy lay in marine engineering, where the development of the compound-expansion engine had given prominence to the problems of boiler design and boiler pressure. One sophisticated answer was to contain the water and steam in a honeycomb of small tubes surrounded by combustion gases, in what became known as 'water-tube' boilers. The early types were not very successful. A simpler solution was to develop the old box or tank boiler into a cylindrical form. On the Clyde, James Howden devised such a cylindrical 'tank' boiler in 1862, his version becoming known as the 'Scotch' boiler. When allied to steel plates in the 1870s, and combined with the 'forced-draught' patented by David Napier in 1851, this became the common installation in merchant vessels. This cylindrical form enabled higher pressures to be sustained, but it was the temperamental water-tube version which led on to the next development in the marine compound engine. John Elder & Co. were asked to build a vessel with water-tube boilers working at 150 lbs per square inch. In order to make full use of the power of the steam, A. C. Kirk devised the triple-expansion engine, to expand the steam in three cylinders instead of two. This was fitted in the *Propontis* in 1874, but it was not till 1882 that Kirk linked his engine to a Scotch boiler in the *Aberdeen*. This was a deep-sea service vessel, and inaugurated the era of triple-expansion engines on the long trade routes. Subsequently, in 1885, Walter Brock, working at Denny's, devised a quadruple-expansion engine which could cope with even higher pressures and yield greater economy. It was, however, suited more to larger vessels, and was most used in the bigger cargo ships before the First World War.

These improvements answered the quest for economy more than speed. They were made effective by proper balancing of engines to reduce vibration and wear and tear. Latterly in 1913 Denny introduced the Mitchell thrust block, a device which ensured that the thrust developed by the propeller was transmitted to the structure of the ship, and did not travel back up the drive shaft to the engine. The aspect of speed was catered for by great increases in power, by installing twin and triple screws driven by separate engines, and by 1900 these refinements had carried the reciprocating marine steam engine to the limit of its capabilities. The Clyde had led the way. In doing so it had raised problems of speed and economy which could only be answered by a departure from the traditional type of marine steam engine.

The most serious loss of power and efficiency in the marine steam engine came in transmitting the up-and-down reciprocating motion of the cylinders to the rotary motion of the screws. The solution was clearly to devise an engine capable of transmitting rotary motion direct to the propeller, and this stage was reached with the development of the steam turbine. In this machine the expanding steam imparted a rotary motion by impacting on a series of angled blades or vanes arranged in the form of circular fans or wheels. In the 1890s Parsons in Britain and Carter in America were working on similar devices; Parsons' was the first to be adopted. His steam turbine was demonstrated at the Naval Review at Spithead in 1897 when his launch, the *Turbinia*, zig-zagged at 34½ knots between the dreadnoughts. It was installed in a few torpedo-boat-destroyers in the next few years, but its commercial application was innovated on the Clyde, where in 1901 Denny installed a direct action turbine in the *King Edward*, a Clyde steamer.

This was built on licence from Parsons, and marks the beginning of the transition in Clydeside marine engineering from a reliance on internal, to dependence on external technology. The turbine offered the only available solution to the need for greater power to drive the larger vessels. Once more the Clyde led the way in pioneering the new marine engine. In its first form the turbine transmitted power directly to the propeller, but since the turbine was capable of higher revolutions than the screw, it had to be worked well below its maximum efficiency to adapt itself to the speed of the revolving propeller. The answer was to introduce gearing, to effect a reduction in speed between the turbine and the propeller shaft. Parsons first applied such a device commercially to a cargo ship in 1910, and in 1912 Fairfields designed and built the Clyde's first two ships with geared turbine machinery. The full benefits of turbines and gearing had not yet been achieved, but once again Clyde shipyards were leading the way, and in 1911, almost half the entire horse-power installed in the Clyde was supplied by steam turbines.

The other significant departure from the traditional marine steam engine was the oil-driven diesel engine, patented by the German, Rudolph Diesel, in 1892. Its advantages lay in the lower cost of oil over coal, and in the ability to deliver very small powers from compact engines. This again was a development conceived outside Clydeside. It could scarcely be otherwise, for the Clyde was the home of marine steam technology. The first seagoing diesel-driven ships were built in Italy and Holland in 1910, and Barclay Curle & Co. powered the *Jutland* with diesels built on licence in 1912. In the same year, the *Glasgow Herald Supplement* reported that the single-screw cargo steamer, driven by the reciprocating engine, still held the lead in world tonnage. The Clyde was pioneering an alternative, the steam turbine. The other choice was the diesel, whose full development lay, like that of the turbine, in the future. The turbine was the Clyde's solution for large vessels and high speeds; the diesel was already best for small vessels. It remained to determine what balance was best for vessels of intermediate size and purpose. The end of the era of reciprocating marine steam engines, the foundation of Clydeside success, was in sight. However, in 1913, the local marine engineers were active in improving the turbine, and in increasing the economy of their vessels. In a sense the link between local invention and innovation was being severed. The lead in invention appeared to be passing beyond the bounds of Clydeside but, as yet, vigorous innovation of outside technical development kept the Clyde yards in the forefront of world shipbuilding.

During these years shipbuilding on the Clyde was carried out by a large number of fairly small but highly competitive firms. There were forty-three firms in 1870, and thirty-eight in 1913. Towards the end of the period some yards were taking steps to minimise competition. As we have seen, Beardmore sought a sure outlet for large castings, plates, bars and sections by buying up the Napier yard and then establishing a new yard at Dalmuir. John Brown of Sheffield did the same by buying up J. & G. Thomson's yard at Clydebank in 1899. Then in 1905 Cammel Laird & Co. of Birkenhead purchased half the ordinary shares in the Fairfield Shipbuilding and Engineering Co. at Govan, while Fairfields took an interest in the Coventry Ordnance Works, jointly owned by Cammels and John Brown & Co. A community of interests was growing among steelmakers and shipbuilders, and this was to be a link more strongly developed at a later date.

In spite of trends of deterioration in leadership in marine engineering, and moves towards combination among firms, the Clyde shipyards led the growth of the regional economy between 1870 and 1913. The demands of the shipyards boosted the growth of steel and dictated the changing production patterns of the pig-iron and malleable-iron producers. Marine engineering and shipbuilding lay at the centre of a complex concentration of heavy engineering and finishing trades. In the years before the First World War the regional economy prospered when the shipyards were busy, and faltered when the flow of ships slackened.

8

Dislocation

Dimensions of distress

The war effort with its ceaseless demand for output strained the regional economy and its labour force. But the peace that followed almost drove it to breaking-point through failure of demand and lack of work. Between the wars the unimaginable happened: the region which had enjoyed expanding production for a century found its great industries going into decline. Coal, iron, and ships never again equalled their 1913 output. Between 1913 and 1937 the region's coal output contracted by 40 per cent. Pig-iron, the spur to growth for half a century, suffered a two-thirds reduction, and ships launched declined almost by half (Table 21). Alone of the staple industries, steel increased its output from 1·4 million to 1·8 million tons. But in steel the peak year was 1920 with over 2 million tons produced, and this was not surpassed during the next twenty years.

The pattern of contraction reveals that coal and iron were in difficulty mainly through a process of longer-run decline, while the distress in shipbuilding and steel arose largely from cyclical slumps. Sectoral decline became marked for coal and iron during the war when the output of both was curtailed by one-quarter and one-third respectively. Then in the 1920s coalmining proved surprisingly stable, output declining by only 10 per cent, while pig-iron diminished by a further third. In the cyclically-affected industries, steel was cut back by one-quarter from its inflated 1920 output, while ship tonnage launched decreased by just over 10 per cent. Cyclical influences were in fact relatively weak in the 1920s, biting severely only in the down-turn of 1921–2.

TABLE 21   *Output of coal, iron, steel and ships, 1911–37 (annual average production)*

Period	West Scotland coal (million tons)	Scotland pig-iron (million tons)	Scotland steel (million tons)	Clyde launchings (000 tons)
1911–13	22·7	1·32	1·3	676·0
1918–20	17·1*	0·97	1·8	617·2
1927–29	16·8	0·61	1·5	544·3
1935–37	14·0	0·45	1·6	293·3

* 1919 only
Sources: Glasgow Herald, Annual Trade Review; Mineral Statistics of the United Kingdom and Ireland

In contrast, the 1930s were dominated by cyclical depression. Coal production contracted by 28 per cent from 1929 to 1932, and recovered weakly to 1937 before resuming its progressive decline. In iron and steel, the reduction was much sharper, with three bad years from 1931 to 1933, while the deepest effects of the cyclical down-turn were felt in shipbuilding where launchings were at a low level for five long years. At the bottom of the slump in 1933 tonnage launched was less than 10 per cent of the 1929 output. In general terms, it can be said that the problems of coal and iron arose from a sectoral decline in which their structural difficulties were exacerbated by the influence of cyclical depression, while both steel and shipbuilding suffered more from cyclical down-turns, the effects being deepened by certain structural weaknesses within the industries. The result was prolonged and extensive unemployment in all the major trades in the region.

The foretaste of disaster came with the coal strike of 1921 and the severe deflationary measures operating through 1922. By then one-third of the workforce in shipbuilding, one-quarter of the men in engineering, iron and steel, and one-fifth of the miners were out of work. Throughout the 1920s there was never less than 14 per cent of the region's insured workforce unemployed, and the worst was still to come. In the 1930s cyclical depression threw great numbers out of work, and heaped these on top of the already large numbers unemployed through sectoral decline. Between 1929 and 1932 the proportion of insured workers registered as unemployed increased from 12 to 25 per cent in Ayrshire, and from 10 to 50 per cent in Dunbartonshire; in Lanarkshire unemployment doubled from 14 to 33 per cent of the workforce, and a similar proportion was out of work in Renfrewshire. Throughout the 1930s unemployment in Scotland averaged 20 per cent: in the west, over a quarter of the workforce, some 190,000 persons, were out of work.

The dimensions of distress are staggering. The major industries were truncated; coal and shipbuilding barely operated at half the pre-war level in the late 1930s, and pig-iron was reduced by two-thirds: steel at best was in a stagnant condition, and unemployment averaged over 20 per cent of insured labour throughout two decades. Such a reversal of the region's fortunes must be explained.

The downward spiral

In the 1920s events were powerfully influenced by three widely-held beliefs. It was thought that most industries suffered from excess capacity generated by the exigencies of war; that wartime inflation had weakened the competitive position of British goods by increasing their price; and that the road back to economic health lay in a recovery of world demand and a growth of world trade. These premises fostered the conviction that if prices could be reduced this would stimulate demand for British goods in world markets, and that a resurgence of world trade would employ the enlarged productive capacity of British industry.

Government policy was therefore designed to act on prices. The measures were carried out in two stages. In the first instance in 1921 and 1922, the government placed sharp restrictions on credit, pursued economies in public expenditure, and brought powerful deflationary pressures to bear on the economy; as a consequence, prices declined by half between June 1920 and February 1922, and money wages were reduced by 40 per cent. This was a preliminary step designed to bring British prices back into line with American levels, and to make it possible in the second stage for Britain to re-establish the pound at its 1914 gold value, and make it once more convertible to gold. The return to the gold standard was believed to be a prerequisite for stabilising the world's monetary arrangements, for promoting the rapid expansion of world trade, and for rehabilitating sterling as the leading world currency.

The acceptance of such policies, and the hope which Scottish manufacturers entertained for their success, rested on two further assumptions. It was firmly believed that the regional economy of the west of Scotland was an export economy, and that the problem of its industries was one of cyclical contraction of demand capable of being overcome by measures designed to regenerate world trade.

The belief that the key to the revival of the staple industries lay in a recovery of world trade permeated the British mind in the 1920s. However, the volume of world trade grew only very slowly in this period, and in spite of measures taken by the government, the region's exports stagnated. The average tonnage of goods handled by Clyde ports was 7·3 million between 1918 and 1920 and 7·1 million between 1923 and 1929. Since the policies were believed to be correct, this unhappy

G*

situation was rationalised by reference to two impediments. The first was the increase in protection of foreign markets, and the second the persistence of uncompetitive prices for Scottish and British goods in world markets. On the first of these, the *Glasgow Herald Annual Trade Review* pointed out as early as 1921 that, 'As a result of the war, walls of adverse circumstances have been raised round every country which are invulnerable to the old commercial weapons . . .'. The raising of tariffs certainly progressed rapidly in the 1920s as many states sought to protect emergent industries and to limit imports to stabilise their balance of payments. The tendency for the international economy to break up into small national trading preserves undoubtedly made it more difficult for British and Scottish industry to sell their products overseas. Even more serious, however, was the price situation since the demand for British exports proved to be relatively price-inelastic in the inter-war years. In spite of the drastic deflation of the early 1920s, and the moderate deflation that was persistently applied for most of the period, Scottish and British prices were not pulled down below American and German levels. This, together with the modest overvaluation of the pound when the gold standard was re-adopted in 1925, clearly contributed to sales resistance to British goods in world markets.

When the international economy disintegrated in the world depression of 1929–32 the solution through a renewal of world trade no longer appeared feasible. Thus, while the 1920s had been imbued with hope placed in external factors, the 1930s saw governments despair of international solutions, and seek remedies in cultivating the home market behind protective tariffs and in reducing the scale of industry to suit the new demands. The emphasis was no longer on schemes to bring surplus capacity into use, but on proposals to eliminate redundant plant. Scottish problems in the 1930s were therefore to be seen as a result of the collapse of foreign demand.

Such an explanation is persuasive, relating the stagnation of the 1920s to weak cyclical expansion of world demand, while the 1930s depression is to be explained by the structural failure of world markets. However, such an emphasis on exports fails to distinguish clearly between the ebb and flow of demand, that is, cyclical problems, and the more deep-seated structural weaknesses which affected every major Scottish industry. The export stagnation and collapse thesis is of least direct application to coal and iron in the west of Scotland, and of most significance in explaining the developments in shipbuilding, steel, engineering and textiles.

The export industries all suffered between the wars, but shipbuilding demonstrates most clearly the connection between failure of world demand and stagnation of regional production. The core of the problem lay in the sheer size and productive capacity of world shipbuilding. At the end of the war demands for new tonnage, port congestion and slow turn-round times created the appearance of a great shortage of mercantile tonnage to carry the world's goods. In two short years, 1919 to 1921, world mercantile tonnage swelled from 51 million to 62 million tons, an increase of over 20 per cent. By 1923, the momentum of orders placed had carried it up to 65 million tons, an increase of 28 per cent over 1919. The world was glutted with ships, and for the remainder of the years between the wars, potential demand for new tonnage hardly grew at all. A minor upsurge between 1927 and 1931 added 5 million tons, but this was cut away by contraction in tonnage to 64·8 million tons in 1935, though this had been completely replaced by 1939.

This pattern was followed by the British mercantile marine. Tonnage increased from 16·5 million to 19·5 million between 1919 and 1921, then stagnated at a little below this level till 1928. Between 1928 and 1930 it grew to 20·4 million before contracting to 17·3 million in 1936. Additions to British-owned tonnage were proportionately less than that to world tonnage, with the result that while Britain owned 39 per cent of world tonnage in 1914, she held only 26 per cent in 1938. Thus, within a dismal world picture of mercantile tonnage launched, British additions were less buoyant than foreign construction. In spite of this, the Clyde rode the storm extremely well, building about one-third of the total tonnage launched in Britain. The main weakness was a failure to hold on to the lion's share of world tonnage built. The Clyde launched about 20 per cent of world tonnage before the war, but this had declined to 14 per cent by 1934–8. Both features can largely be explained in terms of the overall strength, direction and type of demand, and the competitiveness of foreign shipyards.

Demand for ships has already been reviewed, being generally stagnant following the early post-war boom in construction. After the initial expansion, British yards retained over half the world tonnage under construction from 1927 through to 1930, and the Clyde produced nearly 20 per cent on its own. This resilience was linked to the direction of demand. Before the war, British and Clyde construction was ordered generally in the proportion of two-thirds by British owners and one-third by foreign buyers. In the 1920s, British orders were maintained better than foreign contracts, and fed a steady high share of new tonnage to British and Clyde yards. Moreover, the type of demand also favoured the Clyde. The worst effects of excess tonnage were felt in a decline of tramp cargo freights, but passenger-liner and cargo-liner tonnage was in steady demand. Since the Clyde specialised in these types of construction, Clyde launchings remained generally above 500,000 tons per year, except in 1921 and 1922 following upon the severe coal strike, and in 1926 and 1927 as a consequence of the General Strike and prolonged coal stoppage.

In the 1930s, however, the strength and direction of demand moved irresistibly against Scottish and British interests. The average world tonnage launched was 1·8 million tons per year in the 1930s, a million tons less than the average of the 1920s. The pure cargo steamer was the type of ship least in demand, and in the shortfall of a million tons per year, British yards lost their grip on world production, their share declining from 45 per cent in the 1920s to 36 per cent of world tonnage launched in the 1930s. Within this decline, the Clyde retained its position precisely, contributing 36 per cent of British output, but launchings then averaged only 245,000 tons per year as against 465,000 in the 1920s. Both the British and Clyde shipbuilding industries were barely running at half the level of the 1920s, and in the worst period the Clyde launched 62,000 and 49,000 tons in 1932 and 1933 respectively, a mere 9 and 7 per cent of the 1913 tonnage. In the recovery that followed, the Clyde was helped by passenger-liner orders, notably the completion of the *Queen Mary* which had lain idle at Clydebank from 1931 to 1934, and the sister ship, *Queen Elizabeth*, ordered in 1936. However, the wide range of Clyde capacity was also important, and passenger/cargo vessels and tankers were among the most significant orders from 1934 to 1939, pulling the river out of the depths of depression. As far as can be judged, few foreign orders came to the Clyde, and most of the recovery was based on the slender home orders: indeed in 1938, tonnage placed abroad by British shipowners exceeded for the first time that built in Britain on foreign account.

The drying up of foreign orders, and the placing by home owners of orders with foreign yards links the changes in strength, direction, and type of demand, to competitiveness. Between 1934 and 1938, the average price per ton of merchant ships built in British yards increased steeply from £23·41 to £34·24. This was partly due to a coincidence of commercial recovery and re-armament pressures forcing up prices of steel plates from under £9 to over £11 per ton. This placed great strain on the competitiveness of British yards in comparison with foreign builders, where direct subsidies in building together with lower costs due to more efficient production kept prices down. Moreover, exchange controls forced many British owners to place orders abroad, since that was the only way of recovering credits earned in the course of trade. Consequently, both foreign and British orders went to foreign rivals. Germany was by no means the most dangerous of these. Holland, Sweden, Denmark and Japan all built for Britain. Consequently all of these countries greatly increased their share of mercantile tonnage launched, partly at Britain's expense.

In the absence of similar subsidies British shipbuilders were forced to attempt to relieve themselves of the burden of unused capacity. It had been the hope in the 1920s that the normal economic regulator of depression would edge out the small, the uneconomic and the inefficient firms. However, the extraordinary tenacity of small- and medium-sized family firms kept the surplus capacity in existence, awaiting a more ruthless form of weeding-out. This came in 1930 in the form of National Shipbuilders Security Ltd, an organisation supported by most shipbuilders and a consortium of bankers. The aim was to raise funds by charging a 1 per cent levy on sales, the capital to be used to purchase redundant and obsolete shipyards and close them down. On the Clyde, the immediate consequence was the purchase of the assets of Beardmore's Dalmuir shipyard. By 1933, seven Clyde yards were closed, two were in mothballs, and another three worked under restricted quotas. In all, capacity had been cut by about 19 per cent. Since the aim of the project was to weed out surplus capacity and enable the industry to reduce its costs, the success of the venture is debatable; the saving in costs was reckoned to be less than 5 per cent, and this was more than taken up in the rapid price rises from 1934 to 1938.

The other scheme which aimed at rationalising the industry and encouraging economic and efficient production was the government-sponsored 'scrap and build' plan, contained in Part II of the 1935 British Shipping (Assistance) Act. The objective was mainly to aid the builders of cargo steamers by encouraging owners to scrap old tonnage and replace it with new orders. The Treasury offered favourable loans in return for an undertaking to scrap 2 tons of existing tonnage for every 1 ton of new construction placed on order. The Act operated for two years, and only contributed 4 per cent of tonnage built in these years; hardly a major contribution to the health of the industry.

By 1938 the industry on Clydeside had slimmed down marginally in its capacity. Its launchings were dominated by five or six firms who regularly built over half the tonnage. Though retaining its position within Britain the Clyde was no longer the dominant force in world shipbuilding it had been before the war. The explanation so far has been given in terms of changed demand conditions. To what extent was the Clyde's reduced position also due to technical backwardness?

The Clyde's supremacy before 1914 rested substantially on the pioneer work in construction, both in design and materials, and in the innovations in marine steam engines. As far as design is concerned there is little evidence that the Clyde fell behind in the years between the wars. The Clyde in common with other British yards adopted tank testing for all types of ships, and the emphasis was on economy of operation. Hull and superstructure forms were streamlined, steering gears were refined, and electric-arc welding was introduced in vessels up to 250 feet long, and for bulkheads, and generally in tankers to produce water-tight seams.

In propulsion the Clyde still led in refinements of the triple-expansion steam engine for general cargo purposes, and in the steam turbines for the great passenger liners. The development of the motor vessel was also pursued, though perhaps not so rapidly as in some foreign yards. In 1921, motor ships represented only 10 per cent of Clyde tonnage; by 1927, 30 per cent of merchant tonnage was motor powered. In the recovery from 1934 to 1938, over 41 per cent of total mercantile tonnage was represented by motor vessels. This compares with a figure of 54 per cent for the rest of the world. However, if the Clyde figures are confined to cargo vessels, since passenger liners operated best on geared turbines, then the Clyde was not at any noticeable disadvantage in innovating and using the diesel engine. It has sometimes been argued that the Clyde was losing its world lead through loss of leadership in marine-engine design. There is little to support this view in the inter-war period, and two diesel engines of Scottish design, the *Glennifer* and *Kelvin* engines, were among the most successful in operation, though mainly for smaller vessels.

In the final analysis the contraction of shipbuilding on the Clyde was not due in any significant measure to poor price competitiveness, inferior technology or inefficient working, though shipyard design was old fashioned. Even positive leadership in price, technology and efficiency would not have preserved the industry in its pre-war position with its pre-war capacity. The overriding influences were depressed world demand arising out of excess tonnage in existence by 1923, and foreign competitors using protective subsidies and credit measures to capture new tonnage at any price. In such circumstances the failure of demand could not be corrected by measures taken by independent producers. The inter-war problems of the shipbuilding industry on the Clyde were largely outside the control of the shipbuilder or the shipworkers.

Since shipbuilding lay at the heart of the region's industries its faltering performance could not help but be transmitted to the metal and engineering industries. The weakness of shipyard demand produced locally slack markets, but even within this context, the metal industries wrestled with a range of problems which in themselves held down production.

The Scottish steelmakers found themselves under pressure from three directions: excess capacity, flagging demand, and high costs of production. Since the industry had greatly extended its capacity during the war many companies found that in conditions of sagging demand their works were operating at too low a load factor, and hence had to carry relatively higher overhead charges per ton of steel produced. Excess capacity was clearly made worse by lack of demand, and in concert, both exacerbated the cost problem which in itself was linked to resources, technology, and the organisation of the industry.

The resource problem was fundamental to the cost position of the industry, for fuel and raw materials represented the largest portion of the finished cost of steel at the works. Here, the steelmasters were faced with almost insuperable problems. The making of steel could not use the raw splint coal of the district, itself in decreasing supply, but had to rely on hard metallurgical coke. Less than half the industry's needs for this were produced locally, and large quantities had regularly to be imported from the north of England. Similarly, Scotland was not self-sufficient in its supplies of pig-iron for the steel industry. The local producers could only supply half the industry's needs, at very high costs, and the remainder had to be imported.

To these cost problems must be added the organisational weakness of the metallurgical industries. Few steelworks had blast furnaces near them. There were no integrated steel works and, hence, neither hot waste gases from the blast furnaces, nor hot metal charged direct to the steel furnace could be employed. When these factors are linked to relatively small works, small steel furnaces, on average some 60 tons per charge, and inefficient layout of plant, it is not surprising that in the 1920s, at the peak of the post-war boom, English and Welsh steel plates and angles could undercut Scottish products by between £3 and £4 per ton.

The Scottish steelmakers reacted in two ways. They took action against costs, and they set about slimming the capacity of the industry by rationalisation.

The high costs partly reflected the fact that the Scottish steel industry had grown up on the production of high-quality acid steel made by the open-hearth furnace. As such, it rested on high-quality haematite pig-iron produced from imported Spanish and north African ores smelted by high-cost pig-iron manufacturers. During the war the shortages of iron ore had enforced a move into some basic steel production, using cheaper phosphorus iron ores mined in England. In the 1920s the Scottish steelmakers attempted to reduce their raw material costs by shifting sharply towards basic steel production. In 1913 basic steel represented only 10 per cent of output. In 1920, 38 per cent of ingots were basic steel, and by 1930, 62 per cent of all open-hearth steel was made from basic pig-iron. The adoption of basic steel permitted greater flexibility in sources of supply of iron ore, hence a greater latitude to adjust supplies to variations in market price. Other directions in which raw material costs were capable of adjustment were in the replacement of high-cost Scottish pig-iron by imports, and also in the more intensive use of scrap steel. By 1935, 51 tons of scrap were used for every 100 tons of steel produced, a much higher input than in any other steel-making district.

The manufacturers also attacked the unused capacity by rationalisation. The concentration of control had begun in earnest in the war years, and by 1933 four companies controlled all Scottish steelmaking capacity. These were the Scottish Iron and Steel Co. at Coatbridge, the Lanark-shire Steel Co. at Motherwell, the Steel Company of Scotland with works at Blochairn and Newton, and the largest, Colvilles Ltd, formed as a public company in 1930 to take over the private companies of David

Colville and James Dunlop & Co. Colvilles operated works at Mother-well, Cambuslang, Tollcross and Glengarnock.

Between 1933 and 1937 consolidation progressed steadily, partly aided by the 33⅓ per cent tariff, which from 1932 stemmed the flood of cheap foreign steel into the British market. In 1934, Stewart & Lloyds succumbed to the attraction of setting up a new steel and tube works at Corby, on the iron-ore fields of Lincolnshire, and Colvilles acquired their Scottish steel-plate business. In the same year Colvilles took over Beard-more's Mossend works, and by 1936, Colvilles controlled over 90 per cent of Scottish steel capacity; only the Scottish Iron and Steel Co. at Coatbridge remained outside Colville's control. The concentration of ownership was accompanied by a closure of old plants. The Calderbank works, formerly operated by James Dunlop & Co., were closed, as were the Mossend works and the Motherwell Iron and Steel Co. In addition, the Clydesdale works of Stewart & Lloyds were partially closed down. This vigorous rationalisation was accompanied by modernisation. In 1937 new steelmaking capacity was added at Glengarnock to bring the firm's capacity up to 2,500 tons per week, and at the Dalzell works, a new rod mill was brought into operation. Even more significant, in 1937 Colvilles embarked on plans to lay down modern blast-furnace and steel-furnace capacity at Clydebridge, to create the first integrated steel mill in Scotland.

Ambitious as both the cost-reducing policies and rationalisation pro-grammes were, the effects were not dramatic. The full advantages of cost reductions were frustrated by persistently high fuel costs, the situation made insoluble by reliance on heavy imports of coke from England on which high freight charges had to be paid. Even the plans in the 1937 extension of Clydebridge only aimed at producing 1,000 tons of coke per day, about half that work's requirements, and the other works were less favourably placed. Moreover, the inland sites meant double handling of ore from freighter to rail, and this also increased charges. There was no escape from this, for the persistent inability of Scottish pig-iron pro-ducers to supply more than half the pig-iron requirements committed the steelmen to a reliance on imports and on scrap. About half the pig-iron imports came from England, a quarter from India, and a quarter from other foreign suppliers. The Scottish steel industry had become the epitome of industrial inertia. It was no longer based on local raw materials, nor was it conveniently sited to make efficient use of imported supplies. Fixed capital investments and local markets were its only sure founda-tions in the district.

The efforts to reduce costs and the programme of rationalisation failed to overcome the problems of excess capacity, stagnant markets, and uncompetitiveness. Since costs and capacity proved stubborn of adjust-ment, only the control of markets remained for manipulation. Before the war the main outlet for Scottish steel had been in the Clyde's shipyards, and in the inter-war years there grew an astonishing interlinkage of ownership and control among the shipbuilders and steelmakers. In the 1920s Scottish steel firms fell into the hands of shipbuilders who apparently feared a shortage of steel when their industry appeared to be buoyant immediately after the war. David Colville & Sons were taken over by Harland & Wolff, the Glasgow Iron and Steel Co. by Beardmore, and the Steel Company of Scotland was acquired by a consortium of shipbuilders headed by Stephens of Linthouse. At the same time, the Lithgows gained control of James Dunlop & Co., while the Lanarkshire Steel Co. fell to the Northumberland Shipbuilding Co. The depression in shipbuilding brought a realignment from 1930. David Colville & Sons Ltd and James Dunlop & Co. came together to form Colvilles Ltd, while Harland and Lithgows and their associates were satisfied by an undertaking that Colvilles would supply all their shipbuilding steel as a first commitment for a period of years. Nevertheless, Lithgows then purchased the Steel Company of Scotland from the Stephens consortium, and when in 1934 Colvilles acquired control of both the Steel Company of Scotland and the Lanarkshire Steel Co., the main Scottish shipbuilders were intimately linked to the main Scottish steel producers.

The boards of the steel companies and the shipbuilders were shared by many men from both sides. Sir James Lithgow and Henry Lithgow were directors of Colvilles and of James Dunlop & Co., and Sir William Lithgow was chairman of Beardmore's. Sir James Lithgow was also a director of Fairfield Shipbuilding and Engineering Co., and Henry Lithgow, Sir Harold Yarrow and A. M. Stephen sat on the board of the Steel Company of Scotland. Conversely, a steelman like John Craig, chairman and managing director of Colvilles, also sat on the board of Harland & Wolff.

Such a community of interest between steel producers and shipbuilders could not have been without a strong influence on the development of the steel industry. Trapped as the industry was between stubborn costs and surplus capacity, captive markets provided some guarantee of continued existence, though such markets could not entirely override high costs and relative inefficiency. Such arrangements were sufficient to keep steel production relatively stable throughout the inter-war years, but the industry as a whole failed to grow. While British steel production rose from 9 million to 12 million tons between 1920 and 1937, an increase of 33 per cent, Scottish production was still below the 1920 figure. Even taking the entire period from 1913 to 1937, British output grew by 69 per cent, Scottish by only 32 per cent. Consequently, Scotland's contribution declined from 23 per cent of British output in 1920, to under 15 per cent in 1937.

In spite of the fact that the industry shed 5,000 workers, rationalised, moved into cheaper steel and doubled output per man between 1925 and 1936, its weaknesses continued to be serious. Unintegrated plant, small furnaces and heavy reliance on imported fuel and raw materials kept the industry in a weak competitive position. Even when demand was growing rapidly behind a strong protective tariff the industry could not supply all Scotland's needs at competitive prices, and from 1932 to 1937 imports of iron and steel goods ran at twice the level of exports. Like shipbuilding, the Scottish steel industry needed a long period of buoyant demand to build up the works to a high load factor, to enable the industry to bear heavy overhead charges. The demand was never strong enough; this committed the industry to long years of under-utilisation and high cost between the wars.

Whereas sagging demand lay at the root of the difficulties of steel and shipbuilding, the iron industry was plagued by more intractable problems. They arose from the structure of the industry itself. Local supplies of coal-measure iron ore had been the foundation of the industry, but the supply had weakened before 1913 and between the wars this bulwark crumbled away. Iron-ore production dwindled from almost 600,000 tons in 1913 to a mere 36,000 tons in 1936. Similarly, raw splint coal which had fuelled the pig-iron revolution was now in short supply, and increasing furnace size forced the ironmakers to come to rely on coke. By 1930 no Scottish blast-furnace was fuelled by splint coal.

The pig-iron industry was therefore faced with vanishing resources. Of ore and fuel, it was the fuel problem which proved more severe. Diminishing local ores were easily offset at a not prohibitive price by high-quality imports from Spain and north Africa, but the shortage of local coking coals could only be overcome by costly purchases and construction: by importing coke from the north of England, and by establishing modern coking ovens at the ironworks. The transfer of coke by rail was expensive, and the building of coke ovens was only economic if the large quantities of gas produced could be sold. At this point the unintegrated iron and steel sectors, a heritage from the past, presented grave difficulties. The separation of steelworks from blast-furnace made the economic use of the gas impractical for the steelmen. Private purchasers like the Corporation of Glasgow could not arrive at agreed terms with either Baird or Dixon, two of the largest producers of coke gas, and so the modernisation of iron production was hampered, since ironmasters were unwilling to invest in coke-producing capacity without a market for the gas produced. Costs of production therefore remained high; they were boosted further by the decline of the by-product distillation of tar and ammonia from the blast-furnace gases. Post-war developments in the manufacture of synthetic ammonium sulphate undercut the product of the ironworks and forced the closure of many plants.

Nor was the position eased by the persistent technological weaknesses of the industry. The use of splint coal in the furnace had kept the Scottish unit small, and even in the 1930s when coke was universally employed, and when the ironmasters claimed they had carried out considerable improvements, Scottish furnaces only increased their output from 300 to 600 tons per week. That was only half the average for Britain as a whole. Furnaces therefore remained small, and at a disadvantage in costs of production. Moreover, the layout of the works was notoriously old-fashioned. The first mechanically-charged blast-furnace in Scotland did not come into operation till 1938 as part of Colvilles' extension of the Clydebridge steelworks.

Not only were resources and technology factors in high-cost production, but the iron industry appeared to ignore opportunities for co-operation with steelmakers by persisting in making the type of pig-iron developed between 1870 and 1913. When ore imports had begun in earnest in the 1870s, both the pig-iron and steel industries developed on the basis of acid or haematite ores and pig-iron. But when the steel industry switched to basic pig-iron and basic steel between the wars, the ironmakers remained faithful to haematite pig-iron. While in 1937 three-quarters of Scottish steel was basic steel, less than a quarter of pig-iron production was basic, a mere 117,000 tons as against 198,000 tons haematite and 182,000 tons for foundry and forge. The Scottish iron industry thus signally failed to meet the needs of the steel industry in pig-iron, either in volume or in type.

In the iron industry, in strong contrast to steel and ships, failure of demand was not a significant element. Dwindling resources replaced by higher-cost imports, a relatively backward technology and old-fashioned plant layout, unintegrated production from iron to steel; these were the crippling structural weaknesses. They, together with a narrow product range, rendered the Scottish iron industry incapable of supporting the growth of steel. The production of pig-iron collapsed under an influx of cheaper English, Welsh and foreign pig-iron. Output slumped dramatically from an average of 1 million tons per year during the war to 493,000 tons between 1925 and 1929, and 400,000 tons for the period 1933–7. By then only five pig-iron producers remained, and only sixteen furnaces were in blast.

With the demise of iron a link was broken in the chain of industrial interdependence that had characterised the regional economy. Structural decay had overtaken the cotton-based economy in the mid-nineteenth century; it was now apparent in the heavy-industry complex. The next element to feel the strain was coalmining.

In the first few years of peace there appeared to be solid grounds for the belief that the coal industry would resume its pre-1914 upward climb. A series of short-run factors kept coal in scarce supply and created the appearance of buoyant demand. The three-month strike in Britain in

1921 was followed by a similar stoppage in America in 1922, and European coal supplies were also curtailed in 1923 when the French occupied the Ruhr in response to the German failure to meet reparation payments. This apparent sellers' market for coal stored up problems for the Scottish industry in three main directions: in expectations for continued growth, in an enlarged labour force, and in a damaging wage settlement after the 1921 strike. The latter embodied a flat rate for each district linked to a division of profits between men and owners, the flat rate plus profit share to be not less than an agreed minimum wage, which had to be met come what may. The belief in growth drew men back into the industry, and by 1923, with 79,000 men, the region's coal industry was back to 1913 employment levels and within 2 million tons of that year's peak production, with an output of over 20 million tons.

But expansion was an illusion. Demand, far from increasing, had been affected by a basic structural change. For the first time in the history of coalmining, aggregate demand ceased to grow, held in check by many economies in the use of coal, especially by iron- and steel-producers. Moreover, the market for coal was seriously affected by the growing substitution of gas, electricity and oil in the home and in industry. By 1925 the effects of the short-run scarcities had worked themselves out, and the demand for coal moved downward.

It was not immediately apparent how fundamental these changes in demand were; coal producers everywhere assumed they would be short-lived. This belief threw the efforts of the coalmasters into an attempt to reduce costs, on the assumption that lower prices would regenerate demand and carry the industry forward. This immediately brought them into conflict with the workers over the minimum wage clause in the 1921 Agreement. The clause appeared to be workable in conditions of increasing demand, but when this slackened and prices began to tumble, the owners found themselves between shrinking prices and a minimum wage rate; this double adversity ate heavily into the declining net proceeds of the industry. Between 1924 and 1925 selling prices did not cover costs of production per ton of disposable coal. The industry was only saved from a serious strike against wage reductions by a government subvention in support of wages, this to run from 1 May 1925 to 1 May 1926. The owners firmly believed that the problems of the industry could only be overcome by reducing wages and increasing the hours of work from seven to eight per day. The failure to reach a settlement culminated in the General Strike of 1926, with the miners staying out for seven months.

The miners were ultimately forced to return to work on the owners' terms. Even so, the owners miscalculated the extent of their problem. The share of each £100 of net proceeds going to wages was reduced from £87. 8s. 9·6d. to £87, and more significantly the minimum wage was reduced from 9s. 4d. to 8s. 4·8d. per day with an extra hour's work added.

However, the continued downward pressure on prices soon forced the share of net proceeds going to wages above that intended in the 1926 settlement. The minimum wage clause again squeezed the owners as prices declined, and the industry only made a profit of 3·25*d*. per ton of disposable coal in one year, 1929, in the entire period from 1927 to 1933.

The attempt to regenerate demand by reducing prices was spectacularly unsuccessful. By 1930 the belief that demand would recover to pre-war levels was finally dead. Owners at last recognised that there was a world surplus of coal, and that the industry would have to learn to work within a framework of reduced demand. The attack on costs through wage reductions had run its bitter course, and had been accompanied by a dramatic decline in the workforce and a closure of pits.

Under the influence of the 1930 Coal Act the emphasis switched to rationalisation, an attempt to reduce the overextended and uneconomic capacity of the industry. Part I of the Coal Mines Act set up seventeen districts, of which Scotland was one, to control production by the allocation of quotas to individual collieries, while Part II set up the Coal Mines Reorganisation Commission to encourage amalgamations. The Act also reduced hours from 8 to 7½ per day and attempted to reinstate national rather than district wage negotiations. This was frustrated by opposition from the owners.

Nevertheless the relentless pressure on prices, profits and wages acted to reduce the scale of the industry from its post-war scale. In the west of Scotland employment fell by 34,000 men between 1924 and 1937, while production slumped from 18·9 million to 14·5 million tons. In shedding such a large number of men and in closing down ninety less-productive mines the region's coal industry had dramatically increased the productivity of its labour from 245 to 334 tons per man per year. This large increase was supported by a heavy investment in mechanical mining, especially in Lanarkshire where, in 1937, 83 per cent of coal mined was machine-cut compared with a Scottish average of 79 per cent and a British figure of 54 per cent. This extensive use of machinery was reflected in the fact that average employment per mine decreased from 233 in 1924 to 180 men in 1937 in the west of Scotland.

Rationalisation had been pushed far and fast, and in spite of the small average size of the mines, ownership became increasingly concentrated. By 1933, one firm, Bairds, controlled 70 per cent of the output in Ayr-shire, while in Lanarkshire over a third of employment and output was controlled by four firms, Bairds, Nimmo, Coltness Iron Co., and Shotts Iron Co. The extent of mechanisation, the effective use of labour and the reduction in wage rates, gained for Scotland the second lowest regional costs of production in Britain. Only Northumberland had regularly lower costs of production than the Scottish district between the wars. The reward should have been regular and adequate profits. But this was frustrated by the fact that the west of Scotland coal producers consistently received less for the sale of their coal than was obtained elsewhere in Britain. Consequently, the margin of profit remained slim.

On the supply side, the industry was bedevilled by progressive exhaustion of the best and most economic coal seams. In Lanarkshire, output was reduced from 17·5 million tons in 1913 to 8·7 million in 1938, and the west of Scotland then produced only 44 per cent of Scotland's coal as against 52 per cent in 1913. The profitability of the industry was affected in particular by the absence of certain grades of coal from the range of types produced in the region. Prices for anthracite, coking coal and good-quality navigation coal all remained higher than those for steam and general industrial coal. But it was precisely in the most commercial grades that Lanarkshire and Ayrshire had least to offer. Their coals were predominantly steam, household and general industrial in quality, and this enforced lower profits on the industry through lower selling prices.

Structural weaknesses also hampered the industry on the demand side. The export of coal was never very important from the western coalfields, and shipments from the Clyde declined only slowly from 2·75 million tons in 1924 to 1·67 million tons in 1937, though more may have been lost through diminished shipments from eastward ports. The loss of a million tons in exports was relatively small in comparison to the 4·5 million tons lost in production in the same period. Ironmaking had been a major outlet for local coal, but the demise of iron severely curtailed demand. Steel, ships and engineering were major consumers, but since they languished through a failure of export demand, the coal industry shared their fate.

No rationalisation programme could overcome the structural problem of declining resources, and no pruning of labour and reduction in prices could entirely override the disadvantage of only being able to produce coals which earned the lowest prices. The labour force undoubtedly bore the brunt of the need to adjust the scale of output to new levels and types of demand. Indeed, in every industry attempts to adjust to declining markets concentrated on preserving prices and profits rather than jobs. The consequence was that the region was plunged into severe and persistent unemployment for two decades.

The unemployment which debilitated the region was both structural, flowing from a decline of particular industries, and cyclical, stemming from curtailed activity of industries dependent upon stagnant markets at home and overseas. Lanarkshire, particularly north Lanarkshire, was most affected by structural unemployment in the declining coal and iron industries, though cyclical influences increased the proportion of the labour force out of work between 1931 and 1935 to one-third. Indeed, only Wales had a persistently higher level of unemployment than Lanarkshire in the 1930s. In contrast, Renfrewshire and Dunbartonshire were more heavily depressed by the cyclical collapse of markets for the products of their shipyards and marine engineering works. In 1932 half of Dunbartonshire's workforce was out of work, as was one-third of Renfrewshire's. The severe structural and cyclical influences kept unemployment rates in the west of Scotland at roughly three times the level prevailing in London and south-east England between 1929 and 1937, and about double the rates in the Midlands and south-west England.

Unemployment was regionally concentrated on the coalfield industrial areas, and was clearly most severe among the staple industries. In the west of Scotland unemployment in coalmining was 32 per cent in 1932, and still over 20 per cent in 1937. In shipbuilding it was over 75 per cent in 1932, and more than 30 per cent in 1937; in engineering, iron and steel, over 43 per cent of the workforce was out of work in 1932. In addition to regional and industrial concentration, unemployment was understandably heavy in the large towns. In 1932, Clydebank registered over 12,500 unemployed, about 30 per cent of the county workforce; Greenock had another 12,000 out of work, Motherwell 10,800, Paisley 8,390. The lowest ebb of employment came in January 1933 when 407,284 persons were out of work in Scotland, 30·3 per cent of the insured workforce. Over half were located in the west of Scotland, and Glasgow alone registered 136,331 persons out of work. The extent of deprivation is underwritten by the applications for poor relief, over and above the payments made under national insurance. In Glasgow, in January 1933, 114,113 persons were on poor relief. Even this gives an imperfect idea of the distress in the large industrial towns, for whole districts, dependent upon a single trade, could be thrown entirely out of work. In 1932, Govan and its shipyards were virtually silent and totally without work. In Springburn on the northern rim of the city the same was true around the great locomotive sheds.

Although unemployment affected so many people and so many trades, it was disproportionately severe among the young leaving school, and the old working towards retirement. It affected women at only half the level of males. Throughout the 1920s and 1930s, about 30 per cent of the unemployed were under 30 years of age, and another 20 per cent were over 55 years. It was also precisely in these groups that the period of unemployment was most prolonged. As late as 1938 almost 30 per cent of the unemployed males in the west of Scotland had been out of work for more than a year, and over 10 per cent had been without employment of any kind in excess of three years.

This persistent and severe unemployment existed side by side with an increasing workforce in Britain. The insured labour force grew from 10·8 million to 13·5 million between 1923 and 1937. This was an increase of more than 22 per cent, against which Scotland grew barely half as fast at 12 per cent, and the region slower still, at 4 per cent. The insured workforce in the west of Scotland grew only from 701,000 to 764,000, and the small net increase balanced sharp falls in mining, which shed 34,000 men, shipbuilding 9,000, and iron and steel with 5,000 men. In fact the four counties, excluding Glasgow, only increased their insured workforce by 10,000, while Glasgow alone added another 53,000. In both Glasgow and the counties, most of the new jobs were found in the service and distributive trades, building and contracting and local authority employment. There was consequently a small decline in the dominance of coal, metals and engineering in the region's employment, but the shift was scarcely significant and the industrial structure of the region remained largely unchanged.

Such a prolonged period of depression not only debilitated the staple industries; it cut off new developments, and made the problem of regeneration even more severe. Among the threads of new enterprise that grew into lines of great importance in the British economy between the wars were motor vehicles, aircraft, and the electrically-based industries of engineering apparatus, cables, wires and lamps. Of these three, automobiles and aircraft appeared to have been well established in the region during the First World War. The motor industry indeed seemed set for a large expansion in the west of Scotland. Wm Beardmore & Co. had moved to motor manufacture in a big way and produced private cars, taxis, buses and commercial vehicles at factories in Paisley and Coatbridge as well as at their main works at Parkhead. It was even hoped that Beardmore would also take over the old Argyll factory in the Vale of Leven. But instead, by 1921, car production had ceased at Coatbridge, to be concentrated at Anniesland while taxis were still made in Paisley and other vehicles at Parkhead. The private car production was the least important side of Beardmore's work and, indeed, private car manufacture never gained much ground in the west of Scotland after the war.

The new Argyll Motor Co., formed by J. D. Brownlaw on the liquidation of the Vale of Leven establishment in 1914, introduced a new car in 1920, but had ceased production within ten years. Commercial vehicles gained a dominance during the war when the Albion Motor Co. concentrated on lorries and buses, and there was a smaller but still important company, the Halley Co. at Yoker, also producing commercial vehicles. A number of smaller firms also were engaged in vehicle construction, but with the solitary exception of the Albion Motor Co., all had ceased production by 1930.

This failure of new enterprise was most serious in the case of Beardmore, for they had been the largest manufacturers of automobiles and commercial vehicles. This strange withdrawal from a new industry was paralleled by the developing aero-engine and aircraft industry. Here again Beardmore had been dominant in 1920, producing aero-engines at Parkhead, airships at Inchinnan near Renfrew, and flying boats at

Dalmuir near Clydebank. But without heavy government purchases and in view of the prevalent attitude that commercial aviation should make its own way, Beardmore withdrew from the aircraft industry in the late 1920s. Thereafter the only representative of this new industry was the work of William & J. G. Weir on the de Cierva autogiro, leading eventually to the Weir helicopter in 1938.

This close link in enterprise between the older and newer industries, represented by Beardmore, was critical for the industrial future of the west of Scotland. By the 1920s, the car industry was growing rapidly in the Midlands, requiring large plant, large capital and the support of a host of ancillary component industries. A small nucleus of skill existed in the region, but further development required a bold choice of investments. In the contracting economic climate of the 1920s it appears that Beardmore chose to secure the future not by launching out in new directions, but by eliminating their investment in the small new car and aero-engine sector of their industrial empire, and consolidating on the old. Even shipbuilding, also a relatively new Beardmore venture, went to the wall in a marked move back to the confines of steel forgings, castings, railway material, armour plate and ordnance. In adversity, retrenchment won out over new enterprise. The hope of building a new major industry into the region's economy was lost. Other engineering and metal trades which might well have begun to adjust their structure and products in response to new local demands for cars and aero-engines failed to do so, confronted by the limited demand provided by the Albion Motor Co. Structural change from within the industries of the region was made virtually impossible.

The manifold problems of the region's industries between the wars were therefore only partly due to a failure of demand in export markets. Deep-seated structural problems weakened the resilience of the staple trades and made any adjustment to changing world conditions a slow, difficult and expensive business. The failure of local enterprise in major new industries exacerbated the downward pressure on production and employment, and contemporaries, swayed powerfully by the argument that the dependence on export markets was the major reason for the region's troubles, talked about the 'overcommitment' of the region to the heavy industries. The problem of overcommitment was not seen as one requiring internal change in the nature and product of the existing trades, but was thought of as being analogous to having too many eggs in one basket. The proposals to ameliorate the problem therefore did not so much involve changing the existing industries, but cutting them down to a scale suited to reduced markets, and partly replacing them by an infusion of new industry. Hence 'diversification' became an article of faith with individuals and agencies anxious to relieve the distress of the district.

Such action did not wait for government initiative, for official recognition of a 'regional problem' in Britain emerged only slowly in official thinking. Initial government measures were not specifically regional in any sense. In 1928, the government set up the Industrial Transferences Board and related training centres to encourage voluntary migration from depressed areas. This was a palliative of little consequence, since there were more men out of work than jobs available in Britain. A year later, the 1929 De-Rating Act gave some relief from the pressure of rates in hard-hit areas, but once more this was peripheral to the problem.

In this climate of government uncertainty private bodies stepped in. In December 1930 the Development Board for Glasgow and District was formed with the co-operation of the Corporation, the Chamber of Commerce, the Navigation Trust, and later, representatives of adjacent counties, the Trades House and Trade Council and Merchants' House. The Board hoped to develop existing industries and promote newcomers; it set up a central register of available factories and vacant sites, leased a showroom to display local products, and operated on a shoestring. Its initial funds came by donation to less than £3,500, with a public appeal for funds soliciting a very poor response. Its major promotional gambit was the publication of a booklet, *Glasgow and the Clyde*, designed to advertise the advantages of the area and attract industry. This regional initiative was followed up on a national scale in 1931, with the formation of the Scottish Development Council, which aimed to 'assist in stimulating enterprise in Scottish trade and industry in all its branches and to encourage true reciprocity of trade between Scotland and other countries'. This was a more influential body and Sir James Lithgow, Lord Bilsland and Lord Elgin were among its promoters. Government recognition of the problems which these bodies sought to deal with came first in 1932 when certain 'distressed areas' were designated to be surveyed by bodies commissioned by the Board of Trade. The result was in 1934 the Special Areas (Development and Improvement) Act, which was designed to 'facilitate the economic development and social improvement of certain areas which have been specially affected by industrial depression'.

Four such areas were set up in Britain and two Commissioners appointed to administer them. The first Scottish Commissioner was Sir Arthur Rose, who held office from 1934 to 1936. The Scottish special areas included the counties of Lanarkshire, Renfrewshire and Dunbartonshire, sixteen parishes in Ayrshire north of Kilmarnock, eight parishes in West Lothian and three parishes in Midlothian. The City of Glasgow was specifically excluded. This was particularly unfortunate, since it concentrated within itself the largest single bloc of unemployment in Scotland. Ayrshire too was disappointed at being partially excluded, and in response, in 1934, the Ayrshire Development Council was established with offices in Ayr County Buildings. The Glasgow Development

Board and the Ayrshire Council were primarily promotional and advertising bodies designed to make known the advantages of their respective areas to manufacturers. The agency of the special areas was, however, something further. It represented Britain's first explicit 'regional' policy, since it was believed that the depressed areas could only 'escape from the vicious cycle . . . by means of some positive external assistance'.

Nevertheless, the Commissioner lacked real power, since few funds were allocated to encourage industry to set up in the special areas. Indeed, the legislation did not provide for much direct inducement, but concentrated instead on improving the economic and social environment to make the areas more attractive. Hence, between 1 August 1934 and 31 July 1937 only £2·48 million had been authorised to be expended in the Scottish special areas. A sum of £1·5 million was given towards approved public works, mainly sewerage and sewage-purification schemes. Only £507,143 was specifically allocated for industrial development and £7,952 spent on specific inducements to industrial firms. The 'positive external assistance' adumbrated in the 1934 legislation scarcely materialised, and in the report for the year ending 31 August 1937, the new Commissioner, Sir David Allan Hay, could only claim a net gain of sixteen factories and extensions within the Scottish special areas for the entire period from December 1934 to June 1937.

The benefits from the first three years of effort under the special areas legislation seem slender, but they should not be judged solely on the meagre expenditure, for this represented approval of plans which on completion would represent an outlay of more than twice that sum. Moreover, the weaknesses of the first legislation soon became apparent, and as experience of regional problems increased, a second phase of regional policy began to take shape from 1936. Within Scotland the need for additional planning and investigatory machinery was reflected in the setting up of the Scottish Economic Committee. This was a committee of the Scottish Development Council and was set up at the instigation of the Commissioner of the Scottish special areas and the Secretary of State. The Scottish Economic Committee was asked to consider ways and means of reconstructing the Scottish economy and promoting general economic development. In the same year, Special Area Reconstruction associations were set up, with a Treasury guarantee, and had a remit to provide financial aid to firms coming in to the special areas. This was separate from the work of the Commissioner, but clearly worked towards the same ends. Financial assistance direct to industry at last appeared to be a reality, and also in 1938 the Nuffield Trust set aside £2 million to aid the special areas.

These were preliminaries in an important step forward in regional policy which was fully set out in the Special Areas (Amendment) Act, 1937. This at last gave the special-areas legislation financial teeth. It gave the Commissioner power to rent out factories, to extend assistance towards payment of rent, rates or income tax, and also made it possible to provide factories. These financial inducements were strengthened by another contained in the 1937 Finance Act, which gave discretion to the Treasury to remit all or part of the tax known as the National Defence Contribution.

All of these provisions were important, but perhaps the most significant was that relating to the building and renting of factories. This was particularly important in view of the prevailing conviction that the road to salvation lay in broadening the alleged narrow economic base of the region by diversification into new light industries. Although many factory buildings were vacant, many had been de-roofed to avoid rate charges, and most others were held to be too old and unsuited to the needs of the light industries. The attack on this problem was focused on the provision of small modern standard factories for rent in industrial estates. Such establishments had been pioneered in England where, by 1936, estates at Slough and Welwyn Garden City were already held to be a success. The Scottish Economic Committee, at the request of the Commissioner, set up a subcommittee to investigate the possibilities for Scotland; this body recommended the setting up of an estate at North Hillington near Renfrew Airport. While this was going on, another body, the Clyde Navigation Trustees, were moving in a similar direction. They made available a large tract of ground at Shieldhall, on which it was hoped that firms would build factories to their own requirements.

Plans for an estate at Hillington moved ahead rapidly. A site of 320 acres was secured by mid-1937, and in August a company called Scottish Industrial Estates Ltd was created, its capital guaranteed by the Special Areas Fund. The Commissioner set up a board of directors to administer the work of the estate under the chairmanship of Sir Steven Bilsland. The funds for construction were to come from the Special Areas Fund, and were to be free of interest during the first five years of the estate's development. The factories were to be single-storey and of standard construction in units of 5,000 square feet. They were to be built in blocks of four, capable of being used separately, or of being merged to give a larger factory. Provision was also made to permit tenants either to build, or to have built for them, larger factories to their own design within the estate. Tenants with modest requirements were to be catered for by the construction of 'nest' factories, one block containing between six and eight units of 1,200 square feet each. All roads and services were provided by the industrial estates company who administered the estate, publicised its facilities and rented out the standard factories.

Within eighteen months sixty-seven tenants had been secured for 103 factories built by the industrial estates company. As hoped, small-scale light industries made use of the facilities, firms like Compact Chemicals

Ltd, Glendale Garments Ltd, Sunshine Bleach Co. and Scottish Non-Ferrous Tube Industries Ltd being among the first to take up occupation. The Shieldhall site, though sponsored by the Clyde Navigation Trust, also qualified for assistance under the Special Areas Fund. Firms were attracted there by sites which were convenient both for docks and railway.

The initial success at Hillington encouraged the Commissioner and the industrial estates company to attempt to repeat the experiment in other locations. The Commissioner subsequently purchased three further sites at Carfin, Chapelhall and Larkhall in Lanarkshire. These were much smaller, being only 27, 18 and 11 acres respectively and were intended to bring relief to the heavy unemployment in the towns of north Lanarkshire; Airdrie, Coatbridge, Motherwell, Wishaw and Hamilton were all communities suffering from heavy and prolonged unemployment. These three estates were factored by another company, Lanarkshire Industrial Estates Ltd, incorporated in July 1938; this company shared the same management and offices as the larger Hillington estate.

The demonstration effect of Hillington and Shieldhall brought a further venture at Dalmuir in 1938. This was the site of the redundant Beardmore's shipyard, and under the provisions of the Special Areas Fund it was split up in 1938. Beardmore retained a portion and re-opened their engineering works. Part was purchased by the GPO as a depot for submarine-cable-laying ships. Another part was taken over by a ship-breaking business, and the rest was made available for rent as modern factories with a floor space of nearly nine acres. This was the Dalmuir Trading Estate.

There is no doubt that contemporaries felt the innovation of the industrial estates to be a major step forward in the policy of diversification. However, we should not be misled by the publicity given, and the faith held in these estates, for they were at the outset extremely small. By late 1938, within a year of the start of the Second World War, under £1 million had been authorised for the development at Hillington, the Lanarkshire estates, and all other industrial sites. This was expected to lead to an outlay of £1·3 million on approved undertakings on the four estates, with a potential employment of under 4,000 persons. In addition, the Nuffield Trust had by this time given assistance to the tune of £275,700. The Special Areas Reconstruction Association had contributed £210,500, and the Treasury Committee £45,000. A further £351,000 came from a variety of sources, and by the end of 1938 over £882,500 had been provided for economic assistance in the Scottish special areas in addition to the expenditure by the Commissioner. By that time the Special Areas Fund alone was stretched with commitments of £1·1 million to industry, £2·6 million to public works and over £200,000 to each of land improvement and the social services.

It is impossible to say what changes might have flowed from these beginnings. In 1938 the two industrial estate companies were advertising their benefits under the banner 'Industry Marches North'. They attempted to persuade businessmen to establish their factories in any of the estates 'in the centre of one of the richest markets in the country . . . affording a greater margin of safety from air raid'. This pessimistic advantage was to draw Rolls-Royce north during the war. But in 1939 the estates provided jobs for fewer than 5,000 persons.

We cannot realistically judge of the effect of the estates in attracting new light industries under peace-time conditions. But outside the estates, those new industries which envious Scots watched thriving in the Midlands proved stubbornly resistant to locating in Clydeside and in Scotland in general. The electrical industries, motor vehicles, cycles and aircraft, silk, rayon and scientific industries were the core of the new expanding trades. In 1925 these employed only 33,430 persons in the whole of Scotland and provided 17,803 jobs in the western region. Almost half of this was in public utilities, like gas, water and electricity generation. On the eve of the Second World War 53,640 people found employment in the new trades in Scotland, and again about half of these jobs were in the west of Scotland. Even if hosiery is added to this, and in Scotland this was the traditional Border industry rather than a new industry, these growing trades represented under 5 per cent of the insured labour force in Scotland. This was half the proportion of the labour force employed in these newer occupations in Britain as a whole.

It should be no surprise that the newer industries did not expand quickly in the region between the wars. The tiny scale of the new industries and the virtual absence of the real growth leader, the motor-vehicle industry, highlighted the problems of new industries in old industrial areas. It was not that the coalfield regions lacked labour. There was a massive supply of unemployed manpower. But the men out of work had little skill in the new trades. Retraining facilities were derisory. There was only one government training centre, at Springburn in Glasgow. It provided a six-month training programme in skilled occupations, but it only took in as many men as it could guarantee employment for, and trained only some 400–500 men per year. Even then, it taught the engineering skills of the old crafts rather than the techniques of the newer industries.

Another difficulty was the lack of good industrial sites. Most of these, close to docks and railways, and on major roads, had long since been occupied by established trades. In many cases newer, incoming, industries would have to take second-best sites on the periphery of established communications, or set about developing their own linkages. The industrial estates in fact recognised this problem, and sought to solve it by providing essential services and new factories for incoming manufacturers. The English experience also suggested that in the new industries successful growth demanded considerable scale in plant, together with economies of scale deriving from inter-industry linkages. The new industries in Scotland enjoyed none of these advantages and consequently languished.

The needs of the older and newer industries were divergent at almost every point. It was unreasonable to expect that one small region could provide the radically different supplies of skills, capital, plant resources and organisation required to service two such diverse industrial structures. Perhaps because few could see any supporting links between older and new industries, the emphasis was placed on at least partial replacement of the old by the new. This urge to replace the obsolescent by the new lay at the heart of the policy of diversification and indicates clearly that there was a failure to understand the nature of the region's industrial problem. Contemporaries were convinced that the region's economy was over-committed to a narrow industrial base represented by the heavy industries. Their solution was to implant the successful growth industries from England – the so-called light industries. But the region's economy was by no means undiversified, nor did the Midlands prosper because it had a 'diversified' economic base. The Midlands, like Clydeside, was dependent upon core industries which reinforced each other and gave support to a wide range of ancillary trades. Birmingham, Coventry and the Black Country built their industrial structure around the motor industry, electrical manufactures and miscellaneous metal manufactures. The industries of the whole area were largely interdependent since the finished products of Birmingham and Coventry drew raw materials and components from all over the area. This was no less 'over-committed' than Clydeside, with its interlocking heavy engineering, ships, steel and coal. The difference lay in the nature of demand trends for the products of these quite different industrial complexes at that point in time; the newer products were on the upswing, the products of the first industrial revolution were in declining demand.

Contemporaries clearly perceived this difference and sought to even out what they described as imbalance in the west of Scotland economy. But if there was imbalance it was aggravated by the policy of diversification, which sought to introduce new industries, without attempting to adjust the nature of the established manufactures. The solution adopted for the problems of the staple industries was to let them contract to a scale which was consistent with reduced markets for their conventional products. This may have made the rump industries more efficient, but it did little to adjust their outlook, organisation or product range to make it easier for the newer industries to penetrate the regional economy. As Professor Cairncross has made plain, 'the most disquieting feature of the inter-war period was not the absence of diversification . . . it was to a much greater extent the failure of the new industries to take root, and the lack of soil in which they could hope to flourish.'

The new industries which the Special Areas Commissioner and others were so anxious to introduce could not grow without support from the older-established trades, but this link was not clearly recognised. The new motor-vehicle industry demanded strip steel, precision engineering to minute tolerances, mass-produced components as distinct from batch and one-off products. It also demanded a host of component firms. The industrial estates may have been a beginning in establishing suitable sites for such complexes, but in themselves they did not dissolve the barriers to mutually beneficial reinforcement that existed between the old and new industries. As long as there was a failure to recognise that there were basic structural barriers to new industry inherent in the complex of existing industry, then the effort expended on diversification was likely to produce indifferent results. If the energy directed to attracting light industries to set up in an artificial environment in estates had been devoted to enabling the traditional industries to adjust their internal organisation and product ranges, the inter-industry barriers between the old and the new trades might have been sufficiently lowered to permit of spontaneous encouragement to new industrial growth.

This is not to pretend that the small sums given to promoting industrial estates could have transformed the economic structure of the older industries. Indeed, these staples did receive considerable funds, but most were conditional upon the industry forcibly reducing its scale and capacity. This also suited the businessman in these trades, for it generally consolidated his position and gave some security in very uncertain times. In view of such negative government policy, it would be unrealistic to have expected the established entrepreneurs to persevere with pioneer ventures. Without effective government support how could any individual or group of men be expected to transform the existing economic structure to make it a suitable seed-bed for new growth industries? Beardmore's had tried to grasp both the old and new, and had retreated to the staple established trades. Had they and other individual entrepreneurs persisted in pioneering the new industries it is quite possible that, in attempting to win the new, they would have lost even more of the established industrial structure, and perpetrated an even greater calamity of unemployment upon the region.

The government had been correct in 1934 when it accepted that the depressed regions required positive external assistance to put their economies into good shape. Unfortunately the emerging regional policy favoured diversification and largely neglected structural change within the traditional industries, though diversification would inevitably help change the industrial structure. The consequences were increased imbalance in the regional economy, a failure of the new industries to grow as well as they might, and a maintenance of the stagnation and wastage of resources that had characterised the region's economy for two decades. Regional economic policy had made an unconvincing début. It was the threat of war and finally war itself that was ultimately to draw the region's resources back into employment and temporarily obscure the effects of a generation of economic dislocation.

H

9

The managed economy

The Second World War had profound effects on the regional and national economy. In the short run the urgent demands for materials solved the problems of unused capacity and high unemployment. On the eve of war over 178,000 of the insured workforce appeared to have little prospect of finding work. By mid-1941, fewer than 50,000 were on the unemployed register, and in July 1944 only 16,199 persons were recorded as out of work. This was just over 1 per cent of the insured labour force, and rates as full employment by virtually any standard.

The enormous demands of total war placed great stress on the basic industries of Clydeside and exposed weaknesses which had been obscured in the environment of low-level demand between the wars. In spite of the desperate need for coal the industry in Scotland could not respond with either increased output or productivity. Scottish output slumped from 30·5 million tons in 1939 to 21·4 million in 1945, and the west of Scotland output declined by 1 million tons to 12·5 million in the same period. The workforce dwindled from 88,000 to 80,000 men, and productivity collapsed from 345 tons per man to 266 tons during the war. The iron and steel industries overcame their problems more successfully. The war demands highlighted the vulnerability of the steel industry, arising from the unintegrated iron- and steel-producing sections, the weak support from pig-iron production and the heavy dependence on imported supplies of ore and scrap. In spite of these handicaps, steel output averaged 1·9 million tons between 1940 and 1944 and twice surpassed 2 million tons; this compared with an average of 1·5 million tons in the late 1930s.

Even the pig-iron industry showed unexpected recuperative powers, raising its output from 409,000 tons in 1938 to 659,000 in 1940, and averaging well over 500,000 tons per year during the war.

The demands of war also illuminated the strengths of the regional economy. The great reserves of skill and labour and the highly productive and tightly-integrated metal and engineering complex were capable of meeting a multitude of demands simultaneously. This was nowhere better shown than on the Clyde. A decade of stagnation and capacity reduction was cast aside, and the shipyards launched an average of 493,000 tons each year from 1940 through to 1944, as against 322,000 tons in the five years before the war.

In the short run the Second World War gave a vigorous boost to the region's basic industries, which had been in decline for a generation. It also brought an extension of government intervention and a demonstration that a planned or managed economy could work. The success of government involvement left the central administration with certain important convictions. The first was a commitment to plans for reconstruction after the war to avoid the calamities which befell the nation after 1918, and an overriding determination to maintain high levels of employment. This commitment to manage the economy in the interests of full employment was to dominate economic thinking in Britain till the late 1950s, when it gave way to a certain unease and anxiety about slow growth rates in comparison with other advanced industrial nations.

The immediate post-war years from 1945 to 1947 were times of great austerity. The reconstruction of industry was greatly hampered by severe shortages of fuel, raw materials and certain grades of skilled labour, and by the great scarcity of dollars to purchase essential imports. For a time things looked bleak for the region's industries. In spite of this, all the basic trades, except coalmining, had regained pre-war levels of production by the end of 1946. But this was accompanied by a growing volume of unemployment. At the end of 1946 the Scottish unemployment level increased to 5 per cent and over two-thirds of the 78,702 persons out of work were concentrated in the region. Even more serious, three-quarters of these unemployed were men, one-third of whom were unskilled, and another third of whom by reason of age or impediment were held to be unsuitable for re-employment in their former jobs in heavy industry. But in April 1947 this upward trend in unemployment was quite suddenly reversed. For the next decade the regional economy followed in the wake of Britain in a period of almost continuous expansion.

In striking contrast to the inter-war years, the period from 1945 to 1960 was one of low levels of unemployment for Scotland and for the western region. For a decade from 1947 Scottish unemployment rates were extraordinarily stable, varying only slightly between 2·4 per cent and 3 per cent of a workforce which increased substantially from 1·463 million in 1945 to 2·154 million in 1960.* Unemployment in the region was higher, being on average in the range of 2·5 per cent to 3·5 per cent but that, too, was historically very low for the west of Scotland. Not only was unemployment at a low and stable rate, but the basic industries enjoyed a period of sustained growth, without suffering from the severe fluctuations in output typical of the years between the wars. As a consequence of high employment and sustained growth of output incomes and prices moved ahead in a mildly inflationary fashion quite unlike the deflationary experience of the 1920s and 1930s.

This unexpected prosperity has to be set in the context of a resurgence of world trade and remarkable economic recovery in war-torn Europe after 1947, where American aid through the Marshall Plan, and numerous new international economic organisations, provided a new framework of negotiation, support and co-operation which stimulated the latent production powers of Europe and set it on the path to more than a decade of astonishing economic expansion. In such a favourable international environment, successive British governments adjusted fiscal and monetary policies either to stimulate demand and consumption, or dampen it down when the economy became overheated and the balance of payments seemed threatened. The 1950s have become known as the decade of 'stop-go' precisely because of the way in which monetary and fiscal policy was applied or relaxed to control growth. Given this windfall of new international co-operation, and the transfusion of rapidly expanding world trade, features both absent between the wars, the government was able to support its commitment to high levels of employment with comparative ease. Most industries enjoyed buoyant demand for their products, and fairly moderate adjustments to monetary and fiscal policy appeared to take most of the strain of keeping people in work.

Nevertheless, the government did not depend entirely on such broad measures. The outlines of more specific planning emerged after the election of the Labour administration. The prime vehicle of reconstruction was the policy of nationalisation, in which key sectors of the economy were taken into public ownership. Coal was taken over in 1947, railways and electricity in 1948 and iron and steel in 1949. At the local level, pockets of distress were to be tackled by regional policy under the development areas legislation of 1945, and as industry and industrialists gained confidence in continued growth private development plans began to emerge to promote industrial expansion.

* Some of this growth is attributable to the broadening of industrial insurance in 1948 to embrace all persons in employment, other than the self employed.

Industrial change

Within the region these three strands of planning, nationalisation, regional policy and private-sector programmes affected the major industries in a variety of ways. Outside the public utilities, the influence of nationalisation was most obvious in the coal industry. On 1 January 1947 the dream of a generation of miners was realised when the new National Coal Board (NCB) assumed responsibility for 275 Scottish mines, of which seventy-nine were to be worked under licence by the previous owners. When the NCB completed its survey it found that more than half the collieries in Scotland were far gone in physical and economic decline. It was proposed to phase these out by 1965. This placed the Board in considerable difficulty, for there was an acute shortage of coal. Production was 22·5 million tons in 1946, and it was estimated that an annual output of 35 million tons was required to meet domestic and export demand. For the next decade demand continually outran available supplies. During this time the NCB's policy was to increase output at almost any price.

The NCB's strategy was set out in its long-term 'Plan for Coal' in 1950. Scottish output was to be raised to 30·6 million tons by 1965 at an estimated cost of £64·3 million. Production was to be concentrated in modern units through a programme of new sinkings, involving nine new collieries (four in the west of Scotland) together with four major and thirty-two minor reconstructions. Redundant mines were to be closed slowly, the loss in capacity to be offset by the short-term expedient of developing thirty-eight shallow-drift mines and open-cast workings to win small but accessible pockets of coal. These smaller projects had been begun in 1947, and about thirty were in operation at the end of 1948, mainly in the west of Scotland in the Shotts, Cambuslang, Drongan, Muirkirk and Cumnock districts.

The coal industry seemed set for a new prosperity. Market conditions were favourable and planned investment and reconstruction seemed likely to secure the future. Contrary to all expectations, however, total output continued to decline, productivity did not improve significantly, and the modernisation programme was unexpectedly slow and expensive. Some old pits were closed faster than new capacity could be brought into operation, substantial manpower engaged in modernisation did not contribute to short-term production, and many highly uneconomic pits were kept in operation from fear of losing scarce manpower. The NCB consequently made a loss on its operations in Scotland in every year from 1950 (Table 22).

The NCB in 1956 revised its planned output downward to 26·5 million tons, and moved its estimated expenditure upward to £185 million, the aim still being to create an economically viable coal industry in

TABLE 22   *Output, employment, productivity and profitability, coal, 1948–60*

Year	Scotland output†	West Scotland output†	Employment (000)	OPMS tons	Profit/Loss* s.	Profit/Loss* d.
1948	23·8	13·0	82·4	1·12	2	8·9
1951	23·6	11·4	82·2	1·12		−5·5
1957	21·3	9·7	86·7	0·99	−11	7·0
1960	18·0	8·1	73·1	1·12	−11	11·7

* Per saleable ton before charging interest   † M. tons
OPMS = Output per manshift
Source: NCB, annual reports

Scotland. Unfortunately these proposals ran into collapsing demand from 1958. The world had moved abruptly from coal shortage to a coal surplus, the transition being hastened by a remarkable shift towards an increased use of oil, gas and electricity as substitute fuels. Moreover, British fuel policy had consistently encouraged the railways to switch from coal-burning to diesel engines, and had aimed to persuade industrial and domestic consumers to economise on the use of scarce coal. These trends also accelerated from 1958.

These changes reduced industrial consumption of Scottish coal by over 1·5 million tons between 1957 and 1960 and forced the NCB to restrict recruitment, reduce open-cast mining, and speed up the closure of uneconomic pits. Nearly 2·5 million tons of capacity was closed between 1958 and 1960, more than in the whole period up to 1957. Even this did not stabilise the situation. In 1959 official policy became that of matching output to current demand, and Scotland's contribution was expected to be about 19 million tons.

Fourteen years of planning had met with little success. Scottish output declined by 5·8 million tons between 1948 and 1960 and nearly 5 million tons of this was accounted for by pit closures in the west of Scotland. Productivity failed to increase in spite of an extension of mechanically-cut coal from 86 per cent of output to 90 per cent between 1947 and 1957. Heavy over-manning, manpower employed in unproductive modernisation schemes, and the persistence of uneconomic old mines in the central field, all contributed to this situation. Only the radical reduction in mines and workforce after 1958 enabled productivity to begin to move ahead for the first time since nationalisation. The industry in the west of Scotland bore the brunt of this pruning, and Lanarkshire was worst affected: the county mined half Scotland's coal in 1945, but less than a third in 1960. The region lost over 100 mines through closure, and its workforce declined by 14,000 between 1940 and 1960, in spite of the heavy investment in new collieries at Kingshill in Lanarkshire, and Little Mill and Killoch in Ayrshire. No plan or policy could long delay the contraction, for the structural decline evident between the wars accelerated after 1945 and brought mining in the west of Scotland to the edge of extinction.

The plans for nationalisation also included iron and steel. The ensuing uncertainty as to ownership much delayed the immediate post-war development of the industry. Public ownership was not attained till 15 January 1951. Then the return of the Conservative administration put the policy in reverse; the Iron and Steel Act, 1953, denationalised the industry, and set up the Iron and Steel Holding Realisation Agency to supervise the return of the firms to private ownership, a task accomplished in Scotland by 1955. The return to private ownership was easy, since operational control had never been removed from the existing companies.

The objectives of the industry were laid out in three main development plans in 1946, 1954 and 1957, each chiefly comprising the individual proposals of the various companies. The 1946 plan aimed to extend capacity over a five-year period; Scottish output was to be expanded from 2 million to 2·3 million tons with an outlay of £30 million. The scheme advocated scrapping certain old plant and establishing a new integrated riverside works at Erskine Ferry to be the nucleus for the future development of the industry. But neither the political nor economic climate was favourable. The uncertainty over nationalisation delayed political approval, and the enormous and insistent demand for steel placed emphasis on stretching capacity at existing plants by modest outlays on modernisation. Even this was difficult, since there were critical shortages of fuel and scrap metals, a situation which did not ease till 1948–9. At that point the government gave approval to development proposals costing £11 million, £4 million of which was allocated to extensions at Clyde Iron and Clydebridge, and most of the remainder to modernisation at Motherwell. When the decision was taken to denationalise in 1952 these policies had carried the production of pig-iron to 886,000 tons, and steel to 2·1 million tons: this was very close to the projections of the 1946 plan, which had aimed at 900,000 tons of iron and 2·3 million tons of steel.

The steelmakers, with the industry apparently secure in their hands, formulated new proposals in 1952 and 1953. These were given government approval in 1954. The Scottish plan embraced an expenditure of £34 million, up to £25 million to be allocated for a new integrated iron-and steelworks at Motherwell. This plant, at Ravenscraig, was to be brought into production in the autumn of 1957, and was intended to attack the perennial problems of supplies of raw materials, poor integration of iron and steel production, and obsolete technology. The related

railway and ore-terminal developments were intended to ease the assembly
of raw materials: enlarged blast-furnace capacity would reduce the
industry's dependence on scrap steel; and the entirely new plant would
offset the age and small scale of much of the technical equipment of the
remainder of the industry. Even so, the plan committed the industry to the
old inland location, and to the continuing cost problems of assembling
and transporting large tonnages of ore, coal, scrap, limestone and other
materials. Ravenscraig came into production on schedule in 1957.
An outlay of £22·5 million had provided Scotland with its first fully-
integrated iron and steel plant. The initial capacity was 400,000 tons
of crude steel and this enabled the industry to achieve its target of 2·6
million tons of steel in 1957.

The sustained demand for steel inspired a third post-war development
plan in 1957, which aimed to increase annual capacity to 3·1 million tons
in 1961. Most of this was to flow from the second stage of the Ravenscraig
project, and £32 million was set aside to provide a second blast-furnace,
duplicate sets of coke ovens and steel furnaces, and a slabbing and bloom-
ing mill. Perversely, this new initiative coincided with the first serious
contraction in demand for steel in the post-war period. As in the case of
coal, a decade of developing capacity quite suddenly moved the world
into a surplus of steel, and for the first time since before the war, serious
price cutting was resorted to in world markets. More perplexing still, the
domestic market, which had been secure from foreign competition since
the war, now came under severe pressure. The licensing of exports was
abandoned and import duties re-introduced. The 1958 recession cut back
on capital goods projects at home and abroad, and the Scottish steel industry was only able to operate at 75–80 per cent of capacity in 1958–9.

The severity of this setback brought an unexpected addition to the
development proposals. One feature of the 1957 plan had been the
decision to establish a fourth continuous strip mill, probably in South
Wales. Scotland appeared to have neither a claim on, nor an ambition to
attract, this project in 1957. But in 1958, when unemployment rose,
when the steel industry in England and Wales recovered more rapidly,
depending less on the demand of capital-goods industries, it seemed de-
sirable to protect the Scottish steel industry from a sudden collapse in
demand for its heavier steel products by giving it some strip-steel capacity.
Trade unions and other bodies made powerful representations to the
government who, in November 1958, announced a compromise of two
smaller mills, one to be developed at Newport by Richard Thomas
and Baldwins Ltd, the other at Ravenscraig to be built by Colvilles Ltd.
It is difficult to avoid the conclusion that Colvilles had the project thrust
upon them by a political decision, and that the group had not actively
sought to attract or embark upon such a scheme.

Many people believed that the ability to supply strip steel would attract many new industries, but this confidence did not rest on any secure foundation. There was no local market for large quantities of strip steel, and none has subsequently emerged. The site was inland, and the proposed capacity of 500,000 tons was only half of what was then regarded as the minimum size for economic production. Even a £50 million loan from the government was little comfort, since this carried Colvilles beyond its own financial resources for the first time. Nevertheless, the scheme was pushed forward. It involved a semi-continuous hot-strip mill at Ravenscraig, and a cold-reduction plant at Gartcosh: this meant that pig-iron capacity and steelmaking facilities both had to be extended, and in the midst of a serious recession, the Scottish industry's development plan was given a dramatic boost.

The iron and steel industry in 1960 was greatly changed from that existing in 1945. Fifteen years of planning and investment had brought great strides in overcoming the basic problems of unintegrated iron and steel production, obsolete technology, and raw material difficulties. A progressive concentration of ownership bound the iron and steel sectors closely together, production being dominated by four companies in 1960. This gave great support to steel production, and the increased output in both iron and steel rested on considerable advances in organisation and technology. Between 1938 and 1960 blast-furnace productivity grew from 33,000 tons to 194,000 tons per year, taking Scotland from last to fourth place among the ten iron and steel districts. This was partly achieved by closing old plants at Shotts ironworks in 1952, and at Govan in 1958, together with constructing new furnaces at Clyde Iron, Ravenscraig and Gartsherrie. The fuel problem was alleviated by blending crushed coals and introducing the use of 'sinter', a mixture of ore fines, coke and other iron-bearing substances to effect economies in the furnace. Oil firing of furnaces was also introduced in 1948, and by 1960 Scottish blast-furnaces consumed 127,000 tons of oil.

The efficiency of the industry was greatly increased by the extended use of the hot-metal process, made possible by the fully integrated plant at Ravenscraig, the partial integration at Clyde Iron and Clydebridge, and the linking of the pig-iron production at Gartsherrie to steel mills at Coatbridge, this last being controlled by Bairds and Scottish Steel. Hot metal charged increased from 0·5 per cent in 1938 to 47 per cent in 1960, although this was still far below the British level of 87 per cent. The increased use of hot metal also encouraged a reduction in the use of scrap metal in steel production: the addition of scrap metal to the open-hearth furnace had been as large as 79 per cent of the charge in 1938, compared with a British average of 58 per cent. In 1960, this had been cut back to 62 per cent, as against 52 per cent for Britain as a whole.

In spite of the fact that the industry passed through a decade of uncertainty regarding ownership, the development plans had increased

H*

production by 1 million tons to 2·7 million between 1947 and 1960. Although this was substantial, it was slower than the rate achieved elsewhere, and Scotland's share of total British output declined from over 15 per cent to 11 per cent. This reflected the severity of the problems confronting the steelmakers. The industry in 1960 was not a perfect model of efficiency, but in view of the constraints of an inland location, and the dependence on large quantities of imported raw materials, the re-organisation had produced a surprising degree of integration and quite astonishing improvements in productivity.

This degree of success was not to be shared by shipbuilding, even though peace-time brought unprecedented demands for vessels and set the industry on course for two decades of unparalleled prosperity. The underlying support was the enormous growth of world trade at more than 7 per cent per year. This created extensive demands for bulk carrying capacity, first for oil, and then for iron and other minerals. World merchant tonnage consequently nearly doubled from 69·4 million tons in 1939 to 129·8 million tons in 1960.

This should have presented great opportunities for the Scottish industry, but British and Clyde shipbuilders' output remained stationary, and the yards moved from a surfeit to a scarcity of orders between 1946 and 1960. Thus, while British and Clyde yards built 57 per cent and 18 per cent respectively of world tonnage in 1947, they supplied a mere 15 per cent and 4·5 per cent in 1958. Clyde launchings remained remarkably stable during this period at an average of 416,000 tons per year, and this was about 30 per cent of British building throughout.

A number of features help explain this failure to respond to market opportunity. In the replacement boom after the war the Clyde was said to have an annual capacity of between 600,000 and 700,000 tons, but chronic shortages of ship steel and skilled labour kept launchings down to an average of 369,000 tons between 1946 and 1950. These scarcities affected the industry to some extent throughout the 1950s, and in addition, deliveries of steel out of sequence presented difficulties in the scheduled assembly of vessels and kept the yards below capacity production. The bunching of orders also presented problems in maintaining a steady employment of men and resources: this was most severe in 1950–1 and 1956–7, when the Clyde acquired over 2 million tons of orders, enough to last for three years of normal production. Inevitably, this led to a lengthening of delivery times, and pressure to negotiate contracts on a cost plus profits basis, rather than at a fixed price.

During the 1950s three factors came to play a critical role in obtaining new orders: credit arrangements, the quotation of fixed prices, and quick delivery dates. Clyde yards were at a disadvantage in all three. German yards benefited from special taxation relief and low interest rates: Holland and Sweden enjoyed long-term credit arrangements backed by either the government or local municipalities. In Japan the industry was officially controlled under a system of indirect subsidies on raw materials, low interest on loans, and reduced taxation. In Britain, the Ship Mortgage Finance Co. and the Export Credit Guarantee Department were weak supports compared with the comprehensive range of subsidies and allowances available to builder and purchaser in foreign yards. The latter were frequently enabled to quote fixed prices and early delivery dates which Clyde and British yards could not meet, and orders were redirected to the recovering yards in Europe and Japan. In the later 1950s delivery from a German or Japanese yard was frequently only half the period quoted by British builders. This performance by rivals was related to extensive mechanisation and the well-planned layout of modern yards, designed to give a 'flow-line' production, akin to an assembly line in a modern factory. This also favoured standardisation and larger vessels. These characteristics to a considerable degree ran counter to arrangements on the Clyde, and explain part of the Clyde's deteriorating position. Only twelve of the twenty-three yards on the Clyde had a sizeable capacity, and two, Lithgows at Port Glasgow, and Browns at Clydebank, launched 30 per cent of Clyde tonnage between 1946 and 1960. But none of the yards was very extensive, and most were physically confined with short frontages on a narrow river. This made it difficult to adopt a flow-line layout and large berths without resort to amalgamation: the relative prosperity of the 1950s preserved the independence of the firms, and amalgamation had to await the enforced groupings of the 1960s in a belated attempt to save the industry from collapse.

Although this type of improvement was not easy for the Clyde shipbuilders, they did invest in other modernisation schemes. In the 1940s there was emphasis on replacing riveting by welding, and in increasing mechanisation in the yards. The 1950s brought improvements in prefabrication and heavy lifting gear, and in yard transport and layout. No yard, however, was entirely rebuilt to match the new European and Japanese yards and, relatively, Clyde and British shipbuilders lost ground to their competitors. Indecisive management clearly must bear some responsibility in these matters. Inter-union demarcation disputes must also have made it difficult to gain acceptance for new methods.

In view of these facts, Clyde builders were less well placed than foreign rivals to withstand the unfavourable market conditions which set in from 1957. World shipbuilding capacity had finally outrun the growth in world trade, bringing cancelled orders in its wake. Only tanker orders remained buoyant and saved the Clyde from a severe contraction of work (Table 23): unfortunately, this support began to weaken after 1955, and by 1960 the Clyde had only 232,000 tons of work in hand, barely sufficient for six months. New orders were scarce, and yards which could rarely quote fixed prices or offer firm delivery dates, were left with little work. Many of the orders which were obtained in 1960 were for the first time taken at prices which could not cover costs, in an effort to keep workforces together pending a revival. Surplus world building capacity ensured that the recovery did not quickly materialise, and though it was not immediately clear, Clyde shipbuilding was on the brink of a disastrous decline. It had arrived there through its own weaknesses in a highly competitive world.

TABLE 23 *Merchant tonnage launched and tanker tonnage launched on River Clyde, 1946–60*

Period	Merchant tonnage		Tankers (000 tons)	% Tankers
	(000 tons)	Annual Average		
1946–50	1,846	369	395	21·4
1951–55	2,229	446	1,161	52·1
1956–60	2,005	401	781	38·9
1946–60	6,080	405	2,337	38·4
1951–60	4,234	423	1,942	45·8

Source : Compiled from *Glasgow Herald*, Annual Trade Reviews

Regional policy

The framework of public and private enterprise planning which embraced the mining, metals and engineering industries was designed either to stabilise or expand the output of the various trades. But the measures employed were frequently *ad hoc* responses to trends set in motion by external factors. Such plans were not designed as part of a coherent policy of regional regeneration. But the third thread of planning did have this broader objective in view. This was regional policy. It was this feature of government involvement that brought the region closest to the position of a managed economy.

The foundations of regional policy were laid in the 1934 Special Areas Act, and although the Second World War delayed further action, the government's intentions were made explicit with the passing of the Distribution of Industry Act in June 1945. This designated certain 'development areas', which were broadly the old 'special areas', together with their large towns and a few additions of territory at their peripheries. The Act empowered the Board of Trade to acquire land, erect new factories for rent at the 1939 value of 1s. 0d. per square foot, construct ancillary buildings, and provide services such as water, electricity and roads. The legislation also made available some financial assistance to firms for capital equipment. The Act itself did not direct new industrial building away from congested areas, and industrialists were only obliged to advise the Board of Trade when erecting buildings in excess of 10,000 square feet. However, the Board was able to use the war-time licence controls to influence decisions in new building, and these remained in force till 1954. This was reinforced in 1947 when the Town and Country Planning Act introduced the requirement of planning permission for all industrial plant over 5,000 square feet; permission took the form of an Industrial Development Certificate, and the granting or withholding of these was for some time a powerful instrument in guiding the location of new industrial building.

Regional policy was given a wide range of new powers. The agents of the Board of Trade in applying the policy were to be the industrial estates companies. The Hillington Estate Co. retained its former position, but the Lanarkshire Industrial Estate Co. was dissolved and re-incorporated as Scottish Industrial Estates Ltd, with responsibility for extending the scope of a number of trading estates, and assisting new industrial endeavour throughout the Scottish Development Area. The commitment to regional assistance was continued under the second Distribution of Industry Act, 1950, which substantially enlarged the Scottish Development Area, including Highland areas for the first time. This framework remained in force till 1960, having been changed modestly by the Distribution of Industry (Industry and Finance) Act, 1958, and was finally replaced by a new body of legislation in the Local Employment Act, 1960.

The initial plans set aside £10 million to aid regional development in Britain. Newhouse Industrial Estate was begun in 1945, Blantyre, Port Glasgow, Vale of Leven, Carntyne and Queenslie in 1946, together with another at Dundee. Sites were acquired for another eight estates in the region, and by the end of 1946 projects were in hand for developments on nineteen trading estates and eighteen individual factories.

The region benefited from the new policies, and from several inherent advantages. While the national economy was severely hampered by shortages of labour, factory space and materials, the west of Scotland, like most other development areas, had surplus labour, particularly female labour. It also had factory space available, through the programme of advance factory building and de-requisitioning of government factories. Scarce materials were more readily on hand because of priority allocations. This vigorous regional policy was checked abruptly by the grave financial crisis in the autumn of 1947, when the government was faced with a serious balance of payments deficit. Large cuts were made in all industrial building programmes, the construction of advance factories was halted, and emphasis was switched to developing export and import-substitution industries to take the strain off the balance of payments.

Some attempt was made to re-establish the initiative after the devaluation of 1949 with the second Distribution of Industry Act in 1950, but the coming to power of the Conservatives in 1951 heralded a decade of neglect for regional planning, and indeed a retreat from planning on all fronts.

Although regional spending declined after 1947, the initial surge produced a vast building programme. By 1950 there were 22 estates, 15 ex-government factories and 18 individual factory sites in operation in the region. Factory floor space grew eleven-fold, the average size of factories trebled, and the Scottish Development Area had attracted over 13 per cent of all new industrial building undertaken in Britain. It is doubtful if such a momentum could have been maintained, even if regional policy had not been cut back. By 1950 the surplus labour pool was virtually exhausted, and readily available factory space disappeared with the final absorption of ex-government establishments and the ending of advance factory building after 1947.

The check given to regional policy by the financial crisis in 1947 was reinforced by the renewed prosperity of the traditional industries from 1948. This reduced unemployment and encouraged the complacent belief that the existing measures had largely solved the regional problem. There followed the dormant decade of the 1950s in which annual government expenditure on British regional development declined from £8·5 million between 1945 and 1951 to £4 million between 1951 and 1958. Following upon the easing of building controls only 8·5 per cent of new factory building came to Scotland in the 1950s, and in the absence of government support, the industrial estates companies had to encourage more development by private enterprise. This effort was strikingly successful: by 1960, government finance had provided 11 million square feet of new factory space, while private enterprise contributed 38 million, all but 4 million square feet of this coming in the 1950s, when government initiative slackened. The estate companies then factored a total of 17·5 million square feet of factory space, and the region contained 18 industrial estates and 29 other factory sites, giving employment to about 65,000 persons.

This large injection of employment had called for large capital investments. Between July 1945 and March 1958 the government provided £7·8 million in grants and loans to firms, and £24·8 million for new factories. This represented 22 per cent of the new industrial building in the Development Area, and private enterprise must have invested three or four times as much again up to 1960. The new jobs were strongly concentrated in the engineering and electrical groups, which represented a third of all companies located in the industrial estates. Non-Scottish companies had made a striking contribution to these developments. Ten American companies had set up by 1949, and forty-one by 1960: five other companies were in joint Anglo-American control, and four had been taken over by American interests. These fifty concerns employed 25,000 persons and occupied six million square feet of factory space, half of which had been financed by the government: thirty-five of the companies were located within the region.

The infusion was more important than the simple figures of employment suggest, since some of the companies had introduced industries which were entirely new to the region. Euclid, for example, brought in massive earthmoving equipment at Newhouse, as did Caterpillar at Tannochside. Honeywell Controls developed micro-switches and industrial instrumentation at Newhouse, while IBM, United Kingdom, introduced electronic data-processing equipment in Greenock. Others built on well-established Scottish strengths, such as Joy Sullivan in power-driven mining machinery, and Goodyear in tyres at Garscadden.

The regional policy measures clearly brought new supports to the regional economy. The inter-war desire had been for more jobs and more diversification and much had been achieved on both counts by 1960. But many of the jobs in the new factories were simple transfers from older sites, and only 45,000 entirely new jobs had been created in Scotland between 1945 and 1960. Even the 65,000 employees in the west of Scotland's industrial estates were only 18 per cent of all manufacturing employment, and 6 per cent of the entire regional workforce. In spite of the successful attraction of industry, the total input was small in relation to the economy as a whole, and while industrial diversification was increasing, the net effect was not yet sufficient to alter the existing industrial structure materially.

The regional economy

The period 1940–60 was an interlude of comparative prosperity for the west of Scotland. The basic industries recovered in a way few had ever dreamed could be possible after the dismal experience of the years between the wars. Sustained demand for the region's products introduced a new feeling of security, few men were regularly unemployed, and public and private investment slowly upgraded the productive machinery of the staple industries. Even more encouraging, the framework of regional measures seemed to be successful in building new and growing industries into the regional economy. Even so it could not be claimed that the region's problems had been solved. Although the rate of unemployment was much lower than between the wars, averaging 3 to 3·5 per cent, it was still normally at least double the British figure, falling marginally short of that dismal record on only two occasions in 1952 and 1957.

The record would have been much worse but for another disquieting feature. There was a massive loss of manpower by net outward migration, some three-quarters of the natural increase leaving the region between 1951 and 1960. Consequently, the region's occupied labour force grew only from 1·053 million in 1951 to 1·071 million in 1961. The region failed to generate enough jobs to offer to the economically-active age-groups, and had a smaller proportion of its males in this group in employment than any other major region in Britain.

The slow growth, or lack of growth, in job opportunity suggests, too, that in spite of the apparent prosperity the regional economy was growing more slowly than that of the nation as a whole. Local figures are not available to give precise information on this, but estimates of the rate of growth of the Scottish gross domestic product (GDP) indicate that Scotland did lag behind. In aggregate, Scottish GDP increased from £1,238 million to £1,964 million between 1951 and 1960, an increase of 59 per cent. Over the same period British GDP increased by 70 per cent. Scotland's share of that GDP declined from 9·3 per cent to 8·7 per cent in a single decade. One consequence was that *per capita* income on Clydeside was only 90 per cent of that of the British average in 1961. These disturbing features clearly signpost the regional problem: persistently high unemployment running at twice the national average, a failure to create sufficient jobs for the available labour force, a continuing outflow of population, taking place within a framework of slower than average economic growth, which resulted in lower than average incomes.

These were not new problems. They had been a source of concern since the First World War, and they had repeatedly been diagnosed in terms of an unfavourable industrial structure. Since the regional economy seemed on the brink of further deterioration, the question of an unfavourable regional economic structure assumed prominence once more. The peculiar features of the industrial structure seemed to lie in a heavy representation of some trades, and in a relatively slight contribution in others. In terms of employment, the region was dominated by its manufacturing sector. While manufacturing employed a third of the British workforce in 1961, 40 per cent of the region's labour was dependent on manufacturing, and within the Clydeside conurbation the proportion was as high as 42·7 per cent. Moreover, the region depended heavily on a very narrow range of employment within the manufacturing sector. Five major industries were heavily over-represented in comparison with the national pattern. Metal manufacturing, engineering and electrical goods, shipbuilding and marine engineering, textiles, and food, drink and tobacco provided 28·5 per cent of the region's total employment and over two-thirds of all manufacturing jobs. Decay was built into this employment structure, for in three of these groups, shipbuilding and marine engineering, metal manufacture, and textiles, there had been serious employment contraction in the country generally during the 1950s. At the other end of the scale there was a range of industries relatively poorly represented in the west of Scotland. Vehicles, chemicals and allied trades, printing and publishing, and the broad range of professional and service occupations employed only 29 per cent of the region's workforce as against over 36 per cent nationwide. This deficiency was particularly serious in the case of motor vehicles, which was a growth leader in employment in Britain, but which up to 1960 was represented solely by the commercial vehicle sector within Scotland.

Regional imbalance, as a feature of the local economy, emerged first in the broad concentration on a few industries within older manufacturing trades, and in the marked deficiencies in newer industries and services. The imbalances became even more pronounced within the industrial groups, irrespective of their degree of representation in the region. In the well-represented food, drink and tobacco sector, 51 per cent of employment was concentrated in the two areas of bread and flour confectionery and the drink industries. A whole range of employment, including milk products, sugar, fruit and vegetable products, and animal and poultry foods, were weakly represented. Within the core sector of engineering and electrical goods over half the jobs were in two blocks: industrial plant and steelwork, and other machinery. The remaining jobs were in a wide range of trades, but most were on a very small scale. The electronics side, represented by radio equipment, domestic electric apparatus, telegraph and telephone apparatus, employed under 10 per cent of the engineering workforce. Similar concentrations and omissions were evident within poorly represented groups. Within the chemicals and allied industries group, 71 per cent of employment fell within the explosives and fireworks, and chemicals and dyes industries. Synthetic resins and plastics, pharmaceutical and toilet preparations, lubricants, oils, fats, soaps, detergents and polishes were only scantily represented. In the same manner, the vehicle group owed over 56 per cent of its jobs to locomotive and railway rolling-stock construction.

This type of concentration and deficiency is typical of every broad industrial group represented in the region. Indeed, one ought to expect regional specialisms to produce this type of employment pattern. However, the real problem appears to be that in too many cases the region had a high proportion of its labour force employed in slow-growing or declining industries, and relatively too few in the expanding sectors. Comparing Scotland with Britain between 1950 and 1958, the Toothill Report found that almost 44 per cent of total employment in Britain was in industries which had increased their labour force by 10 per cent or more: in Scotland, the proportion was under 39 per cent. Correspondingly, Scotland had almost 62 per cent of her workforce in the slow-growing, static and declining group, as against 56 per cent for the rest of the country. Even more serious, many industries which were growing rapidly in Britain registered a decline in employment in Scotland. These included the vehicle group and a number of the electrical apparatus trades.

Since the region's growth sector was composed of a few large and many small new establishments widely dispersed throughout the area, the encouragement to service industries and ancillaries was limited. The problems of scale and location meant that many of the newer industries were, to an extent, not integrated with the region's economy. They virtually worked in a vacuum, drawing components from England, and hence were in many cases subject to increased costs, lower efficiency, and slower growth than their equivalents in England, which were surrounded by their complex of supporting and related industries.

Seen in these terms the problem was severe. But few planners or politicians believed that it was insoluble. Such structural decay should be capable of repair by a slow process of replacement, by encouraging indigenous and migrant companies to expand in new and growing areas of employment. The short-run penalties of higher costs, small scale, slower growth and poorer efficiency could be offset by regional incentives, an idea implicit in all the regional measures designed since 1934. If the policies were maintained long enough, the belief was that the regional economic structure could be altered to match the new export and domestic demand patterns which fostered and sustained rapid growth.

However, a quarter century of effort in changing the industrial structure had not produced very remarkable results. Though structural changes had been pursued only indirectly and inconsistently between 1934 and 1960, the patent lack of achievement by this means suggests that the region's problems should not be analysed and explained entirely in terms of its industrial structure. Recent research into regional growth and decay has revealed a range of obstacles which cut right across the industrial structure, whether it be in the old and declining sectors or among the representatives of the newer industries. The level of productivity was found to be low in comparison with general British levels, and as a result most industries were burdened with wage costs which were high in relation to output, that is, their efficiency wages were relatively high, making for a poor competitive position. Further, in spite of the host of advantages which regional measures had created to encourage industrial growth, the west of Scotland, and the Clydeside conurbation in particular, appeared to attract a decreasing proportion of the new indigenous and migrant companies from the mid-1950s.

The productivity problem was perhaps the most worrying feature for industrialists, politicians and planners. The most obvious expression of this was the fact that in a wide range of industries the net output per head in Scotland was lower than that of Britain in general. It is not clear why this should be, although certain indicators suggested that a low level of fixed capital investment had meant a persistence of older and less-efficient machinery and inferior factory organisation and working conditions. Certainly, in the 1950s, fixed investment in manufacturing industry in Scotland ran between 7 and 8 per cent of the British total, considerably less than Scotland's share of manufacturing industry and manufacturing employment. Relatively less capital was being invested per worker than was the case in Britain generally, contributing to lower productivity. It has also been suggested that difficult labour relations, hard-line attitudes on manning arrangements, restrictive practices and demarcation must all have reduced productivity. It is difficult to measure the effect of such factors. But one indicator could be the days lost per thousand workers in mining, manufacturing, construction and transport industries. Over the period 1947–59, the annual average in days lost in Scotland was 448, while the average for Great Britain was only 226 days. This might well have had some bearing on productivity and the attractiveness of Scotland to incoming companies. But internationally, only West Germany, with an average of 75 days lost, was better off than Scotland. In Japan the loss was 671 days, while in the USA a total of 1,473 days was lost per thousand workers.

The explanations of low productivity are elusive. For many years there was no great concern at Scotland's poor record, since it was assumed that low labour costs counteracted this disadvantage. However, it appears that from about the mid-1950s, Scottish wage costs began to converge on those of Great Britain. This seems to have resulted from the practice of beginning to negotiate wage deals which left little room for downward differentials to be applied in the different industrial districts. Shop-floor and plant negotiations frequently took place from the base level of the national agreement with a view to revising it upward, rather than to attempt an independent regional wage settlement. Even so, hourly earnings for male manual workers in manufacturing industry in Scotland were only 93 per cent of the British rates in 1960, and the wage costs could not have been a crippling burden at that stage. More seriously, the convergence of Scottish wage rates on the British average was not accompanied by an improvement in output, and the efficiency wage position deteriorated, making Scotland a higher cost-of-production area. Total output was also adversely affected. This was reflected in Scotland's slower overall growth and declining contribution to Britain's gross national product (GNP) in the 1950s.

The remaining feature hindering growth in the region was the deterioration in the attraction of new companies, and slow growth of indigenous companies. The Lanarkshire experience is revealing here. In the short post-war period of 1945–9 new companies invested nearly £41 million in Lanarkshire. In the entire decade of the 1950s new companies invested only £22·7 million. The rate of entry was about six companies per year before 1949, and only half that in the 1950s. Clydeside as a whole

attracted roughly 50 per cent of all new companies coming to
Scotland up to the mid-1950s, but thereafter, in spite of the persistence of the regional incentives, the attraction rate slipped slowly
to only one company in every three. This was particularly serious
since the incoming companies represented the main hope for restructuring the regional economy and pushing it toward more rapid
growth. At the same time, indigenous company growth barely kept
pace with indigenous company closures, and hence contributed little
to restructuring the regional economy. The failure to attract a
larger share of the newer industries seems to be related less to any
structural defect in the economy, than to the image which prospective
employers had of life and work in the west of Scotland. The overriding
impression of urban congestion, poor housing, health and environment,
allied to a reputedly difficult labour situation, seems to have acted to
discourage some investment in the region.

By the 1950s the west of Scotland came to display all the worst features
of a region in decline. Inadequate capital investment, high efficiency
wages, a low rate of entry of newer industries, a preponderance of
declining heavy industries: these combined to create a high-cost, low-
productivity industrial region. These intractable problems are clearly
based in the industrial structure, but are exacerbated by features which
cannot be eradicated by tackling the structural problem alone. This
makes the management of the declining regional economy extraordinarily
difficult. While governments have been successful in maintaining a high
level of employment, they have not only been less successful in adjusting
the defective structure, but seem also to have been largely unaware of
non-structural obstacles. The resulting persistent pressure on costs and
on jobs has weakened the resilience of the economy and stimulated the
outward flow of manpower.

A yet further consequence has been a gradual elimination of Scottish
enterprise from the region. As late as 1939 most companies in it were
controlled by Scottish interests, generally resident in the region. By
1960, over 60 per cent of all manufacturing firms employing more than
250 persons were controlled by non-Scottish interests. The failure of
local enterprise and the inability to regenerate the staple industries has
committed a once vigorous region to the status of a branch-factory
economy. The policies which had sought to protect the region from
dependence on too few staple industries succeeded instead in introducing a new kind of vulnerability, reliance upon firms which largely
kept top management and research and development units out of the
region, and hence gave it no local foundation for new and independent
growth.

Neither the old nor this new vulnerability seemed likely to be too
serious in the late 1950s. But the times were deceptive. The regional

policies had been designed to benefit the newer incomers rather than the indigenous older trades, and the long years of attempting to encourage the regional economy had offered scant protection to the staple industries.

The failure to pursue a consistent regional policy, or to attempt to eradicate real and imagined obstacles to the introduction of new industry, made inevitable a savage amputation of the older industries in the difficult decade of the 1960s.

10

The region's people

Population

The population of the west of Scotland between 1871 and 1961 had a quite different history from that of the preceding century. It grew twice as fast as that of Scotland as a whole, doubling from 1·2 to 2·4 million, increasing its share of total population from 36 per cent to almost half in 1961. But the trends of the main factors affecting population growth were reversed in this period. Birth- and death-rates moved downward; the rate of natural increase was halved. The inward tide of migrants was replaced by a massive outflow of people. The only factor constant since the earlier period was the movement of people into the towns.

The effect of these changes was not immediate, it became evident first in the trend of birth- and death-rates. The first deep cut in death-rates came in the 1870s, with the impact of sanitary reform, first in Glasgow, and then in the landward area of the adjacent counties in the 1880s and 1890s. Glasgow's death-rate declined sharply from about 30 per thousand in the 1860s to 25 per thousand in the 1870s: this was paralleled by a more modest contraction in the counties in the following decade. The real breakthrough to low levels of mortality came, however, immediately after the First World War, when the infant mortality-rate was dramatically reduced from a regional average of about 112 to less than 85 per thousand live births (Table 24). This was a remarkable and universal improvement, and followed the creation of the Maternity and Child Welfare Service in 1915. The Notification of Births Act, 1915, enabled local authorities to obtain a 50 per cent grant to make arrangements for supervising the health of expectant and nursing mothers and of children under five years: these provisions were further extended under the

TABLE 24 Rates of birth, death, infant mortality and natural increase, 1871–1960

Period	Scotland				West Scotland				Glasgow			
	BR	DR	IMR	NI	BR	DR	IMR	NI	BR	DR	IMR	NI
1871–80	34·9	21·6	123	13·3	38·5	24·0		14·5	37·4	25·2	161	12·2
1881–90	32·3	19·2	119	13·1	34·5	19·9		14·4	35·0	25·3	144	9·7
1891–1900	30·2	18·5	128	11·7	32·8	19·0		13·8	31·8	20·6	148	11·2
1901–10	28·4	16·6	116	11·8	30·1	16·4		13·7	28·4	16·4	149	12·0
1911–20	24·1	15·3	106	8·8	25·7	14·5	112	11·2	31·5	14·5	134	17·0
1921–30	21·5	13·7	89	7·8	22·2	13·0	85	9·2	21·4	14·2	106	7·2
1931–40	17·9	13·4	78	4·5 ⎱	19·1	12·6	80	6·5*	18·6	13·9	101	4·7
1941–50	18·8	13·3	57	5·5 ⎰					18·4	13·8	111	4·6
1951–60	18·5	12·1	30	6·4	19·9	12·3	38	7·6	19·4	12·3	46	7·1
1960	19·4	11·9	26	7·5	20·4	11·5	28	8·9	21·6	12·2	31	9·4

* Figures for 1931–50

IMR = Infant Mortality-Rate: NI = Natural Increase

Sources: Annual Reports of the Registrar General for Scotland; J. Cunnison and J. B. S. Gilfillan (eds), Glasgow; Third Statistical Account of Scotland, Glasgow 1958

Maternity and Child Welfare Act, 1918. These measures, together with the Midwives (Scotland) Act, 1915, took simple hygiene and post-natal care into the homes of the working classes. The infant mortality-rate was again greatly reduced during and after the Second World War, this time by new medical and pharmaceutical discoveries in the control of bacteria. Consequently, infant mortality in 1961 was only one-fifth that of 1871, and the overall death-rate had been more than halved.

The birth-rate also decreased steadily in these decades, though the reasons are less easy to discern. The main down-turn again came in the decade 1911–20. The absence of young men in the forces overseas and the employment of young women in the munitions factories must have had some effect on the number of births. The maintenance of low levels for the next twenty years undoubtedly reflected the economic hardship of the inter-war years as a barrier to marriage. Further, the large volume of emigration from the region sent out mostly people in the main reproductive age-groups. This downward pressure on births was not relieved till after the Second World War. Then renewed prosperity, regular work, and a returning fashion for larger families swept the birth-rate upward for the first time in thirty years.

The immediate result of declining death-rates and an even more rapid shrinkage in births was to halve the region's rate of natural increase (Table 24). This turned abruptly downward in the 1920s, averaging 7·7 per thousand from 1921 to 1960. The growth of the region's population was brought almost to a halt. The population had increased by 85 per cent from 1871 to 1921, but grew only by 9 per cent between 1921 and 1951. This was a remarkable reversal for a region which had experienced such explosive population growth for over 150 years, and the change in fortune was directly linked to migration.

Net inward migration continued to add to the region's population before 1901, but to a much more reduced extent than before 1871. Indeed, in one decade, the 1880s, the region lost almost 32,000 persons by net emigration. This was the result of a boom of investment and development in the dominions and colonies attracting Scotsmen overseas. In spite of this the region gained 75,500 persons by net migration in the thirty years between 1871 and 1901, about 10 per cent of the total population increase for the period. This compared with a net loss of 483,000 for Scotland as a whole, about a quarter of the total natural increase. The region's pull on people clearly weakened before 1901, and after that was replaced by a net loss of some of the natural increase in each decade. The west of Scotland, like the country at large, became a source of net emigration. Over 763,000 people left the region between 1901 and 1961, a loss of almost 60 per cent of the total natural increase: this compared with a Scottish outflow of 1,388,000, some two-thirds of the natural increase for the country.

TABLE 25   *Net gains and losses by migration, 1871–1960 (figures in 000)*

Period	Ayr*	Dun-barton*	Renfrew*	Lanark,* incl. Glasgow	Glasgow†	Lanark‡
1871–80	− 17·2	+ 7·2	+ 19·9	+ 10·9	− 38	− 48·9
1881–90	− 25·5	+ 5·9	− 4·0	− 8·2	− 11	+ 3·2
1891–1900	− 6·3	+ 4·6	− 52·5	+ 120·8	+ 29	+ 91·8
1901–10	− 23·7	+ 7·7	+ 10·3	− 98·7	− 82	− 16·7
1911–20	+ 1·9	− 7·0	− 47·5	− 82·7	− 67	− 15·7
1921–30	− 39·8	− 16·6	− 36·2	− 110·2	− 51	− 59·2
1931–50	− 4·0	− 2·1	+ 2·2	− 194·5	− 139	− 55·5
1951–60	− 1·1	+ 4·7	− 10·1	− 115·7	− 112	− 3·6

Sources: * Annual report of the Registrar General for Scotland, 1953, Appendix IX
     † A. K. Cairncross, *Home and Foreign Investment, 1870–1913*; D. J. Robertson, 'Population Past and Present', in *Glasgow*, Third Statistical Account of Scotland, ed. J. Cunnison and J. B. S. Gilfillan
     ‡ Obtained by subtracting Glasgow results from the combined Lanarkshire and Glasgow data
Note: Net migration is arrived at by comparing estimates of the natural increase of the population with the actual recorded increase between two censuses. If the recorded increase is greater than the estimate of natural increase there has been a net gain (+) by migration. If the recorded total is less than expected by natural increase there has been a net loss (−) of some of the natural increase by migration

The pattern of gains and losses among the counties is complicated by boundary changes which transferred large numbers of people to Glasgow. An attempt has been made to eliminate these from the migration patterns in Table 25. Ayrshire lost part of its natural increase in every decade save 1911–20, while Dunbartonshire gained consistently up to the First World War, and Lanarkshire still attracted migrants till 1900. In the latter case it was the expanding steel and engineering industries around Motherwell, and the new mining investment in the middle Clyde valley, which pulled workers into the county. In Dunbartonshire migrants were attracted by the booming shipyards and marine-engineering industry. The draw of these industries is also reflected in the late gain in the county of Renfrewshire between 1901 and 1910. Glasgow, in contrast, lost part of its natural increase steadily throughout the period, making only one small gain in 1891–1900. It clearly became the second city of the Empire more by transfers of population from adjacent counties than by its own natural increase. Glasgow gained 60,000 persons from Renfrewshire in 1891, and a further 38,000 in 1912: at the latter date Glasgow also added 185,000 persons from Lanarkshire. The city increased its total population, but its natural increase still drained away as lack of work and intolerable pressures on housing drove people out of the region between the wars. The small gain in Renfrewshire and Dunbartonshire at the end of the period reflects a movement of people into the new suburban housing developments, particularly in middle-class areas like Newton Mearns, Milngavie and Bearsden.

This outward movement of people much reduced the importance of the immigrant in the region's population. In 1871 nearly 30 per cent of all persons in the west of Scotland were immigrants, but in 1961 they represented only 15 per cent of the total population. This reflected the greater attraction of new job opportunities in England and overseas, and the fact that the type of work available in the region had changed significantly. In the nineteenth century poor Irish and Highlanders had been attracted by unskilled work in factories and mines. Consequently, the Irish represented 43 per cent of all immigrants in 1871, and a third in 1901. The Highlanders added another fifth. These two groups represented two-thirds of all the incomers in 1871. In strong contrast, the Irish represented less than 15 per cent of the immigrants in 1961, and together with the Highlanders, only a third of all incomers. The balance had swung in favour of the English as the main immigrant group: this reflected the importance of small gross additions in the post-Second World War years, as the new industries demanded new skills in management and operation, and attracted a new kind of middle-class immigrant to live in the region. However, even this significant incursion could do little to offset the outward flow of people from the region, or reverse the slowing down of the rate of growth of the population. After making every allowance for changes in the birth- and death-rates, it is clear that both the growth and stagnation of the population in the west of Scotland was dominated by the ebb and flow of migration.

These major movements of people into and out of the region were paralleled by a continuous internal shift of population into the towns in a third phase of urbanisation between 1871 and 1914. The basic framework of towns was extended by the expansion of existing and newer towns in response to the influence of new investment in coalmining, the erection of the modern steel industry, and the huge expansion of marine engineering and shipbuilding. In the central Clyde valley mining settlements like Cambuslang, Blantyre, Burnbank and Larkhall quickly grew to prominence. On the northern edge of the coalfield their growth was overshadowed by the expansion of the new steel towns from Mossend in the west to Motherwell–Wishaw in the east. The combined population of Motherwell and Wishaw was 17,511 in 1871, but 65,643 in 1911, a growth of almost four times. Even this spectacular increase was dwarfed on the west side of Glasgow in the shipbuilding towns. Govan grew over four-fold from 19,200 in 1871 to 89,600 in 1911: Renfrew increased more than three times from 4,100 to 12,600, and on the north bank, Dumbarton doubled in size from 11,400 to 20,600. Most striking of all was the progress of Clydebank: it grew from total obscurity, with only two farms on the site of J. & G. Thomson's yard in 1871, to a town of 37,500 in 1911. No other town in Britain grew so fast in these years.

The urban network had been clearly delineated in 1871, but the considerable growth to 1914 brought about a coalescence of the urban settlements in the confined lowland of the Clyde valley, to create what is now called the Central Clydeside or Glasgow conurbation. It is in this complex of urban areas that the extent and speed of urbanisation has been most evident. In 1961 the Clydeside conurbation contained 35 per cent of Scotland's population, twice the proportion of the population of England and Wales living in London. With Glasgow at its centre, and tentacles of heavily built up country stretching out along the major urban axes described earlier, the conurbation compressed 1·8 million people into a tiny area of 150 square miles. This huge concentration of population has persisted in recent decades, despite a fourth phase of urban development since the end of the First World War. Some towns like Greenock and Gourock began to decline absolutely in population from 1921, and Glasgow's population slipped downward from its peak of 1,128,000 in 1939. The main characteristic, however, was that all the main urban areas in the region experienced a slackening in their rate of growth, as inward migration gave way to emigration.

The end product was a very highly urbanised region in 1961 (Table 26). Lanarkshire was the most completely urbanised of the counties, and even Ayrshire, the most rural of the counties in 1901, shared the high proportion of urban living common throughout the west of Scotland. Over 95 per cent of the region's people were urban dwellers in 1961, compared with just over 85 per cent for Scotland. The tendency for the population to concentrate in a few large towns had also continued. By 1961, the west of Scotland contained thirty of Scotland's fifty-eight towns with populations in excess of 10,000; these thirty towns housed 78 per cent of the entire regional population and over 80 per cent of the urban population. This was slightly less than the proportion in the larger

TABLE 26   *Percentage urban population by county in West Scotland, 1871–1961*

County	1871	1901	1961
Ayr	65·1	67·7	87·4
Dunbarton	63·7	81·4	94·2
Lanark	87·9	92·1	97·3
Renfrew	84·0	89·5	95·2
West Scotland	82·4	88·0	95·4

Source : Compiled from censuses of Scotland

towns in 1901, and reflects the substantial move of population out of the town centres toward the suburbs in search of more pleasant living conditions.

After two centuries the urbanisation of west-central Scotland was almost complete. Industrial towns continued to grow in the 1950s because of the natural excess of births over deaths, and the movement of people from less to more favoured localities. But the number of people who remained to be made urban dwellers, as distinct from rural dwellers, was very small. Moreover, the inter-war and post-war drift to the suburbs had not reduced the congestion of urban living; it had merely filled in most of the remaining open spaces. In fact by 1961 the central core of the conurbation was gradually losing the appearance of separate and readily-identifiable towns. It was becoming more a complex mixture of built-up territory and open spaces, where total coalescence was prevented only by the happy accident of a local geography in which numerous deeply-entrenched streams broke up and separated the sprawling mass of brick and mortar. These natural green belts had, by the 1950s, been complemented by others laid down by planners who grasped at the breathing space provided by the slowing down of urban growth to begin the long task of rehabilitating and reshaping the urban environment. The problem was tackled on many fronts, including the construction of new towns at East Kilbride and Cumbernauld, the redevelopment of Glasgow, and the introduction of the 'overspill' policy, by which people displaced by slum clearance in Glasgow were received in other towns within and outside the region. These efforts focused attention once more on the continuing attempt to overcome the twin problems of housing and health in the heavily-urbanised society of west-central Scotland.

Housing and health

Efforts to improve housing and health in the west of Scotland proceeded in three phases after 1870. The first stage of amelioration stretched to the First World War; the second extended from 1919 to 1945; the third covered the post-war period between 1945 and 1960.

Each stage derived part of its character from the legislative framework in operation at the time. The first period began with the 1867 Act 'to consolidate and amend the law relating to Public Health in Scotland'. This enabled local authorities to appoint sanitary inspectors and medical officers of health: it also gave some authority to remove nuisances on receipt of complaints, including the demolition of old and insanitary houses. Little use was made of this power, the larger burghs preferring to shoulder the expense of obtaining more specific Burgh Police Acts from parliament. A more formal framework did not emerge till the reconstruction of local government twenty years later, after which there flowed a series of 'Housing of the Working Classes' Acts in 1890, 1900 and 1903. The Public Health (Scotland) Act, 1897, was also relevant, for the first time giving local authorities power to control the type and amenity provision of houses constructed in their areas. The Housing Acts permitted the local authorities to prohibit the continued use of property pronounced unhealthy by their inspectors, as well as enabling them to undertake substantial improvement schemes by slum clearance. These powers were further extended in the Housing, Town Planning, etc. Act, 1909. By then the local authority could act in three ways to remove defects in housing revealed by the sanitary inspectors. It could force owners to make improvements by obtaining an order under the Public Health Act from a magistrate, sheriff or justice; under the Housing Acts the authority itself could issue an order prohibiting the habitation of a dwelling till improvements were carried out; for dwellings of under £16 annual rent the local authority could call on the owners to make repairs, or close the house down if the situation merited it.

Unfortunately, this body of legislation was largely permissive; local authorities could condemn and remove defective property, but no legislation obliged them to provide replacement housing. The powers at the disposal of local authorities therefore remained primitive during a period of extraordinarily rapid urban growth. This left the provision of housing mainly in the hands of private-enterprise builders, who met the demand in two gigantic building booms in 1868–77 and 1893–1904.

Changes in the census definition of a 'house' make it difficult to give an overall figure for the net increase in housing in the region. In Glasgow, however, over 65,000 houses were added between 1871 and 1911, though this included transfers through boundary extensions. Judging from the applications made to the Dean of Guild Court for building in this period, at least two-thirds of the new housing was undertaken in the two housing booms. Most of the new construction was for tenements to be rented to the working classes, mainly in two- and three-room apartments, though up to a quarter of all houses built in Glasgow in the first building boom were single-ends, that is, one-apartment houses.

The private builders in Glasgow housed over 10,000 persons each year in the building booms, but even this could not contain the demand for house room. The poorest of the working classes still supported an active making down, or subdivision, of existing property into single apartments. Lodgers remained a feature, but diminished in importance in the face of the spread of the model lodging house system in Glasgow and the surrounding counties. The Corporation opened its first two municipally-controlled lodging houses in 1871, and by 1902 owned seven establishments. There were another sixty lodging premises on the register at this time, giving accommodation for 9,705 men and 577 women, about 1 per cent of the city's population.

The desperate need of the poorest classes for cheap, rented and 'furnished' accommodation also fostered the growth of the 'farmed' house system. This practice was again most common in Glasgow and the larger towns like Paisley and Greenock. It involved owners farming out their property to factors in return for a fixed rent. The house farmers then subdivided the property, filled it with the most basic of household goods, and rented the accommodation to sub-tenants. These houses offered the most dismal of shelter to a transient population at rents of 8d. to 12d. per double room per night. The daily rental was partly in response to the fact that the labourers who made use of the facility were paid daily, and factors feared the rent money would be expended in drink if not collected regularly. House farmers controlled about 900 houses in Glasgow in 1900, providing living space for about 2,700 persons.

Model lodging houses and farmed houses were the last resort of men and women who were frequently out of work. Many of these houses also came within the category of 'ticketed houses' in the oldest and most congested parts of the city. Dwelling houses of up to three rooms and less than 2,000 cubic feet of air capacity were measured and ticketed to show the maximum number of persons who could legally sleep there. The minimum allowance was upgraded in 1890 to 400 cubic feet per adult, children under ten years counting as half a person. In 1902 Glasgow had 20,000 ticketed houses, sheltering 74,000 persons, about 10 per cent of the entire population. Ticketing did give a meagre control over congestion and overcrowding. Paisley began to apply the system at the end of 1901.

In the city and large towns, the housing needs of the workmen in steady employment were mainly met by the private builder. But he did not have an entirely clear field. Local authorities, improvement societies, and co-ownership tenancy schemes also began to provide some housing for the working classes.

The City Improvement Trust began its demolition of slums in earnest in 1871. By 1874 over 15,000 persons had been displaced, and two years later, another 10,000 had had their houses pulled down. The intention had been to clear congested slum property and to sell the sites to private builders for redevelopment. Unfortunately, the credit crisis which followed on the failure of the City of Glasgow Bank in 1878 coincided with a sharp decline in building activity and a fall in land prices. This left the Trust with much land and slum property on its hands throughout the inactive years from 1877 to 1887. The burden of owning so much expensive city-centre property eventually forced the Trust to begin to build tenement property on its own. It erected two small buildings in the Drygate in 1887, and another two in the Saltmarket in 1888. This was the beginning of municipal house building. A second Improvement Act was obtained in 1897 to further the work, and by 1914, the Trust had expended nearly £600,000 on erecting new tenements. This outlay had enabled it to build 2,199 new houses, providing accommodation for about 10,000 persons. These were mainly from the more prosperous tradesmen class, paying rentals of about £5 per year for a single apartment and £8 for a two-roomed house. The Housing Acts also enabled other local authorities to move in this direction.

But only 3,484 families were in local authority housing in the large towns in 1914, out of a total of 346,387 households. This was barely 1 per cent of the families: in Glasgow the proportion was 1·3 per cent, and in Greenock 1·5 per cent. In Clydebank, Hamilton and Kilmarnock the proportion was well below 1 per cent.

The local authorities were quite cold-blooded in their housing policies. There was no attempt to cater for the impoverished classes. These houses were for a few selected tenants: those in regular work, on good income, and of impeccable habits. This type of provision was extended in Glasgow by a private building and improvement society, the Glasgow Workmen's Dwelling Co. Ltd. This non-profit-making enterprise was established in 1890 with a capital of £40,000. It aimed to prove that adequate housing could be provided at reasonable rents; the refurbishing of old property was its main concern, though it did build two new blocks, one near the Cathedral, in Rottenrow, the other in Bridgeton. By 1902 the company owned 669 houses, which had cost it £54,000, and returned a rental of over £4,600 per year. The Company, like the Corporation, carefully selected its tenants: further, it charged four weeks' rent deposit plus a week's rent in advance before entry. Each of its properties had a resident caretaker. The rents charged varied between £4 17s. 0d. and £7 per year for single apartments, depending on whether they were in new or re-claimed property, while the two-apartment rents ranged from under £8 to £11 per year. This compared with about £6 for single-ends and £9 for two apartments in private tenement property. The society proved its point that good-quality houses could be provided, but it did not significantly lower the rents at which such accommodation was made available.

Compared with this, the costs of housing in the co-ownership schemes were well beyond the average workman. Under the provisions of the 1909 Housing, Town Planning, etc. Act, any public utility society could borrow up to two-thirds of the cost of houses erected. A public utility society was defined under the Industrial and Provident Societies Act of 1893 as any society whose rules prohibited paying a dividend in excess of 5 per cent. When it obliged its members to take up shares of loan stock for the purpose of qualifying for a house built by it, it became a co-partnership or co-ownership society. The idea of low-density garden-suburb housing built out of the funds of subscribers grew out of the co-operative movement in 1888, and was applied by Cadbury's at Bournville in 1900, and by Henry Vivian in the garden suburb development at Ealing. It spread to Scotland after 1900, and about eight societies were in existence in 1914. The earliest in the west of Scotland appears to have been the Gourock and Greenock Tenants Ltd, established in 1912 to provide housing for Admiralty workers at the new torpedo plant. It was followed in 1913 by the Glasgow Garden Suburb, which opened its first sixty houses at Westerton in 1914. The promoters also established the Greenock Garden Suburb in 1914, and other schemes were begun at Renfrew and Irvine. The lowest annual rent at Westerton was £18 18s. 0d. and the average tenant's wage was £2 10s. 0d. per week, far beyond the earnings of the mass of the working class. The following year the war, by putting a stop to government loans, brought the expansion plans of the society to a halt.

These experiments contributed little to the housing of the working classes, who were utterly dependent upon private-enterprise building. Unfortunately this virtually ceased after about 1904. The reasons are not clear, but contemporaries adduced rising building costs, high interest rates, increasing feu duties and landlord taxes. The working classes were unable, or unwilling, to meet the new higher costs with higher rentals. Tenement building continued after 1904, but was mainly for the middle classes, of substantial red standstone properties with discreet tiled closes and spacious rooms. The consequences of this piecemeal response to rapid urban growth are evident. In 1911 over 80 per cent of the families in the west of Scotland still lived in houses of one to three rooms. However, the proportion of one-roomed apartments had diminished sharply from over 40 per cent in 1870 to 18 per cent in 1911. Further, the two- and three-roomed house had become more common, almost two-thirds of all families living in houses in this group by the later date. It should also be added that the average size of room increased substantially in the newer tenements. The density of occupation per room also declined from 1·9 to 1·7, though this was still above the Scottish average of 1·4. Both the improvement in density of occupation and in average house size had been achieved by modest slum clearance of the oldest and smallest houses in most large towns, together with substantial building of new tenement property with houses bigger than one apartment.

In spite of this, housing conditions in the large towns were still grim. People still lived at appalling densities in the heart of Glasgow. The 1902–3 Municipal Commission on the Housing of the Poor revealed that in congested areas dominated by ticketed and farmed-out houses, densities ranged from 508 to 876 persons per acre. In parts of Greenock densities rose to 717 per acre, and in Coatbridge to between 635 and 650 per acre. Taking even the high level of three or more persons per room as a definition of overcrowding, the 1911 census revealed that 30 per cent of Ayshire's population was officially 'overcrowded'. The proportion in Dunbartonshire was a quarter, and reached nearly 40 per cent in Lanarkshire, including Glasgow. Individual communities, Airdrie, Hamilton and Motherwell, registered 40 per cent overcrowding, Coatbridge and Wishaw 45 per cent.

Mere figures convey very little of the great pressure this placed on life. Alexander McCallum, a sanitary inspector in Glasgow, declared to the Municipal Commission in 1903 that the nightly inspections of ticketed houses revealed 'both men and women concealed in every corner ... hidden in the cupboard, in presses, under the bed, and even on the house-tops. In the worst case ... we took 7 off an adjoining roof, 11 adult persons being found in the house which contained only 880 cubic feet ...'. Such conditions meant a total lack of privacy, and in single-ends meant that the children were forced out of doors. A minister on his evening visitations found 'children everywhere – sitting in closes and on the stairs, trying to play, often half asleep, on bitter winter nights'. The problem was at its most extreme at birth and death. Mrs Mary Laird giving evidence to the Commission on behalf of the Women's Labour League maintained of living in one room: 'if decency at the beginning of life is ... made difficult, decency at the end is made impossible. The beloved dead is laid on the bed and all the usual domestic duties ... has to be done with ever that still pale form before them'. This went on for three days, the body being moved to the table or coal bunker at night to enable the family to get to sleep.

The deprivation did not end there, for the test of household amenity omitted much. In 1915, 93 per cent of one-roomed houses and nearly two-thirds of two-roomed flats in Glasgow shared the use of a water closet, frequently between four families. In Clydebank, which was a 'new-tenement' town built since 1870, few houses had separate sculleries, the sink commonly being in the kitchen. In Paisley, water closets were shared by up to three families, and in Motherwell between three and four tenants shared this facility. These were among the most progressive towns according to the report of the 1917 Royal Commission on Housing of the Industrial Population in Scotland; much of the population must have been less well provided for.

Housing conditions eased only slowly in this period, old houses deteriorating into slums faster than new houses could be built and older property cleared. In spite of this the health of the urban population appeared to improve fairly rapidly, and the overall death-rate in the region declined by a fifth between 1871 and 1910. Further, there was a substantial decrease in the rates of death from the major diseases, though Glasgow, as representative of the west of Scotland's congested industrial towns, retained rates above the national averages (Table 27).

There were three important shifts in the nature and treatment of the public-health problem. First, the virulence of the major epidemic diseases receded in the 1870s as the sanitary reform movement gained

I

momentum. This induced a fall in the adult death-rate and released fever hospitals, especially in Glasgow, to begin to make provision for other cases. Second, as epidemic fever waned, childhood infectious diseases came to the fore, and the population of hospitals became younger as more cases of scarlet fever, diphtheria, measles and whooping cough began to be treated. Third, the death-toll from pulmonary tuberculosis declined sharply, as did that from bronchitis: but pneumonia advanced again, affecting children as a complication of measles or whooping cough. These three changes revealed a close and depressing relationship linking ill health, the young age-groups, and poor housing conditions.

TABLE 27   *Death-rate per 100,000 of population in Scotland from the principal epidemic diseases and certain others, 1871–1915*

Disease	Quinquennial Averages				
	1871–5	*1881–5*	*1891–5*	*1901–5*	*1911–15*
Typhoid fever	42	27	19	11	5
Typhus fever	23	4	1	0	0
Smallpox	38	0	1	3	0
Measles	39	36	51	32	33
Scarlet fever	106	36	20	9	13
Whooping cough	60	61	53	49	41
Diphtheria	62	45	37	17	18
Respiratory tuberculosis	254	213	175	148	110
Bronchitis	258	211	186	124	108
Pneumonia	91	109	128	146	129
All diarrhoeal diseases	95	74	79	71	53
Cancer	47	55	69	86	110

Comparisons with Glasgow at related dates

Disease	*1885–94*		*1916–25*	
	Scotland	*Glasgow*	*Scotland*	*Glasgow*
Typhus fever	1·5	2·9	0·0	0·3
Smallpox	0·5	0·3	0·4	1·1
Scarlet fever	21·5	39·0	6·5	6·2
Whooping cough	59·5	106·0	29·0	42·9
Diphtheria	39·0	43·9	13·0	13·7
Measles	46·0	78·0	26·0	43·3
Diarrhoeal diseases	74·5	51·5	33·0	47·4

Sources: Annual reports of the Registrar General for Scotland; W. A. Horne, 'Health', in *Glasgow*, Third Statistical Account of Scotland, ed. J. Cunnison and J. B. S. Gilfillan, Glasgow, 1958

The concentration of death in the smaller houses was quite striking. In the 1880s Dr J. B. Russell reported in his pamphlet *Life in One Room* that, 'Of all the children who die in Glasgow before they can complete their 5th year, 32 per cent die in houses of one apartment and not 2 per cent in houses of five apartments and upwards.' In the 1890s, while the overall death-rate in congested areas like Cowcaddens and High Street was over 30 per thousand, it was less than 10 per thousand in the spacious districts of Blythswood and Woodside. Later still, in 1911, the male infant mortality-rate in Glasgow was 210 per thousand in one-roomed houses, but only 103 in those of four rooms. This discrepancy was widespread in the west of Scotland. In Renfrewshire, for example, the infant mortality-rate in the upper district was 81 per thousand in 1913: but in villa areas within the same district there had been no infantile deaths that year.

The recognition of this relationship coincided with a change in medical thinking towards the prevention of disease as distinct from its treatment. This made clear the need to improve housing standards to make possible the successful treatment of disease. It also emphasised the need to extend hospital accommodation. An entirely new phase of public health activity was ushered in in the 1890s with a widespread reform of the administrative machinery. The Local Government Act, 1889, carried the stimulus of sanitary reform into the counties, where almost the first effect was to begin to replace the wet ashpit privies by the water closet. In the same year, the Infectious Diseases (Notification) Act enabled local authorities to determine the occurrence of certain diseases directly they were identified, and this was made obligatory throughout Scotland in the revised Public Health Act of 1897. The 1890s consequently witnessed the recognition that the promotion of public health was a definite function of local government. This laid the foundation for a successful first attack on the main causes of mortality in the industrial towns and villages.

The changes in the causes of death away from epidemic fevers towards childhood ailments quickly revealed that diseases of the lungs were a serious factor. In the 1880s and 1890s deaths from respiratory diseases represented over a fifth of all deaths in Glasgow, and up to half of all the respiratory deaths were among children under five. It was argued that the tenement was an ideal spreading ground for all forms of disease, but that poor ventilation and the close proximity of people, especially prepared the way for lung complications. The Housing Act, 1890, moved to ameliorate this relationship by requiring the removal of doors from the box-beds, which were common in tenements, and in Glasgow the 1892 Building Act prohibited enclosed beds in new buildings.

For the moment this was as far as general provision for remedying the causes of lung disease went. Treatment for such diseases was also neglected at this point, for the major emphasis in the public health movement was still on fever and the more infectious diseases. The transfer of responsibility for public health from the parishes to county districts in 1889 enabled new county hospitals to emerge, but almost without exception their concern was for cases of scarlet fever, measles, whooping cough and diphtheria, while the epidemic diseases of smallpox, typhoid and typhus were still treated in isolation units. Nevertheless, any extension of hospital services was an improvement. Lanarkshire acquired a site for a central hospital at Dalserf near Motherwell in 1890, together with three others for smaller local hospitals at Stonehouse, Longriggend and Shotts. In Ayrshire the private hospitals at Kilmarnock and Ayr were supplemented by a number of smaller local units, and a similar extension occurred in the other counties.

The relative neglect of lung diseases, and especially pulmonary tuberculosis, by the hospital services was surprising. The tubercular patient was generally left to spread his consumption by contact, in spite of the fact that Koch had identified the tubercle bacillus in 1882, and there had followed an early suspicion that the disease was transmitted by sputum and coughing in confined places. Moreover, the link between animal tuberculosis and its transfer to man through meat and milk was also mooted at this time. Glasgow, indeed, prohibited the sale of tubercular carcases for human consumption in 1890, and as early as 1899 the Local Government Board prohibited the sale of milk from cows with tubercular udders. However, it was not till 1912 that pulmonary tuberculosis was made a notifiable disease. Since the National Health and Insurance Act, 1911, provided for Treasury grants in aid of treatment, there followed a new phase of hospital building. The tubercular patient at last began to be isolated from the general community in an attempt to speed recovery and prevent the transmission of the disease in the crowded towns.

The public health movement developed on two planes in this period, one at the level of the man in the street, the other within the medical and hospital services. In the first instance there was a sustained effort to improve the sanitary conditions of the towns and villages through piping in pure water, extending scavenging and cleansing services and in attempts to improve the quality of housing. Within the medical sphere the hospital services changed from being general fever establishments in the 1870s towards becoming units for the treatment of infectious diseases of children in the 1880s and 1890s. After 1910 they moved to a third phase, where tuberculosis sanatoria gained prominence. This was paralleled by a general change in medical philosophy, placing more emphasis on the prevention of illness.

These developments combined to save young lives. Sources of infection were removed from the home and isolated in hospital, and the contemporary improvement in diet, as more protein became available with imports of meat, also contributed to improving health. The first result was a lowering of the general death-rate after 1870. When this generation of more robust young men and women began to have their own children, the timing coincided with the beginnings of the Maternity and Child Welfare Scheme in 1915. A generation after the adult death-rate had begun to decline, the infant mortality-rate also began to come down in the decade after the First World War.

The worst features of public ill health, which had grown out of rapid industrialisation and urbanisation, were lessening by 1915. But although epidemic fevers had been largely eradicated, and while even pulmonary tuberculosis had been much reduced, another lung and respiratory disease, pneumonia, had assumed new prominence. Further, cancer as a cause of death appeared to be on the increase, as did heart disease. High death-rates had been brought under control in the major nineteenth-century illnesses, but the full benefits of the considerable advances springing from the reorganisation of public health administration were only to be felt after the First World War.

Ill health and low vitality lay in wait for those who survived into the working age-groups in the industrial towns. Life there meant 'insufficient supplies of water, unsatisfactory . . . drainage, grossly inadequate provision for the removal of refuse . . . the unspeakably filthy privy-midden in many . . . mining areas . . . gross overcrowding and huddling of the sexes together in the congested villages and towns'. These deficiencies were based on a building style which had produced 'groups of lightless and unventilated houses in the older burghs, clotted masses of slums in the great cities . . . streets of new tenements . . . developed with the minimum regard for amenity'.

These were the terms in which the commissioners reported on the Housing of the Industrial Population in 1917. They found that the tenement, old or new, lay at the heart of the problem: yet they did not completely condemn this building style. The evidence suggested that the tenement was solidly built, was warmer than cottage-style housing, and housed the workman close to his place of employment. On the other hand, the tenement was inextricably mixed up with industrial buildings. Its normal form of a hollow square with enclosed back-court excluded much light and ventilation, and the predominance of small apartments encouraged overcrowding. In addition, the solidity of the structure tended to permit the outer shell to outlive the useful life of the interior, hence encouraging a gradual and serious deterioration in living conditions. The commissioners therefore recommended that no more single-apartment houses should be built; that tenements should not exceed three storeys, and that the hollow-square building pattern should be abandoned. They favoured a single block, or terrace construction, to admit light and air to front and rear of the structure. To promote this they advocated that future building for the working classes should be vested in the local authorities. These recommendations were to form the basis of the Housing, Town Planning, etc. (Scotland) Act, 1919.

This obliged local authorities, or in default the Scottish Board of Health, to undertake house-building for the working classes: it was intended that the building should meet the general housing needs of the population; and the Act embodied subsidies in aid of construction. These provisions were consolidated in the Housing (Scotland) Act, 1925, which has remained the basis of all subsequent legislation. A further enactment in 1930 briefly restricted subsidies to houses replacing unfit dwellings, but the Housing (Scotland) Act, 1935, broadened the provision again, and introduced a new concept. Subsidies would, in future, aid two types of construction. The first type, as previously, was to replace unfit houses; the second was to build houses to end overcrowding. This was an open-ended commitment. It confirmed the acceptance of the view that local authorities had a continuing responsibility to meet the housing needs of the working classes, and indeed to improve the overall quality of the housing stock.

The second major phase of house construction therefore followed on the passing of the Housing Act, 1919, which inaugurated the real beginning of local authority house building. Some 120,000 local authority houses were built in the region between 1919 and 1945, and this represented 70–80 per cent of all new building undertaken in these years. These new houses were entirely different from previous dwellings in four ways: in the constructional material; in type of house; in density of building; and in size of house. Building in stone was abandoned in favour of brick. The old type of tenement was replaced by the two-storey, semi-detached and terraced cottage-style of house. Nearly all had some garden ground, and the density of construction was normally to house less than 100 persons per acre. Experimental steel houses, like the Weir House, were also constructed in small numbers, as were occasional batches of timber houses. This latter type was frequently of single-storey, semi-detached cottage construction, as at Carfin in Lanarkshire. These developments could not properly be described as garden suburbs, but the idea of low-density garden-city layouts clearly influenced the local authorities in their rejection of high-density tenement building.

In Glasgow the Corporation wavered between the new cottage-style of low-density building which dominated their efforts in the 1920s, and a new type of three-storey flat-tenement, which was more common in the 1930s. Nearly 70 per cent of their construction was cottage-style in the 1920s, and was at its lowest densities of less than fifty persons per acre in Knightswood and Mosspark. Conversely, in the 1930s, much of the building was on cleared tenement sites, and over 68 per cent of new houses were of the new flatted three-storey type. The Blackhill, Haghill and Balornock schemes were typical of this new style, at densities of up to 100 persons per acre. This innovation was influenced not only by the growing shortage of building land, but also by reductions in government subsidies and a steep rise in building costs. The cost of three-apartment dwellings had more than halved from £800 in 1920 to just under £300 in 1935, but then rose steeply by over a third to more than £400 in 1938.

Another departure from previous habits was the building by the local authorities of larger houses. The single apartment was virtually abandoned, fewer than 100 being built in Glasgow between 1919 and 1944 out of a total of over 54,000 units. Construction throughout the region was dominated by the three- and four-roomed house, the three-roomed apartment representing over 60 per cent and the four-roomed house about one-quarter of all construction. This was typical of the whole of Scotland, where 344,209 new houses were built from 1919 to 1941. Seventy per cent of these were local-authority houses, the remainder being privately built. This was the reverse of the situation in England and Wales, where 4·2 million houses were constructed, only 28 per cent being built by local authorities.

In spite of this massive phase of new house building Scotland's housing situation was still desperate. The Housing (Scotland) Act, 1935, laid down detailed standards of occupancy, and on this basis it was found that more than one-quarter of all houses in Scotland were overcrowded, while the proportion was just over 4 per cent in England and Wales. With only one-ninth of the population of England and Wales, Scotland had 259,000 overcrowded houses, compared with 341,000 in the rest of the country. The gap between building achievement and housing need left Scotland with an estimated requirement of 300,000 houses in 1938. Under the provisions of this Act an overcrowding survey was conducted in Glasgow. This revealed that 31 per cent of all families were found to be in overcrowded dwellings, and 70 per cent of these were declared unfit for occupation.

This notwithstanding, the inter-war housing programme made possible a substantial improvement in the public health of the community in the west of Scotland. The general death-rate and the infant mortality-rate both declined by about a third. The improvement was particularly marked in the large towns and in Glasgow. Between 1911 and 1931 the infant mortality-rate in Glasgow fell from 134 to 106 per thousand live births. In Kilmarnock the rate was reduced from 97 to 78, and Coatbridge registered a massive decline from 140 to 84. In every case, however, the rate increased slightly by 1941, owing to the initial deterioration of living standards at the start of the Second World War.

While better housing helped, much of this improvement could be traced to the extension of the Child Welfare Scheme after 1915, and to the development of the health-visitor services in the 1930s. The health of the young members of society was also greatly improved by the growing supervision of illness under the schools health services. Education authorities could form health departments from 1908, but it was mainly after the Local Government (Scotland) Act, 1929, that the provision gained ground. School meals for 'necessitous' cases also expanded in the 1930s, and the Milk Act, 1934, made available free milk to the same schoolchildren. Some authorities, notably Glasgow, extended this by making milk generally available in schools at the cost of ½d. for a third of a pint.

Within the hospital services much of the effort continued to be concentrated on the treatment of tuberculosis. Improved X-ray equipment gave better results from the 1920s, and the extensive development of sanatoria and hospital care halved the death-rate from pulmonary tuberculosis from 110 to 56 per 100,000 of the population between 1915 and 1939. However, the disruption of the tuberculosis service with the onset of war, together with the congestion of military camps and war-time conditions, forced the rate upward again to 62 per 100,000 between 1941 and 1945. Other forms of tuberculosis also yielded rapidly to the improvements stemming from enactments affecting dairies, the pasteurisation of milk, and the beginning of tuberculin-tested milk herds.

However, as tuberculosis was controlled and the infant mortality-rate decreased, other killers became more prominent. Heart disease claimed less than 10 per cent of all deaths in 1925, but took nearly one-quarter in 1945. Cancers also increased their toll, and deaths from vascular lesions of the nervous system doubled. Even while overall mortality-rates were waning, incapacity through ill health remained a chronic problem. In 1936, 18 per cent of all days lost at work among the insured population were caused by respiratory complaints, including tuberculosis. Rheumatism accounted for a further 12·5 per cent, and diseases of the nervous system 10·8 per cent. Over 40 per cent of all days lost at work were the result of endemic debility stemming from overcrowding, a polluted and damp atmosphere, and poor nutrition.

The gains made by the public health movement had been impressive, but much remained to be done. Although the infant mortality-rate had greatly decreased, the Boyd Orr Report on Infant Mortality in Scotland (1943), prepared for the Department of Health in Scotland, found that Scotland had a poor record. The quinquennial average rate for 1934–8 was 77 per thousand live births. This was the highest of seventeen countries, including the Dominions, the USA and all the countries of western Europe except Spain and Portugal. The west of Scotland had the highest infant mortality-rate of any region in Britain, and Glasgow the highest rate of any town in the country. The committee felt that this adverse situation was primarily the result of 'poverty, faulty feeding and poor housing'.

Poor housing had once more been placed at the centre of social deprivation and poor health, and though the war years severely restricted
house building, the government had already committed itself in 1935 to
the ending of overcrowding. The necessity for this was emphasised in
1940 with the publication of the report of the Royal Commission on the
Distribution of the Industrial Population, the Barlow Report. This
advocated a decentralisation of people and industries to relieve urban
squalor. It also supported the concept of urban planning. In 1943, the
Secretary of State for Scotland invited the constituent local authorities
of the Clyde valley to set up a Regional Advisory Committee to consider
the planning problems of the region.

At the same time Glasgow's Town Clerk prepared a report on the
post-war planning problems of the city. This revealed that 700,000
persons were crushed into an area of 1,800 acres in the centre of the city.
They existed at an average density of 400 per acre, rising to over 700 per
acre in some districts. This meant that one-third of the region's population
was squeezed into a tiny area of three square miles in the middle of
Glasgow. Other large towns, like Paisley, Greenock, Motherwell and
Wishaw, shared very high central densities, and throughout the region
there was a clear need to decentralise the urban population. Glasgow
reckoned that over half its population, some 550,000, would have to be
displaced by redevelopment, and allowing for new building on the cleared
areas, this left 250,000–500,000 Glaswegians to be housed beyond the
boundaries of the city. The problem was to find somewhere for the
people to go.

Glasgow's problem was particularly acute, and Bruce, the city engineer,
produced a detailed redevelopment plan in 1945. This advocated a 50-
year phased development programme, including the redevelopment of
existing housing schemes to take higher densities of occupancy. The
Bruce plan maintained that high-density redevelopment would enable
Glasgow to rehouse all its population within its own boundaries, but
this was contrary to the policies put forward in the Clyde Valley Plan in
1946. Sir Patrick Abercrombie and his team of planners recommended
freezing the land use of the remaining unbuilt land around Glasgow to
provide a minimal green belt: they also proposed a range of densities
for redevelopment schemes within the region. Within Glasgow they
advised densities of up to 120 persons per acre in the centre, diminishing
to half that at the periphery. The range for the large burghs was from
90 to 60 per acre from the centre outward, and in the less-heavily
urbanised landward areas of the counties they recommended net residential densities of 75 down to 45 per acre.

These proposals meant that Glasgow could not hope to resettle all its
population within the city boundaries. In order to meet the overspill, the
Clyde valley planners recommended the establishment of one or more new

towns, the selected sites being at Bishopton, Cumbernauld and East Kilbride. Even then the planners thought that at least 100,000 persons would have to be rehoused entirely outside the region, owing to lack of building space.

The Secretary of State for Scotland accepted the idea of a perimeter green belt to prevent the total coalescence of the region's towns. Outside Glasgow the main industrial towns were thought to have available sufficient building land to comply with the recommended redevelopment densities. It was intended that they would build away from Glasgow to prevent the merging of the settlements and retain the integrity of the flimsy green belt. To help ease Glasgow's problem, the new town of East Kilbride was designated in 1947. Unfortunately, no provision was made to help pay for the transfer of households. Houses were only made available if jobs had been secured in East Kilbride, and since Glasgow did not like the idea of overspill, Glaswegians were reluctant to move.

The collection of data in the 1951 census highlighted just how difficult was the whole problem of urban planning and renewal in the west of Scotland. The Scottish Housing Advisory Committee had, in 1944, advised the acceptance of a new occupancy index of not more than two persons per room, the first room in the house being excluded from the calculation. On this basis, in 1951, 20 per cent of the region's population, and almost 25 per cent of the population in the Central Clydeside conurbation was living in overcrowded conditions. This compared with only 1·7 per cent in Greater London, and 5·8 per cent on Tyneside, the most 'officially' overcrowded conurbation in England. Further, the region was dominated by very small houses of few rooms. Almost 70 per cent of all houses were in the 1–3-room size, compared with under 40 per cent in Tyneside, the English conurbation with the highest proportion of small houses. Within the Clydeside conurbation no fewer than 42·7 per cent of all houses were of 1–2 rooms, and another 30 per cent of 3 rooms. The test of household amenity added even more weight to the need for redevelopment; even when shared households are excluded, the Central Clydeside conurbation emerged in a far worse plight than any of the other British conurbations (Table 28). Throughout the west of Scotland over one-third of all households had to share a water closet, and almost half the households did not have the exclusive use of a fixed bath. Indeed, 42·5 per cent of all households in the region had no bath at all, and in Glasgow the proportion was 50 per cent.

The dispute over redevelopment densities, and the unwillingness of Glasgow to contribute financial aid to families wishing to take up residence in East Kilbride, confined the bulk of Glasgow's population to the building that was still possible within the city, between 1947 and 1952. The Corporation would have built at high densities to retain the popula-

TABLE 28   *Percentage of households without exclusive use of household amenities in 1951*

	Cooking stove	Piped water	Kitchen sink	Water closet	Fixed bath
West Scotland	10·6	9·4	9·1	35·5	49·0
Glasgow	9·5	7·8	7·8	37·6	55·9

Percentage households in British conurbations without exclusive use of amenities: 1951 (excluding shared households)

Conurbation	Cooking stove	Piped water	Kitchen sink	Water closet	Fixed bath
Central Clydeside	2·1	0·6	0·6	29·2	43·0
Greater London	0·6	3·2	1·5	2·6	14·4
West Midlands	1·8	5·8	3·6	8·9	32·2
West Yorkshire	1·8	2·7	0·6	24·1	39·4
S.E. Lancashire	2·1	1·7	0·4	5·1	37·3
Merseyside	1·6	2·0	1·4	1·1	23·9
Tyneside	0·9	3·2	6·7	9·0	34·4

Sources: Census, 1951; R. Grieve, *The Clyde Valley – A Review*

tion of the city, but the shortage of bricks and the uncertainty over the strengths of the newly-adopted prefabricated building techniques enforced relatively low-density building. Consequently, Glasgow Corporation built two-, three- and four-storey houses on the diminishing land resources at the edges of its own territory.

Between 1945 and 1949 the city built over 12,000 houses, 7,600 of which were of the cottage type in semi-detached and terraced blocks. One-third of these were of three apartments, and 58 per cent of four apartments. Much of the cottage-style housing was in relatively low-density schemes like Penilee, Berryknowes and Mansewood. Then, as land began to run out, the Corporation reverted to a concentration on three- and four-storey tenement-style flats at densities of up to 120 persons per acre. Over 24,000 houses were built from 1950 to 1954. Some 18,500 of these were of three and four storeys in huge peripheral housing schemes like Easterhouse, Barlanark, Castlemilk and Drumchapel. These were high-density housing units, tenements on the edge of the countryside, with neither the amenity of the old city and its services, nor the recreational facilities of better-planned garden-suburb estates.

As the city's building land diminished, its planners estimated, in 1952, a requirement of 209,000 houses to meet immediate and future needs: the Corporation recognised that at least 135,000 of these could not be built within the city limits. By 1956 the problem had reached an acute stage. The Corporation and the Secretary of State came to an agreement to set up a second new town at Cumbernauld. Unlike East Kilbride, Cumbernauld was to be a high-density development; Glasgow agreed to contribute to the removal costs of its citizens. Even with two new towns, it was realised that not all of Glasgow's displaced inhabitants could be rehoused as redevelopment proceeded. Consequently, the Housing and Town Development (Scotland) Act, 1957, made provision for overspill agreements. Towns agreeing to accept Glasgow families, and to offer them new homes, qualified for annual housing subsidies. By 1960, Glasgow Corporation had signed twenty-two overspill agreements with towns throughout Scotland.

In this way the ten-year dispute between Glasgow Corporation and the Scottish Development Office over redevelopment densities, the green belt and the policy of overspill, was finally resolved. The strategy for the region's towns was now clear. The burghs and landward areas of the counties could mostly extend their housing programmes within the densities recommended by the Clyde Valley Plan, while Glasgow was permitted to ring itself round with large-perimeter housing schemes of relatively high density, and at the same time to clear its central slums, housing part of the displaced population in redevelopments on the same site, the remainder being housed in the new schemes, the new towns and in overspill-agreement areas. The long-term plan was to reduce Glasgow's population by between 250,000 and 300,000 persons, to turn it into a city of some 750,000 persons.

A series of Housing Acts of 1946, 1950, 1952 and 1957 developed a complex system of grants and subsidies, and with this assistance new housing estates mushroomed around and within every town in the region. Between 1945 and 1961 over 132,000 permanent new homes were built, all but 25,000 being undertaken by the local authorities. In this third phase of home provision the local authorities built houses at an extraordinary rate. The benefits were clearly evident within a decade. In 1951, 39 per cent of all households in the region had been still in one- and two-roomed houses; this proportion had declined to 29 per cent by 1961. Conversely, three- and four-roomed households increased from 49 per cent to 59 per cent of the total, and the density of occupation improved from 1·14 persons per room in 1951 to 0·99 in 1961. The amenities also improved substantially as new houses replaced the old. The proportion of families without exclusive use of a water closet decreased from 35·5 per cent to 18·7 per cent, and those without exclusive use of a fixed bath declined from 49 per cent to 30 per cent: the proportion with no bath changed from 42 per cent to 27·6 per cent. These were immense advances in a short space of time.

But the region had by no means solved its housing problem. The planners' dilemma was that, as standards of what was acceptable in housing rose, houses formerly regarded as satisfactory had to be added to the already long list for clearance and redevelopment. It was partly by these higher standards of acceptability that, in 1958, Glasgow's Medical Officer of Health classed 30 per cent of the existing housing stock as either totally unfit, or unacceptable and incapable of improvement. Glasgow already had a housing waiting-list of 100,000 families in 1958, and her problem was compounded by reclassification. All the local authorities suffered from this. In addition, the problem was further aggravated when the region's population began to grow again, after 1945, when all the predictions had been that it would decline.

More people and new classifications of housing standards inevitably meant that yet more houses had to be erected on diminishing supplies of building land. This turned the planners' eyes towards a new style of high-density building: the multi-storey flat. The Housing Act, 1957, extended subsidies to cover this type of construction. In Glasgow, plans were made to incorporate multi-storey dwellings in the proposals for the comprehensive redevelopment areas, that is, central areas which were to be entirely cleared and rebuilt at lower densities and higher standards than the existing nineteenth-century tenements permitted. The multi-storey flat was, of course, a vertical tenement, permitting high residential densities in association with some open space. The Hutchesontown-Gorbals Comprehensive Redevelopment area was the first to include some multi-storey buildings, thus enabling the overall density of occupation to be set at 164 per acre. The plans for this were approved in 1957, and in 1959 the Anderston Cross plans were accepted by the Secretary of State at redevelopment densities of 166 per acre. These were up to twice the density common in the inter-war and early post-war housing schemes, and reflected Glasgow's great shortage of building land. By 1960 the Corporation had submitted plans for twenty-nine such development areas for approval by the Secretary of State, thus carrying the housing programme of the city into the 1990s.

The type of house and form of building selected to tackle the region's housing problem did not please everyone. New towns were not initially popular: extensive housing schemes, far from the shops, entertainments and diversions of the city, did not meet with universal approval. Subsequently, the multi-storey flat has been compared unfavourably with the more traditional housing styles. There were undoubtedly shortcomings in the housing programme, but planning the social fabric of a complex and overcrowded industrial-urban society was no easy task. The planners aimed to preserve amenity and open space consistent with improved housing, and the local authorities hoped to provide a separate house for every family in need. The two aims were not entirely consistent, but had worked surprisingly well together between 1946 and 1960. Whatever the criticisms levelled at the planners and local government, they had to be set against the undoubted contribution made by these bodies to better health and a decent life style in the community at large.

With the gradual removal of slums, the dismantling of old miners' rows, and the extensive building of new and modern houses, the worst features of inadequate sanitation and defective public-health provision began to disappear. The sizeable extension of water filtration and sewerage works in the inter-war years was an important factor in this. These steady and sometimes unspectacular advances contributed to the better health of the community. However, their impact was immeasurably increased by dramatic developments in the medical services after 1945.

In 1948 the provision of medical care for the community at large was revolutionised with the introduction of the National Health Service, which extended free treatment to every person. Hospital services, formerly split up between the counties and large burghs, were unified in a regional administration, the Western Regional Hospital Board. The general practitioner services were co-ordinated under the control of an executive council, which also had responsibility for the administration of the dental, ophthalmic, and pharmaceutical services. Larger local authorities were designated as local health authorities, and though they lost control of the hospitals, they retained the maternity and child welfare services, the provision of midwives and health visitors, and were responsible for home nursing, care and after-care facilities, vaccination and immunisation. Moreover, under the Education (Scotland) Acts of 1945 and 1947, the local education authorities were empowered to extend the schools' medical services, and insist on the medical inspection of pupils. They could also make available their own free medical and dental treatment in addition to that provided under the general health service.

The consequences of this bold step were real and lasting. In the 1930s the indexes of backwardness in public health had been high infant mortality-rates and the continual drain on adult life by tuberculosis. By 1960 there had been immense improvements in both areas. Scotland registered an infant mortality-rate of 26 per thousand live births in 1960, the same as the USA. Compared with 1934–8, Scotland had brought her rate close to that of England and Wales, though not yet into line with the very low rates of countries like Sweden and the Netherlands. The improvement was closely tied to the extension of ante-natal and post-natal care. Medical opinion held that the rate was unlikely to be reduced further until there was closer liaison among hospitals, doctors, and child clinics in an attempt to instruct expectant mothers in diet and mother-craft. On the other front, tuberculosis had been successfully contained.

In 1945 deaths from tuberculosis represented over 6 per cent of all deaths in Scotland, while in 1960, the proportion was only 0·8 per cent. The overall death-rate per 100,000 of the population had declined from 82 to 13, and for respiratory tuberculosis, from 56 to 12. The success with this disease was based largely on the effectiveness of streptomycin, introduced in 1947, together with the mass radiography campaigns in schools and towns in the 1950s.

In spite of these advances, the general death-rate declined only slowly, from 12·6 per thousand in 1941 to 11·5 per thousand in 1960. This was low for the region, and on a par with England and Wales, but since countries like Canada, the Netherlands and Japan already had death-rates of under 8 per thousand, there was still room for considerable improvement in the region. None the less, the achievement was remarkable. In 1960 not a single life was lost to typhoid or typhus fever, scarlet fever, smallpox, whooping cough or diphtheria. The great killers of the nineteenth and early twentieth centuries had been overcome, and only tuberculosis remained as a small threat from that time.

Further reductions in the general death-rate were likely to prove difficult to achieve, for three groups of disease – heart disease, cancers, and vascular lesions of the central nervous system (cerebral haemorrhage etc.) – showed massive increases in the short period from 1945 to 1960. These three groups accounted for 52 per cent of all deaths in 1945, but over 68 per cent in 1960. In the same time the virtual ending of tuberculosis had elevated deaths by violence to fourth place in the fatality table. These trends signposted the beginning of a new phase in problems of public health and hospitalisation. The hospitals and public health services had, for over 100 years, sought to deal with the physical illnesses of the people who paid the cost of physical deprivation in congested urban living. But as the problems of physical health stabilised, new dangers from stress and strain and the pace of modern life began to emerge. The heart diseases, the cancers, the vascular lesions fall at least in part in this new category. Already in the 1950s, mental disturbances showed an alarming increase. These were likely to occupy the medical and welfare services as much in the future as physical ailments had done in the past: the stress illnesses appeared to be at least part of the cost of life in an old region undergoing rapid and sometimes violent change in its physical and social environment.

The growth of income

We have seen how the benefits of industrialisation had barely touched the mass of the workers in terms of advances in their real income before 1870: were the rewards more widely spread in the succeeding century? This is no easy question to answer, in spite of the growing volume of facts and figures on wages and prices, but the task is made a little less difficult if the changes are looked at in three periods: 1870–1920, 1920–45, and 1945–60.

In the first stage, there are two contrasting periods dividing around the years 1900–5. In the earlier phase the region's workers enjoyed a broad advance in money wages, which ranged from as low as 20 per cent in the cotton-spinning sector to between 25 and 50 per cent in mining, engineering and the building industries. The average advance in money wages seems to have been in the order of 30–40 per cent. Simultaneously, prices dropped steeply for virtually all commodities between the mid-1870s and late 1890s. Evidence given to the Municipal Commission on the Housing of the Poor in Glasgow in 1903 claimed that Professor Smart of Glasgow had estimated the average price fall at 30 per cent. This was supported by other evidence. A local builder submitted a chart showing the comparative price of provisions, prepared by a grain miller, which suggested an average price decrease of 28 per cent between 1857 and 1903.

It is not possible to move from this to an estimate of advances in real income. We do not know how consumer preferences changed in response to such price movements. Moreover, there is the complication of rents. Rent, as an item of expenditure, took between 10 and 14 per cent of the weekly wage, and moved sharply upward between 1870 and 1900. In the northern districts of Glasgow, rents for single apartments were £3 17s. 6d. in 1866 and £6 in 1901, an advance of 55 per cent: two-apartment rentals advanced by 38 per cent from £6 10s. 0d. to £9 in the same period. This must have eaten deeply into incomes, notwithstanding that they themselves had increased substantially in money terms. The balancing of these diverse changes is virtually impossible, but most people must have experienced a growth in real income of 30–50 per cent. A. L. Bowley placed the advance at 40–45 per cent for Britain as a whole between 1880 and 1896, and the scanty Glasgow data suggest a change of similar dimensions.

The next twenty years were not so favourable for the working population. Between 1900 and 1913 wages and prices advanced rapidly together, and while engineers and miners possibly kept just ahead, most of the workforce may well have experienced some deterioration in real income. Certainly, on balance, there could have been little or no overall gain in the decade before the First World War. The war itself induced a doubling of most wage rates. The average weekly wage of all underground workers in coalmines increased from £1. 16s. 6d. in 1914 to £3. 8s. 3d. in 1918. Rates for fitters and turners in shipyards doubled from £1. 19s. 0d. to £3. 17s. 0d. per week, while the tonnage rate for iron puddlers increased from 9s. 0d. to 18s. 0d. Every trade registered an advance of two or two-and-a-half times in wage rates and earnings during the war. But it was barely enough to keep up with prices. Bowley estimated that prices outran wages in the first three years of war, were caught up by wages in 1918, and that wages only pulled ahead in 1919 and 1920. It appears that wages and prices moved upward together for much of the time between 1900 and 1920, sometimes one ahead, sometimes the other. The unhappy conclusion is that real income seems barely to have grown throughout these twenty years.

This still left the region's people with a substantial gain in real income over the half century, 1870–1920, but most of the progress had come in the years of steadily falling prices from about 1876 to 1896. The meagre evidence also suggests that the region's wage earners improved their position a little more rapidly than those in the main industrial districts of England. The evidence of wage-rates and earnings in the 1870s, together with the findings of the 'Returns of Wages' published between 1813 and 1886 (C-5172), indicated at the later date that the wages in all the main trades in the west of Scotland were 5–10 per cent lower than the average for Britain. By 1900, the vigorous expansion of the major Clydeside industries appears to have pulled most wage rates and earnings to a rough parity with those elsewhere in Britain.

The phase of quickly-advancing wage rates and prices was brought abruptly to an end in the savage deflation of 1921. The next period 1920–45 was dominated by low or declining prices for much of the time. Wage-rates also came down, and the question is whether wages declined by less or more than prices in these years. We have two advantages in assessing the changes in this period, which were absent previously. After 1914, the regional diversity in wage rates declined in Britain with the growth in nationally-negotiated wage settlements, and from 1924, we have estimates of the growth of national income for Scotland. These advances make it possible to use indexes of British retail prices to judge the Scottish experience, since we can assume that regional divergence was no longer so large as had been the case in the nineteenth century.

The national income figures, which represent estimates of Scotland's contribution to, or share of, the total national income of Britain, allow us to leave the juggling act of balancing diverse wage-rates, and to take a view of the growth of the income per head of the total population. This conceals the experience of individual groups, but enables us to take a better view of average change. The evidence suggests that, even allowing for the heavy unemployment of the inter-war years, there was a modest growth in real income (Table 29). The stationary money wages in the 1920s were converted into a 9 per cent real income advance by declining prices, but this was cut away in the catastrophe of the Depression. Real income fell by about 16 per cent between 1929 and 1932, but recovered by almost 30 per cent to 1938. Over the whole period both money and real income per head of the population advanced by about 15–16 per cent. This was a quarter slower than for the entire country, and consequently

TABLE 29   *Estimates of income per head of population, 1924–60 (Scotland)*

Year	Income/ head (£)	Real income/* head (£)	% of UK* real income/ head
1924	83	74	93
1932	67	67	90
1938	86	86	89
1948	182	104	91
1952	249	282	90
1960	377	329	85

* 1924–48 at 1938 prices; 1952–60 at 1956 prices
Sources: 1924–48 adapted from A. D. Campbell, 'Income', in *The Scottish Economy*, ed. A. K. Cairncross, Cambridge University Press, 1954; 1952–60 compiled from G. McCrone, *Scotland's Economic Progress*

Scottish real income per head declined from 93 per cent of the British average in 1924 to 89 per cent in 1938. This indicated that the gap between rates of earnings in Scotland and England had opened up again: the discrepancy was back to the level of the 1870s, at somewhere between 5 and 10 per cent.

This deterioration was briefly halted during the Second World War when money income per head doubled from £86 in 1938 to £170 in 1944. When adjusted for prices, this meant an advance in real income of about 25 per cent. Consequently, real income per head for Scotland grew by about 40 per cent between 1924 and the end of the Second World War. Most of the improvement came after 1936, and the advance was especially rapid during the war. The benefits appear to have been in favour of the wage earner as distinct from the salaried group. Wages represented 32 per cent of the national income in 1924, but nearly 37 per cent by 1948.

The sustained advance of the war years was unhappily followed by a contraction in real income in the austerity years between 1945 and 1948, when in Scotland the fall was about 9 per cent compared with only half that for the country as a whole. This was balanced by a growth of similar magnitude from 1948 to 1952, and followed by a jump of 18 per cent to 1960. However, Scotland had been doing less well than the rest of the country throughout this third phase from the end of the war. The gap in average rates of pay remained pronounced, Clydeside rates averaging 93 per cent of the British level in 1960. Moreover, Scottish real income per head grew only half as fast as the British advance, with the result that

Scotland fell further behind. In simple money terms, income per head in Scotland was 92 per cent of the British average in 1952, but only 88 per cent in 1960. When allowance is made for price changes, real income per head in Scotland had decreased from 90 to 85 per cent of the British average. This was back to the gap which existed in the depths of the Depression in 1932.

The complexity of changes in wages and prices makes it impossible to give an estimate of the advance of real income for the whole period from 1870 to 1960. The most we can say is that real income probably grew by about 40 per cent between 1870 and 1920, and by another 40 per cent from 1924 to 1948. In the last period, the increase appears to have been in the order of 25 per cent. Throughout the entire period, real income per head in Scotland was lower than the average for the country as a whole. The standard of living of the region's people was continually depressed, in the present century, by lower average wage-rates, a higher proportion of declining and slow-growing industries, higher levels of unemployment, and a lower proportion of the active age-groups entering into the workforce.

The contrast between the two centuries on either side of 1870 could not be greater. The vigorous growth of the century of industrial revolution paid almost no dividend to the workers who helped make the changes possible. The second century of difficulty and decay has distributed the rewards of industrialisation in a remarkable way, embracing all sections of the community in the large advances in real income. Unfortunately, the failure of the region's economy to grow rapidly has meant that the advances have been less than they otherwise could have been. The people of the west of Scotland have been obliged to accept a lower standard of living than the British average partly because of the region's past, and partly because of the inadequacy of regional policy. This is yet another charge which the people of the region have had to bear as part of the price of progress in the west of Scotland.

Select bibliography

General

BREMNER, D., *Industries of Scotland*, Edinburgh, 1869.
CAIRNCROSS, A. K., *The Scottish Economy*, Cambridge, 1954.
CAMPBELL, R. H., *Scotland since 1707*, Oxford, 1965.
HAMILTON, H., *The Industrial Revolution in Scotland*, Oxford, 1932.
—— *An Economic History of Scotland in the Eighteenth Century*, Oxford, 1963.
SINCLAIR, SIR JOHN, *The Statistical Account of Scotland*, 21 vols, Edinburgh, 1791–8.

Trade

CAMPBELL, R. H., 'The Anglo-Scottish Union of 1707: the economic consequences', *Economic History Review*, 2nd series, 16, 1964.
PRICE, J. M., 'The rise of Glasgow in the Chesapeake tobacco trade, 1707–1775', *William and Mary Quarterly*, 3rd series, 11, 1954. Reprinted in *Studies in Scottish Business History*, ed. P. L. PAYNE, London, 1967.
ROBERTSON, M. L., 'Scottish commerce and the American War of Independence', *Economic History Review*, 2nd series, 9, 1956.

Transport

DEAS, J., *The River Clyde*, Glasgow, 1876.
KELLETT, J. R., *The Impact of Railways on Victorian Cities*, London 1969.
LINDSAY, J., *The Canals of Scotland*, Newton Abbot, 1968.
REED M. C. (ed.), *Railways in the Victorian Economy*, Newton Abbot, 1969.
THOMAS, J., *Scotland: the lowlands and the borders*, A Regional History of the Railways of Great Britain, Vol. 6, Newton Abbot, 1971.

Banking

CAMERON, R., *et al.*, *Banking in the Early Stages of Industrialisation. A study in comparative economic growth*, Oxford, 1967.

CAMPBELL, R. H., 'Edinburgh bankers and the Western Bank of Scotland', *Scottish Journal of Political Economy*, 2, 1955.
GOURVISH, T. R., 'The Bank of Scotland, 1830–45', *Scottish Journal of Political Economy*, 16, 1969.

Agriculture

BOARD OF AGRICULTURE, County Surveys, under the title *General View of the Agriculture of the County of* . . . , Two Series, 1793, 1812.
HANDLEY, J., *The Agricultural Revolution in Scotland*, Glasgow, 1963.
SMOUT, T. C., and FENTON, A., 'Scottish agriculture before the improvers', *Agricultural History Review*, 13, 1965.
SYMON, J. A., *Scottish Farming Past and Present*, Edinburgh, 1959.

Textiles

BAINES, E., *History of the Cotton Manufacture of Great Britain*, London, 1835.
CLOW, A. and N. L., *The Chemical Revolution*, Edinburgh, 1952.
ROBERTSON, A. J., 'The decline of the Scottish cotton industry 1860–1914', *Business History*, 12, 1970.
WARDEN, A. J., *The Linen Trade Ancient and Modern*, London, 1864.

The heavy industries

BIRCH, A., *The Economic History of the British Iron and Steel Industry 1784–1879*, London, 1967.
BURN, D., *The Economic History of Steelmaking, 1867–1939*, Cambridge, 1961.
BUTT, J., 'The Scottish iron and steel industry before the hot blast', *West of Scotland Iron and Steel Institute*, 73, 1965–6.
CAMPBELL, R. H., 'Investment in the Scottish pig iron trade, 1830–43', *Scottish Journal of Political Economy*, 1, 1954.
—— 'Developments in the Scottish pig iron trade, 1844–48', *Journal of Economic History*, 25, 1955.
—— 'Scottish shipbuilding', *Scottish Geographical Magazine*, 80, 1964.
DUCKHAM, B. F., *A History of the Scottish Coal Industry, Vol. 1, 1700–1815*, Newton Abbot, 1970.
GIBSON, I. F., 'The establishment of the Scottish steel industry', *Scottish Journal of Political Economy*, 5, 1960.
MILLER, A., *The Rise and Progress of Coatbridge*, Glasgow, 1864.
ROBB, A. M., 'Shipbuilding and Marine Engineering' in *Glasgow*, ed. J. CUNNISON and J. B. S. GILFILLAN, Glasgow, 1958.
SEXTON, A. H., 'The Metallurgical Industries', in *Local Industries of Glasgow and the West of Scotland*, ed. A. MCLEAN, Glasgow, 1901.

Population

CAIRNCROSS, A. K., *Home and Foreign Investment 1870–1913*, Cambridge, 1953.
ROBERTSON, D. J., 'Population Past and Present', in *Glasgow*, ed. J. CUNNISON and J. B. S. GILFILLAN, Glasgow, 1958.
TIVY, J., 'Population Distribution and Change', in *The Glasgow Region*, ed. R. MILLER, and J. TIVY, Glasgow, 1958.

Housing and health

BAIRD, R., 'Housing', in *The Scottish Economy*, ed. A. K. CAIRNCROSS, Cambridge, 1954.
—— 'Housing', in *Glasgow*, ed. J. CUNNISON, and J. B. S. GILFILLAN, Glasgow, 1958.
BUTT, J., 'Working Class Housing in Glasgow 1851–1914', in *The History of Working Class Housing*, ed. S. D. CHAPMAN, Newton Abbot, 1971.
CHALMERS, A. K., *The Health of Glasgow, 1818–1925: An Outline*, Glasgow, 1930.
CRAMOND, R. D., *Housing Policy in Scotland 1919–1964*, University of Glasgow Social and Economic Studies Research Paper No. 1, Edinburgh, 1966.
FERGUSON, T., *The Dawn of Scottish Social Welfare*, Edinburgh, 1948.
—— *Scottish Social Welfare 1864–1914*, Edinburgh, 1958.
HORNE, W. A., 'Health', in *Glasgow*, ed. J. CUNNISON and J. B. S. GILFILLAN, Glasgow, 1958.

The return to labour

BOWLEY, A. L., 'Changes in average wages (nominal and real) in the United Kingdom between 1860 and 1891', *Journal of the Royal Statistical Society*, 58, 1895.
CAMPBELL, A. D., 'Income', in *The Scottish Economy*, ed. A. K. CAIRNCROSS, Cambridge, 1954.
—— 'Changes in Scottish incomes 1919–1949', *Economic Journal*, 65, 1955.
GOURVISH, T. R., 'A note on bread prices in London and Glasgow, 1788–1915', *Journal of Economic History*, 30, 1970.
—— 'The cost of living in Glasgow in the early nineteenth century', *Economic History Review*, 2nd series, 25, 1972.
HOUSTON, G., 'Farm wages in Central Scotland from 1814–1870', *Journal of the Royal Statistical Society*, 118, 1955.
ROBERTSON, D. J., 'Wages', in *The Scottish Economy*, ed. A. K. CAIRNCROSS, Cambridge, 1954.

Between the wars

ALFORD, B. W. E., *Depression and Recovery? British Economic Growth 1918–1939*, Studies in Economic History, London, 1972.
BOARD OF TRADE, *An Industrial Survey of the South West of Scotland*, prepared by the Political Economy Department of the University of Glasgow, London, 1932.
BUXTON, N. K., 'The Scottish shipbuilding industry between the Wars. A comparative study', *Business History*, 10, 1968.
—— 'Entrepreneurial efficiency in the British coal industry between the Wars', *Economic History Review*, 2nd series, 23, 1970.
LESER, C. E. V., and SILVEY, A. H., 'Scottish industries during the inter-war period', *Manchester School of Social and Economic Studies*, 18, 1950.
SCOTTISH ECONOMIC COMMITTEE, *Scotland's Industrial Future: the Case for Planned Development*, Glasgow, 1939.

The economy after 1945

CAMERON, G. C., and REID, G. L., *Scottish Economic Planning and the Attraction of Industry*, Glasgow, 1966.
CAMERON, G. C., 'Economic analysis for a declining urban economy', *Scottish Journal of Political Economy*, 18, 1971.

JOHNSTON, T. L., BUXTON, N. K., and MAIR, D., *Structure and Growth of the Scottish Economy*, London, 1971.

MCCRONE, G., *Scotland's Economic Progress 1951-1960: A Study in Regional Accounting*, London, 1965.

ROBERTSON, D. J., and GRIEVE, SIR ROBERT, *The City and the Region*, University of Glasgow Social and Economic Studies Occasional Papers, No. 2, Edinburgh, 1964.

SCOTTISH COUNCIL (DEVELOPMENT AND INDUSTRY), *Inquiry into the Scottish Economy 1960-1961* (The Toothill Report), Edinburgh, 1961.

Index

A

Abbotshaugh, 32
Abercrombie, Sir Patrick, 249
Aberdeen, 50
Agriculture, 58–78;
cropping patterns, 75–6; enclosure,
67–8; farming practice, 62–4;
feu tenure, 60; implements, 69–70,
74–5; improvement of, 6, 7, 64–7;
infield-outfield system, 59–60;
landholding, 60–2; landownership,
76; leases, 62, 71; livestock
improvement, 71–2; rentals, 62;
rotations, 69; run-rig, 59; 'Society
for Improving of Agriculture and
Manufactures in the Shire of Ayr',
65; 'Society for Improving in the
Knowledge of Agriculture', 65, 81;
tenancies, 61; wages, 78; workforce,
77
Ainslie, John, 34, 39
Aircraft industry, 200, 201
Airdrie, 97, 145, 146, 205, 241
Albion Motor Co., 200, 201
Alexander, Claud, 65, 89
Alexander, William & Sons, 22
Alexandria, 85
Anderson, Dr Thomas, 74

Anderston, 149, 166
Annandale, 45
Ardeer, 171
Ardrossan, 32, 34, 35
Argyll, Duke of, 61, 65
Argyll Motor Co., 200
Arkwright, Richard, 87, 93
Arrochar, 1
Arrol, William, 175
Ayr, 41, 51, 76, 145, 146, 150
Ayrshire, 9, 10, 37, 38, 39, 40, 44, 46,
48, 60, 61, 68, 69, 70, 71, 72, 73,
75, 76, 86, 94, 98, 118, 120, 121,
124, 125, 138, 139, 141, 142, 143,
167, 169, 184, 198, 203, 233, 235, 240

B

Baird, Alexander, 56
Baird & Co., 197
Baird, James, 117, 120
Bairds and Scottish Steel, 217
Ballantrae, 1
Ballindalloch, 88, 89, 90, 102
Ballochmyle, 89
Banking, 48–57; bills of exchange, 57;
cash credits, 50; development of
branches, 50, 52; development of
chartered banks, 48; development of

joint-stock banks, 52–4; development of private banks, 52; Glasgow banks, amalgamations, 54; Glasgow banks, rise of, 54–5; investment in, 6; merchant involvement, 48; policy of Edinburgh banks, 53–4

Banks: Alexander & Sons, 50; Arms Bank (Cochran, Murdoch & Co.), 6, 48, 50, 52; Ayr Bank (Douglas, Heron & Co.), 34, 51, 52, 55; Ayrshire Banking Co., 54; Bank of Scotland, 48, 52; British Linen Co., 50; City of Glasgow Bank, 54, 55, 238; Clydesdale Banking Co., 54; Commercial Bank of Scotland, 52, 54; Coutts & Co., 50; Edinburgh & Glasgow Bank, 54; Galloway Bank, 91; Glasgow Banking Co., 52, 54; Glasgow Commercial Bank, 52; Glasgow Joint-Stock Bank, 54; Glasgow Merchants Bank, 52; Glasgow and Ship Bank, 54; Glasgow Union Bank, 54; Greenock Union Bank, 54; Hunter & Co., 54; Kilmarnock Banking Co., 52; Mansfield, Hunter & Co., 50; National Bank of Scotland, 54; Neale, James, Fordyce & Brown, 51; Paisley Commercial Bank, 54; Paisley Union Bank, 54; Renfrewshire Banking Co., 52; Royal Bank of Scotland, 22, 48, 52–3; Ship Bank (Dunlop, Houston & Co.), 6, 48, 50; Thistle Bank (Maxwell, Ritchie & Co.), 6, 48, 54; Union Bank of Scotland, 54; Western Bank of Scotland, 54, 55, 108

Bannatyne, Dugald, 148
Barclay Curle & Co., 181
Barrhead, 96, 146
Beardmore, William & Co., 129, 176, 178, 182, 189, 193, 200, 201, 205
Bearsden, 234
Beattock, 39
Beith, 86, 138
Belfast, 128
Bell, Henry, 10, 126
Bell, Patrick, 74
Bell, William, 85
Bentham, Jeremy, 102
Berthollet, C., 82
Bessemer, Sir Henry, 173, 174
Bilsland, Lord, 202
Bilsland, Sir Steven, 204

Birmingham, 207
Bishopton, 250
Black, Professor, 82
Blackhill, 34, 42
Blaenavon, 174
Blantyre, 89, 90, 93, 94, 99, 101, 102, 221, 234
Blantyre, Lord, 61
Bleachfields, 81
Bleaching powder, 133
Bleaching process, 81–2
Blochairn, 191
Board of Trustees for Improving Fisheries and Manufactures, 7, 32, 80–3, 85
Bogle, Robert, 88
Bo'ness, 32
Bonhill, 85
Bournville, 239
Bowley, A. L., 256
Bowling, 35
Boyd Orr, Sir John, 248
Bridgeton, 149, 166
Bridgewater, Duke of, 31, 36
British Linen Co., 82–3
Brock, Walter, 180
Brown, A., 91
Brown, John & Co., 182
Brownlaw, J. D., 200
Bruce, J. (Glasgow City Engineer), 249
Buchanan, Andrew & Co., 22
Buchanan, Archibald, 99
Buchanan, Hastie & Co., 25
Buchanan, James, 33
Burnbank, 234
Burns, Robert, 3
Bute, Lord, 102

C

Cadbury's Ltd, 239
Caddell, William, 115
Cairncross, Professor A. K., 207
Calder, 146
Calico printing, 85
Calton, 149
Cambuslang, 94, 168, 175, 192, 213, 234, 241
Cambusnethan, 146
Cammel Laird & Co., 182
Campbells of Blythswood, 148
Canals, 31–6; Forth and Clyde, 6, 32, 33, 42; Glasgow-Paisley-Ardrossan, 32, 34; Monkland, 33, 34, 36, 42,

118; Union Canal, 42, 44
Carfin, 154, 246
Carlisle, 39, 40
Carmacoup, 94
Carron Co., 115, 116, 118
Carronshore, 32
Cartwright, Edmund, 98
Caterpillar Tractor Co., Ltd, 223
Cathcart, Lord, 61, 65
Catrine, 89, 93, 94, 99, 102, 146
Causewayend, 42
Clark, J. & J., 164
Cleland, James, 97, 103
Clyde Iron, 217
Clyde Navigation Trustees, 30, 31,
204, 205
Clyde, River: improvement of, 6,
29–31; unimproved state, 28–9
Clyde Valley regional plan, 249
Clydebank, 164, 166, 188, 199, 200,
201, 219, 234, 239, 241
Clydebridge, 217
Coal: costs of production, 169; exports,
114, 123, 167, 198; markets, 114,
123, 166–7, 213–14; output, 9, 11,
113, 122–3, 167, 196, 197, 198, 214
Coalbrookdale, 115
Coalmining, 111–15, 122–5, 166–9,
195–8, 213–15; development plans,
213–14; employment in, 113–14,
122–3, 167, 196, 197, 214;
mechanisation, 168, 197;
productivity, 168, 197, 214;
profitability, 214; rationalisation,
197; serfdom, 113; wage policy,
196–7
Coatbridge, 33, 118, 122, 146, 191, 200,
205, 217, 240, 247
Coats Iron Works, 174
Coats, J. & P., 164
Cochran, Andrew (Lord Provost of
Glasgow), 37
Collieries: closures, 213–14;
in operation, 123, 167; ownership of,
123–4, 197
Coltness, 177
Colville, David, 176, 192, 193
Colvilles Ltd, 193, 216
Commissioners for Highland Roads
and Bridges, 39
Commissioners of Port Glasgow
Harbour, 28
Communications, see Canals, Roads,
Railways

Condie, John, 117
Conurbation: Central Clydeside, 3,
224, 226, 235, 250, 251
Convention of Royal Burghs, 80
Cook, James, 126
Corby, 192
Cordale, 85
Cort, Henry, 9
Cotton, 86–110; capital, 88–92, 96;
competition in, 105–7; consumption
of, 109; Cotton Operatives Union,
106–7; decline of, 163–6; effects of
American Civil War, 108–9;
employment in, 165; entrepreneurs,
88–91; Glasgow Cotton Spinning
Co., 165; hand-loom weavers, 97, 98,
103–5; hand-loom weaving,
organisation of, 97–8; imports, 92,
93, 96–7; labour supply, 7, 8; mills:
cost of, 91–2, establishment of, 93,
location of, 7, 93, in operation, 96;
ownership pattern, 102; power
looms, 103; power weaving, 106–7;
spindle capacity, 96–7; technical
innovation, 87, 95–6, 98–9, 106;
wage policy, 106–7
Coventry, 207
Cowan, Professor, 150, 151
Craig, John, 193
Creelman, James, 56
Crompton, Samuel, 87, 93
Crum, Messrs, 85, 99
Cullen, William, 82
Cumbernauld, 15, 236, 250, 252
Cumnock, 146, 213
Cunard Line, 129
Cunninghame & Co., 25, 48
Cunninghame, Finlay & Co., 22
Cunninghame, William & Co., 22

D

Dale, David, 56, 89, 102
Dalmuir, 32, 178, 182, 189, 200, 201,
205
Dalquhurn, 81, 85
Dalry, 94
Dalserf, 244
Dalsholm, 85
Darby, A., 9, 115
Deanston, 90, 102
Dempster, George, 89
Denny, William, 126, 179, 180
Diesel, Rudolph, 181

Diseases, *see* Health
Diversification, *see* Economic policy,
    Regional policy
Dixon, John, 41
Dixon, William, 41, 56, 118, 120, 148,
    174
Dobie, George, 126
Dolphinton, 1
Douglas, 47, 94, 146
Douglas, Sir William, 89
Drongan, 213
Drumpellier, 33, 34
Dubs, Henry, 175
Dumbarton, 32, 126, 146, 234
Dumfries, 39
Dunbartonshire, 10, 61, 70, 72, 76, 85,
    98, 139, 141, 142, 143, 169, 184,
    198, 199, 202, 233, 234
Dunblane, 99
Dundas, Sir Lawrence, 33
Dundee, 50, 89, 221
Dundonald, Lord, 73
Dunlop, Colin, 116, 120
Dunlop, James & Co., 192, 193
Dunlop, John, 71
Dunmore, Robert, 88

E

Ealing, 240
East Kilbride, 15, 93, 236, 250, 252
East of Scotland Malleable Iron Co., 122
Economic policy: diversification, 12,
    201; inter-war, 12, 185–6;
    nationalisation, 212, 213; regional
    policy, 202–9
Eddington, Thomas, 115
Edinburgh, 32, 37, 39, 40, 42, 48, 50,
    51, 52, 54, 82, 106, 126, 145, 169
Eglinton, twelfth Earl of, 34, 44, 61,
    64, 65
Elder, John, 129, 130, 179
Elderslie, 96
Elgin, Lord, 202
Elphinstone, Lord, 61
Employment, *see* separate industries
Enclosure Commissioners, 73
Engels, Friedrich, 154, 155
Epidemics, 150–3
Euclid (Great Britain) Ltd, 223

F

Fairfields Ltd, 129, 181, 182, 193

Fairlie, 126
Fairlie, Alexander, 70
Fife, J. W., 126
Finlay, Kirkman, 90, 107
Finnie & Co., 124
Flounders, Benjamin, 90
Foster & Corbet, 99
Freeland, John, 90
Fullarton, Colonel William, 68, 70

G

Gartcosh, 217
Gartsherrie, 42, 217
Germiston, 33
Gillespie, William, 90
Gillies, John, 115
Girvan, 76, 97
Glasgow Building Company, 148
Glasgow, city of: Chamber of
    Commerce, 24; development as a port,
    27; economy of, 1; housing:
    comprehensive redevelopment areas,
    253, cost of construction, 247,
    house types, 149, 251–3, house-
    building, 147–8, 251–3, housing
    requirements, 249, housing schemes,
    245, 251, overcrowding, 247;
    Improvement Trust, 152, 238–9;
    infant mortality, 138, 151; population
    of, 5, 8, 145, 146, 147; property
    developers, 148; public health
    legislation, 152; roads in, 37;
    Royal Infirmary, 137; shipping in
    harbour, 30, 31; tobacco trade, 6,
    21, 22, 23; trade of, 29;
    unemployment in, 199; water supply,
    152; Workmen's Dwelling Co. Ltd,
    239
Glasgow, Earl of, 61
Glassford, John & Co., 22, 32, 33
Glengarnock, 192
Golborne, John, 6, 29, 30
Gorbals, 148
Gourock, 235
Gourock and Greenock Tenants Ltd,
    240
Gourvish, Dr T. R., 158
Govan, 41, 129, 146, 178, 182, 217,
    234
Graham, Sir James, 73
Grangemouth, 35
Gray, J., 74
Greenock, 5, 21, 24, 26, 27, 28, 31,

126, 130, 145, 150, 199, 223, 235, 238, 240, 249
Greenock Garden Suburb, 240

H

Halley Motor Co., 200
Hallside, 10, 175
Hamilton, 40, 74, 86, 205, 239, 241
Hamilton, Dukes of, 61
Hamilton, Hugh, 91
Hamiltonhill, 33
Hamiltons of Dalziel, 65
Handley, J. E., 144
Hargreaves, James, 87
Harland and Wolff, 193
Harley, William, 148
Hay, Sir David Allan, 203
Health, 150–4, 230, 232, 241–5, 247–8, 254–5
Highland and Agricultural Society, 74
Highlanders: in West Scotland, 143
Home, Earl of, 61
Home, Francis, 82
Honeywell Controls Ltd, 223
Hood, James, 165
Hope, James, 39
Horrocks, J., 99
Hospitals: extension of services, 244; Glasgow Royal Infirmary, 137; Parliamentary Road Hospital, 153
Hot-blast: patent, 117; royalties, 120
Houldsworth, Henry, 91, 101, 120
Housing, 147–50, 236–41, 245–7, 249–54; amenities, 241, 252–3; building contractors, 148; construction booms, 237; co-ownership schemes, 239–40; densities per acre, 149, 240, 246; densities per room, 149, 240, 252; densities, redevelopment, 249–50; farmed houses, 238; Glasgow Municipal Commission on the Housing of the Poor, 240–1; house sizes, 149, 240, 252; local authority building, 239, 246–7, 252; lodgers, 149; lodging houses, 149–50, 151, 237; miners' housing, 153–4; multi-storey flats, 253; new towns, 250; overcrowding, 149, 240–1, 247, 250; overspill policy, 250, 252; rents, 149, 239, 240, 256; Royal Commission on Housing of the Industrial Population in Scotland (1917), 241, 245; Scottish Housing

Advisory Committee, 250; slum clearance, 152; subdivision of property, 149; tenements, backlands, 149; tenements, faults of, 245; ticketed houses, 152, 238
Houston, 90
Houston, Alexander, 48
Howden, James, 180
Hunter, John, 126

I

IBM, United Kingdom, 223
Inchinnan, 200
Income, 154–9, 255–9; money wages, 155–6, 256; national income estimates (Scotland), 257–9; real income per head, 258–9; standard of living, 157; trend of real wages, 158–9
Industrial estates: Carfin, 205; Chapelhall, 205; Dalmuir, 205; effects of, 206–7; employment in, 206, 222; Hillington, 12, 204–5; Hillington Estate Co., 221; investment in, 205; Lanarkshire Industrial Estates Ltd, 205; Larkhall, 205; Scottish Industrial Estates Ltd, 204, 221; Shieldhall, 205
Industrial Revolution: regional characteristics, 5; regional effects of, 8; regional origins, 19
Ingram, Archibald, 85
Irish: in West Scotland, 144–5
Iron industry, 115–22, 169–73, 194–5; competition in, 170; costs of production, 117; development of malleable iron, 121–2; entrepreneurship in, 120; furnace capacity, 172, 217; furnaces in blast, 115, 116, 118, 121; hot-blast technique, 9, 116–17; Iron and Steel Holding Realisation Agency, 215; pig iron: exports of, 121, imports of, 172, prices, 170, production, 9, 115, 116, 118, 120–1, 171, 172, 195, 215; profits in, 120; puddling, 9; technical backwardness, 170–1
Iron ore: black-band ores, 9, 116; imports of, 170; production of, 169, 194
Ironworks: Balgonnie, 118; Blair, 44,

120; Blochairn, 176; Calder, 115, 116, 117, 120; Calderbank, 121; Carron, 115; Chapelhall, 118; Clyde, 115, 116–17, 215; Coltness, 120; Dalmellington, 120; Devon, 115; Dundyvan, 36, 120, 121; Eglinton, 44, 120; Gartsherrie, 36, 118, 120; Glenbuck, 115, 118; Glengarnock, 44; Govan, 120, 121; Langloan, 36; Lugar, 120; Markinch, 115; Monkland, 118; Mossend Iron & Steel Co., 121–2; Muirkirk, 115, 116, 120; Omoa (Cleland), 41, 115; Portland, 120; Shotts, 41, 115; Wilsontown, 41, 115, 118, 120
Ironworks, closures, 217
Irvine, 41, 94

J

Jackson, Thomas, 56, 174
Jenner, Edward, 137
Johnstone, 34, 35, 93, 96

K

Kelly, William, 95, 102
Kenyon, James, 102
Kilbarchan, 94
Kilbowie, 166
Kilmarnock, 52, 138, 145, 146, 239, 247
Kilmaurs, 65
Kilwinning, 34, 44, 94, 137
Kimball & Morton Ltd, 164
Kincaid, Captain J., 130
Kinloch, Andrew, 99
Kirk, A. C., 129, 180
Kirkintilloch, 33, 42
Knightswood, 41
Koch, R., 244

L

Lace industry, 165
Lanark, 40, 47, 146, 150
Lanarkshire, 1, 9, 10, 32, 36, 39, 40, 41, 45, 48, 60, 61, 68, 69, 70, 72, 76, 86, 87, 94, 96, 97, 98, 118, 121, 122, 124, 125, 138, 139, 142, 143, 144, 146, 167, 168, 169, 184, 197, 198, 202, 214, 215, 227, 233, 235, 240, 246

Larkhall, 168, 205, 234
Laurie, David, 148, 149
Laurieston, 148
Leblanc, N., 133
Lennoxtown, 85
Lesmahagow, 47, 114
Linen, 79–86; British Linen Co., 84; costs of lint mills, 84; expansion of, 7; finance of, 84; heckling, 80; production, 83–4; scutch mills, 81; yarn merchants, 7
Linwood, 93
Lithgow, Henry, 193
Lithgow, Sir James, 193, 202
Lithgow, Sir William, 193
Lithgows Ltd, 193
Liverpool, 23
Lloyds of London, 132, 176, 178, 179
Lochwinnoch, 93
Lockerbie, 45
London, 37, 39, 40, 51, 128, 129, 199, 235, 250
Loudon, Earl of, 61, 64, 65
Lugar, 120
Luss, 70

M

McAdam, John Loudon, 38, 39
MacArthur, D. 126
MacGregor, John, 129
Mackintosh, Charles, 82, 116
McLauchlan, Archibald, 126
Manchester, 31
Marchmont, Earl of, 71
Marine engineering, see Shipbuilding
Martin, Pierre, 174
Maryhill, 35, 85
Meikle, Andrew, 70
Meikle, James, 70
Merry & Cunninghame, 120, 176, 177
Merry, James, 44
Miller, Captain, 150
Miller, Patrick, 126
Miller, Robert, 99
Milngavie, 234
Milton, 99
Milton, Lord, 82
Monklands, 9, 33, 34, 42, 86, 118, 119, 120, 153
Monkton, 94
Monteith, James, 88, 90
Monteith, John, 99
Morton, Andrew, 165

Mossend, 146, 234
Motherwell, 191, 192, 199, 205, 215, 233, 234, 241, 244, 249
Muirkirk, 8, 39, 41, 116, 120, 146, 213
Munn, James, 126
Murdoch, Andrew, 48
Murdoch, Peter, 48
Mushet, David, 9, 56, 116

N

Naismith, John, 69, 70
Napier, David, 126, 127, 128, 131, 180
Napier, James, 128
Napier, Lord, 32
Napier, Robert, 129
National Coal Board, 213
Neilson, J. B., 9, 116, 117, 120, 122
Neilston, 93, 96, 97
New Lanark, 89, 91, 93, 94, 95, 96, 101, 102, 146
Newcomen, Thomas, 112
Newhouse, 221, 223
Newton, 191
Newton Mearns, 234
Newton Stewart, 89, 90, 91
Nimmo & Co., 197
North British Locomotive Co., 166
Northumberland Shipbuilding Co., 193
Nuffield Trust, 203, 205

O

Omoa, 41, 115
Overspill policy, 250, 252
Owen, Robert, 91, 101, 102

P

Paisley, 5, 9, 80, 85, 86, 90, 92, 93, 96, 97, 98, 100, 101, 103, 105, 142, 145, 146, 164, 165, 199, 200, 238, 241, 249
Paisley Shawl, 100, 164–5
Paisley Thread Industry, 164
Parkhead, 200
Parsons, Charles, 181
Pearce, William, 129
Pennicuik, 93
Perth, 40
Pococke, Richard, 147
Pollokshaws, 85, 99
Population, 3, 4, 5, 8, 135–47, 230–6;

birth-rates, 136–40, 230–2; death-rates, 137, 230–2, 255; immigrants, 142–5, 234; infantile mortality, 138, 230–2, 248, 254; migration, 140–2, 232–4
Port development, 28–31
Port Dundas, 34, 35
Port Glasgow, 21, 24, 26, 27, 28, 29, 30, 31, 126, 219, 221
Portland, Duke of, 61, 65, 73, 154
Portland ironworks, 120
Prestonpans, 82

R

Radcliffe, William of Mellor, 98, 99
Railway companies: Ardrossan to Johnstone Railway, 44; Ardrossan Railway, 47; Ardrossan Railway Co., 34; Ayr and Dalmellington, 47; Ballochney, 42; Caledonian, 36, 40, 45, 46, 47; City of Glasgow Union, 46; Clyde Junction and Coatbridge, 46; Clydebank Junction, 46; Edinburgh and Glasgow, 44–5; Garnkirk and Glasgow, 42, 43, 44; General Terminus and Glasgow Harbour Railway, 46; Glasgow Barrhead and Neilston, 46; Glasgow Dumbarton and Helensburgh, 47; Glasgow Dumfries and Carlisle, 45; Glasgow Paisley and Greenock, 44; Glasgow Paisley Joint Line, 44; Glasgow Paisley Kilmarnock and Ayr Railway, 34, 44, 45; Glasgow and South Western, 36, 45, 47; Monkland and Kirkintilloch Railway, 42, 44; Monkland Railways, 45; North British Railway, 45, 46–7; Slamannan, 42; Wishaw and Coltness, 42
Railways, 41–8; amalgamation of, 45; Anglo-Scottish routes, 45–6; economic effects of, 47–8; finance of, 44–5; interest in canals, 36; operating spheres, 46; rates, 42–3; revenue of, 47; stations in Glasgow, 46–7; traffic on, 43–4, 47; tramways, 41
Randolph, Charles, 129, 130
Ravenscraig, 217
Regional policy, 201–9, 220–3
Renfrew, 29, 200, 234
Renfrewshire, 10, 40, 60, 61, 68, 76,

85, 90, 93, 96, 97, 98, 124, 139, 141, 142, 146, 184, 198, 199, 202, 233, 234, 243
Rennie, John, 6, 29, 30, 34
Renton, 85
Richard Thomas and Baldwins Ltd, 216
Ritchie, James, 65
Ritchie, James & Co., 48
Ritchie, John, 32
Roads, 36–41; benefits of, 40; charges on, 39; effects on journey time, 39–40; mileage of, 40; railway involvement, 40; statute labour roads, 37; turnpike debts, 40; turnpike trusts, 37–8; turnpikes, administration of, 40
Roberts, Richard, 95
Robertson, John, 126
Robertson, John Lewis, 99
Robertson, William, 115
Roebuck, Dr, 82
Rolls-Royce Ltd, 206
Rose, Sir Arthur, 202
Rothesay, 89, 90, 93
Royal Commission on the Distribution of the Industrial Population (Barlow Report), 249
Royal Commission on Hand Loom Weavers, 150
Russell, Dr J. B., 243
Rutherglen, 115

S

St Rollox, 42, 44, 133, 175, 176
Sanquhar, 39
Scott, Stevenson & Co., 95
Scotts of Greenock, 125
Select Committee on Manufactures, Commerce and Shipping, 91, 107
Sheepford, 33
Shieldhall, 204
Shipbuilding, 125–33, 178–82, 186–90, 218–20; construction costs, 130, 131, 188; introduction of iron, 131–3; introduction of steam power, 125–6; introduction of steel, 179; marine engineering, 127–30; National Shipbuilders Security Ltd, 189; orders for ships, 187, 188; origins on R. Clyde, 125; origins of shipbuilders, 129; rationalisation, 189; technical innovation in, 179–82, 189–90;

tonnage built, 132, 133, 178, 187, 188, 220
Shotts, 213
Siemens, C. W., 174, 175
Sinclair, Sir John, 99, 101, 137
Singer Ltd, 164, 166
Small, James, 70
Smeaton, John, 6, 29, 32
Smith, Adam, 3, 139
Smith, James, 73, 74
Smith, Robert, 148
Snodgrass, Neil, 96
Spalding, James, 80
Special areas: expenditure in, 203, 205–6; extent of, 202; power of Commissioner, 203, 204; Special Areas Reconstruction Association, 205
Spiers, Alexander, 39, 68
Spinningdale, 88, 89, 90
Springburn, 166, 206
Stair, Earl of, 65
Stanley, 89, 93
Steel, 173–8, 190–4, 215–18; Bessemer process, 173, 174; competitive position, 177–8; development plans, 215, 216; formation of companies, 175–6; Gilchrist-Thomas process, 176; nationalisation, 215; ownership pattern, 177; production of, 178, 193, 215, 218; rationalisation of, 191–2, 217; Scottish Steel Makers' Association, 178; shipbuilding links, 176–7, 178, 193; Siemens-Martin process, 175
Steel companies: Colvilles Ltd, 191; Glasgow Iron & Steel Co., 176, 177, 193; Lanarkshire Steel Co., 191; Monkland Iron & Steel Co., 173; Scottish Iron and Steel Co., 191; Steel Company of Scotland, 10, 175–6, 191, 193; Stewart, A. J. & Menzies, 177; Stewart & Lloyds, 192; Summerlee & Mossend Iron Co., 176
Steelworks: Clydebridge, 192, 195, 215; Glengarnock, 176; Ravenscraig, 216
Stephen, A. M., 193
Stephens of Linthouse, 193
Stirling, 97
Stirling, Andrew, 34
Stirling, James, 34

Stirling, John, 34
Stirling, William, 85
Stockingfield, 33
Stockport, 95, 98
Stonefield, Lord, 61
Strang, Dr John, 155, 158, 159
Strathaven, 39, 47, 86, 94, 97
Sutherland, 88
Swindells, John, 95
Symington, William, 126
Symonds, J. C., 150

T

Tancred, Thomas, 119, 120, 153
Tannochside, 223
Taylor, James, 126
Telford, Thomas, 34, 39
Tennant, Charles, 44, 82, 133, 175
Textiles, *see* Linen, Cotton
Tharsis Sulphur & Copper Co., 175
Thom, Robert, 102
Thomson, James, 129
Thomson, J. & G., 166, 179
Thomson, John, 126, 148
Thornliebank, 85, 99
Tobacco trade, 20–6
Tod, David, 129
Tod & MacGregor, 131
Tollcross, 192
Toothill Report, 225
Trade, 20–8; Navigation Acts, 20, 23, 25; significance of, 20; in tobacco, 6, 20–6; trading spheres, 26–7; to West Indies, 6, 24–5
Tradeston, 34
Tyneside, 250

U

Uddingston, 74
Unemployment, 12, 14, 184, 198–200, 210, 211, 212, 223
Union of Parliaments, 20

Urbanisation, 145–7, 234–6
Ure, John, 98

V

Vale of Leven, 164, 200, 221
Vessels: *Aberdeen*, 180; *Active*, 127; *Aglaia*, 128, 131; *Charlotte Dundas*, 126; *Comet*, 10, 126; *Despatch*, 127; *Fingal*, 127; *Fire Queen*, 131; *Great Eastern*, 179; *Jutland*, 181; *King Edward*, 181; *Propontis*, 180; *Queen Elizabeth*, 188; *Queen Mary*, 188; *Rob Roy*, 127, 128; *Robert Bruce*, 127; *Rotomahana*, 179; *Servia*, 179; *Talbot*, 127; *Turbinia*, 181; *Vale of Leven*, 131
Vivian, Henry, 239

W

Watt, James, 3, 28, 29, 33, 95, 96, 112
Webster, Dr Alexander, 135
Weir, J. & G., 201
West of Scotland Malleable Iron Co., 122
Westerton, 240
Whitehaven, 23
Wigtownshire, 144
Wilkie of Uddingston, 74
Wilson, John, 115, 116, 120
Wilson, Robert, 115
Wilson, William, 115
Wilsontown, 8
Windmillcroft, 41, 148
Wishaw, 146, 177, 205, 234, 241, 249
Wood, John, 126
Woodhall, 33
Woodside, 93
Woolf, Arthur, 130

Y

Yarrow, Sir Harold, 193
Yoker, 32, 41, 200
Young, Arthur, 139

For Product Safety Concerns and Information please contact our EU representative GPSR@taylorandfrancis.com Taylor & Francis Verlag GmbH, Kaufingerstraße 24, 80331 München, Germany

Printed and bound by CPI Group (UK) Ltd, Croydon, CR0 4YY

08/05/2025

01864444-0001